Robert Eisenman is Professor of Middle East Religions and Chair of the Religious Studies Department at California State University, Long Beach. He has published several books on the Scrolls, including *Maccabees, Zadokites, Christians and Qumran: A New Hypothesis of Qumran Origins* and *James the Just in the Habakkuk Pesher*, and he is a major contributor to a *Facsimile Edition of the Dead Sea Scrolls*.

Michael Wise is an Assistant Professor of Aramaic – the language of Jesus – in the Department of Near Eastern Languages and Civilization at the University of Chicago. He is the author of *A Critical Study of the Temple Scroll from Qumran Cave Eleven* and has written numerous articles on the Dead Sea Scrolls which have appeared in journals such as the *Revue de Qumran*, *Journal of Biblical Literature*, and *Vetus Testamentum*.

THE
DEAD SEA SCROLLS
UNCOVERED

The First Complete Translation and
Interpretation of 50 Key Documents
Withheld for Over 35 Years

Robert H. Eisenman

and

Michael Wise

E L E M E N T
Shaftesbury, Dorset • Rockport, Massachusetts
Melbourne, Victoria

© Element Books Limited 1992
Text © Robert Eisenman and Michael Wise 1992

First published in Great Britain in 1992 by
Element Books Limited
Shaftesbury, Dorset SP7 8BP

Published in the USA in 1992 by
Element Books, Inc.
PO Box 830, Rockport, MA 01966

Published in Australia in 1992 by
Element Books Limited
and distributed by
Penguin Australia Limited
487 Maroondah Highway, Ringwood, Victoria 3134

Reprinted December 1992
Reprinted February 1993
Reprinted March 1993
Reprinted April 1993
Reprinted 1994
Reprinted 1997
Reprinted 2000

Cover photograph *The Temple Scroll*
courtesy Z. Radovan, Jerusalem
Cover design by Barbara McGavin
Typeset by Footnote Graphics, Warminster, Wiltshire
Hebrew and Translation text produced by Element Books Ltd
Printed and bound in the USA by
Edwards Brothers Inc.

British Library Cataloguing in Publication
data available

Library of Congress Cataloging in Publication
data available

ISBN 1-85230-368-9

Contents

Abbreviations, Symbols and Ciphers

Beyer, *Texte* K. Beyer, *Die aramäischen Texte vom Toten Meer*
(Göttingen: Vandenhoeck & Ruprecht, 1984)

DJD *Discoveries in the Judaean Desert (of Jordan)*

DSSIP S. A. Reed, *Dead Sea Scroll Inventory Project: Lists of
Documents, Photographs and Museum Plates* (Claremont:
Ancient Biblical Manuscript Center, 1991–)

ER R. H. Eisenman and J. M. Robinson, *A Fascimile
Edition of the Dead Sea Scrolls*, 2 Volumes
(Washington, D.C: 1991)

Milik, *Books* J. T. Milik, *The Books of Enoch: Aramaic Fragments of
Qumrân Cave 4* (Oxford: Clarendon Press, 1976)

Milik, *MS* J. T. Milik, 'Milki-sedeq et Milki-resha dans les
anciens écrits juifs et chrétiens,' *Journal of Jewish
Studies* 23 (1972) 95–144.

Milik, *Years* J. T. Milik, *Ten Years of Discovery in the Wilderness of
Judaea* (London: SCM, 1959)

PAM Palestine Archaeological Museum (designation used
for accession numbers of photographs of Scrolls)

4Q Qumran Cave Four. Texts are then numbered, e.g.,
4Q390 = manuscript number 390 found in Cave
Four

[ ] Missing letters or words

vacat Uninscribed leather

{ }	Ancient scribal erasure or modern editor's deletion
< >	Supralinear text or modern editor's addition
|||	Ancient ciphers used in some texts for digits 1–9
¬	Ancient cipher used in some texts for the number '10'
3	Ancient cipher used in some texts for the number '20'
. . .	Traces of ink visible, but letters cannot be read
¬	Ancient cipher used in some texts for the number '100'

Introduction

Why should anyone be interested in the Dead Sea Scrolls? Why are they important? We trust that the present volume, which presents fifty texts from the previously unpublished corpus, will help answer these questions.

The story of the discovery of the Scrolls in caves along the shores of the Dead Sea in the late forties and early fifties is well known. The first cave was discovered, as the story goes, by Bedouin boys in 1947. Most familiar works in Qumran research come from this cave – Qumran, the Arabic term for the locale in which the Scrolls were found, being used by scholars as shorthand to refer to the Scrolls.

Discoveries from other caves are less well known, but equally important. For instance, Cave 3 was discovered in 1952. It contained a Copper Scroll, a list apparently of hiding places of Temple treasure. The problem has always been to fit this Copper Scroll into its proper historical setting. The present work should help in resolving this and other similar questions.

The most important cave for our purposes was Cave 4 discovered in 1954. Since it was discovered *after* the partition of Palestine, its contents went into the Jordanian-controlled Rockefeller Museum in East Jerusalem; while the contents of Cave 1 had previously gone into an Israeli-controlled museum in West Jerusalem, the Israel Museum.

Scholars refer to these manuscript-bearing caves according to the chronological order in which they were discovered: e.g. 1Q = Cave 1, 2Q = Cave 2, 3Q = Cave 3, and so on. The seemingly esoteric code designating manuscripts and fragments, therefore, works as follows: 1QS = the Community Rule from Cave 1; 4QD = the Damascus Document from Cave 4, as opposed, for instance, to CD, the recensions

1

of the same document discovered at the end of the last century in the repository known as the Cairo *Genizah*.

The discovery of this obviously ancient document with Judaeo-Christian overtones among medieval materials puzzled observers at the time. Later, fragments of it were found among materials from Cave 4, but researchers continued using the Cairo *Genizah* versions because the Qumran fragments were never published. We now present pictures of the last column of this document (plates 19 and 20) in this work, and it figured prominently in events leading up to the final publication of the unpublished plates.

The struggle for access to the materials in Cave 4 was long and arduous, sometimes even bitter. An International Team of editors had been set up by the Jordanian Government to control the process. The problems with this team are public knowledge. To put them in a nutshell: in the first place the team was hardly international, secondly it did not work well as a team, and thirdly it dragged out the editing process interminably.

In 1985–86, Professor Robert Eisenman, co-editor of this volume, was in Jerusalem as a National Endowment for the Humanities Fellow at the William F. Albright Institute for Archaeological Research – the 'American School' where the Scrolls from Cave 1 were originally brought for inspection in 1947. The subject of his research was the relationship of the Community at Qumran to the Jerusalem Church. This last is also referred to as the Jerusalem Community of James the Just, called in sources 'the brother of Jesus' – whatever may be meant by this designation. Prior recipients of this award were mostly field archaeologists, but a few were translators, including some from the International Team. Professor Eisenman was the first historian as such to be so appointed.

Frustratingly, he found there was little he could do in Jerusalem. Where access to the Scrolls themselves was concerned, he was given the run-around, by now familiar to those who follow the Scrolls' saga, and shunted back and forth between the Israel Department of Antiquities, now housed at the Rockefeller Museum, and the École Biblique or 'French School' down the street from the American School. Had he known at that time of the archive at the Huntington Library in California, not far from his university – the existence of which had never been widely publicized, and was not even known to many at the library itself – he could with even more advantage have stayed at home.

It was from the ranks of the French School – the École as it is called, an extension of the Dominican Order in Jerusalem – that all previous editors were drawn, including the two most recent, Father Benoit, head of the École before he died, and John Strugnell. The International Team had been put in place by Roland de Vaux, another Dominican father. In several seasons from 1954–56 De Vaux did the archaeology of Qumran. A sociologist by training, not an archaeologist, de Vaux had also been head of the École.

After the conquest of East Jerusalem in the Six Day War in 1967, some might call the Israelis the greatest war profiteers; the remaining Scrolls were perhaps their greatest spoil, had they had the sense to realize it. They did not. Because of the delicacy of the international situation and their own inertia, they did little to speed up the editing process of the Scrolls which had, because of problems centring around the Copper Scroll mentioned above, more or less ground to a halt. The opposite occurred, and the previous editorial situation, which seemed at that point on the verge of collapse, received a twenty-year new lease of life.

In the spring of 1986 at the end of his stay in Jerusalem, Professor Eisenman went with the British scholar, Philip Davies of the University of Sheffield, to see one of the Israeli officials responsible for this – an intermediary between the Antiquities Department (now 'Authority') and the International Team, and the Scrolls Curator at the Israel Museum. They were told in no uncertain terms, 'You will not see the Scrolls in your lifetimes.'

These words more than any others stung them into action and the campaign to free up access to the Scrolls was galvanized. Almost five years to the day from the time they were uttered, absolute access to the Scrolls was attained. This is a story in itself, but it must suffice for our purposes to say that the campaign gathered momentum in June 1989, when it became the focus of a parallel campaign being conducted by the *Biblical Archaeology Review* in Washington DC and its editor, Hershel Shanks, and caught the attention of the international press. Unbeknowns, however, to either Shanks or the press, behind the scenes events were transpiring that would make even these discussions moot.

Eisenman had been identified in this flurry of worldwide media attention as the scholarly point man in this struggle. As a result, photographs of the remaining unpublished Dead Sea Scrolls were made available to him. These began coming to him in September of 1989. At first they came in small consignments, then more insistently, until by the autumn of 1990, a year later, photographs of virtually the whole of the unpublished corpus and then some, had been made over to him. Those responsible for this obviously felt that he would know what to do with them. The present editors hope that this confidence has been justified. The publication of the two-volume *Facsimile Edition* two years later, together with the present volume, is the result.

At this juncture Professor Michael Wise of the University of Chicago, a specialist in Aramaic, was brought into the picture. Eisenman began sharing the archive with him in November 1990. Professor Wise describes the impression the sight of the extensive photographic archive made on him when he came to California and mounted the stairs for the first time to the sunny loft Eisenman used as a study:

'The photographs were piled in little stacks everywhere around the room. They were so numerous that stacked together, they would have topped six feet in height. Someone should have taken a picture and recorded the scene, the two of us standing on either side of a giant stack of 1800 photographs of previously sequestered and unpublished Dead Sea Scrolls – the big one that did not get away.'

Two teams immediately set to work, one under Professor Eisenman at California State University at Long Beach and one under Professor Wise at the University of Chicago. Their aim was to go through everything – every photograph individually – to see what was there, however long it took, leaving nothing to chance and depending on *no one else's work*.

At the same time, and in pursuance of the goal of absolutely free access without qualifications, Eisenman was preparing the *Facsimile Edition* of all unpublished plates. This was scheduled to appear the following spring through E. J. Brill in Leiden, Holland. Ten days, however, before its scheduled publication in April 1991, the publisher inexplicably withdrew and Hershel Shanks and the Biblical Archaeology Society stepped in to fill the breach. But valuable time had been lost and other events were now transpiring that would render the whole question of access obsolete.

Independently and separately, the Huntington Library of San Marino, California, in pursuance of a parallel commitment to academic freedom and without knowledge of the above arrangements – though aware of the public relations benefits implicit in the situation – called Eisenman in as a consultant in June 1991. Thereafter, in September 1991, the Library unilaterally decided to open its archives. The monopoly had collapsed. B.A.S.'s 2-volume *Facsimile Edition* was published two months later.

What was the problem in Qumran studies that these efforts were aimed at rectifying? Because of the existence of an International Team, giving the apearance of 'official' appointment, the public naturally came to see the editions it produced (mainly published by Oxford University Press in the *Discoveries in the Judaean Desert* series) as authoritative. These editions contained interpretations, which themselves came to be looked on as 'official' as well. This is important. Those who did not have a chance to see these texts for themselves were easily dominated by those claiming either to *know* or to have *seen more*.

This proposition has been put somewhat differently: control of the unpublished manuscripts meant control of the field. How did this work? By controlling the unpublished manuscripts – the pace of their publication, who was given a document to edit and who was not – the International Team could, for one thing, create instant scholarly 'superstars'. For another, it controlled the interpretation of the texts. For example, instead of a John Allegro, a John Strugnell was given access; instead of a Robert Eisenman, a Frank Moore Cross; instead of a Michael Wise, an Emile Puech. Without competing analyses, these interpretations grew almost inevitably into a kind of 'official' scholarship.

A conception of the field emerged known as 'the Essene theory' dominated by those 'official' scholars or their colleagues who propounded it. As will be seen from this work, this theory is inaccurate and insufficient to describe the totality of the materials represented by the corpus at Qumran. Another unfortunate effect of this state of affairs was that it gave the individuals involved, whether accidentally or by design, control over graduate studies in the field. That is to say, if you wanted to study a given manuscript, you had to go to that institution and faculty member controlling that manuscript. It could not be otherwise. Out of this also grew, again inevitably, control of all new chairs or positions in the field – few enough in any case – all reviews (dominated in any event by Harvard, Oxford, and the École Biblique), publication committees, magazine editorial boards, and book reviews. Anyone opposing the establishment was dubbed 'second-rate'; all supporting it, 'first-rate.'

Whatever the alleged justification, no field of study should have to undergo indignities of this kind, all the more so, when what are at issue are ambiguous and sensitive documents critical for a consideration of the history of mankind and civilization in the West. We had, in fact, in an academic world dedicated to 'science' and free debate, where 'opposition' theories were supposed to be treated honourably and not abhorred, the growth of what in religion would go by the name of a 'curia' – in this case 'an academic curia', promoting its own theories, while condemning those of its opponents.

These were the kinds of problems in Qumran studies that Eisenman decided to resolve, unilaterally as it were, by cutting the Gordion Knot once and for all by publishing the 1800 or so previously unpublished plates he had in his possession. The present work is a concomitant to this decision, and the fifty documents it contains represent in our judgement the best of what exists. Reconstructed between January 1991 and May 1992, these give an excellent overview of what there is in the previously sequestered corpus and what their significance is.

The fifty texts in this volume were reconstructed out of some 150 different plates, most of the numbers for which are given in the reader's notes at the end of each chapter. Twenty-five of the most interesting of these plates are presented in this volume not only for the reader's interest, but also so that he or she can check the accuracy of the transliterations and translations. The rest can be located in *A Facsimile Edition of the Dead Sea Scrolls*, published by the Biblical Archaeology Society of Washington DC in 1991, to which the corresponding plate numbers are provided.

Thirty-three of these texts are in Hebrew (including one in a cryptic script that required decoding) and seventeen in Aramaic. Aramaic was apparently considered the more appropriate vehicle for the expression of testaments, incantations, and the like. More sacred writings were more typically inscribed in Hebrew, the holy language of the Books of Moses. Writers of apocalyptic visions also often preferred Aramaic, probably because of a tradition that Aramaic was the language of the Angels. This division, while by no means hard and fast, can be seen as characterizing the present collection as well.

Texts and fragments are translated as precisely as possible, as they are; nothing substantive is held back or deleted. A precise transcription into the modern Hebrew characters conventionally used to render classical Hebrew and/or Aramaic writing, is also provided, so the reader can compare these with the original photographs or check translations, if he or she so chooses. Every translation might not be perfect, and the arrangement of fragments in some cases still conjectural, but they are precise and sufficient enough to enable the reader to draw his or her own conclusions, which is indeed the point of this book.

Also towards this end commentaries on each text are provided, some lengthy, some less so, which should help the reader pass through the shoals of what are often quite esoteric allusions and inter-relationships. These commentaries also attempt to put matters such as these into a proper historical perspective, though in these matters, it should be appreciated that Professor Eisenman and Professor Wise have ideas concerning these things that, while complementary, are not always the same. Both agree as to the 'Zealot' and/or 'Messianic' character of the texts, but one would go further than the other in the direction of 'Zadokite', 'Sadducee', and/or 'Jewish Christian' theory.

Every effort is also made to link these new documents with the major texts known from the early days of Qumran research which were published in the fifties and sixties, including the Damascus Document, the Community Rule, the Habakkuk *Pesher*, the War Scroll, and Hymns, which can be found in compendiums in English available from both Penguin Books and Doubleday. Through these commentaries the reader will be able to see these earlier works in a new light as well. Without commentaries of this kind, linking one vocabulary complex with another, one set of allusions with another — sometimes esoteric, but always imaginative — and new documents like those we provide in this work, the interpretation of these early texts must remain at best incomplete.

Nor is the number of documents presented here insubstantial. It compares not unfavourably with the numbers of those already published and demonstrates the importance of open archives and free competition even in the academic world. It also makes the claim that more time was required to study these texts than the thirty-five years already expended, and pleas to the public for more patience, somewhat difficult to understand.

Nor are these documents, as the reader will be able to judge, dull or unimportant. They absolutely gainsay any notion that there is nothing interesting in the unpublished corpus, just as their style and literary creativity gainsay any idea that these are somehow inferior compositions. On the contrary, some, particularly ecstatic and visionary recitals, are of the most exquisite beauty. All are of unique historical interest.

Of the Cave 4 materials in the *DJD* series and the 1800 photographs or so in the *Facsimile Edition*, about 580 separate manuscripts can be identified. Of these, some 380 are non-Biblical, or 'sectarian' as they are referred to in the field; the rest Biblical. Non-Biblical or sectarian texts are those not found in the Bible. Except for those apocryphal and pseudepigraphic works that have come down to us through various traditions, most of these are new, never seen before.

During the somewhat acrimonious exchanges that developed in the press in the 1989 controversy over access, some claimed that they were willing to share the documents assigned to them. This was sometimes disingenuous. It may have been true concerning Biblical manuscripts to some extent, which were not particularly new or of ground-breaking significance. It most certainly was *not* true where non-Biblical or sectarian documents were concerned. These last always remained firmly under the control of scholars connected in one way or another with the École mentioned above, like de Vaux's associate Father Milik, Father Benoit, Father Starky, John Strugnell, and Father Emile Puech.

But these non-Biblical writings are of the greatest significance for historians, because they contain the most precious information on the thoughts and currents of Judaism and the ethos that gave rise to Christianity in the first century BC to the first century AD. They are actual eye-witness accounts of the period. While those responsible for the almost quiescent pace of scholarship may have felt themselves justified from a philological perspective in proceeding in this way, the interests of the historian were in many cases completely ignored.

Most philologists, who are primarily interested in reconstructing a single text or a given passage from that text, just could not appreciate why historians, after waiting some thirty-five years for all materials to become available, did not wish to wait any longer, regardless of the perfection or imperfection of their translation efforts. The historian needs the materials relating to the given movement or historical current before drawing any conclusion or making a judgement about that movement.

Sometimes even philological efforts, by ignoring the relationships of one manuscript with another, one allusion to another, end in inaccuracy. This is often the case in Qumran studies. Without all the relevant materials available, nothing of precision can ultimately really be said, either by the philologist or the historian, so access to all materials benefits both. In our opinion the results of our labours in this work confirm this proposition.

The same is the case for works in this collection which make actual historical references to real persons. The members of the International Team knew about these references, and occasionally mentioned them over the years in their work, but saw no need to publish them, because they seemed either irrelevant to them — matters of passing curiosity only — or they could make nothing of them. This is illustrative — as anyone who looks at what we have made of these will see. To the outsider's eyes or those of an editor with a different point of view, these materials are of the most far-reaching, historical import. As a matter of fact they go far towards a *solution* to the Qumran problem.

This should be clear even to the most dull-minded of observers. The same can be said for the disciplinary text at the end of this work, which actually mentions names of people associated with the Community. All references of this kind, together with the actual circumstances of their occurrence, manifoldly increase our understanding of the Qumran Community.

This is also true of the two Letters on Works Righteousness in Chapter 6. Parts of these letters have been circulating under one name or another for some time, but no complete text was ever made available. In fact, efforts to publish them have been incredibly drawn out − insiders knew of their existence over thirty years ago. To see from their public comments what these insiders made of these letters, proves yet again the argument for open access. The implications of these letters, for solving the basic problems of Qumran and also of early Christianity are quite momentous as we shall see below. For our part, in line with our previously announced intentions in this work, we have gone through the entire corpus of pictures completely ourselves and depended on no one else's work to do this. We made all the selections and arrangements of plates ourselves, including the identification of overlaps and joins. The process only took about six weeks. Contrariwise, the information contained in these two letters should have been available thirty years ago and much misunderstanding in Qumran studies would have been avoided.

The same is true for the last column of the Damascus Document with which we close Chapter 6. This was the subject of the separate requests for access Eisenman and Davies addressed to John Strugnell, then Head of the International Team, and the Israel Antiquities Department − in the spring of 1989 − only to be peremptorily dismissed. It was after these 'official' requests for access to this document that this access issue boiled over into the international press.

What difference could having access to a single unknown column of the Damascus Document make? The reader need only look at our interpretation of this column below to decide. It makes *all the difference*. Before translating every line and having all the materials at our disposal, we could never have imagined what a difference it actually could make. As it turns out, analysed in terms of the rest of the corpus and compared with certain key passages in the New Testament, we have the basis for understanding Paul's incipient theological approach to the death of Christ, which in turn stands as the basis of the Christian theological understanding of it thereafter.

From the few crumbs the International Team was willing to throw to scholars from time to time, we knew that there was a reference of some kind in this text to an important convocation of the Community at Pentecost – much as we heard rumours about bits from other unpublished texts – but never having been shown it, we did not know that the text was an excommunication text or that the Damascus Document ended in such an orgy of nationalistic 'cursing'. This makes a substantial difference.

Certain theological constructions which Paul makes with regard to 'cursing' and the meaning of the crucifixion of Christ are now brought into focus. With them, notions of the redemptive nature of the death of Christ as set forth in Isa. 53 – that a majority of mankind still considers fundamental – are clarified (the reader should see our further discussion of these matters at the end of Chapter 6). This is the difference having all of the documents at one's disposal can make.

So what in effect do we have in these manuscripts? Probably nothing less than a picture of the movement from which Christianity sprang in Palestine. But there is more – if we take into consideration the Messianic nature of the texts as we delineate it in this book, and allied concepts such as 'Righteousness', 'Piety', 'justification', 'works', 'the Poor', 'Mysteries', what we have is a picture of what Christianity actually *was* in Palestine. The reader, however, probably will not be able to recognize it because it will seem virtually the opposite of the Christianity with which he or she is familiar. This is particularly the case in documents such as the two Letters on Works Righteousness above, and others in Chapter 6 which detail the legal minutiae reckoned as Righteousness or 'works that will justify you'.

The reason again for this is simple. We cannot really speak of a 'Christianity' *per se* in Palestine in the first century. The word was only coined, as Acts 11:26 makes clear, to describe a situation in Antioch in Syria in the fifties of the present era. Later it was used to describe a large portion of the overseas world that became 'Christian', but this Christianity was completely different from the movement we have before us – well not *completely*.

Both movements used the same vocabulary, the same scriptural passages as proof texts, similar conceptual contexts; but the one can be characterized as the mirror reversal of the other. While the Palestinian one was zealot, nationalistic, engagé, xenophobic, and apocalyptic; the overseas one was cosmopolitan, antinomian, pacifistic – in a word 'Paulinized'. Equally we can refer to the first as Jamesian, at least if we judge by the letter ascribed to James' name in the New Testament, which both Eusebius and Martin Luther felt should not be included in the New Testament. Of course in their eyes it should not have been, as its general thrust parallels that of many documents from Qumran and it is full of Qumranisms.

It is for these reasons that we felt it more appropriate to refer to the movement we have before us as the 'Messianic' one, and its literature as the literature of 'the Messianic Movement' in Palestine. In so far as this literature resembles Essenism, it can be called Essene; Zealotism, Zealot; Sadduceeism, Sadducee; Jewish Christianity – whatever might be meant by this – Jewish Christian. The nomenclature is unimportant and not particularly relevant.

But what should be clear is that what we have here, regardless of the date one gives it, is an archive of impressive dimensions. If not first century, it certainly leads directly into the principal movements of the first century, all of which adopt its vocabulary and ethos as their own. For instance, as we have noted, it is impossible to distinguish ideas and terminology associated with the Jerusalem Community of James the Just from materials found in this corpus.

But the archive as it is has very clear connections with the 'Zealot Movement' as we shall point out below, a theory Professor Wise has been championing for some time. In fact, this was a theory of Qumran origins proposed very early in the history of Qumran research. Those supporting the establishment 'Essene theory' thought they had vanquished it twenty-five years ago by ridiculing its proponents, Cecil Roth and G. R. Driver of Oxford. There were shortcomings in the theory as they propounded it then, because it did not take into account the entire expanse of the literature represented by the corpus at Qumran. However, if our presentation in this volume of this movement as the Messianic one, having both 'Zealot' and 'Jewish Christian' propensities, is taken into account, then a good many of these shortcomings can be made good.

In fact, what one seems to have reflected in this Qumran literature is a *Messianic* élite retreating or 'separating' into the wilderness as per Isa. 40:3's 'make a straight Way in the Wilderness for our God.' This élite seems to have inhabited 'desert camps', where they were actually 'preparing' to be joined by the Angels, referred to by them as 'the Heavenly Host', and for what appears to be a final apocalyptic Holy War against all evil on this earth. This would appear to be the reason they are practising the regimen of extreme purity in the wilderness in these texts – not the somewhat more retrospective presentation in the New Testament as it has come down to us. This movement consists of a small cadre of committed 'volunteers' or 'Joiners for war', of 'Holy

Ones' or 'Saints' preparing in the wilderness through 'Perfection of the Way' and 'zeal for the Law for the time of the Day of Vengeance'.

The militancy of this spirit will be unfamiliar to many readers – although those with a knowledge of militant Puritanism of seventeenth-century England – particularly under Cromwell – and thereafter in America will recognize it. It is a militancy that is still very much part of the Islamic spirituality as well. It is this kind of spirit which shines through the texts as we have them, a proposition which both editors have been attempting to put forward in their separate analyses of Qumran materials. It is also probably at the core of the movement behind Judas Maccabee's similar military endeavours, coming down through the descendants of his nephew John Hyrcanus – his successors – to so-called 'Zealots' of the war against Rome in the first century, and beyond. These, if you like, were the Holy Warriors of their time. They are the cadre of those willing to live the regimen of extreme purity in preparation for 'the last times'. They are perhaps more akin to the Crusading movement in the Middle Ages – and other like movements – than a sect. It is difficult for those accustomed to a more Gentile Christian overseas approach to conceive that this was the nature of Christianity at its formative moment in Palestine.

Where dating and chronology generally are concerned, we have not relied on the methods of paleography at all. These methods have in the past too often been employed illegitimately in Qumran research to confuse the non-specialist. The paleographic sequences that were developed, while helpful, are too uncertain to have any real relevance to such a narrow chronological period. In addition, they depend on the faulty assumption of a 'rapid' and 'straightline' development of scripts at this time, a proposition that is by no means capable of proof.

'Book' or scribal hands are notoriously stubborn, often lasting centuries beyond the point of their initial creation; and informal or 'semi-cursive' hands are just not datable in any precise way on the basis of the kind of evidence we have before us. In other words the fact of accurately being able to date the origin of a given scribal hand – a dubious proposition in any time or place – tells us nothing about when a given individual within, for instance, a community such as that represented by the literature at Qumran actually *used* that hand. It is the same for the equally popular subject in Qumran research, coin data. Dropping a coin with a given date on it only tells us that the coin was not dropped before it was minted, *not* how long afterwards. All the more so in paleography. Even if it were possible to date a given handwriting style with any precision, we can only know that the handwriting was not used *before* the date of its theoretical development, not how long after. The whole construction is a tautological absurdity.

Similar problems obtain for AMS Carbon 14 dating techniques. Eisenman and Davies first proposed the application of this technique in the 1989 letter to the Israel Department of Antiquities referred to above. But the process is still in its infancy, subject to multiple variables, and too uncertain to be applied with precision to the kind of materials we have before us. Even the tests that were conducted were neither extensive nor secure enough to be of any real use in making definitive determinations. As always in this field, one is finally thrown back on the areas of literary criticism, textual analysis, and a sure historical grasp — debatable enough quantities in any field, almost totally lacking in this one — to make determinations of this kind.

Among the documents in the present collection are several of the most sublime and incredible beauty. The Hymns and Mysteries in Chapter 7 are examples, as are the visionary recitals in Chapters 1, 2, 3 and 5. In fact, the visionary nature of the Qumran corpus is much under-estimated. Texts of this kind border on what goes in Judaism under the name of *Kabbalah*, and indeed it is difficult to see how there cannot have been some very direct relationship albeit an underground one. In addition, the allusions and ideas contained in the documents of this collection hang together to an astonishing degree. Correspondences are precise; vocabulary clusters, regular. The ideas and images move so consistently from document to document as to awe the investigator. Everything is so homogeneous and consistent that there can be little doubt that what we have before us is a movement and the archive, its literature.

Since the situation in this field is so fluid, it is always possible that a text included in this work may have been published elsewhere or be in the process of being published, and parts of texts or a whole text included in this work, in fact, were already published or were published after we began working on them. Since we were already working on the text (or texts) in any event and since no complete English translation was readily available, and it was important to have a fuller literary context by which to judge that text, we have included them. We have also provided a section at the end of each chapter containing publication and technical information. Generally we limited this bibliography to those books and articles where such a text was published or in which a detailed description, if not every single word, of the text was provided.

We have, also, attempted to keep our translations as faithful to the original as possible. This may result in what seems to be an uneven style. For instance, we have not turned sentences around or reversed them in favour of more fluent English. In pursuance of this, too, we have capitalized concepts we considered particularly important and relevant to the Qumran ethos, so the reader would also be able to take note that a particular word was recurring across the breadth of the Qumran corpus. Examples of words of this kind are 'Righteousness', 'Piety', 'Truth', 'Knowledge', 'Foundations', 'the Poor', 'the Meek, 'Mysteries', 'Splendour', and 'Fountain'. Often these are terms of very considerable historical import.

Unlike many translators — who appear to go out of their way to be inconsistent or confusing, and seem to have no idea what was an *important* concept at Qumran and what was not — we have attempted to use familiar expressions to translate key words, for example 'Holy Spirit' instead of 'spirit of holiness', 'the Way' instead of 'the path', 'works' instead of 'deeds', and 'Messiah' instead of 'anointed one'. When we came upon a word such as 'justification', being used in a manner known to early Christian theology, we called it 'justification', not something else. Nothing less would do. Where we saw 'works Righteousness', as for instance in the two letters we entitled by that name, we called it that, however unfamiliar the 'works' therein enumerated might appear.

We have also tried to render familiar words consistently. For instance, some texts refer to 'the *Torah*'. Sometimes these same texts or others refer to '*Hok*'/'*Hukkim*', that is ordinance(s) or Law(s). Since occasionally an important terminology for the development of the Zealot Movement like 'zeal' is associated with these last, we often render them, too, as 'Law' or 'Laws', that is the individual legal requirements of *Torah* and/or Covenant.

To add to this confusion, there is a further ambiguous legal usage '*Mishpat*'. Depending on the context, this can be rendered 'Judgement' or 'ordinance' once again. Since, when used eschatologically, it most often refers to what is, in English usage, 'The Last Judgement', we have preferred to render it as 'Judgement' throughout, so that the reader would be able to recognize the underlying Hebrew word in the translation, even though this occasionally leads to imprecision when applied to everyday, mundane affairs. For instance, the individual we shall discuss in Chapter 6 below, called 'the *Mebakker*' or 'Bishop', when judging individual cases and making individual rulings is, also, referred to as making 'Judgements'.

A key ideology is *Hesed*. In most cases it means 'Piety', but sometimes, especially when applied to God, it can actually mean that 'Grace' which Paul embraces so heartily in his letters. For the sake of consistency, we have translated it 'Piety' throughout. There are also innumerable instances of the use of the key terminologies: *Ebion*, *'Ani*, and *Dal*, all referring to 'the Poor' or 'poverty'. For the purposes of consistency and precision, we have preferred 'Poor' for the first, 'Meek' for the second, and 'Downtrodden' for the third. Such are the editorial decisions that must be made in a work of this kind.

Finally there is the reconstruction of various fragments into a single rationalized whole. Often the order of these is arbitrary, representing what seemed in the circumstances the most rational. It is sometimes not sure whether all of these really even belong to the same text. For instance, in a splendid mystic and visionary recital, the Chariots of Glory below, there is an excommunication text comparable to the last column of the Damascus Document, imbedded in somewhat more prosaic material. What are we to do with such a fragment? Yet, the columns in question were preserved contiguously – such is the nature of the material before us.

Often we decided simply to leave such passages as part of the same manuscript, even though it is possible they were not. This is true, in some instances too – but certainly not all – as concerns the order of fragments in a given document. But we did not feel this was sufficient cause to hold up work as some 'official' editors seem to have felt for so long, and decided that matters such as these were relatively minor (of greater interest to the specialist than the general reader), as compared with the right of the public to *know*. It was more important to translate a given manuscript, provide commentary, get it out, and leave the public to judge such fine points for itself, as we ourselves would do in other forums.

In closing, the editors wish to thank the members of both teams which worked on these texts, one at California State University and Long Beach and one at the University of Chicago. The first included Rabbi Leo Abrami, Eron Viner, Ilan Cohen, Eyran Eylon, and Dr James Battenfield. The second included David Clemens, Deborah Friedrich, Michael Douglas, and Anthony Tomasino. Where the second team is concerned, Professor Wise wishes especially to thank Mr Douglas and Mr Tomasino. They shared his labours on many manuscripts. Mr Tomasino in particular contributed to all aspects of his work on many manuscripts along every step of the way. They also acknowledge the help and suggestions offered by Professor Norman Golb, Professor Dennis Pardee, Dr Douglas Penny, and Dr Yiftah Zur. These colleagues and students have helped make this a better book.

Translations of this kind are difficult. Work – albeit preliminary – was accomplished here under very difficult circumstances and in very short order that has been 'on the back burner', as it were, for the better part of thirty-five years. Those who helped deserve only credit and none of the blame for any errors in reading or interpretation in this work. Final responsibility for all readings, translations and commentary, however, must and does, of course, lie with the authors. Professor Wise also wishes to express his gratitude to his brother Jamie and wife Cathy, for whom in the words of the poet in the deepest sense, *matre pulchra filia pulchrior*; Professor Eisenman, to his wife Heather and children, Lavi, Hanan, Nadav, and Sarah. The work in this field is now at a beginning. We hope our efforts in this volume will be of help in further illuminating 'the Way'.

Fountain Valley, California
Des Plaines, Illinois
June 1992

CHAPTER 1

Messianic and Visionary Recitals

These texts constitute some of the most thought-provoking in the corpus. We have placed them in the first chapter because of the importance of their Messianic, visionary and mystical — even Kabbalistic — content and imagery. These are not the only texts with such import. This kind of thrust will grow to a climax in Chapters 5 and 7.

But the Messianic theorizing these texts exhibit is particularly interesting — it has heretofore either been underestimated or for some reason played down in the study of the Scrolls. In at least two texts in this chapter (not to mention other chapters), we have definite Messianic allusions: the Messianic vision text we call, after an allusion in its first line, the Messiah of Heaven and Earth, and the Messianic Leader (*Nasi*) text. In both there are clear correspondences to recognized Messianic sections in the Prophet Isaiah.

Interestingly, we do not have the two-Messiah doctrine highlighted in a few of the texts from the early days of Qumran research, like the Damascus Document found in two recensions at the end of the last century in the Cairo *Genizah* or the Community Rule from Cave 1, but rather the more normative, single Messiah most Jews and Christians would find familiar. Though in the Messianic Leader (*Nasi*) text, this figure is nowhere declared to be a 'Messiah' as such, only a Messianic or eschatological 'Leader', the Messianic thrust of the Biblical allusions underpinning it and the events it recounts clearly carry something of this signification. Its relation to the Damascus Document, further discussed in our analysis of the Messianic Florilegium in Chapter 4, do as well.

But even in the published corpus, there is a wide swath of materials, particularly in the Biblical commentaries (the *pesharim*) on Isaiah, Zechariah, Psalms, etc., and compendiums of Messianic proof texts,

17

that relate to a single, more nationalist, Davidic-style Messiah, as opposed to a second with more priestly characteristics that has been hypothesized. This last is, of course, in evidence too in the Letter to the Hebrews, where the more eschatological and high-priestly implications of Messiah-ship are expounded.

Even in the Damascus Document, there is some indication in the first column of the Cairo recension that the Messianic 'Root of Planting out of Aaron and Israel' has already come. The 'arising' or 'standing up' predicted in the later sections can be looked upon, as well, as something in the nature of a Messianic 'return' – even 'resurrection' (see Dan. 12:13 and Lam R ii.3.6 using *'amod* or 'standing up' in precisely this vein and our discussion of the Admonitions to the Sons of Dawn below). Nor is it completely clear in the Cairo Damascus Document that the allusion to 'Aaron and Israel' implies dual Messiahs, and not a single Messiah out of two genealogical stalks, which was suggested by scholars in the early days of research on it, and is, as we shall see, the more likely reading.

The very strong Messianic thrust of many of the materials associated with Qumran has been largely overlooked by commentators, in particular the presence in the published corpus in three different places of the 'World Ruler' or 'Star' prophecy from Num. 24:17 – that 'a Star would rise out of Jacob, a Sceptre to rule' the world – i.e. in the Damascus Document, the War Scroll, and one of the compendiums of Messianic proof texts known as a Florilegium. There can be little doubt that the rise of Christianity is predicated on this prophecy. Our own Genesis Florilegium, playing on this title, also ends up with an exposition of another famous Messianic prophecy – the 'Shiloh' from Gen. 49:10, which also includes the 'sceptre' aspect of the above prophecy.

The first-century Jewish historian Josephus, an eye-witness to the events he describes, identifies the world ruler prophecy as the moving force behnd the Jewish revolt against Rome in AD 66–70 (*War* 6.317). Roman writers dependent on him, like Suetonius (*Twelve Caesars* 10.4) and Tacitus (*The Histories* 2.78 and 5.13) do likewise. Rabbinic sources verify its currency in the events surrounding the fall of the Temple in AD 70 (*ARN* 4 and b. Git 56b). However, reversing its thrust, these last present their hero, Rabbi Yohanan b. Zacchai as applying it – as Josephus himself does – to the destroyer of Jerusalem and future Roman Emperor Vespasian! The Bar Kochba uprising in AD 132–6 can also be thought of as being inspired by this prophecy, as Bar Kosiba's original name seems to have been deliberately transmuted into one incorporating this allusion, i.e. Bar Kochba – 'Son of the Star'.

The other texts in this section are all visionary and eschatological, most often relating to Ezekiel, the original visionary and eschatological prophet and a favourite in Qumran texts. Whatever else can be said of them, their nationalist, militant, apocalyptic and unbending thrust canot be gainsaid, nor should it be overlooked.

1. THE MESSIAH OF HEAVEN AND EARTH (4Q521)
(Plate 1)

This text is one of the most beautiful and significant in the Qumran corpus. In it many interesting themes that appear in other Qumran texts reappear. In the first place, there is continued emphasis on 'the Righteous' (*Zaddikim*), 'the Pious' (*Hassidim*), 'the Meek' (*'Anavim*), and 'the Faithful' (*Emunim*). These terms recur throughout this corpus (in particular see the Hymns of the Poor below) and should be noted as more or less interchangeable allusions and literary self-designations. The first two are important in the vocabulary of Jewish mysticism; the last two in that of Christianity.

New themes also appear, such as God's 'Spirit hovering over the Meek' and 'announcing glad tidings to the Meek', themes with clear New Testament parallels. These also include the Pious being 'glorified on the Throne of the Eternal Kingdom', which resonates as well with similar themes in the New Testament and the *Kabbalah*, and God 'visiting the Pious' and 'calling the Righteous by name', both paralleled in the Damascus Document. In CD,i.7 God is said to have 'visited' the earth causing, as we have seen, a Messianic 'Root of Planting' to grow, and following this, in iv.4, 'the sons of Zadok' are described as being 'called by name'. This phrase 'called by name' is also found in column ii.11 of the Damascus Document, where it is followed by the statement that God 'made His Holy Spirit known to them by the hand of His Messiah' – words which resonate with the language of the present text as well.

Not only do parallel allusions confirm the relationship of the 'sons of Zadok' with the '*Zaddikim*' ('the Righteous'/'Righteous Ones'), but 'naming' and predestination are important themes in both the early columns of CD and Chapters 2–5 of Acts, where, for instance, the predestination of Christ and the language of the Holy Spirit are signalled. If the additional fragments of this text – which may or may not be integral to it – are taken into consideration, then there is some allusion to 'anointed ones' or 'messiahs' plural, probably referring to the priests doing service in the Temple. The two columns of the major fragment on this plate (no. 1) very definitely, however, evoke a singular, nationalist *Messiah*, as does the interpretation of the 'Shiloh Prophecy' related to it in the Genesis Florilegium below.

He is to a certain extent a supernatural figure in the manner of Dan. 7's 'Son of Man coming on the clouds of Heaven'. This imagery is recapitulated in Column xif. of the War Scroll from Cave 1 at Qumran, which interprets the 'Star Prophecy' in terms of it and the rising of 'the Meek' in some final apocalyptic war. The War Scroll, of course, also uses eschatological 'rain' imagery to identify these 'clouds' with the 'Holy Ones' ('the *Kedoshim*' or 'Heavenly Host'). In the Messiah of Heaven and Earth text, not only are the 'heavens and the earth' subsumed under the command of the Messiah, but so, too, are these presumed '*Kedoshim*' or 'Holy Ones' from the War Scroll.

There are also the very interesting allusions to 'My Lord'/*Adonai*, referred to in Isa. 61:1, which seems to underly much of the present text; but since the sense of this is often so imprecise, it is impossible to tell whether the reference is to God or to 'His Messiah' whom it so celebrates. If the latter, this would bring its imagery closer still to similar New Testament recitations. The reader should note, however, that for Josephus mentioned above, one of the determining characteristics of those he calls Essenes and Zealots was that they would not 'call any *man* Lord' (italics ours).

By far the most important lines in Fragment 1 Column 1 are Lines 6–8 and 11–13, referring to 'releasing the captives', 'making the blind see', 'raising up the downtrodden', and 'resurrecting the dead'. The last allusion is not to be doubted. The only question will be, who is doing this raising, etc. – God or 'His Messiah'? In Lines 6–8 the reference seems to be to God. But in Lines 11–13, it is possible that a shift occurs, and the reference could be to 'His Messiah'. The editors were unable to agree on the reconstruction here.

In any event, language from Isa. 61:1 (see above) is also clearly identifiable in both line 8 and line 11. But likewise, there are word-for-word correspondences to the Eighteen Benedictions, among the earliest strata of Jewish liturgy and still a part of it today: 'You will resurrect the dead, uphold the fallen, heal the sick, release the captives, keeping faith with those asleep in the dust. . .', referring obviously to God. It should be noted too that these portions include reference to the *Hassidim*, also evoked several times in the present text. It is also interesting to note that Isa. 60:21, which precedes Isa. 61:1, contains the 'Root of Planting' imagery used in the first column of the Damascus Document referred to above and the 'Branch' imagery that will be so prominent in the Messianic Leader (*Nasi*) text that follows below.

The reference to 'raising the dead' solves another knotty problem that much exercised Qumran commentators, namely whether those responsible for these documents held a belief in the resurrection of the dead. Though there are numerous references to 'Glory' and splendid imagery relating to Radiance and Light pervading the Heavenly abode in many texts, this is the first definitive reference to resurrection in the corpus. It should not come as a surprise, as the belief seems to have been a fixture of the Maccabean Uprising as reflected in 2 Macc. 12:44–45 and Dan. 12:2, growing in strength as it came down to first-century groups claiming descent from these archetypical events.

TRANSLITERATION   Fragment 1 Column 2

1. [הש[מ]ים והארץ ישמעו למשיחו
2. [וכל א[שר] בם לוא יסוג ממצות קדושים
3.   התאמצו מבקשי אדני בעבדתו   *vacat*
4.   הלוא בזאת תמצאו את אדני כל המיחלים בלבם
5.   כי אדני חסידים יבקר וצדיקים בשם יקרא
6.   ועל ענוים רוחו תרחף ואמונים יחליף בכחו
7.   יכבד את חסידים על כסא מלכות עד
8.   מתיר אסורים פוקח עורים זוקף כ[פופים]
9. ל[עו]לם אדבק [בו   ]שלים ובחסדו [אבטח]
10. וט[ו]בו [   ] הקדש לוא יתאחר [   ]
11. ונכ>ב<דות שלוא היו מעשה אדני כאשר י[   ]
12. אז ירפא חללים ומתים יחיה ענוים יבשר
13. [   ].ש.[קד]ושים ינהל ירעה [ב]ם יעשה
14. [   ] וכלו כ.[   ]

Fragment 1 Column 3

1. ואת חק יתרדף ואתר אותם ב[[
2. נכבדו באדם אבות על בנים [[
3. אשר ברכת אדני ברצונו [[
4. גלה ה[אר]ץ בכל מק[ו]ם   [
5. וכל ישראל בגול[ה   [
6. ו .. שב] [מכו]   [
7. מ[[

Fragment 2

1. [	]ים ונחליה[ם
2. [	[ממנו ה.]
3. [	[.נה]

Fragment 3 Column 1

1. [	]ם
2. [	
3. [	
4. [	ל<ו>א יעב<ו>ד עם אלה .]
5. [	כוח
6. [	ינדלו

Fragment 3 Column 2

1. [	ו[
2. [	]
3. [	ופ[
4. [	.[
5. [	ו...[
6. [	ואשר ת.]
7. [	קפדו אדיר[ים
8. [	וקדמי שמים]
9. [	[ו]לכל אביכ[ם

Fragment 4

1. [	
2. [	
3. [	
4. [	
5. [	יפיעו [
6. [	את אדם [
7. [	יעקוב [
8. [	וכל כלי קודשו [
9. [	וכל משיחיה .]
10. [	[ש ידבר אדני] [
11. [	את אדני בנבר[תו] [
12. [	עיני [

Fragment 5

1. [	י[ר]או [א[ת כל]
2. [	וכל אשר בה ..]
3. [	וכל מקורי מים ונחלים]

[ ] ועושים [א]ת ה... לבני אד[ם]   [ ] .4

[ ] .באלה מקל[לים] ולמה לה[ן]   [ ] .5

[ ] *vacat*   [ם ה.ד.ה את מני עמי   [ ] .6

[ ] [דה ונו.ד. לכם   ע] [אדני ...]   [ ] .7

[ ] [יתה ופתח]   [ ] .8

TRANSLATION

Fragment 1 Column 2 (1) [. . . The Hea]vens and the earth will obey His Messiah, (2) [. . . and all th]at is in them. He will not turn aside from the Commandments of the Holy Ones. (3) Take strength in His service, (you) who seek the Lord. (4) Shall you not find the Lord in this, all you who wait patiently in your hearts? (5) For the Lord will visit the Pious Ones (*Hassidim*) and the Righteous (*Zaddikim*) will He call by name. (6) Over the Meek will His Spirit hover, and the Faithful will He restore by His power. (7) He shall glorify the Pious Ones (*Hassidim*) on the Throne of the Eternal Kingdom. (8) He shall release the captives, make the blind see, raise up the do[wntrodden.] (9) For[ev]er will I cling [to Him . . .], and [I will trust] in His Piety (*Hesed*, also 'Grace'), (10) and [His] Goo[dness . . .] of Holiness will not delay . . . (11) And as for the wonders that are not the work of the Lord, when He . . . (12) then He will heal the sick, resurrect the dead, and to the Meek announce glad tidings. (13) . . . He will lead the [Ho]ly Ones; He will shepherd [th]em; He will do (14) . . . and all of it . . .

Fragment 1 Column 3 (1) and the Law will be pursued. I will free them. . . (2) Among men, the fathers are honored above the sons . . . (3) I will sing (?) the blessing of the Lord with his favor . . . (4) The l[an]d went into exile (possibly, 'rejoiced') everywh[ere . . .] (5) And all Israel in exil[e (possibly 'rejoicing') . . .] (6) . . . (7) . . .

Fragment 2 (1) . . . their inheritan[ce . . .] (2) from him . . .

Fragment 3 Column 1 (4) . . . he will not serve these people (5) . . . strength (6) . . . they will be great

Fragment 3 Column 2 (1) And . . . (3) And . . . (5) And . . . (6) And which . . . (7) They gathered the noble[s . . .] (8) And the eastern parts of the heavens . . . (9) [And] to all yo[ur] fathers . . .

Fragment 4 (5) . . . they will shine (6) . . . a man (7) . . . Jacob (8) . . . and all of His Holy implements (9) . . . and all her anointed ones (10) . . . the Lord will speak . . . (11) the Lord in [his] might (12) . . . the eyes of

Fragment 5 (1) . . . they [will] see all . . . (2) and everything in it . . . (3) and all the fountains of water, and the canals . . . (4) and those who make . . . for the sons of Ad[am . . .] (5) among these curs[ed ones.] And what . . . (6) the soothsayers of my people . . . (7) for you . . . the Lord . . . (8) and He opened . . .

2. THE MESSIANIC LEADER (*NASI* – 4Q285)
(Plate 2)

We released this text at the height of the controversy over access to the Dead Sea Scrolls in November 1991. Since then much discussion has occurred concerning it. Our purpose in releasing it was to show that there were very interesting materials in the unpublished corpus which for some reason had not been made public and to show how close the scriptural contexts in which the movement or community responsible for this text and early Christianity were operating really were.

However one reconstructs or translates this text, it is potentially very explosive. As it has been reconstructed here, it is part of a series of fragments. There is no necessary order to these fragments, nor in that of other similar materials reconstructed in this book. Such materials are grouped together on the basis either of content or handwriting or both, and the criterion most often employed is what seemed the most reasonable.

Here, the key question is whether Fragment 7 comes before or after Fragment 6. If after, as we have placed it in our reconstruction, then the Messianic *Nasi* or 'Leader' would be alive *after* the events described in Fragment 6 and could be the one 'put to death'. This was our initial assessment. If before, then it is possible that the Messianic Leader does the 'putting to death' mentioned in the text, though such a conclusion flies in the face of the logic of the appositives like 'the Branch of David. . .' grouped after the expression 'the *Nasi ha-ʿEdah*', which would be clumsy even in Hebrew.

Another question that will arise concerning this text is whether the individual who appears to be brought before 'the Leader of the Community' in Fragment 6 is the same as the one referred to in Fragment 7 by the pronoun 'him', if in fact a 'him' can be read into this line at all and not simply the plural of the verb, 'kill/killed'. In Hebrew the spelling is the same. The reader should keep in mind that whether there is any real sequentiality in these fragments or whether they even go together at all is conjectural, and these questions will probably not be resolved on the basis of the data before us.

In favour of the *Nasi ha-ʿEdah* being killed – which, all things being equal, makes most sense if Fragment 7 is considered by itself only, even without the accusative indicator in Biblical Hebrew, *'et'* – there are many texts at Qumran and from the Second Temple period generally that are not careful about the inclusion of the object indicator in their Hebrew, including the Messiah of Heaven and Earth above and the Eighteen Benedictions mentioned above. Another counter example where the object indicator is not employed occurs in Column ii. 12 of the Damascus Document, where reference is made to 'His Messiah making known the Holy Spirit', also mentioned above.

Concerning whether our reconstruction of Line 4 of Fragment 7 attaching 'the Branch of David' to 'the Leader of the Community' is correct, it is interesting to note that not only is 'the Prophet Isaiah' mentioned in Line 1, but Line 2 quotes 11:1: 'A staff shall rise from the stem of Jesse and a shoot shall grow from his roots.' There even seems to be an allusion to its second line, 'the Spirit of the Lord shall rest upon Him', in Line 6 of the Messiah of Heaven and Earth above, and we will see this same passage actually evoked at the end of the beautiful Chariots of Glory text in Chapter 7 below. This prophecy was obviously a favourite proof text at Qumran, as it very definitely was in early Christianity. But this prophecy has already been subjected to exegesis in the already-published Isaiah Commentary[a] from Cave 4. There are many such overlaps in Qumran exegeses, including that of the 'Star Prophecy' already noted.

In 4QpIs[a], the exegesis of Isa. 11:1–3 is preceded by one of Isa. 10:33–4 about 'Lebanon being felled by a Mighty One' amid allusions to 'the warriors of the Kittim' and 'Gentiles'. This seems to be the case in the Messianic Leader (*Nasi*) text as well, where allusions to 'the Kittim' in other fragments – including 'the slain of the Kittim' – abound, showing the context of the two exegeses to have been more or less parallel. These kinds of texts about 'the falling of the cedars of Lebanon' or 'Lebanon being felled by a Mighty One', as it is expressed in both texts, usually bear on the fall of the Temple or the priesthood. In Rabbinic literature, Isa. 10:33–4 is interpreted in this way, and specifically – and one might add definitively – tied to the fall of the Temple in AD 70 (see *ARN* 4 and b. Gitt 56a).

Sometimes 'Lebanon' imagery, which like 'Kittim' is used across the board in Qumran literature, relates especially when the imagery is positive, to the Community leadership. The reference is to the 'whitening' imagery implicit in the Hebrew root 'Lebanon'. This is played upon to produce the exegesis, either to Temple, because the priests wore white linen there, or to the Community Council, presumably because its members also appear to have worn white linen. Readers familiar with the New Testament will recognize 'Community' and 'Temple' here as basically parallel allusions, because just as Jesus is represented as 'the Temple' in the Gospels and in Paul, the Community Rule, using parallel spiritualized 'Temple' imagery in viii. 5–6 and ix.6, pictures the Qumran Community Council as a 'Holy of Holies for Aaron and a Temple for Israel'. This imagery, as we shall see, is widespread at Qumran, including parallel allusions to 'atonement', 'pleasing fragrance', 'Cornerstone', and 'Foundation' which go with it.

Completing the basic commonality in these texts, 4QpIs[a] also sympathetically evokes 'the Meek' and goes on to relate Isaiah 11:1's 'Staff' or 'Branch' to the 'Branch of David' in Jeremiah and Zechariah. Highlighting these Messianic and eschatological implications, it describes the Davidic 'Branch' as 'standing at the end of days' (note the language of 'standing' again). In the process, it incorporates 'the Sceptre' language from the 'Star Prophecy', which will also reappear, as we shall see, in the Shiloh Prophecy in the Genesis Florilegium below. The 'Star Prophecy', too, as the reader will recall, was quoted in a passage in the War Scroll with particular reference to 'the Meek'. The War Scroll too makes continual reference to 'Gentiles' and 'Kittim'.

To complete the circularity, 4QpIs[a] ends with an evocation of 'the Throne of Glory', again mentioned in the Messiah of Heaven and Earth text above and alluded to in Jer. 33:18 — which in turn also evokes 'the Branch of David' again — and other texts below like the Hymns of the Poor and the Mystery of Existence. We are clearly in a wide-ranging universe here of interchangeable metaphors and allusions from Biblical scripture.

The reference to 'woundings' or 'pollutions' in Line 5 of Fragment 7 of the present text and the total ambiance of reference to Messianic prophecy from Isaiah, Jeremiah, Zechariah, etc. heightens the impression that a Messianic 'execution' of some kind is being referred to. This is also the case in Isa. 11:4 where the Messianic Branch uses 'the Sceptre of his mouth . . . to put to death the wicked', however this is to be interpreted in this context.

The reader should appreciate that the *Nasi ha-'Edah* does not necessarily represent a *Messiah per se*, though he *is* being discussed in this text in terms of Messianic proof texts and allusions. '*Nasi*' is a term used also in Column v.1 of the Damascus Document when alluding to the successors of David. In fact, the term '*Nasi ha-'Edah*' itself actually appears in CD's critical interpretation of the 'Star Prophecy' in Column vii, which follows. In its exegesis CD ties it to 'the Sceptre' as we shall see in Chapter 3 below. Not only is it used in Talmudic literature to represent scions of the family of David, but coins from the Bar Kochba period also use it to designate their hero, i.e. '*Nasi* Israel' — 'Leader of Israel'. Today the term is used to designate the President of the Jewish State.

This reference to *meholalot* (woundings) in Line 5 of Fragment 7, followed by an allusion to *ha-cohen* (the priest) — sometimes meaning the high priest — would appear to refer to an allusion from Isa. 53:5 related to the famous description there of the 'Suffering Servant', so important for early Christian exegetes, i.e. 'for our sins was he wounded' or 'pierced'. Though it is possible to read *meholalot* in different ways, the idea that we have in this passage an allusion to the 'suffering death' of a Messianic figure does not necessarily follow, especially when one takes Isa. 11:4 into consideration. Everyone would have been familiar with the 'Suffering Servant' passages in Isaiah, but not everyone would have used them to imply a *doctrine* of the suffering death of a Messiah.

In fact, it is our view that the progenitors of the Qumran approach were more militant, aggressive, nationalistic and warlike than to have entertained a concept such as this in anything more than a passing manner. It has also been argued that this Messianic *Nasi* text should be attached to the War Scroll. This would further bear out the point about violent militancy, because there is no more warlike, xenophobic, apocalyptic and vengeful document — despite attempts to treat it allegorically — in the entire Qumran corpus than the War Scroll.

There can be no mistaking this thrust in the present document, nor the parallel 4QpIs[a]. Its nationalistic thrust should be clear, as should its Messianism. If these fragments do relate to the War Scroll, then they simply reinforce the Messianic passages of the last named document. The 'Kittim' in the War Scroll have been interpreted by most people to refer to the Romans. The references to Michael and the 'Kittim' in the additional fragments grouped with the present text simply reinforce these connections, increasing the sense of the Messianic nationalism of the Herodian period. However these things may be, the significance of all these allusions coming together in a little fragment such as this cannot be underestimated.

TRANSLITERATION　　　　　　　　　　　　　　　　**Fragment 1**

[	‏]ה לוייאים וחצ[יה	] .1
[	‏יו]בל לריע בהמ]	] .2
[	‏[. כתיים ו..ם]	] .3

　　　　　　　　　　　　　　　　　　　　　　　　　Fragment 2

[	‏[ם ועל]	] .1
[	‏[ם למען שמכה]	] .2
[	‏[את מיכאל נ]	] .3
l	‏[עם בחירי]ם	] .4

Fragment 3

[[טו.]   ] .1
[מטר] [ומלקו[ש   ] .2
[כהר לרוב והארץ]   ] .3
[   ]. לאין משכלה]   ] .4
[   ] לוא יראה בתבונ[ה   ] .5
[   ] מן הארץ ואין דב[ר   ] .6
[   ] קודשו נקרא . [   ] .7
[   ]לכם ובקרבכם]   ] .8

Fragment 4

[   ]למו עד]   ] .1
[   ] אתכם אל ע[   ] .2
[   ]ר ובשמים]   ] .3
[   ] בעתו ולת.]   ] .4
[ל[בב ל[   ] .5
[   ]. ולוא]   ] .6
[   ]ון כול נג.]   ] .7
[   ]ך כיא אל .]   ] .8
[   ]. .ל. ..]   ] .9

Fragment 5

[   ] מתוך] ה[עדה]   ] .1
[   ]ב הון] ו[בצע]   ] .2
[   ]ר ואכלכם א[   ] .3
[   ] להם קברי[ם   ] .4
[   ]..ל חלליה[ם   ] .5
[   ]כי עון ישובו]   ] .6
[   ] ברחמים ו[   ] .7
[   ]. יש[ר]אל עו[   ] .8
[   ]ש וא[   ] .9

Fragment 6

[   ]ת תנגף רשעה]   ] .1
[נשי[א העדה וכול ישר[אל   ] .2
[   ]ה כת..]   ] .3
[   ] על הרי]   ] .4
[ה[כתיים]   ] .5
[נש[י]א העדה עד הים ה[גדול   ] .6
[   ]ו מפני ישראל בעת ההיאה]   ] .7
[   ]יעמוד עליהם ונעכרו עליהם]   ] .8

9. [   ] ישבו אל היבשה בעת הה[י]אה   [

10. [   ] יביאוהו לפני נשיא [העדה   [

Fragment 7

1. [   ] ישעיהו הנביא וניקפ[ו סבכי היער בברזל [

2. [ולבנון באדיר י]פול ויצא חוטר מטע ישי [ונצר משרשיו יפרה [

3. [   ] צמח דויד ונשפטו את [[

4. [   ] והמיתו נשיא העדה צמ[ח]ח דויד   [

5. [   ] ם ובמחוללות וצוה כוהן [[

6. [   ] ח[ל]ל[י] כתיי[ם [ל]   [

TRANSLATION

Fragment 1 (1) ... the Levites, and ha[lf ...] (2) [the ra]m's horn, to blow on them ... (2) the Kittim, and ...

Fragment 2 (1) ... and against ... (2) for the sake of Your Name ... (3) Michael ... (4) with the Elec[t ...]

Fragment 3 (2) ... rain ... and spring [rain ...] (3) as great as a mountain. And the earth ... (4) to those without sense ... (5) he will not gaze with Understand[ing ...] (6) from the earth. And noth[ing ...] (7) His Holiness. It will be called ... (8) your ... and in your midst ...

Fragment 4 (1) ... until ... (2) you, to (or 'God') ... (3) and in Heaven ... (4) in its time, and to ... (5) [he]art, to ... (6) and not ... (7) all ... (8) for God ...

Fragment 5 (1) ... from the midst of [the] community ... (2) Riches [and] booty ... (3) and your food ... (4) for them, grave[s ...] (5) the[ir] slain ... (6) of iniquity will return ... (7) in compassion and ... (8) Is[r]ael ...

Fragment 6 (1) ... Wickedness will be smitten ... (2) [the Lea]der of the Community and all Isra[el ...] (4) upon the mountains of ... (5) [the] Kittim ... (6) [the Lea]der of the Community as far as the [Great] Sea ... (7) before Israel in that time ... (8) he will stand against them, and they will muster against them ... (9) they will return to the dry land in th[at] time ... (10) they will bring him before the Leader of [the Community ...]

Fragment 7 (1) ... Isaiah the Prophet, ['The thickets of the forest] will be fell[ed with an axe] (2) [and Lebanon shall f]all [by a mighty one.] A staff shall rise from the root of Jesse, [and a Planting from his roots will bear fruit.'] (3) ... the Branch of David. They will enter into Judgement with ... (4) and they will put to death the Leader of the Community, the Bran[ch of David] (this might also be read, depending on the context, 'and the Leader of the Community, the Bran[ch of David'], will put him to death) ... (5) and with woundings, and the (high) priest will command ... (6) [the sl]ai[n of the] Kitti[m] ...

3. THE SERVANTS OF DARKNESS (4Q471)

This is a text of extreme significance and another one related to the War Scroll. The violence, xenophobia, passionate nationalism and concern for Righteousness and the Judgements of God are evident throughout. Though these may have a metaphoric meaning as well as an actual one, it is impossible to think that those writing these texts were not steeped in the ethos of a militant army of God, and hardly that of a peaceful, retiring community. Their spirit is unbending, uncompromising. They give no quarter and expect none.

There is the particularly noteworthy stress on 'Lying', a theme one finds across the spectrum of Qumran literature, in particular where the opponents of the community or movement responsible for these writings are concerned. There is also the actual use of the verb *ma'as* (meaning to 'reject' or 'deny') in Fragment 2.7, paralleling similar usages in the Community Rule, the Habakkuk *Pesher*, etc.

In texts such as these, *ma'as* is always used to portray the activities of the ideological adversary of the Righteous Teacher, the 'Liar'/ 'Spouter' who 'rejects the Law in the midst of the whole congregation' or the parallel activities of those archetypical 'sons/servants of Darkness' who do likewise. Here it is used in contradistinction to 'choosing' – in this case the groups' opponents reverse the natural order; they 'choose the Evil', instead of 'the Good', which they 'reject'.

Similar reversals occur across the board in Qumran literature – one particularly noteworthy one in Column i of the Damascus Document, where 'justifying the Wicked and condemning the Righteous' on the part of 'the Breakers' of both 'Law and Covenant' is juxtaposed in Column iv with the proper order noted below of 'justifying the Righteous and condemning the Wicked'. This last is definitive of 'the sons of Zadok', itself synonymous probably too with 'the *Zaddikim*' in Line 5 of the Messiah of Heaven and Earth text. Both texts use the same reference, 'called by name', as descriptive of these respective terminologies.

There is the usual emphasis on fire, presumably the Judgements of Hell fire, and there is no shirking the duty for war, which is to be seen in some sense, if Fragment 4 is taken into account, as being fought under levitical or priestly command (cf. War Scroll ii.1–3). There is the usual emphasis on 'works' (Fragment 2, Column 4 reconstructed) and particularly noteworthy is the reference to 'Servants of Darkness' as opposed presumably to 'Servants of Light'.

The Jamesian parallels to the theme of 'works' should be clear; so too should Paul's characterization in 2 Cor. 11–12 of the Hebrew 'archapostles' – presumably including James – as disguising themselves as 'Servants of Righteousness' (cf. the actual use of this allusion in the Testaments of Naphtali below) and 'apostles of Christ', when in fact they are 'dishonest workmen and counterfeit apostles'. Paul also employs 'Light' terminology in this passage, not to mention an allusion to 'Satan' so important in referring to Mastemoth/Mastema and its parallels below, i.e. 'even Satan disguises himself as an Angel of Light.' Emphasizing 'Truth' (the opposite, it will be noted, of 'Lying') and at the same time parodying the position of *everyman according to his works*, in 11:31 he revealingly insists, 'he does not lie', thus demonstrating his awareness of the currency of these kinds of accusations at this time. His application of such 'Lying' terminology – so widespread in these Qumran documents – to himself, even if inadvertently, is noteworthy indeed.

One should also note, in particular, the widespread vocabulary of 'Judgement', the 'Heavenly Hosts' and even 'pollution'. Notice, too, the consistent emphasis on 'Righteousness' and 'Righteous Judgement', and on 'keeping', i.e. 'keeping the Law' – 'Covenant' in this text. The group responsible for these writings is extremely Law-oriented and their zeal in this regard is unbending. The very use of the word 'zeal' connects the literature with the Zealot mentality and movement.

The terms 'keeping' and 'Keepers of the Covenant' also relate to the second definition in Column 4 of the Community Rule of 'the sons of Zadok', a term with probable esoteric parallels and variations in 'sons of Righteousness', as we have seen above. One should also note the use of the word 'reckoned' in Line 5 of Fragment 1, which resonates with the use of this term in the key Letters on Works Righteousness below in Chapter 6.

TRANSLITERATION   Fragment 1

לעת צויתם לבלתי [	[.1
ם ותשקרו בבריתו[	[.2
אמרו נלחמה מלחמותיו כיא נאלנו[	[.3
יכם ישפלו ולוא ידעו כיא באש[	[.4
תתגברו למלחמה ואתם נחשבתם [	[.5
בקיאי *vacat* משפט צדק תשאלו ועבודת [	[.6
תתנשאו ויבחר ב]כמה [לזעקה [	[.7
ומחוק [ותשור]ף [	[.8

Fragment 2

[	‏[ש ..א‎	] .1
[	‏[לשמר עדוות בריתנו‎	] .2
[	‏[ור כול צבאותם באורך א[פים‎	] .3
[	‏[ולהניא לבבם מכול מ[עשה‎	] .4
[	‏[ע[בדי חושך כיא משפט‎	] .5
[	‏[באשמת גורלו ..‎	] .6
[	‏[למאוס בטו[ב ולבחור ברע‎	] .7
[	‏[ל שנא אל ויצוב ל[‎	] .8
[	‏[כול הטוב אשר‎	] .9

Fragment 3

[	‏[אל ול[‎	] .1
[	‏[עולמים וישימנו‎	] .2
[	‏[שפ[ט עמו בצדק ול[אומו‎	] .3
[	‏[. ם בכול חוקי‎	] .4
[	‏[לנו בנעוות[נו‎	] .5
[	‏[לוע[‎	] .6

Fragment 4

‏[ה מכול אש[ר‎		] .1
‏[כול איש מאחיו מפני‎		] .2
‏[ו והיו עמו תמיד וש[רתו‎		] .3
‏[כול שבט ושב[ט] איש‎		] .4
‏[ששה ועש[רים ומן [ה]לוים שנים‎		] .5
‏[ויש[רתו לפניו] תמיד על‎	[עשר	.6
‏[. ל[מען יהיו מלמדי‎		] .7

TRANSLATION

Fragment 1 (1) . . . the time You have commanded them not to (2) . . . and you shall lie about His Covenant (3) . . . they say, 'Let us fight His wars, for we have polluted (4) . . . your [enemie]s shall be brought low, and they shall not know that by fire (5) . . . gather courage for war, and you shall be reckoned (6) . . . you shall ask of the experts of Righteous Judgement and the service of (7) . . . you shall be lifted up, for He chose [you] . . . for shouting (8) . . . and you shall bur[n . . .] and sweet . . .

Fragment 2 (2) to keep the testimonies of our Covenant . . . (3) all their hosts in forbear[ance . . .] (4) and to restrain their heart from every w[ork . . . (5) Se]rvants of Darkness, because the Judgement . . . (6) in the guilt of his lot . . . (7) [to reject the Go]od and to choose the Evil . . . (8) God hates and He will erect . . . (9) all the Good that . . .

Fragment 3 (2) Eternal, and He will set us . . . (3) [He jud]ges His people in Righteousness and [His] na[tion in . . .] (4) in all the Laws of . . . (5) us in [our] sins . . .

Fragment 4 (1) from all tha[t . . .] (2) every man from his brother, because (3) . . . and they shall remain with Him always and shall se[rve] (4) . . . each and every tribe, a man (5) . . . [twen]ty-[six] and from [the] Levites six-(6) [teen . . .] and [they] shall se[rve before Him] always upon (7) . . . [in] order that they may be instructed in . . .

4. THE BIRTH OF NOAH (4Q534–536)

A pseudepigraphic text with visionary and mystical import, the several fragments of this text give us a wonderfully enriched picture of the figure of Noah, as seen by those who created this literature. In the first place, the text describes the birth of Noah as taking place at night, and specifies his weight. It describes him as 'sleeping until the division of the day', probably implying noon.

One of the primordial Righteous Ones whose life and acts are soteriological in nature, Noah is of particular interest to writers of this period like Ben Sira and the Damascus Document. The first *Zaddik* (Righteous One) mentioned in scripture (Gen. 6:9), Noah was also 'born Perfect', as the rabbis too insist, as is stressed in this passage. Because of this 'Perfection', Rabbinical literature has Noah born circumcized. However this may be, 'Perfection' language of this kind is extremely important in the literature at Qumran, as it is in the New Testament. See, in this regard, the Sermon on the Mount's parallel: 'Be perfect as your Father in Heaven is Perfect' (Matt. 5:48).

'Perfection' imagery fairly abounds in the literature at Qumran, often in connection with another important notation in early Christianity, 'the Way' terminology. For Acts, 'the Way' is an alternative name for Christianity in its formative period in Palestine from the 40s to the 60s AD (Acts 16:16, 18:24f., and 24:22). At Qumran it is widespread and also associated with 'walking', as well as the important 'Way in the wilderness' proof text. One has phrases like 'the Perfect of the Way', 'Perfection of the Way', 'walking in Perfection', and the very interesting 'Perfect Holiness' or 'the Perfection of Holiness' also known to Paul in 2 Cor. 7:1.

In this text, too, the Kabbalistic undercurrents should be clear and the portrayal of Noah as a Wisdom figure, or one who understands the Secret Mysteries, becomes by the end of Fragment 2 its main thrust. Noah is, therefore, one who is involved in Heavenly 'ascents' or 'journeying' or at least one who 'knows' the Mysteries of 'the Highest Angels'. For more on these kinds of Mysteries see Chapters 5 and 7 below, particularly the Mystery of Existence text.

This emphasis on 'Mysteries' is, of course, strong again in Paul, who in 2 Cor. 12:1–5 speaks of his own 'visions' and of knowing someone 'caught up into the Third Heaven' or 'Paradise'. One should also not miss the quasi-Gnostic implications of some of the references to 'knowing' and 'Knowledge' here and throughout this corpus. These kinds of allusions again have particular importance in Chapters 5 and 7.

As the text states, echoing similar Biblical and Kabbalistic projections of Noah, Noah is someone who 'knows the secrets of all living things'. Here, the 'Noahic Covenant' is not unimportant, not only to Rabbinic literature, but also in directives to overseas communities associated with James's leadership of the early Church in Jerusalem from the 40s to the 60s AD. (James also seems to have absorbed some of Noah's primordial vegetarianism.) This abstention from 'blood', 'food sacrificed to idols' (i.e. idolatry), 'strangled things' (probably 'carrion' as the Koran 16:115 delineates it) and 'fornication', which Acts attributes to James in three different places, are also part and parcel of the 'Noahic Covenant' incumbent on all 'the Righteous' of mankind delineated in Rabbinic literature. They survive, curiously enough, as the basis of Koranic dietary regulations, in this sense, the Arabs being one of the 'Gentile peoples' *par excellence*.

The specifics of Noah's physical characteristics are also set forth in this text, and the reference to his being 'the Elect of God' is extremely important. A synonym for *Zaddik* or 'Righteous One' in the minds of the progenitors of this literary tradition, the term 'the Elect' is also used in the Damascus Document in the definition of 'the sons of Zadok' (iv.3f.), showing the esoteric or qualitative – even eschatological – nature of these basically interchangeable terminologies. It also appears in an extremely important section of the Habakkuk *Pesher*, having to do with 'the Judgement God will make in the midst of many nations', i.e. 'the Last Judgement', in which 'the Elect of God' are actually said to participate (x.13).

The reference to the 'Three Books' is also interesting, and certainly these 'books' must have been seen as having to do with the mystic knowledge of the age, or as it were, the Heavenly or Angelic Mysteries. In regard to these, too, the second half of this text has many affinities with the Chariots of Glory and Mystery of Existence texts in Chapter 7.

TRANSLITERATION   Fragment 1

.1 [   ] [מתילד יהוון מרמש כחדה .[   ]
.2 [   ] [ש בליליא מתילד ונפק של]ם
.3 [   ] [ב]מתקל תקלין תלת מאה וחמ]שין
.4 [   ] [יא דמך עד מפלג יומיא ע]
.5 [   ] [ביממא עד משלם שנין ו] [ב]
.6 [   ] [נזחה לה מנה לא ...] [ ] שנ]י]ן]

Fragment 2 Column 1

.1 [   ] [.יא תהוא [ ]
.2 [   ] ק]דישין ידכר]ון]
.3 [   ] [לה יתנלון נהי]רין]
.4 [   ] [י]אלפ>ו<נה כולה זי [ ]
.5 [   ] ח]כמת אנש וכול חכי]ם]
.6 [   ] [במתחא ורב להוא
.7 [   ] י]חזיע אנשא ועד
.8 [   ] [ינלא רזין כעליונין
.9 [   ] [ין ובטעם רזי
.10 [   ] [א ואף
.11 [   ] [בעפרא
.12 [   ] ס]לק רזא
.13 [   ] [. מנתה

Fragment 2 Column 2

.7 [   ] מן ה]
.8 [   ] עבד]
.9 [   ] די אנחה יצף מנה לכול אמ] [ ] .
.10 [   ] כסותה בסוף מחסניך אתקף טובוהי מ..] [ק]
.11 ולא ימות ביומי רשעא וילכה סכלא די פמך ירמנכה
.12 חובה למאמת מן יכתוב מלי אלה בכתב די לא יבלא ומאמרי
.13 תעדה עדי ועדן רשיעין ידעך לעלמין נבר די לעבדיך ל]

Fragment 3 Column 1

.1 [ ] מן [ק]שב]ומה שו] [כמה] [א]די ידא תרתין [ ]
.2 [   ] [שערה] ו]טלופחין על]
.3 ..ליה וש]ומן זוערין על ירכתה]ומן בתר תרת]ין שנין דן מן דן ידע
.4 בעלימותה להוה כלהון [כאנ]וש די לא ידע מדע]ם עד] עדן די
.5 [י]נדע תלתת ספריא   *vacat*   [ ]   *vacat*
.6 [בא]דין יערם וידע שו]כלא[ ]שן חזון למאתה לה על ארכובת]ה[
.7 ובאבוהי ובא]ב]כ]התוהי ..] [חין וזקינה עמה לה]וו]ן מלכה וערמומ]ה[
.8 [ו]ידע רזי אנשא וחוכמתה לכול עממיא תהך וידע רזי כול חייא

9. ‏[וכ]ול חשבוניהון עלוהי יסופו ומסרת כול חייא שניא תהוא
10. ‏[וימטון כול ח]שבונוהי בדי בחיר אלהא הוא מולדה ורוח נשמוהי
11. ‏[ ]   ‏ח]שבונוהי להוון לעלמין[ ]   ‏[
12. ‏[ ]   ‏א] די ל]‏   ‏לין[ ]..[
13. ‏[ ]   ‏ת חשב]ון[
14. ‏[ ]   ‏ב[
15. ‏[ ]   ‏והי[
16. ‏[ ]   ‏.[
17. ‏[ ]   ‏.[

TRANSLATION

Fragment 1 (1) . . . (When) he is born, they shall all be darkened together . . . (2) he is born in the night and he comes out Perfe[ct . . .] (3) [with] a weight of three hundred and fif[ty] shekels (about 7 pounds, 3 ounces) . . . (4) he slept until the division of the days . . . (5) in the daytime until the completion of years . . . (6) a share is set aside for him, not . . . years . . .

Fragment 2 Column 1 (1) . . . will be . . . (2) [H]oly Ones will remem[ber . . .] (3) lig[hts] will be revealed to him (4) . . . they [will] teach him everything that (5) . . . human [Wi]sdom, and every wise ma[n . . .] (6) in the lands (?), and he shall be great (7) . . . mankind shall [be] shaken, and until (8) . . . he will reveal Mysteries like the Highest Angels (9) . . . and with the Understanding of the Mysteries of (10) . . . and also (11) . . . in the dust (12) . . . the Mystery [as]cends (13) . . . portions . . .

Fragment 2 Column 2 (7) from . . . (8) he did . . . (9) of which you are afraid for all . . . (10) his clothing at the end in your warehouses. (?) I will strengthen his Goodness . . . (11) and he will not die in the days of Wickedness, and the Wisdom of Your mouth will go forth. He who opposes You (12) will deserve death. One will write the words of God in a book that does not wear out, but my words (13) you will adorn. At the time of the Wicked, he will know you forever, a man of your servants . . .

Fragment 3 Column 1 (1) . . . of the hand, two . . . it lef[t] a mark from . . . (2) barley [and] lentils on . . . (3) and tiny marks on his thigh . . . [After tw]o years he will be able to discern one thing from another . . . (4) In his youth he will be . . . all of them . . . [like a ma]n who does not know anyth[ing, until] the time when (5) he shall have come to know the Three Books. (6) [Th]en he will become wise and will be disc[rete . . .] a vision will come to him while upon [his] knees (in prayer). (7) And with his father and his forefa[th]ers . . . life and old age; he will acquire counsel and prudence, (8) [and] he will know the Secrets of mankind. His Understanding will spread to all peoples, and he will know the Secrets of all living things.

(9) [Al]l their plans against him will be fruitless, and the spiritual legacy for all the living will be enriched. (10) [And all] his [p]lans [will succeed], because he is the Elect of God. His birth and the Spirit of his breath (11) . . . his [p]lans will endure forever . . . (12) that . . . (13) pl[an . . .]

5. THE WORDS OF MICHAEL (4Q529)

This text, which could also be referred to as 'The Vision of Michael', clearly belongs to the literature of Heavenly Ascents and visionary recitals just discussed regarding the birth of Noah and alluded to by no less an authority than Paul. Such recitals are also common in the literature relating to Enoch and Revelations. They are part and parcel of the ecstatic and visionary tendencies in the Qumran corpus that succeeding visionaries are clearly indebted to, including those going underground and re-emerging in the Kabbalistic Wisdom of the Middle Ages and beyond. In our discussion of the Mystery of Existence text in Chapter 7 we highlight some of these correspondences to the work of a writer like Solomon ibn Gabirol in the eleventh century AD.

This genre can be seen as having one of its earliest exemplars here. The reference to the Angel Gabriel in Line 4 is of particular importance and follows that of one of the first such visionary recitals, Daniel, a book of the utmost importance for Qumran visionaries and in the Qumran apocalyptic scheme generally. Daniel, too, is a work integrally tied to the Maccabean Uprising, as are − at least in spirit − many of the Qumran documents. As in Dan. 8:16, Gabriel is here the interpreter of the vision or, if one prefers, the Heavenly or mystic guide − though by the end of the vision as extant in this fragment, it is no longer clear whether Michael or Gabriel is having the vision.

In the Islamic tradition − a later adumbration clearly owing much to the tradition we see developing here − Gabriel serves as the revealing or dictating Angel co-extensive with what in Christian tradition might otherwise be called the Holy Spirit. Here, whatever else one might say of him, Gabriel is the guide in the Highest Heaven − traditions about Muhammad too are not immune from such Heavenly Ascents − not unlike the role Dante ascribes to Virgil and finally Beatrice in his rendition of a similar ecstatic ascent and vision.

Here the Archangel Michael ascends to the Highest Heaven. Some practitioners of this kind of mystic journeying speak of three 'layers' (again see Paul in 2 Cor. 12:2), some of seven, and some of twelve. He then appears to descend to tell the ordinary Angels what he has seen, though, as we have noted, how his role differs from Gabriel's is difficult to understand in the text as presently extant. While in Heaven Michael beholds the 'Glory of God' — literally 'Greatness' in Aramaic. Ezekiel — a prophet of the utmost importance in Qumran tradition, not only for works of this kind, but also for the notion of the 'sons of Zadok' terminology generally — is one of the first to have had such visions relating to the divine 'Glory'. The terminology is also important in the New Testament and fairly widespread at Qumran.

Most of the vision is incomprehensible, but one idea, which re-appears in Paul and Kabbalistic tradition generally, is found here — that of the New or Heavenly Jerusalem, i.e. while in Heaven Michael learns of a city to be built. This apocalyptic and visionary genre clearly owes much to imagery in Daniel and is reiterated in the pseudo-Daniel works in Chapter 2. But the actual themes of Heavenly Ascents and a Heavenly Jerusalem again go all the way back to Ezekiel's visions. Not only is Ezekiel picked up by an Angel-like 'Holy Spirit' and deposited in Jerusalem as part of his ecstatic visionary experience early in that book (Ezek. 8:3), but at the end of the book ascribed to him, he is picked up again and proceeds to measure out a new Temple (40–48). This theme is the crux of the next work, which was either directly ascribed to Ezekiel or operated as part of a pseudo-Ezekiel genre.

TRANSLITERATION

1. מלי כתבא די אמר מיכאל למלאכי אל [מן בתר די סלק לשמיא עליא]
2. אמר די גדודי נורא תמה השכח[ת]
3. [והא] תשעה טורין תרין למד[נ]חא ותרין לצפונא ותרין למערבא ותרין [
4. [לדר]ומא תמה חזית לגבריאל מלאכ[א אמרת לה[
5. א...א והחזיתה חזוה ואמר לי]
6. בספרי די רבו מרא עלמא כתיב ה.]
7. [ ] בני חם לבני שם והא רבו מרא עלמא]
8. כדי כשבין דמעא מן ..דרא]
9. והא מתבניה קריה לשמה די רבו [מרא עלמא ולא[
10. יתעבד כל די באיש קודם רבו מר[א עלמא
11. וידכר רבו מרא עלמא לבריתה ל[טב ברכתא ויקרא ותשבחתא]
12. [לר]בו מרא עלמא לה רחמין ולה]
13. במדינתא רחיקתא להוא גבר ל]
14. הוא ולהוא אמר לה הא דן ה.]
15. לי כספא ודהבא] והא. [ ]

TRANSLATION

(1) The words of the book that Michael spoke to the Angels of God [after he had ascended to the Highest Heaven.] (2) He said 'I found troops of fire

there . . . (3) [Behold,] there were nine mountains, two to the eas[t and two to the north and two to the west and two] (4) [to the so]uth. There I beheld Gabriel the Angel . . . I said to him, (5) '. . . and you rendered the vision comprehensible.' Then he said to me . . . (6) It is written in my book that the Great One, the Eternal Lord . . . (7) the sons of Ham to the sons of Shem. Now behold, the Great One, the Eternal Lord . . . (8) when . . . tears from . . . (9) Now behold, a city will be built for the Name of the Great One, [the Eternal Lord] . . . [And no] (10) evil shall be committed in the presence of the Great One, [the Eternal] Lord . . . (11) Then the Great One, the Eternal Lord, will remember His creation [for the purpose of Good] . . . [Blessing and honor and praise] (12) [be to] the Great One, the Eternal Lord. To Him belongs Mercy and to Him belongs . . . (13) In distant territories there will be a man . . . (14) he is, and He will say to him, 'Behold this . . . (15) to Me silver and gold . . .'

6. THE NEW JERUSALEM (4Q554)
(Plate 3)

The Aramaic work known as 'The New Jerusalem' has turned up in Qumran Caves 1, 2, 4, 5 and 11 with the most extensive portions coming from Caves 4 and 5. The author is obviously working under the inspiration of Ezekiel's vision of the new Temple or the Temple of the end of days referred to above (Ezek. 40–48), which he elaborates or extends into the ideal picture of Jerusalem. This vision is reminiscent not only of Ezekiel's description of how he measures out the new Temple, but also of parts of the Temple Scroll from Qumran and the New Testament Book of Revelation.

In the New Jerusalem the visionary, most likely Ezekiel himself – though in the extant fragments no name is accorded him – is led around the city that will stand on the site of Zion. His companion, presumably an Angel – possibly even Gabriel or Michael of the previous visionary recitals – points out various structures while measuring them with a cane seven cubits long, i.e. about 10.5 feet.

A precise understanding of the text remains elusive because of several problems: the use of rare or previously unknown vocabulary, the many breaks in the manuscripts, and the inherent difficulty of using words to convey ideas that really require an architectural draw-ing. In spite of these problems, these Cave 4 materials contribute substantially to our knowledge of the city that the author envisaged.

He conceived of a city of immense size, a rectangle of some 13 x 18 miles. Surrounding the city was a wall through which passed twelve gates, one for each of the twelve tribes of Israel. In keeping with the priestly emphasis of the text, an emphasis common to other texts like the Testament of Levi or the Testament of Kohath, which might indicate a Maccabean or at least a pro-Maccabean ethos to the vision, the Gate of Levi stood in the position of greatest honour in the centre of the eastern wall — that is to say, directly in line with the sacrificial altar and the entrance to the Temple.

With the Cave 4 additions to what was previously known of this text, we find that nearly 1,500 towers, each more than 100 feet tall were to guard the city. The final fragment, if it is part of the manuscript in the manner indicated (Column 11 or later), moves into more apocalyptic and eschatological motifs. The 'Kittim' are specifically referred to. It is generally conceded that, as in the Book of Daniel, the Kittim refer to the Romans (Dan. 11:30), though in 1 Macc. 1:1 the expression is applied to Alexander the Great's forces.

These 'Kittim', as noted, are a key conceptuality in the literature found at Qumran, and reference to them, as we have seen, is widespread in the corpus, particuarly in texts like the War Scroll, the Nahum *Pesher*, the Habakkuk *Pesher*, the Isaiah *Pesher*[a], etc., not to mention the Messianic Leader (*Nasi*) text. The reference here reinforces the impression of the total homogeneity of the corpus, i.e. that crucial ideas, concepts, and expressions move and recur from document to document. If the term is used here in the manner of the War Scroll, the Nahum *Pesher* (where they come after Greek Seleucid Kings like Antiochus and Demetrius) and the Habakkuk *Pesher*, then references to Edom, Moab and the like could refer to various petty kingdoms — what in the Damascus Document are called 'the Kings of the Peoples' like the Herodians and others.

At the end of the New Jerusalem the Aramaic equivalent to the word 'Peoples' is also signalled. This is an expression used in the jargon of Roman law to refer to petty kingdoms in the eastern part of the Empire. In both the Damascus Document, where the expression 'Kings of the Peoples' is actually used (viii. 10) and in the Habakkuk *Pesher*, where the terms *ha-ʿAmim* and *yeter ha-ʿAmim* ('the additional ones of the Peoples') are expounded (ix. 5ff.), similar meanings can be discerned. This expression also has to be seen as generically parallel to Paul's important use of it in Rom. 11:11–13 when describing his own missionary activities (i.e. he is 'the Apostle to the Peoples'). However, it is possible that we do not have a chronological sequentiality here.

At the end of Column 11 according to our reconstruction, it is clear that Israel is to emerge triumphant; and there may even be a reference to that Messianic 'Kingdom' that 'will never pass away' first signalled in Dan. 2:45 and, in fact, referred to in the Pseudo-Daniel texts later in this collection. The intense imagery of these great eschatological events centred in some way on Jerusalem might seem strange to the modern reader, but such ideas are directly in line with the scheme of the War Scroll already referred to, not to mention the Book of Revelation, where the same word 'Babylon' occurs and is clearly meant to refer to Rome. That such religious and nationalistic intensity could be bound up with measurement and the matter-of-factness of often barren description is precisely the point: the future could be so certain as to acquire such a patina. This was reassuring indeed.

TRANSLITERATION

Column 2

9. [ ] [ ].[ ] שתת עשר [
10. [ ] נ]ה וכלהון מבינין דן
11. [ ] ומשח מן זוית] מדנחא די בצפונא
12. [לדרומא עד תרעא קדמיא ר]אסין תלתין וחמשה ושם
13. [תרעא דן קרין לה תרע] שמעון ומן ת]רעא דן עד ת]רעא מציע{י}א
14. [משח ראסין תלתין וחמשה] ושם תרעא דן די [קר]ין לה תרע
15. [לוי ומן תרעא דן משח לדר]ומא ראסין תלתין וחמשה
16. [ושם תרעא דן קרין לה תרע יהודה ומן] תרעא דן משח עד זוית
17. [מדנחא די בדרומא ומשח] מן   זויתא דא למערבא
18. [ראסין 3IIII ושם תרעא דן] קרין לה תרע יוסף
19. [ומשח מן תרעא דן עד תרעא מציעא ראסי]ן 3IIII ושם
20. [תרעא דן קרין לה בנימין ומן תר]עא דן משח עד תרעא
21. [תליתיא ראסין 3IIII וקרין לה] תרע ראובן ו[מן תר]עא דן
22. [משח עד זויתא מערבא ראסין 3IIII ו]מן דא זויתא משח עד

Column 3

5. [ ] מש[ח ראסין]
6. [13 III [ ] ושם [תרעא דן קרין לה תרע דן ומשח] מן תרעא [דן עד תרעא]
7. מציעיא רסין [3III] ושם תרעא דן קרי]ן לה תרע נפתלי ומן [דן]
8. תרעא משח עד תרעא ת]ליתיא ר]סין 3 II [ ]II ושם תרעא דן קרין
9. לה תרע   אשר   ומש]ח מן תר]עא דן עד זוית{א} די מדנחא רסין
10. 3IIII   *vacat*
11. ואעלני לנוא קריתא ומ]שח כל פר]זיתא אורכא ופתיא קנין
12. 33ר—1 ב 33ר—[מ]רבעה]   *vacat*   אמין III ר 33ר—
13. IIIIIII ולכל רוח ושבכ [ס]חר סחר לפרזיתא ברית שוק קנין
14. תלתה אמין 13 ו[כ]רן [א]חזיני מש[ח]ת פרזיא כלהן בין פרזא לפרזא
15. שוק פתה קנין שתה [אמין 1133] ושקיא רברביא די נפקין
16. מן מדנחא למערב]א קנין]   עשרה פותי שוקא אמין

17. ‏333 ‎ה־II מנהון ות[לי]חיא   די על [שמא]ל מקדשא משה
18. ‏קנין אמין ה־IIIIIIII פתי אמין [ה־ 3 II]I3 ‎II]II ופתי
19. ‏שוקיא די נפקין מן דרו[מא לצפונא   תרי מנהון קנ]ין IIIIIIII
20. ‏ואמין IIII לשוק חד לאמי[ן שתין ושבע   ומציעיא די במצ]יעת
21. ‏קריתא משה פתיה קנין ה־III   ואמה חדה ואמין 3333 ‎ה־II
22. ‏וכל שוקא וקריתא [רציפין באבן חור]   *vacat*

Column 4

1. ‏[שש ויהלם   ואחזיני]
2. ‏[משחת שפשיא תמנין פותיהון די שפשיא קנין אמין תרין אמין ארבע עשרה]
3. ‏[על כל תרע ותרע דשין תרין די אבן פותיה די דשיא]
4. ‏[קנה חד אמין שבע   ואחזיני משחת ...יא תרי עשר פותי [
5. ‏[תרעיהון קנין תלתה אמין עשרין וחדה   על כל תרע ותרע דשין]
6. ‏[תרין פותי דשיא קנא חד ופלג אמין עשר ופלג [
7. ‏[וליד כל תרע תרי מגדלין חד מן ימינא]
8. ‏[וחד מן שמאלא פותיהון ואורכהון משחה חדה קנין חמשה בחמשה אמין]
9. ‏[תלתין וחמש ודרגא די סלק ליד תרעא בנוא על ימין מגדליא ברום]
10. ‏[מגדליא פתיה אמין חמש מגדליא ודרניא קנין חמשה בחמשה אמין]
11. ‏[חמש לאמין ארבעין בכל רוח תרעא   *vacat* [
12. ‏[ואחזיני משחת תרעי פרזיא פתיהון קנין תרין אמין ארבע עשרה]
13. ‏ופתי .]   [יא משחתה אמין [ומשח] פתיה די כל אספא
14. ‏קני[ן תרין א[מין ה־IIII וית טלולא אמה חדה [ומשח על כל] א[ספא ית]
15. ‏דשין לה ומשח בנוא אספא ארכה אמ[ין ה־II]II ופתיה אמין עש[רים וחד]
16. ‏אעל[ן]י לנוא אספא והא אסוף אחרן ותרעא עוד כתלא גוא די ליד ימינא
17. ‏כמש[ח]ת תרעא בריא פתיה אמין ארבע רומה אמין IIIIIII ודשין לה תרין וקו[דם]
18. ‏[תר[עא דן אסף עללה פתיה קנה ח[ד] אמין שבע וארכה עלל קנין תרין א[מין]
19. ‏ה־IIII ורומה קנין תרין א ה־II]I [I] ותרע לקבל תרעא פתיה לנוא פרזית[א]
20. ‏כמשחת תרעא בריא ועל שמאל מעלה דן אחזיני בית דרג סח[ר וסלק] פ[תיה]
21. ‏משחה חדה קנין תרין בתרין אמין ארבע עשרה ות[רעין לקבל תרעין]
22. ‏כמשח[ת]ה ועמוד [ב]נ[וה די דרגא סחר וסל[ק עלוהי פתיה וארכה]

Column 5

1. ‏[משחה חדה אמין שת בשת מרבע] ודרגא ד[י סלק לידה] פתיה אמין ארבע וסחר
2. ‏[וסלק רום קנין תרין עד   [*vacat*
3. ‏[ואעלני לנוא פרזיתא ואחזיני בה בתין מן תרע ל]תרע חמשת עשר תמניה בחדה
   רוח עד זויתא
4. ‏[ושבעה מן זויתא עד תרעא אחרנא <פותי]הון> ארך בתיא קנין תלתה אמין 13 ופתיהון
5. ‏[קנין תרין אמין ה־IIII וכדן כל תוניא] רומהון קנין תרין אמין ה־IIII ותרעהון
   במציעתא
6. ‏[א]רבע ארך ורום קנה חד אמין שבע
7. ‏[א]רכהון ופתיהון אמין ה־II בית

8. [ ] לידה אמה בריתא [
9. [ ] רו[ם קדמיתא אמין
10. [ ] יא ופותיהון אמין[
11. [ ] קנין תרין אמין ארבע [
12. [עשרה] א[מ]ה חדה ופלג ורומה גו
13. [ ] ...תנא ית טלולא די עליהון[...

Column 9 (or later)

14. [ ] קני[ן] תרין
15. [אמין ארבע עשרה] ואמין[
16. [ ] משחת .[
17. [ ] תח[ומי קריתא

Column 10 (or later)

13. [ ] [מ] [ ] [ן .] [ן .א ..א יסודה פתיה קנין תרין אמין
14. ארבע ע[ש]רא ורומה קנין שבעה אמין ארבעין ותשע וכלה
15. בניה בחש[מל] וספיר וכדכוד ועשיתה דהב ומגדליה אלף
16. [ארבע מא[א]ה תלתין ותרין ופתיהון וארכהון משחה חדה
17. [ ] ורמהון קנין עשרה
18. [אמין שבעין קנין תרין אמין] ד – IIII
19. [ ] אר[כהן
20. [ ] מצעיא אמין
21. [ ] תרין לתרעא
22. [ ] לכל רו[ח]יא תלת תלת מגדליא נפקין

Column 11 (or later)

14. [ ] ... ...[
15. [ ] באתרה ומלכות מ[ן
16. [ ] כתיא באתרה כלהון בסוף כלהון [
17. [ ] אחרין שגיאן ורשין עמהון מ[ן
18. [ ] עמהון אדום ומואב ובני עמון [
19. [ ] די בכל ארעא כלה לא יש.[
20. [ ] ויבאשון לזרעך עד עדן די .[
21. [ ] בכל עממ[ין] מלכות[א] ב.ל[
22. [ ] ויעב[דון] בהון עממין [

TRANSLATION

Column 2 (9) ... sixteen ... (10) and all of them, from this building ... (11) [and he measured from] the northeast [corner] (12) [towards the south, up to the first gate, a distance of] thirty-five [r]es. The name (13) [of this gate is called the Gate] of Simeon. From [this gat]e [until the middle [g]ate

(14) [he measured thirty-five res]. The name of this gate, by which they desig[nate] it, is the Gate (15) [of Levi. From this gate he measured south]wards thirty-five res. (16) [The name of this gate they call the Gate of Judah. From] this gate he measured until the corner (17) [at the southeast; then he measured] from this corner westwards (18) [twenty-five res. The name of this gate] they call the Gate of Joseph. (19) [Then he measured from this gate as far as the middle gate,] twenty-five [re]s. (20) [This gate they call the Gate of Benjamin. From] this ga[te] he measured as far as the [third] gate, (21) [twenty-five res. They call this one] the Gate of Reuben. And [from] this [ga]te (22) [he measured as far as the western corner, twenty-five res.] From this corner he measured as far as . . .

Column 3 (5) . . . he meas]ured (6) [twenty] five [res. They call this gate the Gate of Dan. And he measured] from [this] gate [to] (7) the middle [gate], [25] res. And they call that gate the Gate of Naphtali. From (8) the gate he measured to the th[ird] gate . . . and they call the name of that gate (9) the Gate of Asher. And he meas[ured from] that ga[te] to the northern corner, (10) 25 res. (11) And he brought me into the city, and mea[sured every blo]ck for length and width: 51 (12) canes by 51 canes square, 357 (13) cubits in every direction. And a free space [s]urrounded the squares on the outside of (each) street: (its measurement) in canes (14) three, in cubits 21. In [l]ike manner he [sh]owed me the measurements of all the squares. Between every two squares (15) ran a road, width (measuring) in canes six, [in cubits 42]. As for the great roads which went out (16) from east to wes[t, (they measured) in canes] as to width ten, in cubits (17) 70 for 2 of them; a t[hi]rd, which was on the n[orth] of the temple, he measured (18) at 18 canes width, [which is in cubits one-hundred and twenty s]ix. As for the width (19) of the streets which went out from s[outh to north, two of them were] nine ca[nes] (20) 4 cubits each, [which is sixty seven cu]bits. And he measured [the central one, which was in the mid]dle of the (21) city. Its width: [13 ca]nes [and one cubit, in cubits 9]2. (22) And every street and the entire city was [paved with white stone].

Column 4 (1) . . . marble and jasper. And he showed me (2) the dimensions of the eighty side doors. The width of the side doors was two canes, i.e., fourteen cubits. (3) . . . each gate had two doors made of stone. The width of the doors (4) was one cane, i.e., seven cubits. Then he showed me the dimensions of the twelve . . . The width (5) of their gates was three canes, i.e., twenty-one cubits. Each such gate possessed two doors. (6) The width of the doors was one and one-half canes, i.e., ten and one-half cubits . . . (7) Alongside each gate were two towers, one to the right (8) and one to the left. Their width and their length were identical: five canes by five canes, by cubits (9) thirty five. The staircase that ascended alongside the inner gate, to the right of the towers, was of the same height as (10) the towers. Its width was five cubits. The towers and the stairs were five canes and five cubits, (11) i.e., forty cubits in each direction from the gate. (12) Then he showed me the dimensions of the gates of the blocks of houses. Their width was two canes, i.e., fourteen cubits.] (13) And the width of the . . ., their measurements in cubits. Then he [measured] the width of each threshold, (14) two canes, i.e., fourteen cubits; and the roof, one cubit. [And above each thres]hold [he measured] (15) the doors that belonged to it. He measured the interior structure of the threshold, length four[teen cub]its and width twe[nty-one cubits.] (16) He brought me inside the threshold, and there was another threshold and yet another gate. The interior wall off to the right had (17) the same dimensi[ons] as the exterior gate: its width, four cubits; its height, seven cubits. It had two doors. In fron[t of] (18) this ga[te] was a threshold extending inwards. Its width was [o]ne cane—seven cubits—and its length extended toward the inside two canes or (19) fourteen [cu]bits. Its height was two canes, i.e., fou[r]teen cubits. Gates opposed gates, opening toward the interior of the bloc[ks] of houses, (20) each possessing the dimensions of the outer gate. On the left of this entry way he showed me a building housing a sp[iral] staircase. Its wid[th] was (21) the same in every direction: two canes, i.e., fourteen cubits. G[ate opposed gate], (22) each with dimensions corresponding to those of the house. A pillar was located in the middle of the structure [upon which] the staircase was supported as it spir[aled upward. Its (the pillar's) width and length

Column 5 (1) were a single measurement, six cubits by six cubits square.] The staircase tha[t rose by its side] was four cubits wide, spiraling [upward to a height of two canes until . . .] (3) [Then he brought me inside the blocks of houses and showed me houses there,] fifteen [from gat]e to gate: eight in one direction as far as the corner, (4) [and seven from the corner to the other gate.] The length of the houses was three canes, i.e., twenty-one cubits, and their width (5) [was two canes, i.e., fourteen cubits. Of corresponding size were all the chambers.] Their height was two canes, i.e., fourteen cubits, and each had a gate in its middle. (6) [. . . f]lour. Length and height were a single cane, i.e., seven cubits. (7) . . . their leng[th], and their width was twelve cubits. A house (8) . . . alongside it an outer gutter (9) [. . . The heig]ht of the first was . . . cubits. (10) The . . ., and their width was . . . cubits. (11) . . . two canes, i.e., four[teen] cubits (12) [. . . cu]bits one and one-half, and its interior (?) height (13) . . . the roof that was over them

Column 9 (or later) (14) . . . two [can]es, (15) [i.e., fourteen cubits . . .] cubits (16) . . . the measurement of (17) [. . . the bound]aries (?) of the city

Column 10 (or later) (13) . . . its foundation. Its width was two canes, (14) i.e., fourte[e]n cubits, and its height was seven canes, i.e., forty-nine cubits. And it was entirely (15) built of elect[rum] and sapphire and chalcedony, with laths of gold. Its (the city's) towers numbered one thousand (16) [four hundr]ed thirty-two. Their width and their length were a single dimension, (17) . . . and their height was ten canes, (18) [i.e., seventy cubits . . . two canes, i.e.] fourteen [cubits.] (19) [. . . th]eir length (20) . . . the middle one . . . cubits (21) . . . two to the gate (22) [in every dir]ection three towers extended

Column 11 (or later) (15) after him and the Kingdom of . . . (16) the Kittim after him, all of them one after another . . . (17) others great and poor with them. . . (18) with them Edom and Moab and the Ammonites . . . (19) of Babylon. In all the earth no . . . (20) and they shall oppress your descendants until such time that . . . (21) among all natio[ns, the] Kingdom . . . (22) and the nations shall ser[ve] them . . .

7. THE TREE OF EVIL (A FRAGMENTARY APOCALYPSE – 4Q458)

We close this chapter with another work in the style of the Words of Michael and these final sentences of the New Jerusalem. This Hebrew apocalypse, while fragmentary, again recapitulates themes known across the broad expanse of Qumran literature, most notably *tem'a* (polluted), *teval'a* (swallow or swallowing), 'walking according to the Laws', *yizdaku* (justified or made Righteous), etc. These themes should not be underestimated and reappear repeatedly in the Damascus Document, the Temple Scroll, Hymns, and the like.

'Swallowing' has particular importance *vis-à-vis* the fate of the Righteous Teacher and his relations with the Jerusalem establishment, i.e. 'they consumed him.' 'Justification' also has importance *vis-à-vis* his activities and those of all the 'sons of Zadok' (primordial *Zaddikim* Righteous Ones), who in CD,iv above 'justify the Righteous and condemn the Wicked' – this in an eschatological manner. It also has to do, as Paul demonstrates, with the doctrine of Righteousness generally. 'Pollution' – particularly Temple Pollution – is one of 'the three nets of Belial', referred to as well in Column iv of the Damascus Document, and we shall discuss it below. It usually involves charges against this upper-class establishment, relating to the foreign appointment of high priests, consorting with foreigners and foreign gifts or sacrifices in the Temple.

As fragmentary as the Tree of Evil text is, there are apocalyptic references to 'Angels', 'burning', 'flames', etc. Images like 'burning fire' have an almost Koranic ring to them, as do references to 'the moon and stars'. There is also an intriguing reference to 'the beloved one' — possibly referring to Abraham as 'friend of God' — of the kind one finds in texts like the Damascus Document and notably the Letter of James. We shall meet these references to Abraham as 'beloved' again below. Some might wish to consider its resonances with 'the beloved apostle' in the Fourth Gospel. The text also evokes 'the Tree of Evil', most likely an eschatological reference to the Adam and Eve story.

The language of 'polluting' and 'pollution' runs all through Qumran literature, particularly the Damascus Document, the Habakkuk *Pesher*, the Temple Scroll and the two Letters on Works Righteousness in Chapter 6 below. It use in this text, particularly in relation to the parallel allusions to 'swallowing' and 'foreskins', is important.

One finds the same combination of themes in the Habakkuk *Pesher*, xi. 13–15. There the usage deliberately transmutes an underlying scriptural reference to 'trembling' into an allusion about the Wicked Priest 'not circumcizing the foreskin of his heart'. This image plays on Ezek. 44:7–9's reconstructed Temple vision, also including the language of pollution of the Temple. This last image is specifically related to the demand to ban from it rebels, Law-breakers, foreigners and those 'of uncircumcized heart'. This is also the passage used to define 'the sons of Zadok' in the Damascus Document above. Here in the Habakkuk *Pesher*, what is being evoked is the imagery of apocalyptic vengeance relating to the 'swallowing' of the Wicked Priest and his 'swallowing', i.e. destruction, of the Righteous Teacher (xi.5–7 and xii.5–7). These passages also play upon the image of the 'cup' of the Lord's divine 'anger'. This genre of apocalyptic imagery is also found in Isa. 63:6 and Rev. 14:10.

This 'swallowing' imagery at Qumran is linguistically related too to a cluster of names like Bela^c (an Edomite and Benjaminite king name), Balaam and Belial — this last a name for the Devil at Qumran. For New Testament parallels to all of these names, see Paul on Christ and 'Beliar' in 2 Cor. 6:15, 2 Pet. 2:15, Jude 1:11 (interestingly enough preceded by an allusion to the Archangel Michael disputing with the Devil) and Rev. 2:14. This cluster parallels the more Righteousness-oriented one we have been delineating above.

In this text, too, the allusion that follows is to the fact that 'they were justified' or 'made Righteous', again heavy with portentousness for early Christian history. The 'justification' referred to has, of course, to do with 'walking according to the Laws', a typically 'Jamesian' (as opposed to 'Pauline') notion of justification. It is encountered across the spectrum of Qumran documents – for instance, at the end of the Second Letter on Works Righteousness in Chapter 6 below and in the definition of 'the sons of Zadok' above.

Again, the nationalist, Law-oriented nature of the apocalypse should be clear, but the last line is portentous too. We have read the word *mashuah* in it as 'anointed', but it could just as easily be read '*Mashiah*' – Messiah (*i* and *u/o* being interchangeable in Qumran epigraphy) – which then adds to the weightiness of the text. However this may be, that this text is now moving into some concept of 'Kingdom' or 'Kingship', possibly that 'Kingdom' in Dan. 2:44 mentioned above 'that will never be destroyed', is self-evident.

TRANSLITERATION

Fragment 1

[	‎ב לידיד .]‏	].1
[	‎ה הידיד .]‏	].2
[	‎ באהל]‏ .[‏	].3
[	‎ לוא ידעו א]ת‏	].4
[	‎ שריפות אש]‏	].5
[	‎ ועמדו עמי מ]‏	].6
[	‎א]מר לרישון לאמור]‏	].7
[	‎] להבים ושלך המלאך הריש]ון‏	].8
[	‎ב] מחרבת ויך את עץ הרשע]‏	].9
[	‎צרים ל..]‏	].10

Fragment 2 Column 1

‎ם...[‏	].1
‎היר]ח והכוכבים‏	].2
‎ השנות [‏	].3
‎ו]יברח בקו]]ה‏	]4
‎ח הטמא.[‏	].5
‎ הזות .[‏	].6

Fragment 2 Column 2

‎ את מ.]‏ .1	[
‎ ויאבדהו ואת ח..]‏ .2	[
‎ ותבלע את כל הערלים ותק.]‏ .3	[
‎ ויצדקו והלך על הח] וקים‏ .4	[
‎ משוח בשמן מלכות ה]‏ .5	[

TRANSLATION

Fragment 1 (1) . . . to the beloved one . . . (2) the beloved one . . . (3) in the tent . . . (4) they did not know . . . (5) burning of fire . . . (6) and the peoples of the . . . arose . . . (7) spoke to the first, saying . . . (8) flames, and He will send the first Angel . . . (9) drying up. And he smote the Tree of Evil . . .

Fragment 2 Column 1 (2) [. . . the mo]on and the stars (3) . . . the years (4) . . . he fled in (5) . . . the polluted (one) (6) . . . the harlots (?)

Fragment 2 Column 2 (2) And he destroyed him, and . . . (3) and swallowed up all the uncircumcised, and it . . . (4) And they were justified, and walked according to the L[aws . . . (5) anointed with the oil of the Kingship of . . .

NOTES

(1) The Messiah of Heaven and Earth (4Q521)

Previous Discussion: R. H. Eisenman, 'A Messianic Vision', *Biblical Archaeology Review* Nov/Dec (1991) p. 65. Photographs: PAM 43.604, ER 1551.

(2) The Messianic Leader (*Nasi* – 4Q285)

Previous Discussions: None. A discussion, taking as its starting point our announcement of this text in November 1991: G. Vermes, 'The Oxford Forum for Qumran Research Seminar on the Rule of War from Cave 4 (4Q285)' will be forthcoming in the *Journal of Jewish Studies*. Photographs: PAM 43.285 and 43.325, ER 1321 and 1352.

(3) The Servants of Darkness (4Q571)

Previous Discussions: None. Photographs: PAM 42.914 and 43.551, ER 1054 (43.551 not listed). The *DSSIP* lists the text as 4QM^g.

(4) The Birth of Noah (4Q534–536)

Previous Discussions: J. Starcky, 'Un texte messianique araméen de la grotte 4 de Qumrân', *École des langues orientales anciennes de l'Institut Catholique de Paris: Mémorial du cinquantenaire 1914–1964* (Paris: Bloud et Gay, 1964) 51–66; Milik, *Books of Enoch*, 56. Photographs: PAM 43.572 (bottom), 43.575, 43.590 and 43.591, ER 1520, 1523, 1537 and 1538. Our Fragment 1 is an eclectic text based on Birth of Noah Manuscripts C and D. Fragment 2 represents portions of Manuscript D. Fragment 3 has been known as 4QMessAram; it is not certain – merely probable – that it is a third copy of the Birth of Noah text.

(5) The Words of Michael (4Q529)

Previous Discussion: Milik, *Books of Enoch*, 91. Photograph: PAM 43.572 (top), ER 1520.

(6) The New Jerusalem (4Q549)

Previous Discussions: Milik, DJD 3, 184–93; J. Starcky, 'Jérusalem et les manuscrits de la mer Morte', *Le Monde de la Bible* 1 (1977) 38–40; Beyer, *Texte*, 214–22. Photographs: PAM 41.940, 43.564 and 43.589, ER 521, 1512 and 1536. The restorations of column 4 are possible because it overlaps with preserved portions of the New Jerusalem text from Cave 5.

(7) The Tree of Evil (A Fragmentary Apocalypse – 4Q458)

Previous Discussions: None. Photograph: PAM 43.544, ER 1493.

CHAPTER 2

Prophets and Pseudo-Prophets

Jews in the Second Temple period and Christians thereafter never ceased believing in prophecy. God had never stopped sending His heralds to call the people back to obedience. For Paul and the early churches following him, the usage perhaps implied something a little different. In Antioch, it seems to have been associated with teachers, the 'prophets and teachers' of Acts 13:1. Individuals like the messengers sent down from Jerusalem by James to assess the situation in Antioch are also called 'prophets' in Acts 11:21, as are Philip's daughters in 21:10. Perhaps the paradigmatic 'prophet' of this kind was Agabus who, 'seized by the Spirit' in Acts 11:22, predicted the famine and in like manner later in 21:12, got hold of Paul's girdle to try to dissuade him from going to Jerusalem.

Most Jews at this time appear to have equated prophecy with prediction, and associated it with soothsaying or fortune-telling. Josephus gives a number of examples, beginning, interestingly enough, with Judas the Essene, who 'never missed the truth' in any of his prophecies (*War* 1.78ff.). Among other things, he seems to have predicted the rise of Alexander Jannaeus, the Maccabean priest-king who will figure so prominently in our texts. In fact, for Josephus these early 'Essenes' seem to have constituted a species of fortune-tellers, hanging around the Temple and producing 'prophecies' to flatter the vanity of some important personage. Later, self-proclaimed 'Pharisees' like Rabbi Yohanan ben Zacchai in Talmudic literature, or even Josephus himself, seem to fulfil a similar role.

For the Jews of the Second Temple period, prophecy lived. A true prophet proved himself by accurately predicting the future. What had ceased was the certain knowledge of just which prophets carried on the succession. Josephus, contrasting the relatively small number of Jewish holy books with the situation among the Greeks, also provides the following description: 'The prophets subsequent to Moses wrote the history of the events of their own times in thirteen books . . . From Artaxerxes (464–424 BC) to our own time the complete history has been inscribed, but it is not considered equally trustworthy compared to the earlier records, because of the lapse of the exact succession of the prophets' (*Against Apion* 1.40f.)

The door was open for false prophets and Josephus notes all the 'imposters and deceivers, pretending divine inspiration, provoking revolutionary actions and driving the masses to madness. They led them out to the wilderness, so that God would show them signs of impending freedom [from Rome]' (*War* 2.259). Actually, for Josephus, these kinds of 'imposters and deceivers' were in intent more dangerous even than the bandits he so fulminates against, because they envisaged *both* revolutionary change and religious innovation. This was a dangerous combination, and may, in fact, characterize some of the works we have collected in this book.

When speaking of prophets in ancient Israel, scholars commonly distinguish two types: those who wrote books, and those who did not. Like Elijah, the latter relied on charismatic qualities to gain an audience. Both types of prophets are in evidence in the period of the Scrolls. Although the Qumran texts by definition contain only the records of the first type, it would be rash to conclude that the readers and writers of the Qumran materials were unaffected by the charismatic, miracle-working prophets of the second. As we have seen, such individuals proliferated as the first century progressed and the tensions with Rome grew.

The last participants in the tradition represented by the literature collected in this work almost certainly were a part of this broad, anti-foreign and ultimately anti-Roman movement. The modern name for this movement is derived from the behaviour of the archetypical son of Aaron, Phineas. Because of his 'zeal' in opposing bringing foreign women into the camp, God's wrath was turned away from the community and His 'Covenant of Peace [including the priest-hood] was won for him and his descendants in perpetuity' (Num. 25:10–13).

It is important to catalogue all incidents of this 'zeal' in Qumran texts, where most often it is expressed in terms of 'zeal for the Laws', 'zeal for the Judgements of Righteousness' or 'zeal for the Day of Vengeance'. Fortunately, we are now in a position to study the visionary and prophetic writings that appear to have so motivated and inspired these revolutionary currents of thought. Among the Qumran writings of this kind claiming visionary and prophetic inspiration are numerous pseudo-Moses texts (some previously published, although we provide a new example, the Angels of Mastemoth and the Rule of Belial), Pseudo-Jeremiah, Second Ezekiel, and the cycle of writings related to the Book of Daniel.

8. THE ANGELS OF MASTEMOTH AND THE RULE OF BELIAL (4Q390)

This apocalyptic text, which we have named after the splendid allusions in the text itself, could have been placed in the first chapter because of its visionary nature, or even below in Chapter 7 with Hymns and Mysteries. Since it is written in the first person rather than the third, however, and is evidently meant to be a direct expression of God's words, we place it in this prophetic section. Relating to both Ezekiel and Daniel, it contains an allusion from Hosea as well. The text, which could be referred to as a pseudo-Moses text, or even possibly a pseudo-Aaron one, also has strong thematic parallels with Jubilees and Enoch.

Its parallels with the exhortative section of the introductory columns of the Damascus Document are intrinsic, including an emphasis on 'breaking the Covenant' (CD,i.20), 'pollution of the Temple' (iv.18), 'going astray' (i.15) and 'walking in the stubbornness of their hearts' found there (ii.17, iii.5, 11–12). The expression 'They will pollute My Temple' directly parallels what goes under the heading of one of the 'three nets of Belial' in the Damascus Document. These are 'fornication', 'riches' and 'pollution of the Temple', which Belial is characterized as setting up 'as three kinds of Righteousness' and by which he is said to have 'taken hold of Israel'. Of course, allusion to 'the rule of Belial' is strong in both the Angels of Mastemoth and the Damascus Document texts, as it is in many of the documents noted under our comments concerning 'swallowing' allusion above.

These kinds of allusions are strong in the Habakkuk *Pesher* as well, where many of the same words are used, in particular 'breaking' or 'Breakers of the Covenant' (ii.6, viii.16, as opposed to 'keeping' or 'Keepers of the Covenant' — related to the definition of 'the Sons of Zadok' in the Community Rule), and the general emphasis on 'pollution', 'robbing Riches' (1QpHab,viii.11, xii.10; another of 'the three nets of Belial'), 'profiteering' (ix.5, 12), 'violence' (viii.11, xii.6–9) and that 'anger' linked with 'destruction' in 1QpHab,xi–xii discussed above in the introduction to the Tree of Evil text.

Again the basic homogeneity of images and vocabulary, and their movement from document to document, is confirmed, reinforcing the impression that what we have to do with here is a *movement* – in this instance an apocalyptic, Messianic, eschatological one. The apositives of 'keeping' and 'breaking' the Law or Covenant, not to mention the emphasis on 'doing' ('doing the Law') in evidence in this document, are also the backbone of the Letter of James (1:22–27 and 2:9–11). The same can be said for allusions to 'stubbornness of heart'' and 'Riches'.

In Line 11 of Fragment 1, a new expression is introduced, the Angels of Mastemoth. Based on imagery in Hos. 9:7–8, which, interestingly enough, is preceded by a reference to that 'visitation' mentioned in the Messiah of Heaven and Earth text above and echoed in the Damascus Document, it is based on a variation of the parallel 'Satan', meaning 'to hate', 'be hostile', or 'oppose'. These are obviously the same fallen Angels or heavenly 'Watchers' prominent in Enoch and the Damascus Document. The *mastema* usage moves into the Pseudo-clementine literature (Hellenistic novels ascribed to Peter's assistant Clement, achieving their final form in the third to fourth century AD) as the 'hostile man', 'enemy', or 'adversary' terminology (apparently applying to Paul, i.e. 'the enemy of God'; cf. James 4:5 discussing Abraham as 'the friend of God'). Here the allusion can be understood as the 'Angels of Darkness' or the 'Enemy Angels'.

The chronology of this apocalypse to a certain extent follows Jubilees and brings us down to the same period presaged in the Damascus Document. There is also direct reference to the 'seventy years' of Dan. 9:2. The only question is whether the chronology followed by these literary practitioners is any more exact than that encountered in Josephus or Talmudic traditions, which is often not reliable at all. Do they have a clear idea of seven jubilees in absolute chronological terms?

There is also an anti-priestly thrust to the apocalypse, in the sense that as in Ezekiel the priests have been 'warned', but their breaking of the Law and the Covenant, robbing of Riches, and violence goes even as far as 'polluting the Temple'. Whether this relates to a pre-Maccabean, the Maccabean, or the Herodian period is difficult to say, but the unbending, nationalist and anti-corruption stance is constant. Nor is this stance particularly retiring or uninterested in the affairs of men.

TRANSLITERATION   **Fragment 1**

1. [ ]   [.   ..]   [
2. [שנה שבעים]   [אהר]ון בני   [שוב]   [רים ו]מפ]
3. אשר מצ]ו[ך אנוכי אשר כי]בדר[יתהלכו ולא בהמה אהרון בני ומשלו
4. ישראל עשו אשר ככל הרע את הם נם ויעשו בהם תעיד
5. לבנות שבים מארץ רישונה העולים מלבד הרישונים ממלכתו בימי
6. אשר בכול ויבינו מצוה אליהם ואשלחה בהמה ואדברה המקדש את
7. השביעי ביובל ההוא הדור ומתום ואבותיהם הם עזבו
8. ויעשו הכול ויפרו וברית ושבת ומועד חוק ישכחו הארץ לחרבן
9. והסגרת]ים[איביהם ביד ונתחים מהמה פני והסתרתי בעיני הרע
10. פ]ני[ ]ו[בהסתר בחמתי]ו[כ]ל[לא אשר למע]ן[פליטים <מהם> והשארתי לחרב
11.]ו[וישוב]ו[המש]ט[מות מלאכי בהמה ומשלו מהם
12. [לבם בשר]ירות ויתהלכו]בעיני הרע [את   [ויעשו
13. [   ].. [   ]]ת[[

Fragment 2 Column 1

1. [   ].[ ].[[
2. [הקד]ש מקדש א]ת[ו מזבחי ואת בית]י [אח]
3.]ה[ו]ת[ן[   ] עליהם יביאו אלה]כ[י] [..]כן עשה
4. יהיו ההוא ה]יובל מתחלת   שנ]ים שבוע לחרב להסנירם בהם בליעל ממשלת
5. להם[ואשלח א]ותם אצוה אשר מצותי כל ואת חקותי כול את מפרים
    הנביאים עבדי
6. הברית]ו[ה]חוק ה[הפר מיום שבעים שנים באלה אלה להריב]ו[ל]ח[וי
    ונתחים יפרו אשר
7. במועלם עליהם קצפתי כי יבינו ולא ידעו ולא בהם ומשלו המשטמות אכי]מל[ביד
8. ולבצע להון להתחבר בחרו חפצתי לא ובאשר בעיני הרע ויעשו עז]בוני אשר
9. [   ] יטמאו מקדשי את רעהו את איש ויעשוקו ינזלו]ע[ה]לר[אשר
10. [   ] יחמסו כוהניהם זר]ע[ם את]ו[יחלל הם[וב]בני] [מ ..]מו[עדי את[ ]ו
11. [   ] ואת הם]   [.ה]י   [ ]ו
12. [   ]]..יהם

Fragment 2 Column 2

1. [   ] .1
2. [   ] .2
3. [   ]ת .3
4. [   ] מעליה .4
5. [   ] ובדבר .5
6. [ש]חנו אנ .6
7. [ה]ואשלח ידעו .7
8. [ש]לבק וברחמים .8
9. [   ] .א על]ו[הארץ בקרב .9

10. אחוזתם ויזבחו בה]   [

11. יחללו בה ו[א]ת מזב[ח   [

TRANSLATION

Fragment 1 (2) [and] break[ing . . .] again (?) . . . the sons of Aaron . . . seventy years . . . (3) and the sons of Aaron shall rule them, but they shall not walk in My Wa[ys,] which I comm[an]d you and which (4) you shall warn them about. They also (i.e., sons of Aaron) shall do what is Evil in my eyes, exactly as Israel did (5) in the early days of its Kingdom—apart from those who will come up first from the land where they have been captive, to build (6) the Temple. And I will speak to them and send them Commandments, and they will understand to what extent (7) they have wandered astray, they and their forefathers. But from the end of that generation, corresponding to the Seventh Jubilee (8) since the desolation of the land, they will forget Law and festival, sabbath and Covenant. They will break (i.e., violate) everything, and do (9) what is evil in My eyes. Thus I shall turn My face away from them, and give them into the hands of their enemies, delivering [them] (10) to the sword. Yet I will spare a remnant, so th[at] in My anger and [My] turning a[way from them,] they will not be des[royed]. (11) And the Angels of Mas[t]emoth will rule over them and . . . they will turn aside and (12) do . . . what I consider Evil, walking in the stub[borness of their hearts . . .]

Fragment 2 Column 1 (2) [My] house [and My altar and] the Hol[y] Temple . . . (3) thus it will be done . . .[f]or these things shall come upon them . . . and (4) the rule of Belial will [be] upon them, and they will be delivered to the sword for a week of year[s . . . From the] beginning of that Jubilee they will (5) break all My Laws and all my Commandments that I commanded th[em, though I send them] my servants the Prophets. (6) And they wi[ll be]gin to quarrel with one another. Seventy years from the day when they broke the [Law and the] Covenant, I will give them (7) [into the power of the An]gels of Mastemoth, who will rule them, and they (i.e., the people) will neither know nor understand that I am angry at them because of their rebellion, (8) [because they aban]doned Me and did what was evil in My eyes, and because they chose what displeases Me, overpowering others for the sake of Riches and profiteering (9) . . . They will rob their neigh[b]ors and oppress one another and defile My Temple (10) . . . and] My festivals . . . through [their] children they will pollu[te] their seed. Their priests will commit violence . . .

Fragment 2 Column 2 (4) from it . . . (5) and with a word . . . (6) we . . . (7) they will know, and I will send . . . (8) and with compassion to as[k . . .] (9) in the midst of the land [and] on . . . (10) their possession and they will sacrifice in it . . . (11) they will pollute it and the alta[r . . .]

9. PSEUDO-JEREMIAH (4Q385)

This text, attributed to the prophet Jeremiah, contains many interesting characteristics. In the first place, one should note the seemingly interchangeable references to the Lord and God. The emphasis on 'keeping the Covenant' encountered above is continued – in this case even in captivity. The style shifts in the second and third fragments – if in fact all the fragments are part of the same document – to the first person, where it would appear to become more of a pseudo-Ezekiel than a pseudo-Jeremiah composition, though one could even opine this for the curious historical information presented in Fragment 1.

Of course, in this context, the very term 'pseudo' is perhaps inappropriate, as many people have doubted that the Biblical Jeremiah is entirely the work of a single individual by that name. Presumably after Jeremiah died many of his disciples continued to revere his words and gather his pronouncements, and many people believe they actually arranged or composed some of the portions found in the Biblical book. We do not know how long this process continued, but at a certain point it has to be considered pseudepigraphic. It would be difficult to know where the historical prophet left off and tradition began, and therefore where this fragment fits in. Indeed the present work may have been considered an authentic one, and in fact it does contain many interesting historical details.

In the second and third fragments, not only do we have what appears to be the 'son of Man' terminology from Ezekiel, but also a probable parallel to Dan. 11:2's allusion to resurrection. Again, this is consistent with the ethos of other Qumran documents. In this context, one should note the positive attitude to David, paralleled, for instance, in Column v of the Damascus Document, as well as in Lines 28ff. of the Second Letter on Works Righteousness in Chapter 6 below, where David is referred to as a man of 'pious works', whose sins were 'forgiven' him. Another interesting reference is to 'the land of Jerusalem' in Line 2 of Fragment 1. This greatly enhances the sense of historicity of the whole, since Judah or 'Yehud' (the name of the area on coins from the Persian period) by this time consisted of little more than Jerusalem and its immediate environs.

TRANSLITERATION   Fragment 1 Column 1

ירמיה הנביא מלפני יהוה [	[1.
אש]ר נשבו מארץ ירושלים ויבואו	[2.
]נות נבוזרדן רב הטבחים	[3.
.]ים ויק]ח א]ת כלי בית אלוהים ואת הכהנים	[4.

5. [ ] ו[בני ישראל ויביאם בבל וילך ירמיה הנביא
6. [ ] [הנהר ויצום את אשר יעשו בארץ שביא[ם]
7. [ ] [בקול ירמיה לדברים אשר צוהו אלהים
8. [ ] [ישמרו את ברית אלהי אבותיהם באר[ץ]
9. [שבים] [אשר עשו הם ומלכיהם וכהניהם
10. [ ] [ללו [ ]ו אלהים ל[ ]

Fragment 2

1. מאחרי פני ולא רם לבבו ממנ[י   [
2. וישלמו ימיו וישב שלמה [בנו על כסאו   [
3. ואתנה נפש איביו בנפש]   [
4. ואקחה עידי עול[ה   [
5. [ ] [לל   [

Fragment 3

1. [ ] [....]   [
2. [ ] . יהוה ויקומו כל העם ויד[ברו [.ע]   [
3. [ ] [ל את יהוה צבאת ואף אני מ[ ]תי עמה .]   [
4. vacat ויאמר יהוה אלי בן [אדם   [אלהים]   [
5. [ ] [.תם ישכבו עד אש[ר   [
6. [ ] [.יכם ומן הארץ]   [
7. [ ] [<נאשם> .. מצ[ ]   [

TRANSLATION

Column 1 Fragment 1 (1) . . . Jeremiah the Prophet before the Lord (2) [. . . wh]o were taken captive from the land of Jerusalem, and they went (3) . . . Nabuzaradan the captain of the guard (4) . . . and he too[k th]e vessels of the House of God and the priests (5) [. . . and] the children of Israel and brought them to Babylon. And Jeremiah the Prophet went (6) . . . the river, and he commanded them concerning what they were to do in the land of their captivity (7) . . . to the voice of Jeremiah, concerning the things that God commanded him (8) . . . and they will keep the Covenant of the God of their fathers in the la[nd of] (9) [their captivity . . .] that they did, they and their kings and their priests (10) . . . God . . .

Fragment 2 (1) from following Me, nor did his heart become too proud to serve M[e . . .] (2) and his days were completed, and Solomon [his son] sat [on his (David's) throne . . .] (3) and I gave the soul of his enemies in exchange for the soul . . . (4) and I took the witnesses of Evi[l . . .]

Fragment 3 (1) . . . (2) . . . the Lord, and all the people arose and sa[id . . .] (3) the Lord of Hosts, and I also . . . with them . . . (4) And the Lord said to me, 'Son of [man . . .] God . . . (5) they shall sleep unti[l . . .] (6) and from the land . . . (7) he was rendered guilty . . .

10. SECOND EZEKIEL (4Q385–389)

This text again recapitulates the themes we have been encountering in this chapter. Beginning in Fragment 1 with a more or less familiar vision of Ezekiel's Chariot, in succeeding fragments it moves into more apocalyptic and eschatological themes. In Lines 4ff. of Fragment 3 Column 1, the well-known 'bones' passage from Ezekiel is evoked with an obviously even greater emphasis on the idea of resurrection encountered in several texts above and associated with these passages from Ezekiel in the popular mind. For instance, the 'bones' passage from Ezekiel, also used the tell-tale words 'stand up' we have encountered above, and was found buried under the synagogue floor at Masada, probably not without reason.

Here the passage is actually tied in Lines 1–2 to the reward of those who have 'walked in the ways of Piety and Righteousness', i.e. we are in the framework of eschatological Judgement. The *Hesed* (Piety) and *Zedek* (Righteousness) doctrines are absolutely fundamental to Qumran, as they are to Christianity thereafter, and not surprisingly to the tradition of Jewish *Kabbalah*. They are also the twin underpinnings of the 'opposition' movement in this period; as Josephus puts it, John taught 'Righteousness towards men and Piety towards God' (*Ant.* 18.116). Josephus ties these to 'Essene' practice as well (*War* 2.128ff. and *Ant.* 15.375), and they are the basis of the two 'love' commandments also reported in the Gospels of Jesus' teaching: 'Thou shalt love thy neighbour as thyself' – loving men – and 'Thou shalt love the Lord thy God' – loving God (Matt. 22:37ff., Mark 12:30f., Luke 10:27). Here, too, Piety is defined as 'loving Your Name', showing these concepts to be absolutely consistent across the breadth of Second Temple literature. Under them were subsumed all of one's duties, earthly and heavenly.

At Qumran, as in early Christianity and James 2:8, 'loving one's neighbour as oneself' had an economic dimension ending up in the condemnation of 'Riches' and the 'Poor' terminology. If you made economic distinctions between men it was impossible to be perfectly Righteous. In this context, see Column vi.20–21 of the Damascus Document, where the Righteousness Commandment is immediately followed up by reference to 'the Meek and the Poor'.

The text now moves on to more historical allusions, including a mysterious one to 'a son of Belial'. The language it uses in Fragment 3, Column 3 is typically that found in other Qumran texts. There is the reference to 'Downtrodden' (*Dal*) and 'cup' imagery denoting, as we have seen above, that divine vengeance so important to the Habakkuk

Pesher and recapitulated also with reference to Babylon in Rev. 14:8–11. This 'cup' imagery in the Habakkuk *Pesher* is extremely important, because it has been mistaken by many commentators as denoting drunkenness – the drunkenness of the Wicked Priest. But this is totally inaccurate. It actually denotes, as here, that divine vengeance being visited on the Wicked Priest for his destruction of the Righteous Teacher and his colleagues.

In Line 5 of Fragments 4–6, we have the language of 'rejecting' (*maʾas*) which one finds generally in relation to the activity of the liar in the Habakkuk *Pesher* and other Qumran documents. In Line 15, there is also a reference to 'the priests of Jerusalem' – cf. Habakkuk *Pesher*,ix.4–5: 'the last priests of Jerusalem' – and once again a reference to 'the Angels of Mastemoth', the Satan or Belial we encountered in the Angels of Mastemoth and the Rule of Belial text above. Because of these references and the first person quality of both narratives, it is likely these two texts either belong generically together or are part of the same document.

These references to an Era of Wickedness dominated by 'the Angels of Mastemoth' and to both a 'blasphemous king' and a 'son of Belial' increases these connections and the portentous quality of the text. It has been claimed that allusions from Second Ezekiel reappear in the Epistle of Barnabas, a second-century work brimming with the same kinds of references as this collection. The Epistle of Barnabas is so full of allusions like 'the Way of Light', 'the Way of Darkness', 'the Way of Holiness', 'the Way of death', 'keeping the Law', 'Righteousness', 'the Last Judgement', 'uncircumcized heart' and 'the Dark Lord' (paralleling both Belial and *mastema* above) that is would be difficult not to find parallels.

TRANSLITERATION   Fragment 1

.1   והיו עמי ה[[

.2   בלב טוב ובנ[ופש חפצה   [

.3   וחבא כמעט ק[ט   [

.4   ומבקיעים [.   [

.5   המראה אשר ראה יחזק[אל   [

.6   נגה מרכבה וארבע חיות חית[ובלכתן לא יסבו[

.7   אחור על שתים תלך החיה האחת ושתי רגל[יה   [

.8   [רג]ל[ל] [ל] [..] [ ]ת היה נשמה ופניהם זה בעקר זן]ה ודמות[

.9   הפנ[ים אחד ארי אח]ד נשר ואחד עגל ואחד של אדם והי[תה יד[

.10   אדם מחברת מגבי החיות ודבקה ב[כנפיהן] והא[ופנים   [

.11   אופן חובר אל אופן בלכתן ומשני עברי הא[ופנים שבלי אש[

‫12. ו[ה]יה בתוך נחלים חיות כנחלי אש [כמראה לפידים בינות]‬

‫13. האופנים והחיות והאופנים ויה[י] על ראשם רקיע כעין]‬

‫14. הקרח הנור[א וי]הי קול [מעל הרקיע   [‬

Fragment 2

‫1. [   ] תחת דוני [   ]   ולבי[‬

‫2. הומה את נפשי ויתבהלו הימים מהר עד אשר יאמרו [כל בני]‬

‫3. האדם הלא ממהרים הימים למען יירשו בני ישראל [את ארצם]‬

‫4. ויאמר יהוה אלי לא אש[י]כ פניך יחזקאל ה[נ]ה א[מ]דד [העת וקצרתי]‬

‫5. את הימים ואת השני[ם   [ל]   [‬

‫6. מצער כאשר אמרת ל[[‬

‫7. [כי] פי יהוה דבר אלה [[‬

Fragment 3 Column 1

‫1. [ואמרה יהוה ראיתי רבים מישראל אשר אה]בו את שמך‬

‫2. [וילכו בדרכי צדק ואלה מתי יהיו ו]הכה ישתלמו חסדם‬

‫3. [ויאמר יהוה אלי אני אראה א]ת בני ישראל וידעו‬

‫4. [כי אני יהוה ויאמר בן אדם הנ]בא על העצמות‬

‫5. [ואמרת הקרבו עצם אל עצמו ו]פרק ולפרקו ויהי‬

‫6. [כן ויאמר שנית הנבא ויעל בשר עליה]ם ויקרמו עור‬

‫7. [מלמעלה   ] ויעלו עליהם גדים‬

‫8. [   ] ויהי כן ויאמר שוב הנבא א[ל] ארבע רחות‬

‫9. [השמים ויפחו הרחות בם ויעמוד ע]ם רב אנשים‬

Fragment 3 Column 2

‫1. וידעו כי אני יהוה   *vacat*   ויאמר אלי התבונן‬

‫2. בן אדם באדמת ישראל ואמר ראיתי יהוה והנה חרבה‬

‫3. ומתי תקבצם ויאמ[ר] יהוה בן בליעל יחשב לענות את עמי‬

‫4. ולא אניח לו ומשלו לא יהיה והמן הטמא זרע לא ישאר‬

‫5. ומנצפה לא יהיה תירוש ותזיו לא יעשה דבש [   ] ואת‬

‫6. הרשע אהרג במף ואת בני אוציא ממף ועל ש[א]רם אהפך‬

‫7. כאשר יאמרו היה השל[ו]ם והשדך ואמרו תש[כו]ן הארץ‬

‫8. כאשר היתה בימי [   ] קדם בכן נשיר[]]יהם במ[ ]‬

‫9. [באר]בע רחות השמים [   ] את [   ]   [‬

‫10. [כא]ש בערת כ]   [‬

Fragment 3 Column 3

‫1. ודל לא יחן ויביא אל בבל ובבל ככוס ביד יהוה כדמ[ן]‬

‫2. ישליכנה [[‬

‫3. בכבל והיתה [[‬

‫4. מדור שדיך [[‬

‫5. חרבה [א]רצם [[‬

Fragments 4-6

[ל]והממלכה תשוב לגוי[ם שנים ר]בים ובני ישרא[ל] .2

על כבד בארצות שבים ואין   vacat   משיע להם [ ] .3

יען ב.ען חקתי מאסו ותרתי געלה נפשם על כן הסתרתי .4

פני מ[הם עד] אשר ישלמו עונם   vacat   וזה להם האות בשלם .5

עונם [ ] עזבתי את הארץ ברום לבכם ממני ולא ידע[ו] .6

כ[י   ]..vacat ש[בו ועשו רעה].[ ].[.ש.][ ]ש[ח] .7

[והפרו את הברית אשר כרתי] עם אב[רהם ועם י]צחק ועם .8

[יעקב ובימים] ההמה יקום מלך לגוים נדפן ועשה רעות .9

ב[ ] את ישראל מעם בימו אשבור את מלכות .10

מצרים [ ] ואת מצרים ואת ישראל אשבור ונתתי לחרב .11

[ ] ב[מותי א[רץ]רץ ורחקתי את האדם ועזבתי את הארץ .12

ביד מלאכי המשטמות הסתרתי [את פני מיש]ראל וזה להם .13

האות ביום עזבו את הארץ בד[ ] .14

כהני ירושלים לעבוד אלהים אחרים [ ] .15

מלכים] שלשה אשר ימלכ[ו] .16

TRANSLATION

Fragment 1 (1) and my people shall be . . . (2) with contented heart and with wil[ling soul . . .] (3) and conceal yourself for a little while . . . (4) and cleaving . . . (5) the vision that Ezek[iel] saw . . . (6) a radiance of a chariot, and four living creatures; a living creature [. . . and they would not turn] backwards [while walking;] (7) each living creature was walking upon two (legs); [its] two le[gs . . .] (8) was spiritual and their faces were joined to the oth[er. As for the shape of the] (9) fa[ces: one (was that) of a lion, and on]e of an eagle, and one of a calf, and one of a man. Each [one had the hand of] (10) a man joined from the backs of the living creatures and attached to [their wings.] And the whe[els . . .] (11) wheel joined to wheel as they went, and from the two sides of the whe[els were streams of fire] (12) and in the midst of the coals were living creatures, like coals of fire, [torches, as it were, in the midst of] (13) the whe[e]ls and the living creatures. [Over their heads] was [a firmament that looked like] (14) the terrif[ying] ice. [And from above the firmament] came a sound . . .

Fragment 2 (1) . . . in place of my grief . . . [And my heart] (2) is in confusion, together with my soul. But the days will hasten on fast, until [all humankind] will say, (3) 'Are not the days hurrying on in order that the children of Israel may inherit [their land?'] (4) And the Lord said to me: 'I will not re[fu]se you, Ezekiel. Behold, I will me[as]ure [the time and shorten] (5) the days and the year[s . . .] (6) a little. As you said to . . .' (7) [For] the mouth of the Lord has spoken these things.

Fragment 3 Column 1 (1) [And I said: 'Lord, I have seen many men from

Israel who] loved your Name (2) [and walked in the Ways of Righteousness. And these things, when will they happen, and] how will their Piety be rewarded?' (3) [the Lord said to me, 'I shall show t]he children of Israel, so that they will know (4) [that I am the Lord.' Then he said, 'Son of Man, pro]phesy over the bones (5) [and say: 'Draw together, bone to its bone and] joint to its joint.' And it was (6) [so. Then he said a second time, 'Prophesy, and let flesh cover the]m, and let them be covered with skin (7) [from above . . .] and let sinews come upon them.' (8) [And it was so. Then he said again, 'Prophesy t]o the four winds (9) [of Heaven, and let the winds blow on them, and th]ey will stand up— a great peo[ple], men . . .'

Fragment 3 Column 2 (1) and they will know that I am the Lord.' And he said to me, 'Consider carefully, (2) Son of Man, the land of Israel.' And I said, 'I see, Lord; it is desolate. (3) When will you gather them together?' And the Lord sai[d], 'A son of Belial will plan to oppress my people, (4) but I will not allow him to do so. His rule shall not come to pass, but he will cause a multitude to be defiled (and) there will be no seed left. (5) The mulberry bush will not produce wine, nor the bee honey . . . (6) I will slay the Wicked in Memphis, and leading My sons out of Memphis, I will turn upon the re[s]t. (7) Just as they will say, 'Pe[a]ce and quiet is (ours),' so they will say 'The land r[es]ts quietly.' (8) Just as it was in the days of . . . ancient . . ., so . . . (9) [in the fo]ur corners of heaven . . . (10) [like a] consuming [fi]re . . .

Fragment 3 Column 3 (1) . . . nor shall he have mercy on the Downtrodden, and He shall bring (them) to Babylon. Now, Babylon is like a cup in the Lord's hand; like refu[se] (2) he will hurl it . . . (3) in Babylon, and it will be . . . (4) the dwelling of your fields . . . (5) their land will lie desolate . . .

Fragments 4-6 (2) . . . and sovereignty will devolve upon the Genti[les] for [m]any [years,] while the children of Israe[l . . .] (3) a heavy yoke in the lands of their captivity, and they will have no Deliverer, (4) because . . . they have rejected My Laws, and their soul has scorned My teaching. Therefore I have hidden (5) My face from [them, until] they fill up the measure of their sins. This will be the sign for them, when they fill up the measure of (6) their sin . . . I have abandoned the land because they have hardened their hearts against Me, and they do not kno[w] (7) tha[t . . . they have] done Evil again and again . . . (8) [and they broke My Covenant that I had made] with Ab[raham, I]saac and (9) [Jacob. [In] those [days] a blasphemous king will arise among the Gentiles, and do evil things . . . (10) Israel from (being) a people. In his days I will break the Kingdom (11) of Egypt . . . both Egypt and Israel will I break, (and) give (them) over to the sword. (12) . . . [hi]gh places of the l[and . . .] I have removed (its) inhabitants and abandoned the land into (13) the hands of the Angels of Mastemoth (Satan/Belial). I have hidden [My face from Is]rael. This will be their (14) sign: in the day when they leave the land . . . (15) the priests of Jerusalem to serve other gods . . . (16) three [kings] who will rul[e . . .

11. PSEUDO-DANIEL (4Q243–245)

The pseudo-Daniel portions that follow describe one or more occasions on which Daniel stood before King Belshazzar (cf. Dan. 5). Like Pseudo-Jeremiah, Second Ezekiel, and the Damascus Document, they furnish a tantalizingly mysterious and often apocalyptic view of history. This text refers to: 1. the flood and the tower of Babel; 2. the exodus from Egypt; 3. the exile to Babylon; 4. the first four kingdoms (see also the Vision of the Four Kingdoms below); 5. seemingly the Hellenistic era; and 6. probably the Roman era of the 'last days' or 'end of time'.

The Greek translation of the Old Testament known as the Septuagint, which was used by the Jews of Alexandria and Egypt and later by Christians in the east, includes several additional Daniel stories woven into the Biblical book. Some of these texts might even antedate Daniel, while others simply interpret it. For his part, Josephus provides a glimpse of how Daniel was seen by a first-century Jewish historian: 'One of the greatest prophets . . . for the books that he wrote (note the plural here) and left are read by us even now . . . He not only predicted the future, like the other prophets, but specified when the events would happen' (*Ant* 10.266–8).

This description would not only have relevance for this text, but also for the view of prophets as soothsayers and fortune-tellers with special knowledge about the future in the first century, which we discussed in the introduction to this chapter. The belief that Daniel had predicted not only what would happen, but when, was no doubt a significant factor in the timing of the war with Rome in AD 66. For instance, the 70 years of wrath in Dan. 9:3 – a known interest in the War Scroll at Qumran – could have been seen as the period between the first outbreak of revolutionary activity at the time of Herod's death in 4 BC (not uncoincidentally the time assigned to Jesus' birth) and the final proclamation of the uprising (AD 66); or 'the time, two times, and a half' leading up to 'the End Time' in Dan. 12:7, the 3½ years between the stoning of James the Just in AD 62 and the outbreak of the uprising.

This brings us to the important apocalyptic references to the 'Kings of the Peoples' and 'the Kingdom of the Peoples' in the present text, paralleling references to a 'boastful King' or a 'son of Belial' in the previous text. These references are tantalizing. If they refer to the first century, then there is every possibility, depending on the interpretation and reconstruction of the names, that there is a reference to Herod, and perhaps even his father Antipater, in Lines 30–31.

The reference to 35 years in Line 31 is, of course, very close to the number of years of Herod's rule between 39 BC and 4 BC, but this is only a suggestion and must be treated with care. Whether such a reconstruction is possible is probably tied to the interpretation of these allusions to 'the Kings of the Peoples'/'Kingdom of the Peoples' in Lines 24, 35 and 36. The 'Kings of the Peoples', as we have said, is an allusion found in a crucial section of the Damascus Document (viii. 10) about 'pollution of the Temple', the 'treasury', 'fornication' (even possibly incest), the 'poison of vipers' – the 'Kings' being specifically identified with the vipers – etc. There are also parallel references in the Habakkuk *Pesher* to 'peoples' and 'additional ones of the peoples' as we have noted.

The term 'peoples' used in this manner is known in Roman jurisprudence, where it specifically refers to petty provinces particularly in the eastern part of the Empire, and their kings. Even Paul in Rom. 11:13 uses this terminology in addressing the 'peoples', designating himself as 'Apostle to the Peoples'. Certainly petty kings like the Herodians were referred to in this manner in Roman jurisprudence as a matter of course and have to be considered among these 'Kings of the Peoples'.

On the other hand, the 'Kingdom of the Peoples' may reflect an earlier stage in this usage. Then it would be more obscure. The term is known in Roman administrative practice during this period; for instance in Cicero in *De Domo* 90 or Suetonius, on Caligula, 35.3. Where Paul is concerned, he very likely refers to his own Herodian origins and relationship to such 'peoples' in Rom. 16:11. Indeed such an explanation, if substantiated, is helpful in illuminating his Roman citizenship and easy relations with high Roman officials or their protégés throughout his career.

In Line 12, it is possible that one encounters a 400-year symbolic historical scheme, beginning with the going out from Egypt of the kind one encounters in the Damascus Document (i.5–6; 390 years). As noted above, one should be careful of the chronological precision of these visionary reckonings and take them as symbolic or as approximations only. Where the 390 years in the Damascus Document is concerned, for instance, there can be little doubt that this relates to Ezek. 4:9 – an important prophet at Qumran – having to do with the absence of prophecy in Israel. The reference to 'seventy years' in Line 22, as with similar chronological reckonings in the Angels of Mastemoth and the Rule of Belial text above, ties this text to the Daniel cycle of literature.

TRANSLITERATION

[	דניאל קוד]ם	] .1
[	בלשצר]	] .2
[	].ן.[	] .3
[	מן כתר מבולא]	] .4
[	נ]וח מן לובר]טורא'	] .5
[	.] קריה]	] .6
[	א] מגדלא רו]מה	] .7
[	]...[	] .8
[	ע]ל מגדלא ושל]	] .9
[	לבקרה בבני]	] .10
[	].ס.[	] .11
[	שנין אר]בע מאה ..]	] .12
כולהון ויתון מן גוא]	הו]ן וי.[יח. [.	] .13
ולהוא] מעברהון ירדנא יובל]א[	מצרין ביד .]	] .14
[	ובניהון] .	] .15
[	ית.[ ]	] .16
בחרו בני ישראל אנפיהון מן]אנפי אלוהין]		] .17
והוו דבח]ין לבניהון לשידי טעותא ורזנ עליהון אלוהין וא]מר] למנתן .18
[	אנון ביד נב]וכדנזר מלך ב]כל ולאחרבא ארע<ה>ון מנהון מידי ש] .19
[	בני גלותא] .]	] .20
[	ובדר אנון]	] .21
[	אין שב]ע]ין שנין] .	] .22
[	מלכותא] דה רבתא ויושע אנון]	] .23
[	חסנין מלכות עממ]יא	] .24
[	היא מלכותא קד]מיתא	] .25
[	י]מלך שנין] .	] .26
[	.] בלכרוס]	] .27
[	תה] .[תה]	] .28
[	ש]נין ..]	] .29
[	]רהוס בר]	] .30
[	וימלך]וס שנין תלתין וחמש]	] .31
[	י] מללה]	] .32

[	] . רש[ע]א[[א] אטוע .]	] .33
[	] . בעדנא[דנה יתכנשון קריאי .]	] .34
[	מלכי[עממיא ולהוה מן יום]	] .35
[	קדי[שין ומלכי עממיא]	] .36
[	ע[בדין עד יומא [דנה	] .37
	א.[	] .38
	] . ומה די [	] .39
	דניאל [	] .40
	] כתב די יהב [	] .41
	קהת [	] .42
	].וסי עוזי[ה]	] .43
	]ן א[ב]יתר	] .44
	].[ ]קיה	] .45
	יחוניה [	] .46
	]ן שמעון	] .47
	] דויד שלומוה	] .48
	] אחזי[ה] [	] .49
	].[ ] [	] .50
	] למסף רשעא	] .51
	] אלן בעור יטעו	] .52
	א[לן אדין יקומון	] .53
	ק[רישו]י[א יתובון	] .54
	] רשעא *vacat*	] .55

TRANSLATION

(1) ... Daniel befo[re . . .] (2) Belshazzar . . . (4) after the flood . . . (5) [N]oah from Lubar [the mountain . . .] (6) a city . . . (7) the tower; [its] heig[ht . . .] (9) [up]on the tower and . . . (10) to visit the sons of . . . (12) [fo]ur hundred [years . . .] (13) . . . all of them, and they will go out from (14) Egypt by the hand of . . . and their crossing [will be] (at) [the] River Jordan . . . (15) and their sons . . . (17) the children of Israel preferred their presence (i.e., that of the false gods) to the [presence of God.] (18) [They were sacrific]ing their sons to the Demons of Falsehood, and God was angry at them and de[cided] to give (19) them into the power of Nebu[chadnezzar the king of Ba]bylon, and to lay waste to their land before them by the hands of . . . (20) members of the exilic community . . . (21) and He scattered them . . . (22) an oppression of seve[nt]y years . . . (23) this great [kingdom], and He will save the[m . . .] (24) powerful, a Kingdom of the Peop[les . . .] (25) this is the fi[rst] Kingdom . . . (26) [he wil]l rule (some number of) years . . . (27) Balakros . . . (29) [y]ears . . . (30) . . .rhos the son of . . . (31) [and . . . rh]os [will rule] thirty-five years . . . (32) to say . . . (33) [Evi]l] has led

astray . . . (34) [in] this [time] the called ones will be gathered . . .
(35) [the Kings of] the Peoples, and from (that) day on there shall be . . .
(36) [Holy] Ones and the Kings of the Peoples . . . (37) they shall be doi[ng]
until [this] day . . . (39) and what (40) . . . Daniel (41) . . . a book that he
gave (42) . . . Kohath (43) . . . Uzzi[ah . . .] (44) A[b]iathar . . . (46) Jehoniah
(47) . . . Simeon (48) . . . David, Solomon (49) . . . Ahazi[ah . . .]
(51) to bring Evil to an end (52) . . . these will wander astray in
blindness (53) . . . [th]ese (people.) Then there shall arise (54) . . . [H]oly
O[n]es shall return (55) . . . Evil.

12. THE SON OF GOD (4Q246)
(Plate 4)

This is another Messianic pseudo-Daniel fragment in Aramaic, relating
to the literature centring about that figure. It is full of the language
and heightened imagery of these apocalyptic visionary recitals. In fact,
it takes its cue from a reference in the Biblical Daniel to the 'Kingdom'
that 'the God of Heaven will set up . . . which shall never be destroyed', nor be conquered or absorbed, but rather 'last forever' (Dan.
2:44). There are also parallels in style with the 'little Apocalypse' in
the New Testament, where Jesus is pictured as foretelling the future
woes leading to the destruction of Jerusalem (Luke 21:20).

A key phrase in the text is, of course, the reference to calling the
coming kingly or Messianic figure, whose 'rule will be an eternal rule',
'the son of God' or 'the son of the Most High', while previous
kingdoms, because of their transitoriness, are compared only to
'shooting stars'. Other imagery in the Biblical Daniel also helped
define our notions about Jesus as a Messianic figure, imagery relating
to the 'Son of Man coming on the clouds of Heaven' (Dan. 7:13). This
imagery is strong in the War Scroll, where it is used to interpret 'the
Star Prophecy' (Columns xiff. This is repeated even more forcefully in
Column xixf., where the Heavenly Host is depicted as coming on the
clouds of Heaven and 'shedding Judgement' like 'rain' on all mankind).

There can be no denying the relation of allusions of this kind to the
Lukan prefiguration of Jesus: 'He will be great, and will be called the
son of the Most High; and the Lord God will give him the Throne of
his father David . . . For that reason the Holy offspring will be called
the Son of God' (Luke 1:32–35). Images of this kind, however,

abound in Old Testament scripture, particularly in honouring great kings. See, for instance, Ps. 2:7: 'You are My son; on this day have I begotten you' (in Christian tradition, part of the prefiguration of Jesus' baptism; for a more Jewish Christian presentation of this, see Heb. 1:5 and 5:5). See, too, 2 Sam. 7:14: 'I will be a father to him [David] and he shall be a son to Me', or Ps. 89:27: 'He shall say to Me, "You are my father, my God – the Rock of my deliverance." '

Scriptural prefigurations such as these are also strong in Wisdom and at Qumran, where all 'the Righteous' are reckoned as 'the sons of God'. This is particularly true in the Qumran Hymns where the 'sonship' imagery regarding the Righteous and its putative author 'the Teacher of Righteousness' is strong throughout. In the Son of God text, one should also note the emphasis on 'Truth' or 'Righteousness' – two central Qumran concepts (hence, our capitalization of them throughout this work). Nor can there be any mistaking its eschatological nature and its emphasis on 'judging' or 'the Last Judgement', more key Qumran conceptualities probably stemming from Daniel's proclamation of 'the end time' in 8:20, 11:25, etc.

That the concepts incorporated in words of this kind have gone directly into Christian presentations of its Messiah and his activities is hardly to be doubted. See, for instance, Line 4 in Column 2 and Matt. 10:34: 'I came not to send peace, but a sword.' This kind of 'sword' allusion is also found in Column xix.12 above of the War Scroll, 'the sword of God', used in the war against 'the Kittim'. Further to this, one should note the allusion again to 'Peoples' in Line 8.

One point, however, should be emphasized: the Messianic figure envisaged in texts like the Son of God, War Scroll, etc., whether taken figuratively or otherwise, is extremely war-like. This is in line with the general uncompromising, militant and nationalist ethos of the Qumran corpus; the Messianic figure was to be a triumphant, quasi-nationalist king figure. One should also note that the peace envisaged in this text will only come *after* the cataclysmic Messianic war. As in the War Scroll, God will assist in this enterprise with His Heavenly Host. For the War Scroll, this is the point of the extreme purity regulations and being in camps in the wilderness, which is put in vii.5–6 as follows: 'because the Angels of Holiness are with their hosts,' i.e. 'the war volunteers, the Perfect in Spirit and body ready for the Day of Vengeance'. We shall learn more about the extreme purity regulations required in the 'camps' in the last column of the Damascus Document in Chapter 6 below.

TRANSLITERATION

Column 1

1. ‏[מלכא וכדי רוחה ע]לוהי שרת נפל קדם כרסיא
2. ‏[אדין קם דניאל ואמר מ]לכא עלמא אתה רגז ושניך
3. ‏[מחרק מה להוה אל ר]בא חזיך וכלא אתה עד עלמא
4. ‏[חמס להוה ובאשין רב]רבין עקה תהא על ארעא
5. ‏[עממין יעבדון קרב] ונחשירין רבו [מ]דינתא
6. ‏[עד יקום מלך עם אל ולהוה] מלך אתור ומ[צ]רין
7. ‏[כל עממיא לה יסגדון ו]רב להוה על ארעא
8. ‏[ ] כלא שלם יע[בדון וכלא ישמשון
9. ‏[לה בר אל ר]בא יתקרא ובשמה יתכנה

Column 2

1. ‏ברה די אל יתאמר ובר עליון יקרונה כזיקיא
2. ‏די חזותא כן מלכותהן תהוא שני[ן] ימלכון על
3. ‏ארעא וכלא ידשון עם לעם ומדינה למדינה
4. ‏vacat עד יקום עם אל וכלא יניח מן חרב
5. ‏מלכותה מלכות עלם וכול ארחתה בקשוט יד[ון]
6. ‏ארעא בקשט וכלא יעבד שלם חרב מן ארעא יסף
7. ‏וכל מדינתא לה יסגדון אל רבא באילה
8. ‏הוא יעבד לה קרב עממין ינתן בידה כלהן
9. ‏ירמה קדמוהי שלטנה שלטן עלם וכל תהומי

TRANSLATION

Column 1 (1) [the king. And when the Spirit] came to rest upo[n] him, he fell before the throne. (2) [Then Daniel arose and said,] 'O [k]ing, why are you angry; why do you [grind] your teeth? (3) [The G]reat [God] has revealed to you [that which is to come.] It shall indeed all come to pass, unto eternity. (4) [There will be violence and gr]eat [Evils.] Oppression will be upon the earth. (5) [Peoples will make war,] and battles shall multiply among the nations, (6) [until the King of the people of God arises. He will become] the King of Syria and [E]gypt. (7) [All the peoples will serve him,] and he shall become [gre]at upon the earth. (8) [. . . All w]ill make [peace,] and all will serve (9) [him.] He will be called [son of the Gr]eat [God;] by His Name he shall be designated.

Column 2 (1) He will be called the son of God; they will call him son of the Most High. Like the shooting stars (2) that you saw, thus will be their Kingdom. They will rule for a given period of year[s] upon (3) the earth, and crush everyone. People will crush people, and nation (will crush) nation, (4) until the people of God arises and causes everyone to rest from the sword. (5) His Kingdom will be an Eternal Kingdom, and he will be Righteous in all his Ways. He [will jud]ge (6) the earth in Righteousness, and everyone will make peace. The sword shall cease from the earth, (7) and every nation will bow down to him. As for the Great God, with His help (8) he will make war, and He will give all the peoples into his power; all of them (9) He will throw down before him. His rule will be an Eternal rule, and all the boundaries . . .

13. THE VISION OF THE FOUR KINGDOMS (4Q547)

This is another tantalizing apocalypse in Aramaic relating to the Daniel cycle of literature, as well as to a certain extent Enoch. In it, the king (possibly either Belshazzar or Nebuchadnezzar) sees a vision of four trees, each represented by an Angel. As each tree represents a kingdom, some relationship with the Dan. 7–8 vision of the four kingdoms is evident.

When the text assigns Angels to trees, and thereby to the kingdoms, it is developing an already ancient idea prominent in Daniel. In Dan. 10:13, the seer encounters an Angel, presumably the Heavenly interpreter of visions, Gabriel. This Angel is also of fundamental importance to the heir to many of these traditions, Islam. He tells Daniel that he would have come earlier, but 'the prince of the Kingdom of Persia opposed' him for 21 days. Thus Israel's Angel seems to have been engaged in heavenly combat with the Angel of the Kingdom of the Persians. Only with the aid of another Angel, Michael – already figuring prominently in many of these texts – was he able to advance. A similar understanding of the interplay between the worlds of the seen and the unseen would appear to animate this vision.

It would be interesting to know the identities of all the trees in the Four Kingdoms text, for then one might better appreciate just how the work relates to parallel visions in the Biblical Daniel or Enoch. Only the identity of the first, Babylon, is preserved in Line 5. Does the work end with Alexander of Macedon, or does it come down to the Roman period? Does it contain material of equal antiquity and authority as the Biblical Daniel or Enoch? Or, is this work rather an explication of Daniel, composed later?

The use of trees to represent kingdoms has ample precedent in the ancient motif of the cosmic tree (cf. Ezek. 17 and 31 and Zech. 11:2), and parallels the use of other symbols like animals and horns in Daniel and Enoch. In Dan. 4, Nebuchadnezzar has a dream in which he sees '. . . a tree in the middle of the earth of great size. The tree became large and strong, and its height reached up to the heavens . . .' Daniel later tells the king that this tree represents the king himself and his kingdom, but the book of Daniel does not develop this equation any further.

TRANSLITERATION   **Fragment 1 Column 1**

מן .[	] 1.
חם.[	] 2.
א..[	] 3.
[	] 4.
נ]הור מלאכיא די הוו	] 5.
אמר להון להוא *vacat* כולה	] 6.
..תא רימין הוא *vacat* דן	] 7.
ואמר לי מלכא בדיל *vacat* כדן	] 8.
ד]ך איך כלא עביד הוו קאמין	] 9.
אמר להוון ומפקא להון כפרוש	] 10.
מראיהון ו.. חד מנהון	] 11.
אדין מלאכא די עלו]הי	] 12.

Fragment 1 Column 2

1.	נונהא קאם וארבעה אילני]א מן בתר לה]
2.	קאם אילנא ורקחו מנה ואמ]ר לי מן]
3.	צורתא ואמרת אן אחזא ואתב]י]ן ב]ה וחזית]
4.	אילנא די *vacat* באשים ב] [
5.	ושאלתה מן שמך ואמר לי בכל]אמרת לה]
6.	אנ]תה הוא די שליט בפרס ו]חזית אי]לנא
7.	אחרנא די ת]חות לנא וימא ל] [ ]ואמר
8.	למשנה [ ] ושאלתה מן שמ]ך ואמר לי]ל
9.	ואמרת לה אנתה הוא ד]י שליט ב]ועל]
10.	תקפי ימא ועל מחוזא [ ] וחזית]
11.	אילנא תליתי]א ו]אמרת ל]ה מן שמך ואמר לי]
12.	חזוך] [

Fragment 2

[	מ]חי ואמרת לה היא דא מן ש]ליט	] 1.
[	]ת לעלי]]ת וחזו]ך	] 2.
[	]ל ב]	] 3.
[	]חיל]	] 4.
[	].ל]	] 5.

Fragment 3

[	] מרא [	] 9.

[‏ן אל עליון לא[‏] .10
[‏שא די עליהון ויב. [‏] .11
[‏מר[א די כול מותבה דינין [‏] .12

Fragment 4

‏ה[‏] .8
‏יחדון [‏] .9
‏חזוה [‏] .10
‏[ים מללתא‏] .11
‏מלכ[א די יפלט‏] .12

TRANSLATION

Fragment 1 Column 1 (5) . . . the [Li]ght of the Angels who were (6) . . . he said to them, 'It will all happen . . .' (7) high. It is he who . . . (8) and he said to me, 'O King, because . . .' (9) as everything was done, they would arise (10) . . . he said, 'They shall be.' And he explicated to them clearly (11) . . . their lords. One of them (12) [. . . Then the Angel upon w]hom

Fragment 1 Column 2 (1) (rested) the brilliant Light arose, and the four tree[s after him.] (2) A tree arose, and (the others) moved away from it. He (the Angel) sai[d to me . . . 'What] (3) kind of tree is it?' I replied, 'If only I could see and underst[an]d it.' [Then I saw] (4) a balsam tree . . . (5) I asked it, 'What is your name?' It replied, 'Babylon.' [Then I said to it,] (6) '[Yo]u are he who shall rule over Persia.' Then [I saw another tr]ee (7) [that was be]low where we were standing, and it swore . . . and claimed (8) to be different. (superior to the previous tree?) . . . So I asked him, 'What is [your] name?' [He replied . . .] (9) I said to him, 'You are he wh[o shall rule over . . .'] [By] (10) my power and by the region . . . he swore [. . . And I saw] (11) [the] third tree, [and] I said to [him, 'What is your name?' He replied,] (12) 'Your vision . . .'

Fragment 2 (1) . . . and I said to him, 'This is it. Who is the ruler of . . .'

Fragment 3 (9) . . . the lord of . . . (10) the Most High God . . . (11) which is upon them . . . (12) [the Lor]d of all, he who appoints judges . . .

Fragment 4 (9) . . . they shall seize (10) . . . the vision (11) . . . you have spoken (12) [. . . the kin]g who shall escape . . .

NOTES

(8) The Angels of Mastemoth and the Rule of Belial (4Q390)
Previous Discussions: J. T. Milik, *Books*, 254–5; D. Dimant, 'New Light

from Qumran on the Jewish Pseudepigrapha – 4Q390', in J. Trebolle Barrera and L. Vegas Montaner (eds), *Proceedings of the International Congress on the Dead Sea Scrolls – Madrid, 18–21 March 1991* (Universidad Complutense/ Brill: Madrid/Leiden, 1992). Photograph: PAM 43.506. This text may be called a pseudo-Moses, but it is uncertain that Moses is the 'author' or person addressed. The language of the text is reminiscent of the book of Jeremiah, so this might be a pseudo-Jeremiah text; it may also have been addressed to some other visionary.

(9) Pseudo-Jeremiah (4Q385)

Previous Discussions: None. Photographs: PAM 42.505 and 43.496. Because of the geography of this text and its vocabulary, it can also be viewed as a pseudo-Ezekiel text.

(10) Second Ezekiel (4Q385–89)

Previous Discussions: J. Strugnell and D. Dimant, '4Q Second Ezekiel', *Revue de Qumran* 13 (1988) 54–8; D. Dimant and J. Strugnell, 'The Merkabah Vision in Second Ezekiel (4Q385 4)', *Revue de Qumran* 14 (1990) 331–48. Photographs: PAM 43.493, 43.495, 43.501, 43.503 and 43.504. The order of the fragments is uncertain; we present them roughly as their relation to the book of Ezekiel would suggest. The reference to 'the Angels of Mastemoth' in Fragments 4–6 ties it to the first text we have given this name to.

(11) Pseudo-Daniel (4Q243–245)

Previous Discussion: J. T. Milik, '"Prière de Nabonide" et autres écrits d'un cycle de Daniel. Fragments araméens de Qumrân 4', *Revue Biblique* 63 (1956) 411–15. Photographs: PAM 43.247, 43.249, 43.252 and 43.259. The text presented here is a tentative composite of the three manuscripts. Because these texts are so fragmentary, the order of the portions is uncertain, nor is it certain that Manuscript C is the same literary work as Manuscripts A and B. Manuscript C certainly preserves the end of its text (here, Lines 51–5).

(12) The Son of God (4Q246)

Previous Discussions: J. Fitzmyer, 'The Contribution of Qumran Aramaic to the Study of the New Testament', *New Testament Studies* 20 (1974) 391–4; Milik, *Books*, 60, 213, 261; F. García-Martínez, '4Q246: Tipo de Anticristo o Libertador escatológico?' in *El Misterio de la Palabra. Homenaje a L. Alonso Schökel* (Cristiandad; Madrid, 1983) 229–44. Photographs: PAM 42.601 and 43.236.

(13) The Vision of the Four Kingdoms (4Q547)

Previous Discussion: J. T. Milik, '"Prière de Nabonide" et autres écrits d'un cycle de Daniel. Fragments araméens de Qumrân 4', *Revue Biblique* 66 (1956) 411 note 2. Photographs: 43.576 (Manuscript A), 43.579 (Manuscript B). We present Manuscript A, with reconstructions following Manuscript B. Not all reconstructions, however, are found in Manuscript B. Some reflect our own insight into the text.

CHAPTER 3

Biblical Interpretation

The Jews at the time of the writing of the Scrolls can truly be described as a 'people of the Book'. But which writings were recognized as sacred? The situation represented by the literature before us was still to a certain extent fluid. The Bible recognized by Jews and Protestants was put in its final form around AD 100 after the fall of the Temple in AD 70 by those in the process of developing Rabbinic Judaism. Nor would the decisions made by these heirs of the Pharisee Rabbi Yohanan ben Zacchai, the individual who in Talmudic sources is described as having applied 'the Star Prophecy' to Vespasian – the destroyer of Jerusalem and future emperor in Rome, have been particularly welcome among the supporters of the tradition represented by the literature of the Scrolls.

Yet it is possible to say a few things about which books were already considered holy or authoritative merely on the basis of inspecting the Scrolls themselves. Certainly the Law as we have come to know it (that ascribed to Moses), as well as the Prophets, had already acquired the aura of sacredness, and they are referred to in this manner by the authors of the Scrolls, though additional books like the Temple Scroll and additions like those to Ezekiel above would appear to have still been in the process of being created. Psalms, too, with some additions, would appear to have been recognized.

Most surviving writings from Qumran and later materials about these times, like the Rabbinic *Mishnah* and *Tosefta*, are concerned with understanding and applying the requirements of books and writings already considered sacred. Where the books ascribed to Moses and the Prophets, and to David (the Psalms) were concerned, there appear to have been few sceptics. The problem in the literature before us was not really where to look for God. Writings like the Law, Prophets and

Psalms represented His direct communication with His people. The problem was how to understand that communication.

Various techniques developed to solve this. One method was to extrapolate the basic principles of life from the literature already recognized as sacred and then weave an entertaining story illustrating them. Books like Judith and 3 Maccabees, not so far found at Qumran, represent this kind of approach, as do the stories of Tobit and the Persian Court in this chapter. A related technique was to 'rewrite' Biblical stories, expanding or revising them with new details in accordance with one's own understanding of what God required or how certain aspects of this legacy needed to be interpreted or approached.

The Genesis Apocryphon from Cave 1, published earlier, is an example of such rewriting. So are parts of the document with which we start this chapter, the Genesis Florilegium. Both of them are concerned with rewriting certain aspects of the Genesis narrative which their writers for some reason considered important. As in the story of the Biblical flood, they insert interpretative words into long passages of Biblical text while at the same time paring away what they regarded as dross. In this way, a new, more focused – if tendentious – story emerges; and overlaps, reflecting the amalgam of previous textual traditions, either by design or otherwise disappear.

The various stories involving the mysterious Enoch who, because he was described as 'walking with God' in Gen. 5:24, was thought not to have died, are another variation of this genre. A lively pseudepigraphic tradition developed in Enoch's name, intent on capitalizing on the apocalyptic, visionary and mystical insights implicit in his having visited Heaven and lived. The Jubilees cycle is another example of rewriting and developing aspects of the Genesis tradition with an eye towards enhancing certain parts of it which were considered important by the author. Pseudo-Jubilees in this chapter is a variation of this tradition, though aspects of Enochic literature also shine through the fragmentary document that has survived.

Perhaps the most important method for enhancing previously recognized Biblical texts at Qumran was using the direct interpretative one, called *pesher* because of the constant allusion throughout in the text to the Hebrew word *pishro* ('its interpretation is'). At Qumran this approach usually involved a high degree of esotericism, as the exegesis played on a passage or some vocabulary from older texts like Isaiah, Nahum, Hosea, Habakkuk or Psalms, and developed it in the most intense and imaginative manner conceivable, relating it to the present life of the community, its heroes and enemies, and the people of Israel.

Pesharim (plural for *pesher*) such as these were even embedded in documents like the War Scroll, where 'the Star Prophecy' was treated in this manner, and the Damascus Document, where, as we have seen, Ezek. 44:15's reference to 'the sons of Zadok' and similar prophecies were interpreted in the most graphic and vivid manner in relation to contemporary events and the interests of the community. The document we have called (recalling John Allegro's similar usage) the Genesis Florilegium contains examples of this kind of *pesher* as well, particularly when it comes to interpreting the Messianic 'Shiloh Prophecy' (Gen. 49:10).

Such interpretations often had nothing whatever to do with the underlying Biblical text, often playing on but a few words or an isolated allusion in it to produce the desired commentary. Sometimes words in the underlying text were deliberately changed to produce the desired exegesis having to do with contemporary events and almost nothing to do with the original prophecy, except casually. This is the case in passages in the Habakkuk *Pesher* and Ezek. 44:15 in the Damascus Document above. Parallel processes of this kind can also be said to have taken place in the Gospels.

Finally, an author might wish to launch a direct attack on some overarching problem that particularly exercised him, such as Biblical chronology or genealogy. This approach is again illustrated in the presentation of the flood chronology in the Genesis Florilegium, as well as the Biblical Chronology and Hur and Miriam texts which follow it below. These very easily flow into what it is called later in Rabbinic circles *Midrash* (i.e. homiletic story).

14. A GENESIS FLORILEGIUM (4Q252)
(Plate 5)

This text is one of the most fascinating in the corpus. It consists of some six columns as we have reconstructed it and skims over the main Genesis narrative, alighting only on points and issues it wishes for some reason to clarify or re-present. These include the flood, Ham's son Canaan's punishment, the early days of Abram/Abraham, Sodom and Gomorrah, and Reuben's offence against his father. It ends, perhaps most importantly, with Jacob's blessing of his children. This last, more of an interpretation (*pesher*) than a rewrite, incorporates some of the most telling Messianic pronouncements of any Qumran text in this or any other volume.

In the process, the author picks up some of the major modern scholarly problems in Genesis textual analysis and attempts what in his terms is clearly a resolution. For instance, he attempts to set forth a proper chronology of the flood story, coming up with a 364-day calendar of the Jubilees type. Contradictory elements are either harmonized, passed over or deleted in the interests of rationalizing a coherent calendar and explaining its intrinsic applicability to the flood story. In the process it sorts out inconsistent elements in what modern scholars refer to as the *Yahwist* or *Elohist* (Priestly) parts of the narrative.

Since the main concern of the first two columns about Noah and the flood is calendrical, the traditional story is subordinated to this interest. The calendar is an extremely important matter, and it has been said that whoever controls the calendar, its feast days and rituals, controls the society. Rabbinic literature, building on the Pharisee tradition that preceded it, was originally dependent on a lunar calendar that was only later harmonized, following Roman developments, with a solar year. It should, however, be noted that a 'pre-Rabbinic' form of the lunisolar calendar already existed in our period, as several of the 'Priestly Courses' texts in Chapter 4 below demonstrate.

In theory, this calendar depended on human observation for new moons and the like. Qumran abjured this, attempting a solar harmonization of an intellectual kind and obviously wishing to develop very early on a harmonious total mathematical scheme that did not depend on human failings. In the process, feast days were located at the beginning of weeks, and everything regularized to accord with a full 364-day, one-year scheme including intercalated days.

For instance, the full year, 364-day cycle is completed at the bottom of Column 1 and the beginning of Column 2 with the notice that the earth was completely dry on the seventeenth day of the first month, not the twenty-seventh as in Biblical tradition. The tradition that the flood lasted only one year is known in Jubilees (5:31), but its author seems to have tried to have it both ways and adopt an intermediate position between the text before us and the Biblical tradition of more than one year. For him, though the land was dry on the seventeenth day of the second month, it was not until the twenty-seventh day — the end of the flood in the Biblical text we are familiar with — that Noah sent the animals out of the ark. Noah himself did not really leave the ark until the first day of the third month, two weeks later (6:1).

Our text disagrees, noting in Lines 2–3 of Column 2 that 'on Sunday, on that very day, Noah went forth from the ark'; and as if to further punctuate this point, it adds, 'thereby completing a full year of 364 days'. It returns to this point, showing it to be a major concern, in the next line (4–5), repeating: 'Noah [went forth] from the ark at the appointed time – one full year.' Because the polemic is so emphatic, it would appear that the author of the text is familiar with the traditional text, which is probably the Pharisaic one. That this is the point he wants to hammer home, i.e. that the flood came to an end on the same Sunday the 17th *one full year* after it began, could not be clearer. The rest of the narrative is subordinated to this. Colourful detail, like the size of the ark, the kinds of animals and the raven are discarded.

Because of the author's abstract, mathematical flair and because his calendar is mathematically speaking so harmonized, days of the week do not fluctuate over the month, whatever the year, and he proceeds to give the exact calendrical day of the week for all significant events in the story. In fact, he adds extra days, some perhaps coinciding with significant festival days as in 1.8 or 1.22. For a precise analysis of the scheme of this calendar in this text, see the notes at the end of this chapter. For more on the calendar as it related to courses in the Temple, and other matters of Temple service, see further discussions in Chapter 4.

In the next story from the Noah cycle, the author shows again that his intention is to explain an inherent contradiction in the narrative as it has come down to us, namely why God cursed Canaan, son of Ham, when it was Ham who had actually 'uncovered his father's nakedness' (Gen. 9:26). Though any reasonable person would notice this problem, normative tradition usually does not. Showing that the author both knows the traditional text and is intent on rationalizing certain obvious problems in it, Column 2.7 explains, somewhat triumphantly, that since God had already blessed Noah's sons, He could hardly retract that blessing. Despite its facileness, it is an explanation, and shows that people of this school of thought in the Qumran period (as opposed to some others) were already doing elementary text criticism, a fact which also stands out in the reconstruction of the flood narrative preceding it.

This is again clear in the treatment of the next episode about Abraham; we are dealing with one interesting problem after another in the traditional Genesis text. Column 2.8 shows that the author knows that Abraham will receive a name change in Gen. 17:5. But in 9ff. it switches back to the earlier name Abram as it moves on to the story it is really interested in, Sodom and Gomorrah. In the process, it confronts another problem that seems to have puzzled many commentators, such as Philo in *de migratione Abrahami* 177 and the author of the Book of Acts 7:4, i.e. the apparent implication in Gen. 12:4 that Abraham left Haran *after* the death of his father.

Gen. 11:32 had already put Terah's age at the time of his death at 205. In 11:26 it specified his age at the time of 'Abram's' birth as 70. Some traditions — most notably the version of the Pentateuch possessed by the Samaritans and one Septuagint manuscript obviously related to it — add the number 75 after these two passages to denote Terah's age at the time of *his death* — thereby adding to the conundrum.

Our text is trying to clarify this problem. In the process it rejects the position of Philo and Acts above, that since Gen. 12:4 is placed after Gen. 11:32, it likewise has to be thought of as recording an event that happened *chronologically* after it. Rather, it adds its own more precise, numerical specifications, as it did in the flood narrative preceding it, definitively clarifying this problem in the traditional text. Column 2.8 adds the key piece of numerical data not found in the Bible, *that Terah was 140 years of age when he migrated to Haran*, i.e. that he had lived 70 more years in Ur before migrating to Haran.

In another mathematical rationalization not found in the Bible, the text now deduces Abram's age at the time of Terah's migration as also being 70 (Line 9), i.e. it also fills an important lacuna in Abraham's biographical chronology. It then moves on to add another five years to Abram's age (and by implication Terah's too) to make up the total of 75, his age in Gen. 12:5 when he departed for Canaan. Finally, by implication granting the traditional number 70 for Terah's age at the time of Abram's birth, it affixes some last numerological data, i.e. Terah lived 65 years in Haran after Abram's departure, thereby making up the total of 205 the author started with (2.10). That his concerns are mathematical could not be more apparent.

Another important point it makes, before moving on to even more serious concerns and the second of the two Genesis 'salvation of the Righteous' stories, is that Abraham was the 'friend of God'. The actual terminology used in 2.8 is 'beloved of God'. This is precisely the language the Damascus Document uses to describe Abraham. Interestingly, CD,ii.18ff. does so following an allusion to the 'Heavenly Watchers' and the Noah story just as here. For it, the former fell 'because *they walked in the stubbornness of their hearts*' and '*did not keep the Commandments of God*' (italics ours).

Interestingly too, this is precisely the language James 3:23 and 4:4 uses to discuss how its adversary turned himself into 'the Enemy of God' 4:4. We noted this language above when discussing the meaning of *Mastema* — 'Enemy' or 'Adversary'. For the Damascus Document, Abraham was designated 'beloved of God', language very familiar to Islam, because '*he kept the Commandments*' (language also familiar to the Letter of James), and it proceeds to designate Isaac and Jacob as 'friends of God' as well, just as later Muhammad designates them along with Abraham as 'those who have surrendered to God' i.e. Muslims (Koran 2:133ff.).

The first of these 'escape and salvation' stories in Genesis is, of course, the Noah story. Gen. 6:9 describes Noah as 'Righteous and Perfect in his generation', important terminologies in Qumran literature. The second is the story of Lot. This is picked up in Column 3, which follows in the document before us. This interest, in a compendium as short as the Florilegium, which simply skims Genesis for interesting issues, in the two first escape and rescue stories involving 'Zaddikim' in the bible is probably not accidental. It reflects the pre-eminent position 'the Righteous' play in Qumran ideology generally, as they do in Jewish Christianity to follow, and *Kabbalah* thereafter.

This interest is also apparent in the Gospel of Thomas 12, as is, of course, the parallel interest in *James*: 'In the place where you are to go, go to James the Righteous One for whose sake Heaven and Earth came into existence'. Curiously the best place to look for an explanation of the allusions here is in the medieval Jewish work of mysticism, the *Zohar*. Discussing this Noah episode in 59b, it describes 'the *Zaddik*' in Prov. 10:25's words as the 'Foundation of the world, and . . . the Pillar that upholds it'. In the *Zohar*'s view, and in much of Jewish mysticism thereafter, the very existence of the universe is predicated on the existence of the Righteous/Righteous One.

In the Genesis Florilegium, there is a collateral interest in sexual matters reflecting the condemnation of 'fornication' which one finds in other Qumran documents like that in the 'three nets of Belial' section of the Damascus Document. This is a main concern of James' instructions to overseas communities in Acts, as it is in the letter attributed to his name. This concern is not only prominent in both the Ham/Canaan and Sodom/Gomorrah episodes before us, but also the stories which follow these about blotting out Amalek's name 'from under Heaven' and Reuben's disqualification from his rightful legacy owing to his sexual relations with his father's concubine Bilha. This latter was seemingly as jarring to ancient ears as it is to modern. Referred to in the Blessings of Jacob at the end of Gen. 49:3–4, Reuben's disqualification sets the stage for the blessings on Judah that follow, which are themselves, as we shall see, of very great interest and the climax of the present text as well.

The problem of Reuben's supposed transgression also seems to have disturbed the author of Jub. 33:10ff., who wrestled with the question of why Reuben was not treated according to the Law and stoned as per Lev. 18 and 20. He explains – again somewhat facilely – that the laws of incest had not as yet been revealed. The Damascus Document takes the same approach to David's 'multiplying wives unto himself' (a practice it described as 'fornication' in a previous column), explaining that this ban did not come into effect until 'the coming of Zadok' – whenever this was, it was obviously conceived of as being after David's time (v. 1–5). This approach is portentous for the history of Western civilization, because Paul uses this point and in Gal. 3 and Rom. 4, makes it the centrepiece of his approach to Abraham and the Law, i.e. Abraham came *before* the Law and therefore was not 'justified' ('made Righteous') by it. Muhammad interestingly enough also uses a variation of this to describe his approach to Abraham, namely that he came *before* both Judaism and Christianity.

Here the Genesis Florilegium somewhat laconically adds the words, 'and he reproved him' (Line 5). In other words, it makes it clear that this was all Jacob did. We will find the same words actually used in a text dealing with matters of 'bodily emissions' involving Community discipline at the end of this work. However in noting that Reuben was only first theoretically and implying that Judah would be first in actuality, it again inadvertently reveals its main concern – Jacob's blessings *on Judah* to follow.

The issue of the Amalekites is a different one, but also interesting. Column 4.1 distinctly designates them as the issue of another questionable relationship with a concubine, i.e. 'fornication' again. 4.2–3's almost word-for-word evocation of a speech of Moses from Exod. 17:14 shows the *modus operandi* of the author, i.e. 1. he knows the entire Bible text (at least those books mentioned above), and 2. he is doing Biblical commentary on or exegesis of it.

The addition of the eschatological phrase 'the last days' in the same line, which our text deliberately adds to the speech attributed to Moses in Exod. 17:14, is also instructive. Otherwise both speeches are identical. This, of course, highlights the eschatological themes with which the text ends, as it does what is expected in 'the last times' regarding Amalek.

This leads to another point. Moses predicts the absolute eradication of the Amalekites, i.e. their name would be 'blotted out from under

Heaven'. Though the text in 4.1 refers to Saul's smiting the Amalekites (showing once again that the author knows that Biblical story as
well), and it is possible to think that for him, this fulfilled the Biblical
prophecy, the point is that Saul *did not* do so. Samuel had put the
Amalekites under ban, but Saul did not carry this out, and even
though, according to the Bible, he later repented of this, he was
'rejected' (note – again the use of the tell-tale word *maʾas* repeatedly
throughout the Biblical account).

Saul's failure to do this leads *directly* to the anointment of David in 1
Sam. 16. This is crucial, and the author of our text is most surely
aware of it. But that is what he is interested in – the anointment of
David and the elevation of Judah to be set forth in an eschatological
manner in the interpretation of the 'Shiloh Prophecy' that follows.
With the deftest hand and the most delicate of brush strokes, our
author is doing extremely sophisticated Biblical criticism.

Also illustrative is the completely unbending and militant attitude
in evidence here. This is absolutely characteristic of the attitude of
Qumran and is consistent across the corpus. No peaceful Essenes these.
The addition of 'the last days' or 'end of days' to Moses' speech is also
then purposeful and clearly eschatological. Since Saul failed to do it,
the memory of Amalek will only 'be erased from under Heaven'
properly in 'the last days'. And who will do it? Clearly the Messiah,
with whom the text closes.

Column 5 moves on to Judah. The exegesis it contains has to be
considered the climax of the work and for our purposes, exegesis
generally at Qumran. Nor are we any longer in the realm of Biblical
rewrite or condensation, but exegesis pure and simple. This takes as its
starting point Jacob's blessing on Judah in Gen. 49:10: 'The Sceptre
shall not pass from Judah, nor the Staff from between his feet until the
coming of the Shiloh to whom the peoples will gather.'

In an exegesis of the most far-reaching eschatological significance,
Column 5.1 interprets 'the Sceptre', also mentioned in the Star
Prophecy in Num. 24 – the 'Star' and the 'Sceptre' are equivalent – in
terms of the Government. It will be recalled that the latter prophecy is
also interpreted, as we have seen above, in the Damascus Document.
Though the first part of the exegesis of the Shiloh Prophecy is missing
from the present document, it is clear that this is to involve a Davidic
descendant, i.e. someone from 'the seed' of David mentioned in Line
5.5, which was so important in Christian Messianic expectations we've
mentioned. In 5.2 the 'Staff' or 'Law-Giver' (the *Mehokkek*) in the
Shiloh Prophecy is interpreted in terms of 'the Covenant of the

Kingdom'. In Lines 3–4, the 'feet' in this prophecy are interpreted as the leaders or military commanders of Israel and finally, most significantly of all, 'Shiloh' is distinctly identified as 'the Messiah of Righteousness'. That he is to be *a descendant of David* is made explicit in Line 5.5 as we have seen.

This *Mehokkek* or 'Staff' is also mentioned in another prophecy from Num. 21:18. Like the Star Prophecy from Num. 24 that follows it, this too is interpreted in the Damascus Document (vi.3–11). In Column vii.20 of the Damascus Document, the 'Sceptre' referred to in the Star Prophecy is definitively interpreted in terms of the *Nasi ha-ʿEdah*/'the Leader of the Community', the subject of the text by that name in Chapter 1.

In the interpretation of the *Mehokkek* prophecy that precedes it, 'Damascus' is mentioned, from which the Damascus Document takes its name. So are 'the penitents of Israel', who are also mentioned in the exegesis of Ezekiel's 'sons of Zadok' prophecy two columns prior to this in Column iv. These 'penitents' – called 'the Priests' in the Column iv exegesis – 'go out from the land of Judah' in both exegeses 'to dwell in the land of Damascus'. The 'Staff' is delineated as the 'seeker after the *Torah*'; and the 'well', which he digs in the Num. 21 reference, is again 'the *Torah*'. The 'staves' in Num. 21, i.e. the Laws, are what they (the *Mehokkek*'s followers) are commanded to walk in 'during all the Era of Evil' until 'the One who pours out Righteousness (*Yoreh ha-Zedek*) arises (or stands up) at the end of days.'

Here the 'Messiah of Righteousness', i.e. *Mashiah ha-Zedek* resonating with *Yoreh ha-Zedek* above and other equally pregnant usages, is definitely identified with 'the Branch of David'. But this expression is also mentioned in the Messianic Leader (*Nasi*) text in Chapter 1 above. This now brings all these usages full circle, including the *Nasi ha-ʿEdah* ('the Leader of the Community') called 'the Star' in CD,vii above. As we have seen, too, 'peoples' in the Shiloh Prophecy above is in some sense an important eschatological usage at Qumran. In the present text in Line 5.4, it gives way to 'His people', 'the Covenant of whose Kingdom was given unto him (i.e. the Messianic 'Branch' or 'Star') forever'.

Put another way, one has irrefutable proof here that the Messianic 'Leader', mentioned in the text by that name, is to be identified with this 'Messiah of Righteousness', because the allusion to 'the Branch of David' is used in both as an identifying epithet. This makes the matter of whether the Messianic Leader is doing the killing or being killed more important than ever. Later in this work we shall find additional support for the latter interpretation, when we reconstruct the phraseology *hemitu Zaddikim* at the end of the Demons of Death (Beatitudes) text in Chapter 5 as 'they put to death the Righteous' (plural).

The conjunction of 'the Righteousness' terminology with 'the Messiah', much in the manner that it is co-joined with 'the Teacher' and 'the Pourer' above (the *Moreh* and the *Yoreh*) in the definition of the Shiloh in Gen. 49:10, is of the utmost significance. This is consistent with the total ethos of Qumran and has, in fact, important resonances with presentations of the Melchizedek ideology ('the King of Righteousness') in relation to the eschatological priesthood set forth in Heb. 5:7–10 (including, interestingly enough, reference to 'the Logos of Righteousness' in Line 5:14).

The explanation in the final decipherable line of this exegesis 'because he, i.e. the Messiah of Righteousness, kept . . . the Torah' together with the others 'of the Community' is also important, not only for Qumran Messianic notions but for Qumran ideology as a whole and its overtones with early Christianity of the Jamesian mould. We have already mentioned that the Community Rule defines the 'sons of Zadok' in terms of 'keeping' or being 'Keepers of the Covenant'. This is a qualitative exegesis, not a genealogical one. It is reinforced in the Damascus Document's exegesis of Ezek. 44:15 – also qualitative – and an eschatological element is added, that of 'the last days'.

These also have supernatural connotations, e.g. in CD, iv.3 and 7, 'they stand in the last days' (as does the *Yoreh ha-Zedek*) and 'justify the Righteous and condemn the Wicked'. If these notations are consistent, then the words 'keeping . . . the *Torah*' also imply that the Messiah or Shiloh was also to be reckoned among 'the sons of Zadok'. It should also be clear that *Zedek* and Zadok are to be reckoned as variations of the same terminology – that is, the 'sons of Zadok' and 'sons of Zedek' are equivalent – and that allusions to Melchizedek amount simply to a further adumbration.

Here, too, the allusion in 5.5 to 'the men of the Community' with 'the Messiah of Righteousness' as 'Keepers of the Covenant' implies that the Messiah has either already come, is eschatologically to return, or is, in fact, at that very moment connected to or among 'the *Yahad*' (Community). That the Community honours a Davidic-style, singular Messiah associated in some manner with the concept of Righteousness – a matter of some dispute in Dead Sea Scrolls studies heretofore – is no longer to be gainsaid. All these are very important conclusions indeed with serious implications for Qumran studies. This is the importance of publishing these texts completely and not in bits and pieces.

The text ends in Column 6, a little anticlimactically, with portions from Gen. 49:20–21 about blessings on Asher and Napthali, of which little is intelligible.

TRANSLITERATION Column 1

1. ‏[וכש]נת ארבע מאות ושמונים לחיי נוח בא קצם לנוח ואלוהים
2. ‏[א]מר לא ידור רוחי באדם לעולם ויחתכו ימיהם מאה ועשרים
3. ‏[שנ]ה עד קץ מי מבול ומי מבול היו על הארץ בעת שש מאות שנה
4. ‏לחיי נוח בחודש השני באחד בשבת בשבעה עשר בו ביום ההוא
5. ‏נבקעו כול מעינות תהום רבה וארבות השמים נפתחו ויהי הגשם על
6. ‏הארץ ארבעים יום וארבעים לילה עד יום עשרים וששה בחודש
7. ‏השלישי יום חמשה בשבת ויגברו המ[י]ם על ה[א]רץ חמשים ומאת יום
8. ‏עד יום ארבעה עשר בחודש השביעי [יום] שולשה בשבת ובסוף חמשים
9. ‏ומאת יום חסרו המים שני ימים יום הרביעי ויום החמישי ויום
10. ‏הששי נחה התבה על הרי הוררט ה[וא יום] שבעה עשר בחודש השביעי
11. ‏והמים הי[ו ה]לוך וחסור עד החודש [העש]ירי באחד בו יום רביעי
12. ‏לשבת נרא[ו] ראשי ההרים ויהי מקץ ארבעים יום להראות ראשי
13. ‏הה[רים ויפ]תח נוח את חלון התבה יום אחד בשבת הוא יום עשרה
14. ‏בע[שתי עשר] החודש וישלח [נוח] את היונה לראות הקלו המים ולוא
15. ‏מצאה מנוח ותבוא אליו [אל ה]תבה ויחל עוד שבעת ימים א[חרים]
16. ‏ויוסף לשלחה ותבוא אליו ועלי זית טרף בפיה [הוא יום עשרים]
17. ‏וארבעה לעשתי עשר החודש באחד בשב[ת וידע נוח כי קלו המים]
18. ‏מעל הארץ ומקץ שבעת ימים אחר[ים וישלח נוח את היונה ולוא]
19. ‏יספה לשוב עוד הוא יום א[חד לשנים עשר] החודש [יום אחד]
20. ‏בשבת ומקץ שלוש[י]ם [ואחד יום משלח]ה אשר לא י[ספה]
21. ‏שוב עוד חרבו ה[מים מעל הארץ] ויסר נוח את מכסה התבה
22. ‏וירא והנה [חרבו המים מעל פני האדמה] באחד בחודש הראישו[ן]

Column 2

1. ‏באחת ושש מאו[ת] שנה לחיי נוח ובשבעה עשר יום לחודש השני
2. ‏יבשה הארץ באחד בשבת ביום ההוא יצא נוח מן התבה לקץ שנה
3. ‏תמימה לימים שלוש מאות ששים וארבעה באחד בשבת בשבעה
4. ‏*vacat* אחת ושש *vacat*   נוח מן התבה למועד שנה
5. ‏תמימה *vacat*   ויקץ נוח מיינו וידע את אשר עשה
6. ‏לו בנו הקטן ויאמר ארור כנען עבד עבדים יהייה לאחיו לא
7. ‏קלל את חם כי אם בנו כי ברך אל את בני נוח ובאהלי שם ישכון
8. ‏ארץ נתן לאברהם אהבו *vacat* בן מאה וארב[ע]ים שנה תרח בצאתו
9. ‏מאור כשדיים ויבוא חרן ואב[רם בן ש]בעים שנה וחמש שנה ישב
10. ‏אברם בחרן ואחר יצא [אברם אל] ארץ כנען ששי[ם וחמש שנה]
11. ‏העגלה והאיל והעז[   ] [   ] אברם לאל [   ]

‎.12 האש בעברו]   [.ה ל..ל.]   [

‎.13 לצאת אב]רם אל ארץ[כנען ל]   [

Column 3

‎.1 כאשר כתוב]   [שנים

‎.2 עשר אנש]ים   עמו]רה וגם

‎.3 העיר הזאת]   [צדיקים

‎.4 אנוכ]י[לא]אשחית   [.ים לבדם יחרמו

‎.5 ואם לוא ימצא שם]עשרה צדקים אשחית העיר וכל] הנמצא בה ושלליה

‎.6 וטפיה ושאר .]   [עולם וישלח

‎.7 אברהם את ידו]   מים[

‎.8 ויומר אליו עת]ה   [

‎.9 ....]   [

‎.10 ....]   [

‎.11 [ ]   [

‎.12 [ו]אל שדי יב]רך אותכה ויפרכה וירבכה והייתה לקהל עמים ויתן לכה]

‎.13 א]ת ברכת אביכה]אברהם   [

‎.14 [ ]לם תחי]ה   [

Column 4

‎.1 [ו]תמנע היתה פילנש לאליפז בן עשיו ותלד לו את עמלק הוא אשר הכ]ה[

‎.2 שאול *vacat* כאשר דבר *vacat* למושה באחרית הימים תמחה את זכר עמלק

‎.3 מחחת השמים *vacat* ברכות יעקוב ראובן בכורי אתה

‎.4 ורישית אוני יתר שאת ויתר עוז פחזתה כמים אל תותר עליתה

‎.5 משכבי אביכה אז חללתה יצועיו עלה *vacat* פשרו אשר הוכיחו אשר

‎.6 שכב עם בלהה פלנשו ואמר בכורי אתה]   [ראובן הוא

‎.7 ראשית ערכו ..]   [

Column 5

‎.1 [לוא] יסור שליט משבט יהודה בהיות לישראל ממשל

‎.2 [לוא י]כרת יושב בוא לדויד כי המחקק הוא ברית המלכות

‎.3 [אל]פי ישראל המה הרגלים עד בוא משיח הצדק צמח

‎.4 דויד כי לו ולזרעו נתנה ברית מלכות עמו עד דורות עולם אשר

‎.5 שמר ה]   [התורה עם אנשי היחד כי

‎.6] הוא כנסת אנשי [   ]

‎.7] נתן [   ]

Column 6

‎.1 יתן מעדני ה]מלך נפתלי אילה שלחה הנותן אמרי]

‎.2 שפר ע.]   [

‎.3 את ה]   [

‎.4]. [[

TRANSLATION

Column 1 (1) in the 480th [year] of Noah's life their (Wicked humanity) end came for Noah. And God (2) [sa]id, 'My Spirit shall not dwell among men forever,' and so their days were fixed (at) one hundred and twenty (3) [yea]rs, until the time of the waters of the flood. Now the waters of the flood were on the earth beginning with the six hundredth year (4) of Noah's life. In the second month, on Sunday the 17th, on that very day (5) all the fountains of the great deep burst open, and the windows of Heaven were opened. So there was rain on (6) the earth for forty days and forty nights, until the 26th of the third (7) month, Thursday. The wa[te]rs rose upon the [ea]rth for one hundred and fifty days, (8) until the 14th of the seventh month, Tuesday. And at the end of one hundred (9) and fifty days the waters abated, for two days, Wednesday and Thursday, and on (10) Friday the ark came to rest on the Ararat Range—the 17th of the seventh month. (11) Now the waters [con]tinued to diminish until the [ten]th month. On the first of that month, Wednesday, (12) the peaks of the mountains bec[ame vis]ible. Forty days from the ti[me] when the mou[ntain] peaks became visible, (13) Noah [ope]ned the window of the ark. On Sunday, that is, the 10th of (14) the [eleve]nth month, [Noah] sent forth the dove to see whether the waters had abated, but (15) it did not find any place to alight and so it returned to him [in t]he ark. He then waited seven [mor]e days (16) and once more sent it forth, and it returned to him with a cut olive branch in its bill. [This was on the (17) 2]4th of the eleventh month, on Sunda[y. Therefore Noah knew that the waters had abated] (18) on the earth. At the end of seven mo[re days Noah sent the dove out, but (19) it did not] return again. This was the fir[st day of the twelfth] month, [a (20) Sunday.] At the end of thirt[y-one days from the time he had sent it forth], when it did not (21) return anymore, the wa[ters] had dried up [on the earth.] Then Noah removed the hatch of the ark (22) and looked around, and indeed [the waters had disappeared from the face of the earth], on the first day of the first month,

Column 2 (1) in the six hundred and first year of Noah's life. And on the 17th of the second month, (2) the earth was completely dry. On Sunday, on that day Noah went forth from the ark, thus completing a full (3) year of three hundred and sixty four days. On Sunday, in the seventh (4) <one and six.> Noah (went forth) from the ark at the appointed time, one full (5) year. <> 'Then Noah awoke from his wine and knew what his youngest son (6) had done to him, and he said, "Cursed be Canaan; he shall be his brothers' meanest slave."' He did not (7) curse Ham, but on the contrary, his son, because God had already blessed Noah's sons: 'And in the tents of Shem they will dwell.' (8) He gave the land to Abraham His friend.

<>Terah was one hundred and f[o]rty years old when he left (9) Ur of the Chaldees and came to Haran. And Ab[ram was se]venty, and Abram lived in (10) Haran for five years, and after [Abram] left [for] the land of Canaan, (Terah lived) sixt[y-five years . . .] (11) the heifer and the ram and the she-g[oat . . .] Abram to God . . . (12) the fire when he crossed over . . . (13) Abr[am] to go out [to the land of] Canaan . . .

Column 3 (1) as it is written, . . . twelve (2) me[n . . . Gomor]rah and also (3) this city . . . Righteous (4) I will not destroy . . . only they shall exterminate. (5) And if there are not found there [ten Righteous Men, I will destroy the city and everyone] found in it, along with its booty (6) and its little children. And the remnant . . . forever. And Abraham (7) stretched out his hand . . . (8) And he said to him, 'No[w . . .'] (12) 'And El Shaddai will bless you and make you fruitful and multiply you. You shall become a congregation of peoples. And he will give to you (13) the blessing once given to [Abraham] your father' . . .

Column 4 (1) '[. . . and] Timna was the concubine of Eliphaz the son of Esau, and she bore him Amalek.' It was he whom Saul exterminat[ed] (2) as He said to Moses, 'In the future you will erase the memory of Amalek (3) from under Heaven.' <> The blessings of Jacob: 'Reuben, you are my first born, (4) the first portion of my strength, preeminent in stature and preeminent in power, unstable as water—(but) you shall not be preeminent. You mounted (5) your father's marriage couch, thereby defiling it because he lay on it.' <> Interpreted, this means that he reproved him, because (6) he (Reuben) slept with Bilhah his (father's) concubine. When it says 'You are my first born,' it means . . . Reuben was (7) the first in theory . . .

Column 5 (1) '(the) Government shall [not] pass from the tribe of Judah.' During Israel's dominion, (2) a Davidic descendant on the throne shall [not c]ease. For 'the Staff' is the Covenant of the Kingdom. (3) [The lead]ers of Israel, they are 'the Feet' (referred to in Genesis 49:11), until the Messiah of Righteousness, the Branch of (4) David comes, because to him and his seed was given the Covenant of the Kingdom of His people in perpetuity, because (5) he kept . . . the *Torah* with the men of the Community, because (6) . . . refers to the Congregation of the men of (7) . . . He gave

Column 6 (1) 'he shall yield royal dignities. Naphtali is a doe let loose, who gives (2) beautiful words.' . . .

15. JOSHUA APOCRYPHON (4Q522)

This text contains an assortment of geographical locales and place names that may go back to the period of Joshua or reflect some display or schema connected to the Davidic period. Because of the reference to Eleazar, the high priest often associated with Joshua's activities, we have called it a Joshua Apocryphon, though the text, as it has been preserved in the second column, clearly focuses on the figure of David, his activities, his conquests, his kingship and, in particular, his building of the Temple. Were it not for the fact that much of this seems to be phrased in terms of a prophecy from the earlier conquest period, one might even call it a Samuel Apocryphon.

However, as with the Genesis Florilegium just considered, any idea that there is anything resembling anti-Temple feeling in texts such as these – a notion widespread in the early days of Qumran research based on the incompleteness of the data then available – is simply misguided and fails to come to grips with the ethos of Qumran as it reveals itself in these texts. Nor is there anything remotely suggesting a lack of interest in a Davidic kingship – quite the opposite; the Messianic implications in this text are only a little less overt than the interpretation of the Shiloh Prophecy previously. Note for example in this vein Lines 7–8 of Column 2: 'And the Lord will establish David securely . . . Heaven will dwell with him forever.'

The very reconstruction 'Heaven', if accurate, is interesting when one considers similar constructions in phrases like the Gospel of Matthew's 'Kingdom of Heaven'. It is also interesting that in Line 3 the word 'rock' (*sela'*) – a word not without its own interesting implications in Christianity – is evoked to describe the Mountain of Zion.

David's conquest of Jerusalem, his building the Temple and rich decoration of it is lavishly praised. For those who would refer to this literature as sectarian, the nationalist implications of texts such as this are important, as is the provocative allusion to 'the sons of Satan' in Line 5. This parallels similar references elsewhere in the corpus to 'sons of Belial', and their variation in the 'Mastemoth'/'sons of Darkness' allusions we have encountered above and will encounter further below.

TRANSLITERATION   Fragment 1 Column 1

]ם ואת עין קבר בית	] .1
[בקע]ה] ואת בית צפור את	] .2
]ימו את כול בקעת מצוא את	] .3
[את היכל יצד את יעפור ואת	] .4
]בא ואת מנו את עין כובר	] .5
]ר גרים את חדיתא ואת עושל	] .6
]דון אשר [חי] [.] [.	] .7

.8] [ ].ר] [.בא וא]ת א[שקלון] [

.9] ג[ליל ושנים ש] א[ת השרון

.10] י[הודה את באר שבע [וא]ת בעלות

.11] את קעילה את עדולם ואת

.12] נזר ואת תמני ואת גמזון ואת

.13] חקר וקטר[ון] ואפרנים ואת שכות

.14] בית חורון התחת[ו]ן והעל[יון ו]א[ת

.15] א[ת גילת עליונה [וא]ת התח[תונ]ה

Fragment 1 Column 2

.1 [ ]ן להשכין שם את אה.. ב] [

.2 העתים כי הנה בן נולד לישי בן פרץ בן יה[ו]דה [

.3 את סלע ציון ויורש משם את <כל> האמורי ב] [

.4 לבנות <את> הבית ליהוה אלוהי ישראל זהב וכסף] [

.5 ארזים וברושים יב[י]א מ[לבנון לבנותו ובני הסטן] [

.6 יכהן שם ואיש ..מ] [ ]..[ ] ואות.] [כה] [

.7] [ ]ן מן השמ.] ודוד יהו[ה] ישכין לבטח] [

.8 [ש]מים עמו ישכון [ל]עד ועתה האמורי שם והכנענ[י [

.9 יושב אשר החטיים אשר לוא דרשתי .] [שפ] [..] [[

.10 מאתכה והשלוני וה] נתחיו עבד ע] [א] [

.11 ועתה נ[ש]כינה את א] עד רחוק מן] [

.12 אלעזר] [ע את] [עד מבית] [

.13 ישוב] [צבא מ.] [

TRANSLATION

Fragment 1 Column 1 (1) . . . and En Qeber and . . . (2) . . . Valley, and Bet Zippor, with (3) . . . all the Valley of Mozza (4) . . . and Heikhal-Yezed(?) and Yapur and (5) . . . and Mini and En Kober (6) . . . Garim and Hedita and Oshel (7) . . . which (8) . . . and Ashkalon . . . (9) . . . [G]alil, and the two . . . and the Sharon (10) . . . Judah, and Beer Sheba, and Baalot (11) . . . and Qeilah and Adullam and (12) . . . Gezer and Thamni and Gamzon and (13) . . . Hiqqar and Qittar and Ephronim and Shakkoth (14) . . . Bet Horon, the lower and the upper, and (15) . . . and the Upper and the Lower Gilat

Fragment 1 Column 2 (1) . . . to establish there the . . . (2) the times, for a son is about to be born to Jesse, son of Perez, son of Ju[dah . . .] (3) (He shall capture) the mountain (literally, rock) of Zion, and he will dispossess from there all the Amorites . . . (4) to build the House for the Lord, the God of Israel. Gold and silver . . . (5) cedars and cypress will he bring from Lebanon to build it, and the sons of Satan . . . (6) he will do priestly service there and a man . . . your . . . (7) from the . . . And the Lord will establish David securely . . . (8) [He]aven will dwell with him forever. But now, the Amorites are there, and the Canaanites . . . (9) dwell where the Hittites (do), none of whom have I sought . . . (10) from you. And the Shilonite, and the . . . I have given him as a servant . . . (11) And now, let us establish . . . far from . . . (12) Eleazar . . . forever, from the House (13) . . . army . . .

16. A BIBLICAL CHRONOLOGY (4Q559)

This work attempted to determine the chronology of the people and, in some cases, the events of the Bible. This enterprise was important not only for its intrinsic interest, but also to those who wanted to locate the present in the flow of time toward the Messianic era. They could then predict when the Messiah would come, and when other predictions of the prophets would find fulfilment. Interest in such 'chronomessianism' was great in the period of the Scrolls.

The complexity of Biblical chronology was daunting, because at many junctures the Bible simply did not say how many years passed between events. These 'blanks' could only be filled in by calculation, a process fraught with possibilities for error as well as legitimately different results. In the time of the Scrolls at least three separate systems of Biblical chronology existed: that of the Masoretic text (the Hebrew text normally translated in modern Bibles); that of the Septuagint, the Bible used in Egypt; and that of the Samaritans. Note the correspondence of this text with the Terah reference in the Genesis Florilegium above.

TRANSLITERATION   Column 1 (Fragments 1 and 3)

.1	[ותרח בר]
.2	[שנין 333 ¬ אולד ית אברהם ואברהם]
.3	[בר ש]נין 3 [333¬ III III III אולד ית ישחק]
.4	[ויש]חק ב]ר שנין 333 אולד ית יעקב ויעקב]
.5	[[בר שני]ן 11333 III אולד ית לוי
.6	[[ח.ל]
.7	[ולוי בר שני]ן [3 ¬ [IIII א]ולד ית קהת וקהת בר]
.8	[שנין 13 I[I III III I אולד ית עמ]רם עמ]רם בר שנין]
.9	[ד ¬ אולד] ית אהרון ואהר]ון] נפק ממצ]רין]
.10	[כול שניא] אלן ¬]לף IIIII¬ 3 ¬ III III]

Column 2

.1	[[
.2	[מן אר]ע מרצין]

3. [   ]   [ח שנ]ין

4. [   ]   י]רדנא [

5. [   ]   3[¬||||| בנ>לנ<לא ש]נין

6. [בתמנת סר]ח שנין 3 ומן די מית]יהושוע

7. [   ]   כוש רשעתים מלך]ארם נהרין [   ]

8. [   ]   שני]ן[||| ||| || עתניאל ב]ר קנז

9. [|| ||| ¬|||ן] שנין] 3333 עגלון מלך מואב שנ]ין ¬

10. [אח]וד בר גרא שנין 3333 שמ]גר בר ענת]

TRANSLATION

Column 1 (Fragments 1 and 3) (1) [. . . and Terah was (2) seventy years old when he fathered Abraham; and Abraham (3) was] nin[ety-nine ye]ars old [when he fathered Isaac; (4) and Is]aac was [sixty years old when he fathered Jacob; and Jacob (5) was] sixty-fi[ve year]s old [when he fathered Levi . . . (7) and Levi was thirty-] five [year]s old when he fa[thered Kohath; and Kohath was (8) twenty-] nine [year]s old when he fathered Am[r]am; Am[ram was (9) one hundred and ten years old when he fathered] Aaron, and Aar[on] went out from Egy[pt. (10) (The total of) all] these [years:] eleven thousand, five hundred and thirty-six . . .
Column 2 (2) . . . from the lan[d of Egypt . . .] (3) ye[ars (?) . . .] (4) the [Jo]rdan . . . (5) [in . . .] thirty-five (or more) [years;] in Gilgal . . . ye[ars . . . (6) in Timnath-Sera]h twenty years; and from the time that [Joshua] died . . . (7) Cush-Rishathaim the king of [Aram-Naharain] (8) eight [year]s; Othniel the s[on of Kenaz . . . (9) eighty years;] Eglon the king of Moab eighteen] ye[ars; (10) Eh]ud the son of Gera, eighty years; Sham[gar the son of Anath,]

17. HUR AND MIRIAM (4Q544)

This Aramaic text is difficult to characterize because it is so fragmentary, but it appears to be concerned with genealogies of characters in the Book of Exodus, particularly Hur. If Line 8 is taken with Line 9, the text would appear to make a connection between the Judean hero Hur and Miriam, the sister of Moses, although none is anywhere made explicit in the Bible. According to Josephus, Hur was Miriam's husband (*Ant.* 3.54), and the tradition being signalled here seems to bear this out. Rabbinic literature, identifying Ephrath and Miriam, would have him as her son (Targum to 1 Chr. 2:19 and 4:4). Still, that there is tradition about a relationship between Hur and Miriam is not to be gainsaid.

In Exodus Hur is a passing character. Whether because of his association with the tribe of Judah or the building of the Tabernacle, the text represented here seems to focus on him more than Exodus does. In Exod. 17:10, Hur appears for the first time at the battle with Amalek at Rephidim – mentioned above in connection with Moses' prophecy on the subject and its treatment in the Genesis Florilegium. In Exodus Hur is pictured as supporting the hands of Moses with Aaron (symbolic of the priesthood and his brother-in-law?) to determine the course of the battle being fought by Joshua, Moses' adjutant, in the plain below. When Moses with Joshua ascended the Mountain of Sinai, Hur and Aaron were left in charge of the people (24:14).

Exod. 35:30 makes Hur's connection with Bezalel, the architect of the Tabernacle, explicit. So does 1 Chr. 2:20, where he is listed as the son of Caleb ben Hezron by a second wife, Ephrath (Ephrathah in 2:24) and the father of Uri (probably mentioned in Line 10). These three are credited with founding three well-known Judean towns: Kiriath-jearim, Bethlehem and Bethgader. His connection with the second makes a text focusing on him and connecting him to Miriam (also related in some way to 'Ephrathah') all the more interesting.

TRANSLITERATION   Fragment 1

ודמך]	1. [ד]י יאכל הוא ובנוה]י
[	2. [ב]עלהא שנת עלמה]
[	3. עלוהי ואשכחוה]י
[	4. בנוהי ובני אחו]הי
[	5. יתבו בר שעתהון]
[	6. פטר לבית עלמה]
[	7. *vacat* ומ]
[	8. עשרא ואולד מן מריאם עב.]
[	9. ולסתרי *vacat* ונסב חור]
[	10. ואולד מנה לאור ואהר]ון
[	11. מנה ארבען בנין]

TRANSLATION

Fragment 1 (1) [th]at he ate, he and his son[s . . . (2) [and] her [hu]sband [slept] the eternal sleep . . . (3) upon him, and they found hi[m . . . (4) his sons and the sons of h[is] brother . . . (5) they dwelt temporarily (?) . . . (6) he departed to his Eternal home . . . (8) ten. And with Miriam he became the father of Ab[(?; name incomplete and uncertain) . . . (9) and Sitri. Then Hur took as wife . . . (10) And with her he became the father of Ur and Aar[on . . . (11) with her four (forty?) sons . . .

18. ENOCHIC BOOK OF GIANTS (4Q532)

Enoch was a figure of great interest in the period of the Scrolls, in part because of the mysterious way the Bible refers to him in Genesis 5:24; 'Enoch walked with God, and he was not; for God took him'. Apparently, therefore, Enoch did not die, and was taken alive into Heaven. A substantial literature grew up around this figure, of which part was gathered into the book known as First (or, Ethiopic) Enoch. The Book of Giants was another literary work concerned with Enoch, widely read (after translation into the appropriate languages) in the Roman empire. Among the Qumran texts are at least six, and perhaps as many as eleven, copies of the Book of Giants. The following portion seems to belong to that work. The 'giants' were believed to be the offspring of fallen angels (the Nephilim; also called Watchers) and human women. The story of the giants derives from Genesis 6.

TRANSLITERATION   Column 2 Fragments 1-6

[		]מ[	]	.1
[		[בכש]ר	ר]	.2
[קרל]	[להוון]	נפילי]ן[	כו]ל	.3
[ ]. בדיל כדי מל	[חסיד מנדע]	[הוו קאמ]ין	ע]	.4
[רברבין]	ת>ש<רא בר]	[ארעא תר]	למק[	.5
[א ואנא]	ך על ש]	ה]וו עשיתין ל]	בה]	.6
[ ]א[		]. מן עירין על]מין	ולה]וון	.7
[	[.ו ומיח יאבד בס]וף	].ו	.8
[	[כל רב חנבלו בא]	ה]	.9
[	[שפק לה למא]חא	די]	.10
[[בין] מר מרי]	מן] ארעא ועד ש]מיא	להוון]	.11
[ ].ו בשמיא	[בן ב] [.ו]	[בארעא בכל ב]שר	]	.12
[מן מנדע ור]ב[ ]	[בא וכען לא ש]	]	.13
[ ].ל [	]ו ואסיר תקי]פא	]	.14

TRANSLATION
Column 2 Fragments 1-6 (2) . . . with fles[h] . . . (3) al[l] . . . the Nephili[m] . . . will be . . . (4) they were rising up . . . Pious Knowledge . . . so that when . . . (5) the earth . . . Mighty Ones . . . (6) were firmly decided . . . And I . . . (7) [They] will be . . . by the Ete[rnal] Watchers . . . (8) [in the e]nd he will perish and die. And . . . (9) . . . (10) who . . . allowed him to co[me] . . . (11) They will be . . . [from] the earth as far as He[aven] . . . Lord of Lords . . . between . . . (12) on the earth among all fl[esh] . . . in Heaven. And . . . (13) then there will not . . . and gre[at] Knowledge . . . (14) and the stro[ng] will be bound . . .

19. PSEUDO-JUBILEES (4Q227)

The preserved portions of these two fragments appear to contain information about Enoch similar to the Book of Jubilees 4:17–24. A good deal of the interest centring around Enoch, as we have noted, was connected with his assumption alive into Heaven and the mysterious allusion in Genesis to 'walking with God'. This allowed him to be seen as a mystery figure conversant with 1. Heavenly Knowledge – in particular 'Knowledge' of an esoteric kind, and 2. scientific knowledge of the kind alluded to in this text – knowledge of the heavenly spheres and their courses. Since he had been there, he could actually measure them.

Enoch also becomes one of the precursors of mystical Heavenly journeying or Heavenly Ascents. What is interesting about this text is the reference to 'the Righteous' – the *Zaddikim* – seemingly twice, just in the extant fragments (1.1 and 2.6). This Heavenly journeying moves into early Christian tradition, as it does into both *Kabbalah* and Islam. Not only is Enoch the Righteous a well-known cognomen – as are Noah the Righteous and James the Righteous – but 'the Righteous' would even seem to be a name for the members of the Community represented by the literature at Qumran, a synonym and linguistic variation of the *Bnai-Zadok* ('the sons of Zadok') as we have noted above.

The use of such terminology here in relation to the knowledge of the heavenly bodies and their courses, as well as of the calendar, would appear to carry something of this connotation in Line 2.6, i.e. *the Community leadership* has not and does not err in these matters. The use of *darchei-zev'am* ('the paths of their hosts') in 2.5, meaning the fixed trajectories of the heavenly bodies is interesting too, as a heavenly parallel to some of the more common, earthly adumbrations of this terminology for the Community, such as the *Darchei-Zedek, Darchei-Emet, Darchei-'Or* ('the Ways of Righteousness', 'Truth', 'Light'), etc., as opposed to 'the Ways of Darkness', 'Evil', 'Lying', 'uncleanness', 'abomination', 'fornication' and the like. By implication, these too are fixed, at least in their positive sense, by the Law.

TRANSLITERATION   Fragment 1

[	[כול הצדיקים]	] .1
[	.[לפני מושה]	] .2
[	[את כול ימי]	] .3
[	] *vacat* [	] .4

[   ] *vacat* [   ] .5

[יא[רכו שני]   ] .6

Fragment 2

ח[נוך אחר אשר למדנוהו   ] .1

ששה יובלי שנים [   ].[   ] .2

א[רץ אל תוך בני האדם ויעד על כולם   ] .3

ונם על העירים ויכתוב את כול [   ] .4

ה[שמים ואת דרכי צבאם את [החוד]שים   ] .5

א[שר לוא ישנו הצ[דיקים]   ] .6

TRANSLATION

Fragment 1 (1) . . . all the Righteous . . . (2) before Moses . . . (3) all the days of . . . (6) the years of . . . will be lengthened . . .

Fragment 2 (1) [E]noch after we instructed him (2) . . . six Jubilees of years (3) . . . [ea]rth among all mankind and he witnessed against them all (4) . . . and also against the Watchers. And he wrote down all the (5) . . . [the] heavens and all the paths of their hosts (i.e., the heavenly bodies), all [the mon]ths (6) . . . [in whi]ch the Rig[hteous] have not erred . . .

20. ARAMAIC TOBIT (4Q196)

For Jews and Protestant Christians the book of Tobit is outside the canon of the Bible, being counted among the Apocrypha. Catholics, however, along with the Greek and Russian Orthodox branches of Christianity, regard the book as part of the Bible in the sense that it is 'Deuterocanonical'. Although scholars for the most part believed that Tobit had originally been written in either Hebrew or Aramaic, the Semitic original version was long lost. The book's primary witnesses were two rather different Greek versions (one 'short' version and one 'long'). Thus the significance of the Qumran caches: they include portions of four Aramaic manuscripts of the book, together with one Hebrew manuscript.

All of these manuscripts support the 'long' version of Tobit known from the Greek. It is now clear that the short Greek version never had a Semitic counterpart and is nothing more than an abbreviation of the long Greek text. Until very recently, however, Bible translations into modern languages had always relied upon the short text. In the wake of the Qumran discoveries, translators have begun to work instead with the long text — still, unfortunately, having only the Greek witness; no more than a few isolated phrases of the Qumran Semitic forms have previously been published.

The Semitic texts of Tobit will certainly require adjustments even of those translations that have worked with the superior long Greek text. For example, in the portion presented here (Tobit 1:19–2:2), the latter half of the Aramaic text of 1:22 is preferable to the Greek. The New Revised Standard Version translates the portion in question thus: 'Now Ahiqar was chief cupbearer, keeper of the signet and in charge of administrations of the accounts under King Sennacherib of Assyria; so Esarhaddon *reappointed* him' (italics ours). The Aramaic makes it clear that Esarhaddon did not merely reappoint Ahiqar, but raised him up to a position second only to the king himself (note the translation, Line 8 below). We may expect many such improvements in our understanding of this charming book now that the Semitic texts have brought us much closer to the original.

TRANSLITERATION   Fragment 1

1. ‏[חד מ]ן ב<גי> נינוה וההוי למלכ[א די] אנה קב]ר להון ו[אחוית וכדי ידעת
‏[די] ידע בי

2. ‏[ואתבעית למקטַ]ל ודחלת וערקת [ואתגזל כ]ל [די] הוה לי ולא שביקו
‏לי כל מנד[עם]

3. ‏[די לא נטלו] ל[אוצר מלכא] ל[הן חנ]ה אנתתי וטו[וב]יה ברי ולא הוה יומין
‏א[רבעין]

4. ‏{וחמשה עד די קטלו לה תרין בנו[הי ואנון ערקו לטורי אררט ומלך [ומ]לך}
‏אסרחדון]

5. ‏[כנה חלפוהי   *vacat*   והוא א[שלט] לאחיקר בר ענאל אחי על כל ש[יזפות]

6. ‏[מלכותה ואף אשלט לאחיקר להמרכ]ל והוא על [כ]ל המרכלות מלכא ובעה
‏אחיקר

7. ‏[עלי ותבת לנינוה   *vacat*   אחי]קר אחי הוה רב שקה ורב עזקן והמרכל

8. ‏[ושיזפן קדם אסרחריב מלך אתור ואשלטה אסרחדון תנין לה ארי [הוא]

9. ‏[בר] אחי הוה ומן בית אבי ומן משפחתי וביומי אסרחדון [מל]כא כדי תבת

10. ‏ל[ביתי ואתבת לי חנה אנתתי [ו]טוביה ברי וביום חג שבו[עיא הות לי]

11. ‏שרו טבה ורבעת ל[מאכ]ל ואקרבו פתַו]רא לקודמי וחזית נפתניא די קרבו

12. ‏עלוהי שגיאין ואמ]רת לטו]ביה ברי אזל ברי אזל דבר לכל מן [די ת]השכח באח[ינא]

13. ‏]   [ברי אזל דבר ואתה ויתה ויכל [כחדא עמי וארי]

TRANSLATION

Fragment 1 (1) [one o]f the Ninevites (went) and informed the kin[g that] I was bury[ing them, so] I hid myself. When I discovered [that] he knew about me, (2) [and that I was being sought to be kill]ed, I was frightened and I fled. [Then a]ll [that] I owned [was confiscated,] nothing was left to me. (There was not) one thi[ng] (3) [that they did not take] to the [king's storehouse,] ex[cept Hann]ah my wife and T[ob]iah my son. It was not fo[rty-] (4) [five days before two of] his [sons killed him (i.e., the king). They fled to the mountains of Ararat, and [Esarhaddon his son] ruled (5) [in his place. He em]powered Ahiqar the son of Anael my brother over all the ac[counting] (6) [of his kingdom. He also installed Ahiqar as chief of the (sacred) treas]ury. He was in charge of [a]ll of the king's funds. Aqihar interceded (7) on my behalf, so that I returned to Nineveh. Ahi]qar my 'brother' was the chief cupbearer and the official in charge of the signet rings and the treasurer (8) [and] the accountant for Sennacherib, king of Assyria, while Esarhaddon appointed him second (only) to himself. For [he] (9) was my nep[hew], from the house of my father and my family. In the days of Esarhaddon the [ki]ng, when I returned (10) to my home and Hannah my wife was returned to me, [along with] Tobiah my son, on the day of the festival of We[eks, I had] (11) a fine banquet. I reclined to [ea]t, and they 'set the ta[b]le before me. I saw the many delicacies that they brought, (12) and [I sa]id [to To]biah my son, 'My son, go and bring anyone [whom you] may find among [our] brothers (13) . . . my son, go and get (such), that he may come and eat [together with me . . .]

21. STORIES FROM THE PERSIAN COURT (4Q550)

Apparently these stories concerned the adventures of Jews at the court of the Persian kings. The use of the word 'Jew' (*Yehudi*) in 6.3 is, therefore, probably one of the oldest usages of this term — it is not commonly found in other genres of Qumran literature, which tend either to speak in terms of classical archetypes or to archaize (cf. the allusion to *Beit-Yehudah*/'House of Judah' in the Habakkuk *Pesher*, viii). We will find it in other interesting texts below, and apparently the usage was already becoming common even in Palestine. One also begins to encounter it on the coins of the Maccabeans also discussed below.

The genre of 'the Jew at the foreign court' was very popular during the period of the Scrolls. Such stories encouraged the Jews in the years when they were under foreign domination, for they told of great successes accomplished by their people. Further, they encouraged the Jews to remain loyal to their God in the face of very enticing new cultural alternatives; these stories typically climaxed with the foreign potentate forced to acknowledge the greatness of the Jewish God. Thus these adventures were simultaneously great fun and an argument against idolatry.

As far as can be determined, the structure of the stories presented here was something like the following: a young man raised at the court of the Persian king is at the age when he is about to embark on his career at court. He is instructed as to the adventures of his predecessors, including his father Fratervana, an earlier man named Bagasri and an intermediate figure known as Bagose. Bagasri served in the time of Darius — perhaps the Darius of Dan. 6, who is usually identified as Darius I (522–486 BC) or perhaps one of the later figures by that name: Darius II (423–405 BC) or Dairus III (335–330 BC).

Bagasri had some problem at court, and was in danger of losing his life (Column 6). He triumphed through the greatness of his God, and Darius was forced to acknowledge both his own sins (Column 4) and the power of the God of Israel (Column 8). The king also wrote a scroll telling the whole story much like Nebuchadnezzar in Dan. 4. Bagose served at the court after Bagasri and somehow forfeited all his possessions. Through a series of events now lost, he was vindicated, and like Job his wealth was returned to him in a double measure. Fratervana's tale connects in some way to the servants of the royal wardrobe; perhaps he discovered a conspiracy against the king among those high officials.

The most obvious connections of these stories are with the so-called 'Court Stories of Daniel' (Dan. 1–6). Other didactic tales to which the Qumran texts bears a resemblance are the Books of Tobit and Judith. It should also be remarked that the Book of Esther, which so far has not been found in the Qumran corpus, must also be understood as part of the genre of 'the Jew at the foreign court'. The text before us is not dissimilar to Esther and could even have been a rival to it for inclusion in the canon. Like Esther, there is a king who uses his own memoirs to recall the good services of Jewish courtiers and an evil opponent whom the king ultimately punishes, while at the same time restoring the good name of the Jews.

Why Esther has so far not been found at Qumran has been debated. Since this genre of literature has now been found at Qumran, there most probably was an ideological antagonism to it. Previously one might not have thought so. This objection can best be understood in terms of the militant xenophobia and apocalyptic nationalism of the Community, as well as its condemnation of precisely the kind of 'fornication' Esther indulges in. That Esther could marry and enter the harem of a foreign potentate, even in order to save her people, as the book posits, would have been anathema to a Community or movement such as this.

On the other hand, if Esther is to be considered highly myth-ologized, and if the anti-Herodian animus of the group responsible for many of these writings is confirmed, then a book like Esther would, no doubt, have been looked upon as 'a stalking horse' for Herodian pre-tensions. Herodian princesses like the infamous Berenice and Drusilla (not to mention their aunt Herodias in the previous generation) were making precisely the same kind of marital and extra-marital arrange-ments with people no less despised than Nero's freedman Felix and the destroyer of Jerusalem and emperor to be Titus. Presumably they, too, were making the same excuse, 'to save their people'.

Therefore Esther would have been seen as particularly repugnant in a way that these tales — containing no hint of illicit activity or sexual impropriety — were not. For their part, the Maccabee books present 'the day of Mordechai' as preceded by a feast day they call 'the day of Nicanor'. On this day, which they present like Hannukah as having been ratified by popular vote, the head of a particularly despised foreign enemy of the Jews was *hung* from the citadel of Jerusalem (2 Macc. 15:35, a particularly zealous proponent of this kind of activity).

TRANSLITERATION   Column 2 (or later)

[אנש להן יד[ע] מלכא הן איתי] 1.
[ולא יבד שהד טבא הימנו] 2.
[מלכא איתי לפתרונא בר יש[ו 3.
[נפלת עלוהי אימת בית ספ[רא 4.
[אושי מלכא די תמ[ור] ותתיהב] 5.
[ביתי [ונ]כסי לכול מה די ית.] 6.
[התכול ותקבל עבידת אבוך] 7.

                                   Column 3 (or later)

[   ].ה.[   ] אושי מלכה די תמר לשר.א] 1.
[.] פתרונא א[בוך] מן יומא די קם על עבידת[ה]ה קדם מלכא 2.
[   ].. לה עבד מן קשוט ופ.ה] ק[דמוהי] 3.
[   ]..ואמר אושי] 4.
[   ]נה א.] 5.
[   ].ל.ל. של[ם] 6.
[   ] 7.

                                   Column 4 (or later)

[[הוו] שמעין לפתרונא אבוך] 1.
ל[מעבד   לעבדי לבוש מלכותא ב[כו]ל] 2.
.]ין בה בשתה   עבידת מלכא בכול די קב[ל 3.

4. ארכת רוחה די מלכא אל[   ].י אב[ו]הי [.   ].ק.הי קדמוהי בין

5. ספריא אשתכח מגלה <ח[ד]ה> חתי[מה חתמין] שבעה בעזקתה די
דריוש אבוהי ענינה

6. ש[דר]יוש מלכא לעבדי שלטנא <די כ[ל א]רעא> שלם פתיחת קרית
השתכח כתיב בה דריוש מלכא

7. [כתב לכול] מלכין בתרי לעבדי שלטנא ש[ל]ם ידיע להוא די כול אנוס ושקר

Column 6 (or later)

1. ארי ידע אנתה]   ]לין[[

בחובי אבהתי

2. די חטו קדמין ו]   [שפא ל.]   [וננדת .]   ]יך גבר

3. יהודי מן רברבני מ[לכא]   לה קאם לקבלה וב] [א]   [גב]רא טב[א]

4. נברא טבא עבד]   [חא מה אעבד לכה ואנתה ידע [די כול] אפש[ר]

5. לנבר כות[ר] להתבה[ל]ה גבר] ביתך קאם באתר די אנתה קאם בה אנ] [

6. ק[א]ם מה [ד]י אנתה צ[ב]א פקדני וכדי [אמ]רת אקבדינך ב] [

7. עמר בכול אפשר ויתעל ית עבידתי ק[דם   וכ]ול די] [

Column 8 (or later)

1. עליא די אנתון דחלין ופלחין הו שליט ב[אר]עא כול די יצבא קריב
בידה ל[מע[ב]ד]

2. [ו]כול אנש די ימר מלה [באי]שא על בנסרי כ] יח[קטל בדיל די לא איתי]י [   ]. [[

3.]   [ה< טובה ל[ע]לם .]   [די ח[>ז<]ה]   [תרתין ואמר מלכא
יכת[ו]ב [

4. [ ] חזא [ ]   ].[ ] למ[לכא] אנון בדרת בית מלכ[ות]א רבחא].[[

5.]   [ומן בתר בנסרי קרין בכתבא דנ[ה]

6.]   [ב[אישא באישתה תאבה על]. [ה כו]ל [

7.]   [*vacat* [

Column 9 (or later)

1.].[ ]   [שא גזרת מ[לכא   [א אזלו]   [

2.]   [ל[מכת[ב]ל] [.א אזל]   [בלבוש]   [

3.]   [כליל דה[ב די מתקלה מא]ה וחמ[י]שה אזל]   [

4.]   [בלחודוהי .]   [תיתיא אזל ואמ[ר   [

5.]   [כ[סף ו[ד]הב [ונכס]ין די [אי]תי לבנושי בכפל]   [

6.]   [על בשם בנסרי לדרת מלכא ש.]   [

7.]   [ק[טיל אדין על [ב]נסרי לד[ר]ח מלכא ש.]].[[

8.]   [. רבשקה ענה ואמר בנסרי בנסרי מן]   [

TRANSLATION

Column 2 (or later) (1) a man, unless the king knows; indeed, there exists . . . (2) and the witness shall not perish. They have believed what is upright . . . (3) O king, Fratervana the son of . . . has . . . (4) there fell upon him fear of the (contents of) the archi[ves . . .] (5) the foundations of the king that you shall spe[ak] and be given . . . (6) my house [and] my [po]ssessions for everything that . . . (7) shall you be able to take up your father's occupation? . . .

Column 3 (or later) (1) the foundations of the king that you shall speak to the prince (?) . . . (2) Fratervana [your] father from the day that he took up his occupation before the king . . . (3) for him he did honestly and . . . before him . . . (4) and he said the foundations of . . . (7) pea[ce] . . .

Column 4 (or later) (1) [they used] to listen to Fratervana your father . . . (2) to the servants of the royal wardrobe in [al]l . . . to do (3) the business of the king in all that he recei[ved . . .] in that very year (4) the king's patience . . . his fat[h]er . . . before him; among (5) the books was found a cer[tain] scroll [sea]led by seven seals (impressed by) the signet ring of Darius his father. The matter (6) . . . '[Dar]ius the king to the servants of the kingdom of a[ll] the [e]arth: Peace.' It was opened and read. (The following) was found written in it: 'Darius the king (7) [wrote to all] kings after myself, to the servants of the kingdom: Pe[ac]e. Let it be known to you that all oppression and falsehood . . .

Column 6 (or later) (1) . . . for you know . . . for the sins of my fathers (2) that they sinned aforetime and . . . and I followed after . . . (3) a Jew from among the k[ing]'s officials stood in front of him and . . . [the] good [ma]n. (4) The good man did . . . What shall I do with you? You know [that] it is poss[ible] (5) for a man like [you to hasten (?) everything. A man] of your household (once) stood where you (now) stand . . . (6) Command me (to do) any[thi]ng that you wa[n]t, and when you have [spo]ken, I will bury you in . . . (7) he dwells in all. It is possible that he will bring in my service be[fore . . . and ever]ything that . . .

Column 8 (or later) (1) the highest (God) whom you fear and serve, he is ruler over the [ear]th. It is easy for him to [d]o anything that he desires, (2) [and] anyone who speaks an [e]vil word against Bagasri . . . shall be killed, because there is no . . . (3) Good forever . . . that he saw . . . two. And he said, 'Let the king write . . . (4) he saw . . . to the k[ing . . .] them in the great ro[y]al court . . . (5) and after (the story of) Bagasri, they read in thi[s] book . . . (6) Evil, his Evil shall return upon his . . .

Column 9 (or later) (1) [the] k[ing]'s decree . . . they went . . . (2) [to] writ[e . . .] he went . . . in the clothing . . . (3) a gold[en] crown [weighing one hun]dred and fi[f]ty. He went . . . (4) apart from him . . . he went and sai[d . . .] (5) (he returned the?) [si]lver and [g]old and [possession]s that [bel]ong to Bagose in a double measure . . . (6) he entered the king's court in the name of Bagasri . . . (7) [ki]lled. Then [B]agasri entered the king's co[ur]t . . . (8) the chief butler answered and said, 'Bagasri, Bagasri, from . . .'

NOTES

(14) A Genesis Florilegium (4Q252)
Previous Discussions: J. M. Allegro, 'Further Messianic References in Qumran Literature', *Journal of Biblical Literature* 75 (1956) 174–6; H. Stegemann, 'Weitere Stücke von 4QpPsalm 37, von 4Q Patriarchal Blessings und Hinweis auf eine unedierte Handschrift aus Höhle 4Q mit Exzerpten aus dem Deuteronomium', *Revue de Qumran* 6 (1967–69) 211–17; Milik, *MS*, 138. Photographs: PAM 43.253 and 43.381, ER 1289 and 1375.

We supply the following technical information to help the reader appreciate the author's arguments (references are to primeval dates, columns and lines):

1:1–3 The author understood Gen. 6:3 to mean that only 120 years remained to antedeluvian man before the Judgement of the flood. Whether the replacement of the Masoretic 'he will judge' with 'he will live' represents an interpretation or a textual variant is unclear, but the substitution of 'their days' for 'his days' in Line 2 affects the meaning drastically.

1:10 and following. The author's chronology of the flood (according to the years of Noah's life) is as follows:

(1) 17.2.600 The flood begins (Line 4; Gen. 7:11).

(2) 26.3.600 The rain ceases to fall 40 days after it began (Lines 6–7; Gen. 7:17). The author counted 17.2.600 as the first day in his calculations.

(3) 14.7.600 The waters begin to recede 150 days after the flood began (Line 8; Gen. 7.24, 8:3). Thus the author counted the 40 days of Gen. 7:17 as part of the 150 days. Note that the dates given in the Biblical text work only on the basis of a calendar of 30 days per month; they also allow the intercalation of two days between 17.2 and 14.7 – precisely the calendar of Jubilees and many Qumran texts.

(4) 17.7.600 The ark comes to rest on the mountains of Ararat on the third day of the waters' recession (Line 10; Gen. 8:4). The author calculated the two days mentioned in Line 9 by comparing Gen. 7:24, 8:3 and 8:4.

(5) 1.10.600 The tops of the mountains become visible (Line 11; Gen. 8:5).

(6) 10.11.600 Noah opens a window of the ark and sends the raven (Lines 13–14; Gen. 8:6–7).

(7) 17.11.600 Noah sends the dove out for the first time (Lines 14–15). Thus the author understood the words 'and he sent' of Gen. 8:8 as concealing an unstated lapse of seven days. This is a logical assumption, since there would be no reason to send the dove and the raven at the same time. Further, a seven-day lapse is suggested by what follows.

(8) 24.11.600 The dove goes out a second time, and it returns with an olive branch (Lines 15–18a; Gen. 8:10–11).

(9) 1.12.600 Noah sends the dove out for a third time, and it does not return (Lines 18b–20a; Gen. 8:12).

(10) 1.1.601 Noah removes the covering of the ark (Lines 20b–2:1; Gen. 8:13). The waters have completely receded.

(11) 17.2.601 The land is dry, and Noah leaves the ark at the end of precisely one full year (2:1–3; cf. Gen. 8:14). The date of the Masoretic Text – which the author of the text almost certainly must have had in his scroll of Genesis – was read as a lunisolar date. For Gen. 8:14 to be read this way, it was necessary to presuppose that the flood began in the first year of a three-year cycle, at which point both the solar and the lunisolar calendars agree on the date 17.2. After one year, the two will disagree on the date: solar 17.2 = lunisolar 27.2. After yet another year, the variance will be ten days greater: solar 17.2 = lunisolar 7.3. Between the third and fourth years an intercalated month would return the situation to that of the first year. Thus, only if the flood ended in the second year of the cycle would it be possible to understand Gen. 8:14 as the author did.

(15) Joshua Apocryphon (4Q522)
Previous Discussions: E. Puech, 'Fragments du Psaume 122 dans un manuscript hébreu de la grotte iv', *Revue de Qumran* 9 (1977–8) 547–54; J. T. Milik, *DJD* 3, 179. Photograph: PAM 43.606, ER 1553.

(16) A Biblical Chronology (4Q559)
Previous Discussions: None. Photograph: PAM 43.603, ER 1550.

(17) Hur and Miriam (4Q544)
Previous Discussions: None. Photograph: PAM 43.574 (top), ER 1522.

(18) Enochic Book of Giants (4Q532)
Previous Discussion: J. T. Milik, *Books*, 309. Photograph: PAM 43.573 (top), ER 1521. It is not certain how the fragments should be aligned.

(19) Pseudo-Jubilees (4Q227)
Previous Discussion: Milik, *Books*, 12. Photograph: PAM 43.238, ER 1274.

(20) Aramaic Tobit (4Q196)
Previous Discussions: J. T. Milik, 'La patrie de Tobie', *Revue Biblique* 73 (1966) 522; idem, *Books*, 163 and 186. Photograph: PAM 43.175, ER 1230.

(21) Stories of the Persian Court (4Q550)
Previous Discussions: None. Photographs: PAM 43.584 and 43.585, ER 1530 and 1531.

CHAPTER 4

Calendrical Texts and Priestly Courses

The calendrical texts from Qumran Cave 4 are numerous and significant. They comprise eighteen texts (4Q319–330 and 4Q337), not including many texts which, while not strictly calendrical, presuppose or present a calendrical system. The latter category includes the Genesis Florilegium in Chapter 3 above and the First Letter on Works Righteousness in Chapter 6 and the Brontologion in Chapter 8 below.

Especially noteworthy is the absence among the Qumran caches of any text advocating a different calendar. This absence is striking because the calendar of the Qumran materials was only one of several in use and seems to have represented a minority position. The calendrical texts are, therefore, central to any attempt to understand the significance of the Dead Sea Scrolls. In order to follow the rather technical expositions of these texts, one must know a few facts about the calendar they advocate, and about the priestly courses (*mishmarot*) which served in the Temple at Jerusalem.

The calendar is purely solar, based on a particular understanding of the Creation account found in Genesis. In its exclusive reliance on the sun, it stands in stark contrast to later Rabbinic Judaism, which followed a lunisolar calendar of 354 days relying mainly on the moon. Earlier, the Pharisaic forerunners of Rabbinic Judaism seem to have followed an even more lunar-oriented calendar, though from the evidence of the Qumran texts, the lunisolar calendar seems already to have gained currency during at least some of the period of the Scrolls.

In the system that finally emerged, probably under Greco-Roman influence, in Rabbinic Judaism at the end of the fourth century AD, extra lunar months were intercalated seven times in every nineteen

106

years to produce the kind of harmonization necessary to ensure that the calendar remained fixed to the seasons of the solar cycle. The Muslims, for their part, reflecting probably an earlier phase of this historical process, never made the complicated mathematical and calendrical intercalations necessary for passage from a lunar to a lunisolar calendar.

By contrast, according to the solar calendar at Qumran, the year always contains precisely 364 days. The only question that must be asked is whether this calendar goes back to Maccabean times, as the third text on Priestly Courses implies — or even earlier — and whether the Maccabeans themselves preferred it before the Pharisees took over with the rise of Herod once and for all. However this may be, the anti-Pharisaic and consequently, the anti-Herodian character of the calendar is not to be gainsaid.

Each year consists of twelve months of thirty days each, plus four additional days, one of which is intercalated at the end of each three-month period. Thus the first and second months are 30 days long, while, with its added day, the third month totals 31 days; then the pattern repeats (see Table 1). New Year's Day and the first day of each three-month period always fall on a Wednesday. Wednesday is the day mandated as the first day by the creation order, since the heavenly lights — sun, moon and stars, the basis of any calendar — were created on the fourth day (Gen. 1:14–19). The great advantage of the Qumran calendar over its lunisolar rival is that it results in fixed dates for the major festivals. They cannot fall on a sabbath, thereby avoiding worrisome difficulties affecting sacrifices. In fact, this calendar guarantees that a particular day of any given month will always fall on the same day of the week every year.

Table 1. The 364 Day Calendar

Months	1, 4, 7, 10	2, 5, 8, 11	3, 6, 9, 12
Wednesday	1, 8, 15, 22, 29	6, 13, 20, 27	4, 11, 18, 25
Thursday	2, 9, 16, 23, 30	7, 14, 21, 28	5, 12, 19, 26
Friday	3, 10, 17, 24	1, 8, 15, 22, 29	6, 13, 20, 27
Saturday	4, 11, 18, 25	2, 9, 16, 23, 30	7, 14, 21, 28
Sunday	5, 12, 19, 26	3, 10, 17, 24	1, 8, 15, 22, 29
Monday	6, 13, 20, 27	4, 11, 18, 25	2, 9, 16, 23, 30
Tuesday	7, 14, 21, 28	5, 12, 19, 26	3, 10, 17, 24, 31

Although the authors of the Qumran calendrical texts disdained the lunisolar calendar, a number of their writings synchronize the two versions (see Priestly Courses I and Priestly Courses II, below). The reasons for this synchronization are not entirely clear, but two suggestions may be somewhere close to the mark. First, these authors considered all time holy and its measurement ordained by God. It was probably thought necessary that someone keep a proper record of its passing. Since the opponents of the authors could not be relied upon to do so – following, as they did, an illicit system – the Qumran authors took the responsibility. In order to discharge this responsibility, it would be as necessary to be able to point out errors as to know the correct answers. Thus, they tracked time by the system of their opponents as well as by their own. Second, the authors of these texts certainly expected that at some time they would be in power in Jerusalem. At that time, of course, they would impose the solar calendar, but in order to know where they were in the year, they would have to know both the false lunisolar date and the real solar date. In fact, there is some evidence that at certain points in the Second Temple period the solar calendar actually was imposed, at least for short periods.

In all their timekeeping, the authors of the Qumran calendars reckoned not only by months, but also by the rotation of the priestly courses (*mishmarot*). The courses would come into Jerusalem for service at the temple for one week, then rotate out as the next group arrived to serve. Qumran texts relied upon this 'eternal cycle' not only for their calendar units, but also for their chronography and historiography (see Priestly Courses III). Every sabbath, month, year and feast bore the name of a priestly family (see Priestly Courses IV).

The priestly rotation required six years before the same group would be serving once again in the same week of the year. This sexennial cycle reflects the need to synchronize the solar calendar with the lunisolar version. Since the solar calendar totalled 364 days to the year, while the lunisolar calendar alternated months of 29 and 30 days, the lunisolar calendar would 'fall behind' by ten days per year. After three years, however, the lunisolar calendar was intercalated with an additional 29 or 30 days, bringing the two versions once again into harmony ($364 \times 3 = 354 \times 3 + 30$). Two such cycles fit perfectly with the six years needed for one complete priestly cycle.

The order of the priestly courses was originally determined by lot, and is laid out in 1 Chr. 24:7–18 as follows: (1) Jehoiarib (spelled 'Joiarib' in the Qumran texts), (2) Jedaiah, (3) Harim, (4) Seorim, (5) Malchijah (sometimes spelled Malachijah in the Qumran texts), (6) Mijamin, (7) Hakkoz, (8) Abijah, (9) Jeshua, (10) Shecaniah,

(11) Eliashib, (12) Jakim, (13) Huppah, (14) Jeshebeab, (15) Bilgah, (16) Immer, (17) Hezir, (18) Happizzez, (19) Pethahiah, (20) Jehezkel, (21) Jachin, (22) Gamul, (23) Delaiah, and (24) Maaziah (often spelled Moaziah in the Qumran texts). The Qumran calendars refer to the same names, but vary the order by beginning the cycle with Gamul instead of Jehoiarib. Apparently the reason for this change is that the list as given in 1 Chronicles began the rotation with Jehoiarib in the autumn. The Qumran cycle begins in Nisan (March–April), a vernal New Year. The different beginning derives, as might be expected, from an understanding of the Creation narrative. The Creation happened in the spring; thus an eternal order based on the Creation must of necessity begin at that time. The vernal New Year meant that the priestly cycle would begin with Gamul.

22. PRIESTLY COURSES I (4Q321)
(Plate 6)

The first part of Mishmarot B delineates the equivalences between the solar and the lunisolar calendars. It also preserves information on the 'astronomical observance' of the moon which apparently acted as a check on the tabulated lunar month. The observance ascertained whether or not the full moon was waning at the proper rate, normally confirming the calculation of the day on which that month would end, and, concommitantly, when the subsequent one would begin. Fragment 1 preserves the equivalences starting with the seventh month of the first year and ending with the second month of the fourth year. Fragment 2 begins with the fifth month of the sixth year and completes the cycle. Between the two fragments we learn how the intercalation of the lunisolar calendar was carried out at the end of the third year (by the solar calendar's reckoning; according to the lunisolar reckoning, after the first month of the fourth) and at the end of the sixth year. The remaining portions of Fragment 2 describe the six-year cycle of First Days (of the months) and festivals in terms of the course to which they fall.

TRANSLITERATION   Fragment 1 Column 1

1. ‏[באחד בידעיה בשני]ם עשר בוא בשנים באב[יה בחמשה] ועש[רים בשמיני‏
‏ודוקה בשלושה]‏

2. ‏[במימין בשבעה עשר] בוא בשלושה ביקים באר[בעה ועשרים בתשיעי‏
‏ודוקה בארבעה]‏

3. [בשכניה בעשתי ע]שר בוא בחמשה באמר בשלושה ועשרים בעש]ירי ודוקה
בששה בי]שבאב

4. [בעשרה בו]א ב[ש]שה ביחזקאל בשנים ועשרים בעשתי עשר החודש
ו]דוקה שבת ב[פתח>י<ה

5. [בתשעה בוא] באחד ביויריב בשנים ועשרים בשנים עשר החודש
ו]דוקה בשני]ם בדליה

6. [בתשעה בוא   *vacat*   ה]שני[ת]   הראשון בש[נ]ים במלאכיה בעשר]ים
בוא ו]דוקה

7. [בשלושה בחרים בשבעה] בוא בארבעה בישוע בעשרים בשני ו]דוקה
בחמשה ב]קוץ בשבעה

8. [בוא בחמשה בחופא בתשעה ע]שר בשלישי ודוקה בששה [בא]ל[י]שיב]
ב[ש]ה [בוא שב]ת בפצץ

Fragment 1 Column 2

1. [בשמונה עשר ברביעי ודוקה באחד באמר בחמשה] בוא באחד
ב]גמול בשבעה]העשר בחמישי]

2. [ודוקה בשנים בי]חזק]אל בארבעה בוא בשלושה ביד]עיה ב]שבעה עשר
בששי ודוקה בארבעה]

3. במעזיה בארבעה בוא בארב]עה במימין בחמשה עשר] בשביעי ודוקה
בח]משה בשעורים בשלושה]

4. בוא בששה בשכניה בחמשה [עשר בשמיני ודו]קה שבת באביה בשנים בוא
[שבת בבלגה]

5. בארבעה עשר בתשיעי ודוקה [באחד בחופא באחד] בתשיעי ו]דוק]ה שנית
בשלושה ב]חזיר בשלושים]

6. ואחד ב[וא ב]שנים בפתחיה בש]לושה עשר בעשירי] ודוקה בארבע]ה בי]כין
בתשעה ועש]רים בוא]

7. [בשלושה בדלי]ה בשנים עשר בעשת]י עשר החודש ודו]קה בששה יויר]יב
בת]שעה ועשרים ב]וא בחמשה בחרים]

8. בשנ[י]ם עשר בשנים עשר החודש ודוק]ה[שבת]ב[מימין בשמונה ועשרים
בוא השלישית ב]ששה בקוץ בעשרה]

Fragment 1 Column 3

3. [בשבעה בחמשי ודוק]ה באחד בח]רים בארבעה ועשרי]ם בוא שבת
במלא]כיה בשבעה בששי ודוקה בקוץ בשלושה ועשרים בוא]

4. [באחד בישוע בחמשה] בשביעי ודוקה בארבעה באלישיב בשנים
ועש]רים בוא בשלושה בחופא בחמשה בשמיני ודוקה בחמשה]

5. [בכלנה באחד ועשרים בוא ב]ארבעה בחזיר בארבעה בתשיעי ודוקה שבת
יח]זקאל באחד ועשרים בוא בששה ביכין בשלושה בעשירי]

6. [ודוקה באחד במעזיה בש]ש[ה] עשר בוא שבת בידעיה בשנים בעשתי עשר
החודש ודוקה [בשלושה בשעורים בתשעה עשר בוא בשנים]

7. ‏[במימין בשנים עשר החודש ודו]קה בארבעה באביה בשמונה עשר בוא
‏הרביעית בארבעה בשכנ]יה באחד בראשון ודוקה בששה]

8. ‏[ביקים בשבעה עשר ב]ראשון שבת פתחיה בשלושים בשני
‏ודוקה באח]יר בחז]יר בשבעה עשר בוא באחד בדליה בתשעה]

Fragment 2 Column 1

1. ‏[   ]‏ וד]וקה באחד [בבלנ]א באר[בעה ועשרי]ם בוא שבת בחזיר
‏בשבע]ה בששי

2. ‏[ודוקה בשנים בפתחיה] בשלושה ועשרים בוא באחד ביכין בחמשה
‏בשביעי ודוקה בארבעה

3. ‏[בדליה בשנים ועשרים] בוא בשלושה ביוריב בחמשה בשמיני ודוקה
‏בחמשה בחרים

4. ‏[בששה עשר בוא באר]בעה במלאכיה בארבעה בתשיעי ודוקה שבת
‏באביה באחד

5. ‏[ועשרים בוא בששה בי]שוע [ב]שלושה בעשירי ודוקה באחד ביקים
‏בתשע העשר ב]וא]

6. ‏[שבת בישבאב בשנים בעשתי] עשר החודש ודוקה בשל]ושה באמר
‏בת]שע העשר בוא

7. ‏[בשנים בפצץ בשנים בשנים] עשר החודש ודוקה בארבעה ביחזקאל
‏בשמונה עשר

8. ‏[בוא   *vacat*   השנה הרא]שונה החו]דש הראשון בדל]יה
‏במו]עזיה בו]א]

9. ‏[הפסח בידעיה בוא הנף העומר השני ב]ידעיה [בשעורים בוא הפסח
‏השני השלישי בקון]

Fragment 2 Column 2

1. ‏בי[ש]ו[ע בוא חג השב]ועים הרביעי באלי[שיב החמישי] בבלנה הששי
‏ביחזקאל] השביע] י]

2. ‏במועזיה הואה יום הזכרון ביו]ריב בוא יום הכפורים בידעיה בוא
‏[חג ה]סוכות השמיני [בשעורים]

3. ‏התשיעי בישוע העשירי בחופה עשתי עשר החודש בחזיר שנים עשר
‏החודש בנמול *vacat*

4. ‏השנית הראשון בידעיה בשעורים בוא הפסח ב]מ]ימין בוא הנף העומר
‏ה<ש>ני במ]ימין באביה]

5. ‏בוא הפסח ה]שני השלישי באלישיב] ובחו]פא] בוא חג השבועים [הרביעי
‏בבל]נא החמישי בפתחיה

6. ‏[הששי במועזיה השביעי בשעורים הואה יו]ם הזכרון במלאכיה
‏[בוא יום הכפ]ורים במימין

7. ‏[בוא חג הסוכות השמיני באביה התשיעי ב]חופה העשירי בחזיר ע]שתי
‏עשר החודש ביכין]

8. [שני]ם עשר ה[חו]דש [בידעיה   vacat   ה]שלישית הראשון
ב[מימי]ן באביה בוא

9. הפסח בשכנ[י]ה בוא הנף העומר הש[ני] בשכניה ביקים בוא הפסח
[הש]ני השלשי בבלנא ב[ח]זיר

Fragment 2 Column 3

1. [בוא חג] השבוע[ים הרביע]י ב[פתחיה החמישי בדליה הששי בש[עורים
[השביעי באביה] >[הואה י]ום [הזכרון בישוע]< בוא יום הכפורים]

2. [בשכני]ה בוא חג ה[ס]וכות [ה]שמ[יני ביקים התשיעי בחזיר העשירי
ב[יכין עש[תי עשר החודש ב[יוריריב [שנים]

3. עש[ר] החודש ב[מי]מין [הרביעית הראשון בשכניה ביקים בוא הפסח
בישבאב בוא הנף העומר השני

4. בישבאב ב[א]מר בוא הפסח השני ה[שליש]י בפתחי]ה [ביכין בוא חג
השבועים הרביעי בדליה]

5. [החמישי] בחרים [הששי באביה השביעי] ביקי[ם הואה יו]ם [הזכרון]
בח[ופה בוא יום הכפורים בישבאב בוא חג]

6. [הסוכות] השמיני באמר [התשיעי ביכין העשירי ביוירי]ב עש>תי< [עש]<ר
[החודש] במ[לאכיה שנים עשר החודש]

7. [בשכניה] החמשית הר[א]שון בבלנא באמר] בוא הפסח בפ]צץ בוא] הנף
העומר הש[ני בפצ]ץ ביחזקאל בוא

8. הפסח [הש]נ[י השלישי ב]דליה ביוריריב בוא חג הש[בועים הר[ביעי]
בחרים החמישי בק]וץ הש[שי ביקים השביעי

9. באמר הואה יום הזכר[ון בחזיר בוא יום הכפורים ב[פצץ בוא חג
הסכות השמיני ב[י]חזקאל התשיעי ביויר[י]ב העשירי

Fragment 2 Column 4

4. [הששי באמר השביעי ביחזקאל הואה יום הזכרון ביכין בוא יום
הכפורים בנמול ב[וא חג

5. [הסוכות השמיני במועזיה התשיעי במלאכיה העשירי בישוע] עשתי
עש[ר ה]חודש בחופה

6. [שנים עשר החודש בפצץ]   vacat

7.   vacat

8.   vacat

9.   vacat

TRANSLATION

Fragment 1 Column 1 (1) [on the first of Jedaiah on the twelf]th of it. (The next lunar month ends) on the second of Abi[jah, on] the twe[nty-fifth of the eighth (solar) month. Lunar observation takes place on the third (2) of Mijamin, on the seventeenth] of it (i.e., of solar month eight). (The next lunar month ends) on the third of Jakim, on the [twenty-fo]urth [of the ninth (solar) month. Lunar observation takes place on the fourth (3) of Shecaniah, on the ele]venth of it. (The next lunar month ends) on the fifth day of Immer, on the twenty-third of the ten[th (solar) month. Lunar observation takes place on the sixth day of J]eshebeab, (4) [on the tenth of] it. (The next lunar month ends) on the [si]xth of Jehezkel, on the twenty-second of the eleventh (solar) month. [Lunar observation takes place on the sabbath of] Pethahiah, (5) [on the ninth of it.] (The next lunar month ends) on the first of Joiarib, on the twenty-second of the twelfth (solar) month. [Lunar observation takes place on the seco]nd of Delaiah, (6) [on the ninth of it. The] secon[d] (year): The first lunar month ends on the seco[n]d of Malachiah, on the twentie[th of the first (solar) month.] Lunar observation takes place on (7) [the third of Harim, on the seventh] of it. (The next lunar month ends) on the fourth of Jeshua, on the twentieth of the second (solar) month. [Lunar observation takes place on the fifth of Hakkoz, (8) on the seventh of it. (The next lunar month ends) on the fifth of Huppah, on the ninet]eenth of the third (solar) month. Lunar observation takes place on the sixth of [E]l[iashib,] on the si[xth of it. (The next lunar month ends) on the sabba]th of Happizzez,

Fragment 1 Column 2 (1) [on the eighteenth of the the fourth (solar) month. Lunar observation takes place on the first of Immer, on the fifth] of it. (The next lunar month ends) on the first of [Gamul, on the seventeenth of the fifth (solar) month. (2) Lunar observation takes place on the second of Je]hezk[el, on the fourth of it. (The next lunar month ends) on the third of Jeda]iah, on the [seventeenth of the sixth month. Lunar observation takes place on the fourth of] (3) Maaziah, on the fourth of it. (The next lunar month ends) on the fou[rth of Mijamin, on the fifteenth] of the seventh month. Lunar observation takes place on the fif[th of Seorim, on the third] (4) of it. (The next lunar month ends) on the sixth of Shecaniah, on the fif[teenth of the eighth (solar) month. Lun]ar observation takes place on the sabbath of Abijah, on the second of it. [(The next lunar month ends) on the sabbath of Bilgah,] (5) on the fourteenth of the ninth (solar) month. Lunar observation takes place on the [first of Huppah, on the first] of the ninth (solar) month. A second lun[ar observation] takes place on the third of [Hezir, on the thirty-] (6) first o[f it. (The next lunar month ends) on the] second of Pethahiah, on the thir[teenth of the tenth (solar) month.] Lunar observation takes place on the fourt[h of Ja]chin, on the ninete[enth of it.] (7) [(The next lunar month ends) on the third of Delai]ah, on the twelfth of the eleven[th (solar) month. Lunar obse]rvation takes place on the sixth of Joiar[ib,] on the twenty-nin[th of i]t. [(The next lunar month ends) on the fifth of Harim,] (8) on the twe[lf]th of the twelfth (solar) month. Lunar observ[ation] takes place on the sabbath [of] Mijamin, on the twenty-eighth of it. The third (year): (The next lunar month ends) on [the sixth of Hakkoz, on the tenth . . .]

Fragment 1 Column 3 (3) [on the seventh of the fifth (solar) month. Lunar observat]ion takes place on the first of Ha[rim, on the twen[ty-][fourth] of it. (The next lunar month ends) on the sabbath of Mala[chiah, on the seventh of the sixth (solar) month. Lunar observation takes place on the second of Hakkoz, on the twenty-third of it. (4) (The next lunar month ends) on the first of Jeshua, on the fifth] of the seventh (solar) month. Lunar observation takes place on the fourth of Eliashib, on the tw[enty]-second [of it. (The next lunar month ends) on the third of Huppah, on the fifth of the eighth (solar) month. Lunar observation takes place on the fifth (5) of Bilgah, on the twenty-first in it. (The next lunar month ends) on the fourth of Hezir, on] the fourth of the ninth (solar) month. Lunar observation takes place on the sabbath of Jeh[ezkel, on the twenty-first of it. (The next lunar month ends) on the sixth of Jachin, on the third of the tenth (solar) month. (6) Lunar observation takes place on the first of Maaziah, on the six]teenth of it. (The next lunar month ends) on the sabbath of Jedaiah, on the second of the eleventh (solar) month. Lunar observation takes place [on the third of Seorim, on the nineteenth of it. (The next lunar month ends) on the second (7) of Mijamin, on the second of the twelfth (solar) month. Lunar obser]vation takes place on the fourth of Abijah, on the eighteenth of it. The fourth (year): (The next lunar month ends) on the fourth of Shecan[iah, on the first of the first (solar) month. Lunar observation takes place on the sixth] (8) [of Jakim, on the seventeenth of the] first (solar) month. (The next lunar month ends) on the sabbath of Pethahiah, on the thirtieth of the second (solar) month. Lunar observation takes place on the first of Hez[ir, on the seventeenth of it. (The next lunar month ends) on the first of Deliah, on the ninth . . .]

Fragment 2 Column 1 (1) [Lun]ar observation takes place on the first [of Bilga]h, on the [twenty-] four[th] of it. (The next lunar month ends) on the sabbath of Hezir, on the seven[th of the sixth (solar) month.] (2) [Lunar observation takes place onthe second of Pethahiah,] on the twenty-third of it. (The next lunar month ends) on the first of Jachin, on the fifth of the seventh (solar) month. Lunar observation takes place on the fourth (3) [of Delaiah, on the twenty-second] of it. (The next lunar month ends) on the third of Joiarib, on the fifth of the eighth (solar) month. Lunar observation takes place on the fifth of Harim, (4) [on the sixteenth of it. (The next lunar month ends) on the four]th of Malachiah, on the fourth of the ninth (solar) month. Lunar observation takes place on the sabbath of Abijah, on the (5) [twenty-] first [of it. (The next lunar month ends) on the sixth of Je]shua, [on] the third of the tenth (solar) month. Lunar observation takes place on the first of Jakim, on the nineteenth of [it.] (6) [(The next lunar month ends) on the sabbath of Jeshebeab, on the second of the elev]nth (solar) month. Lunar observation takes place on the thi[rd of Immer, on the nin]eteenth of it. (7) [(The next lunar month ends) on the second of Happizzez, on the second of the twel]fth (solar) month. Lunar observation takes place on the fourth of Jehezkel, on the eighteenth (8) [of it. The fi]rst [year: the first mo]nth (begins) [in Del]aiah. In Ma[aziah] (9) [is the Passover. In Jedaiah is the Lifting of the Omer. The second month (begins) in] Jedaiah. [In Seorim is the Second Passover. The third month (begins) in Hakkoz.]

Fragment 2 Column 2 (1) In Je[sh]ua is the Festival of We[eks. The fourth month (begins) in Elia]shib. The fif[th month (begins) in Bilgah. The sixth month (begins) in Jehezkel.] The seven[th month (begins) (2) in Maaziah. That day is the Day of Remembrance. In Joiarib is the Day of Atonement. In Jedaiah is the [Festival of] Booths. The eighth month (begins) [in Seorim.] (3) The ninth month (begins) in Jeshua. The tenth month (begins) in Huppah. The eleventh month (begins) in Hezir. The twelfth month (begins) in Gamul. (4) The second (year): the first month (begins) in Jediah. In Seorim is the Passover. In [Mi]jamin is the Lifting of the Omer. The second month (begins) in Mi[jamin. In Abijah] (5) is the [Second] Passover. [The third month (begins) in Eliashib,] and in Hu[ppah] is the Feast of Weeks. [The fourth month (begins) in Bil]gah. The fifth month (begins) in Pethahiah. (6) [The sixth month (begins) in Maaziah. The seventh month (begins) in Seorim. That day is the Da]y of Remembrance. In Malachiah [is the Day of At]onement. In Mijamin (7) [is the Festival of Booths. The eighth month (begins) in Abijah. The ninth month (begins) in] Huppah. The tenth month (begins) in Hezir. The el[eventh] month (begins) in Jachin. (8) The [twe]lfth [mon]th (begins) [in Jedaiah.   The] third (year): The first month (begins) in [Mijam]in. In Abijah is (9) the Passover. In Shecan[ia]h is the Lifting of the Omer. The seco[nd] month (begins) in Shecaniah. In Jakim is the [Se]cond Passover. The third month (begins) in Bilgah. In [He]zir is

Fragment 2 Column 3 (1) [the Festival] of Week[s. The [four]th month (begins) in [Pethahiah. The fifth month (begins) in Delaiah. The sixth month (begins) in Se]orim. [The seventh month (begins) in Abijah. That day is the D]ay of [Remembrance. In Jeshua] is the D[ay of Atonement.] (2) [In Shecani]ah is the Festival of [B]ooths. [The] eig[hth month (begins) in] Jakim. The ninth month (begins) in Hezir. The tenth month (begins) in] Jachin. The ele[venth month (begins) in] Joiarib. [The twelfth] (3) month (begins) in [Mij]amin.[The fourth (year): the first month (begins) in Shecaniah. In Jakim is the Passover. In Jeshebeab is the Waving of the Omer. The second] (4) [month] (begins) in Jeshebeab. In [Immer is the

Second Passover. The] third month (begins) [in Pethah]iah. [In Jachin is the Festival of Weeks. The fourth month (begins) in Delaiah.] (5) [The fifth month (begins)] in Harim. [The sixth month (begins) in Abijah. The seventh month (begins)] in Jaki[m. That is the Da]y of [Remembrance]. In H[uppah is the Day of Atonement. In Jeshebeab is the Festival] (6) [of Booths.] The eighth month (begins) in Immer. [The ninth month (begins) in Jachin. The tenth month (begins) in Joiari]b. The elev[en]th [month (begins)] in Ma[lachiah. The twelfth month (begins)] (7) [in Shecaniah.] The fifth (year): the fi[rst month (begins) in Bilgah. In Immer] is the Passover. In Happ[izzez is] the Waving of the Omer. The sec[ond month (begins) in Happizz]ez. In Jehezkel is (8) [the Sec]ond Passover. The third month (begins) in [Delaiah. In Joiarib is the Festival of We]eks. The fou[rth month (begins)] in Harim. The fifth month (begins) in Hakk[oz. The six]th month (begins) in Jakim. The seventh month (begins) (9) in Immer. That day is the Day of Rememb[rance. In Hezir is the Day of Atonement. In] Happizzez is the Festival of Booths. The eighth month (begins) in [Je]hezkel. The ninth month (begins) in Joiar[i]b. The tenth . . .

Fragment 2 Column 4 (4) [The sixth month (begins) in Immer. The seventh month (begins) in Jehezkel. That day is the Day of Remembrance. In Jachin is the Day of Atonement. In Gamul is] the Festival of (5) [Booths. The eighth month (begins) in Maaziah. The ninth month (begins) in Malachiah. The tenth month (begins) in Jeshua.] The eleven[th mo]nth (begins) in Huppah. (6) [The twelfth month (begins) in Happizzez.]

23. PRIESTLY COURSES II (4Q320)
(Plate 7)

Relying largely on ciphers, Fragment 1 of this manuscript preserves three columns. These portions provide the first three years of the correspondence between the lunisolar calendar and the solar calendar. One can observe that the lunisolar calendar loses ten days per year *vis-à-vis* the solar calendar, so that over the period covered by these columns it falls behind a full 30 days. As noted above, it would never fall behind by more. A month was intercalated every three years to bring the two calendars back into alignment.

TRANSLITERATION　　　　　　　　　Fragment 1 Column 1

1. [　　　] [להראותה מן המזרח]
2. .2 [ ] [ל..רה [ב]מחצית השמים ביסוד
3. .3 [ ].מערב עד בוקר בוווו בשבת

4.   [בני ג]מול לחודש הרישון בשנה
5.   [הרישו]נה   *vacat*
6.   [בו]||||| בידעי[ה לו]|||||||||3 ב3ר - בו
7.   [שבת ב]קוץ ל3ר - ב3ר - בשני
8.   [בו]|| באלי]שיב לו]|||||||||3 בו]|||||||||3 בשלשי
9.   [בו]|| בכלנ[ה ל3ר - בו]|||||||||3 ברביעי
10. [בו]|||| בפת]חיה לו]|||||||||3 בו]|||||||3 בחמשי
11. [בו]|||||| בדליה] ל3ר - בו]|||||3 בששי
12. [שבת בשעורי]ם לו]|||||||||3 בו]|||||3 בשביעי
13. [בו]|| באביה ל3ר - [ ] בו]|||||3 בשמיני
14. [בו]|| ביקים לו]||||||| |3| בו]|||3 בתשיעי

Fragment 1 Column 2

1.   בו]||||| <ב><ל><אמר3> בו]|||3 ר - בו]|||3 בעשירי
2.   בו]|||||| ביחזקאל לו]|||||||||3 בו]3| בעשת[י] עשר
3.   בו ביוריב ל3ר - בו]3| בשנים עשר החדש
4.   השנה השנית   *vacat*
5.   בו]|| במלכיה לו]|||||||||3 ב3 ברישון
6.   בו]|||| בישוע ל3ר - ב3 בשני
7.   בו]||||| בחופא לו]|||||||||3 ב-ר]||||||||| [בשלשי]
8.   שבת בפצץ ל3ר - ב-ר]||||||| בר[ביעי]
9.   בו בנמול ל[ו]|||||||||3 ב-ר]||||||| בחמישי]
10. בו]||| בידעיה ל3ר - [ב-ר]||||||| בששי]
11. בו]||||| במימן לו]||||| |3|||| ב-ר]|||||| בשביעי]
12. בו]|||||| בשכניה ל3]ר - ב-ר]||||| בשמיני]
13. שבת בבל[נ]ה לו]|||||||||3 ב-ר]|||| בתשיעי]
14. [בו]|| בפתחיה ל3ר - ב-ר]||| בעשירי]

Fragment 1 Column 3

1.   [בו]|| בדליה לו]|||||||||3 ב-ר]|| בעשתי עשר החדש]
2.   [בו]||||| בחרים ל3ר - ב-ר]|| בשנים עשר החדש]
3.   [השנה השלשית   *vacat*]
4.   [בו]|||| בקוץ לו]|||||||||3 ב-ר ברישון]
5.   [בו ביקים ל3ר - ב-ר בשני]
6.   [בו]|| באמר לו]|||||||||3 בו]||||||| בשלשי]
7.   [בו]||||| ביחזקאל ל3ר - בו]|||||| ברביעי]
8.   [בו]||||| במעזיה לו]|||||||||3 בו]||||| בחמשי]
9.   [שבת במלכיה ל3ר - בו]|||||| בששי]
10. [בו בי]שוע לו]|||||||||3 בו]||||| בשביעי]
11. בו]||| בחפא ל3ר - בו]|||| בשמיני]
12. בו]|||| בחזיר לו]|||||||||3 בו]||| בתשיעי]

13. ‎||||||‎ בו|| ¬ל3 ביכין ‎||||||‎ בו| בעשירי
14. ‎שבת בידעיה ל||||||||||3 בו| בעשתי עשר החדש‎
15. ‎בו|] ב[מימין ל3¬ ביום ||[בשנים עשר החדש‎

TRANSLATION

Fragment 1 Column 1 (1) . . . to show it forth from the East (2) . . . in the midst of Heaven, in the foundation of (3) . . . from evening until morning. On the fourth, on the sabbath, (4) the sons of Gamul (shall serve), in the first month, in the first (5) year. (6) [The fifth day of the course of Jedai]ah = the twenty-ninth day (of the lunar month) = the thirtieth day (of the solar month) in it (i.e., in the first month of the solar year). (7) [The sabbath of Hak]koz (i.e., when the course rotates in; it does not serve until the following sabbath) = the thirtieth = the thirtieth in the second month. (8) [The second of Elia]shib = the twenty-ninth = the twenty-ninth in the third month. (9) [The third of Bilg]ah = the thirtieth = the twenty-ninth in the fourth month (Note: this is a scribal error; the correct equivalence is the twenty-eighth). (10) [The third of Petha]hiah = the twenty-ninth = the twenty-seventh in the fifth month. (11) [The sixth of Deliah] = the thirtieth = the twenty-seventh in the sixth month. (12) [The sabbath of Seori]m = the twenty-ninth = the twenty-fifth in the seventh month. (13) [The second of Abijah = the thirtieth] = the twenty-fifth in the eighth month. (14) [The third of Jakim = the twenty-[nin]th = the twenty-fourth in the ninth month.

Fragment 1 Column 2 (1) The fifth of Immer = the thirtieth = the twenty-third in the tenth month. (2) The sixth of Jehezkel =the twenty-ninth = the twenty-second in the eleven[th] month. (3) The first in Jehoiarib = the thirtieth = the twenty-second in the twelfth month. (4) The second year: (5) The second of Malakiah (sic!) =the twenty-ninth = the twentieth of the first month. (6) The fourth of Jeshua = the thirtieth = the twentieth of the second month. (7) The fifth of Huppah = the twenty-ninth = the nineteenth of [the sixth month.] (8) The sabbath of Happizzez = the thirtieth = the eighteenth of the fou[rth month.] (9) The first of Gamul = the twenty-[ninth = the seventeenth of the fifth month.] (10) The third of Jedaiah = the thirtieth = [the seventeenth of the sixth month.] (11) The fourth of Mijamin = the twenty-[nin]th [= the fifteenth of the seventh month.] (12) The sixth of Shecaniah = the thirt[ieth = the fifteenth of the eighth month.] (13) The sabbath of Bil[gah = the twenty-ninth = the fourteenth of the ninth month.] (14) [The second of Pethahiah = the thirtieth = the thirteenth of the tenth month.]

Fragment 1 Column 3 (1) [The third of Delaiah = the twenty-ninth = the twelfth of the eleventh month. (2) The fifth of Harim = the thirtieth = the twelfth of the twelfth month. (3) The third year: (4) The fifth of Hakkoz = the twenty-ninth = the twentieth of the first month. (5) The first of Jakim = the thirtieth = the tenth of the second month. (6) The second of Immer = the twenty-ninth = the ninth of the third month. (7) The fourth of Jehezkel = the thirtieth = the eighth of the fourth month. (8) The fifth of Maaziah = the twenty-ninth = the seventh of the fifth month. (9) The sabbath of Malakiah = the thirtieth = the seventh of the sixth month.] (10) The first of Je[shua = the twenty-ninth = the fifth of the seventh month.] (11) The third of Huppah = the thirtieth = the fifth of the eighth month. (12) The fourth of Hezir = the twenty-ninth = the fourth of the ninth month. (13) The sixth of Jachin = the thirtieth = the third of the tenth month. (14) The sabbath of Jedaiah = the twenty-ninth = the second of the eleventh month. (15) [The second of] Mijamin = the thirtieth = day [two] of the twelfth month.

24. PRIESTLY COURSES III – AEMILIUS KILLS
(Manuscripts A–E – 4Q323–324A–B)
(Plate 8)

Though extremely fragmentary, this series of manuscripts provides another record of the proper rotation of priestly courses in the sex-annual cycle. This is fairly straightforward and similar to the two preceding ones, though in this one no attempt is made at lunisolar harmonization. It is worth mentioning, too, that its Hebrew is closer to that of early Rabbinic literature than many texts at Qumran. But what is unique about these fragments is that they belong to a select group of Qumran documents mentioning identifiable historical personages, as the Nahum Commentary does with Antiochus Epiphanes and Demetrius and the Paean to King Jonathan below appears to do with Alexander Jannaeus (*c.* 104–76 BC).

In this text, amid over a dozen references to historical events commemorated in the record of rotations, these figures include: 'Aemilius' (Aemilius Scaurus, Pompey's general in Syria and Palestine), 'Shelamzion' (Salome Alexandra, d. 67 BC – Phariseeizing widow of Alexander Jannaeus), her eldest son Hyrcanus II (executed in 30 BC on Herod's orders – also a Pharisee) and possibly Shelamzion's younger son Aristobulus (d. 49 BC, poisoned on his way back from Rome to regain his kingdom by supporters of Pompey – a Sadducee). In addition, too, in Manuscript E, the text possibly contains a reference to John Hyrcanus, Alexander Jannaeus' father (*c.* 134–104 BC), though Hyrcanus II was also known as John. The text also contains fairly negative references to 'Gentiles' and 'Arabs', which increase the sense of its authenticity.

Like others, this text has been known since the 1950s, but for some reason, never published. Withholding it is really quite inexplicable, because we have here a view, however tenuous, of one of the most crucial periods in the Second Temple period. Scaurus was Pompey's adjutant at the time of the conquest of Jerusalem in 63 BC. After it fell and Pompey attached it to Syria, he was left behind as governor.

In turn, Scaurus was closely connected with Herod's father Antipater, who became one of the first Roman procurators in Jerusalem. At one point Scaurus led a campaign on his behalf against the Arabian king at Petra, a locale Paul also refers to as 'Arabia' when describing his own sojourn there in Gal. 1:17. Antipater, who was the intermediary between Hyrcanus II and the Romans, probably began his rise some time earlier under Shelamzion and her Pharisee supporters (*War* 1.110–114).

Of Greco-Idumaean background and married to an Arab (a relative of this same Arab king), Antipater connived at Hyrcanus' survival, played a key role in Aristobulus' discomfiture, and through his intimacies with Pompey and Scaurus, and Mark Antony thereafter, placed his son Herod in a position both to destroy the Maccabeans and succeed them.

For his part, Aristobulus was more hot-headed and popular than his accommodating brother Hyrcanus, and appears to have been the darling of the nationalist-minded Jerusalem crowd. It was the split between these two – and Antipater's adept exploitation of it – that set the stage for the Roman entrance into and occupation of the country and the destruction of the Maccabean family. So ended that independence achieved a century before with Judas Maccabee's legendary acts.

Aristobulus was taken by Pompey to Rome in chains, probably to participate in his triumph. The movement that supported him may be seen as both 'nationalist' and 'Sadducean', while Hyrcanus II and his mother Shelamzion (Lines 4–6 of Fragment 2) are part of a more compromising, less nationalistic, Pharisaic one, willing to live with foreign intervention in the country – in particular, the appointment of high priests.

Seemingly written from the perspective of those who supported Aristobulus II, the present text is hostile to 'Arabs' (with whom Antipater and Hyrcanus were *very* involved), hostile to Shelamzion, under whom the accommodation began, hostile to Hyrcanus II, and without question, hostile to Scaurus and those 'Gentiles' associated with him in the killings he is overtly accused of being involved in (Lines 4 and 8 of Manuscript D Fragment 2 and Line 2 of Manuscript A Fragment 3). Its point of view can most certainly be regarded as 'zealous', if not 'Zealot'.

This is the tantalizing nature of the materials before us. As in the Nahum Commentary, the events recorded would appear to be past history, so much so that they have had a chance to penetrate the commemorative tradition of a zealous lower priesthood holding these memories dear probably not an insubstantial time later. The infractions imputed to Aemilius and the 'leader of Gentiles' have burned deep into its consciousness. After Mark Antony's suppression of the revolutionary activity by Aristobulus' two sons Alexander and Antigonus in the next generation, who like John the Baptist after them were *beheaded*; the priests officiating at the Temple all owed their positions to Roman and Herodian power. They would not and could not have been interested in a literature of this kind.

Where, then, could a text accusing Roman governors of murder have been preserved? Only at a revolutionary outpost such as Qumran. What period could this have been and when did this more 'purist' brand of Sadducees — who apparently ultimately metamorphose into 'Messianic Sadducees' and depending on particular scholars' points of view have been variously called 'Essenes', 'Zealots', or 'Jewish Christians' — write or preserve such materials? We are certainly not in the formative Maccabean period, nor any period linked to personalities like Jonathan or Simon Maccabee, or even Alexander Jannaeus, whom proponents of 'the Essene theory' have previously and tendentiously identified as the *dramatis personae* — most notably the Wicked Priest — of Qumran allusion.

This is consistent and in line with our reading of other Qumran materials, particularly the Testament of Kohath to be discussed in Chapter 5, which condemns foreign involvement and collaboration with foreign invaders in the matter of the priesthood. It is also consistent with our reading of the complex development of the Sadducee movement and a split in this movement between nationalist and collaborating wings coincident with some of the events being outlined here. One pro-Aristobulus, which could easily pass for 'zealot', moves in the first century AD into an 'opposition' and probably even 'Messianic' phase; another, more compromising, owed its existence and the collaborating nature of its ethos to the rise of Herod, who with Antony was responsible for the beheading of Aristobulus' equally nationalistic and Sadducean son Antigonus 25 years later. The second of these, who Josephus confirms 'were dominated in all things by the Pharisees' (*Ant.* 18.17), are the familiar ones pictured by him, the Gospels, and to a certain extent Talmudic sources. They are probably best called *Herodian Sadducees.* The Talmud calls them 'Boethusians' (i.e. Boethusian Sadducees after the name of a priest from Egypt Herod appointed while also marrying his daughter – another instance of the multiplication of wives by the ruler so roundly condemned at Qumran in documents like The Temple Scroll and Damascus Document.)

Whatever else can be said of these unmistakable references to Aemelius' 'killing' – probably while governor, though possibly in the war leading up to this – and to Hyrcanus' rebellion (Line 6 Fragment 2 Manuscript A – almost certainly against his brother Aristobulus), they reveal the text to be hostile to Hyrcanus, hostile to the party of collaboration, and hostile ultimately to the Herodian takeover (perceived as both 'Gentile' and abetted by 'Gentiles'). This approach is consistent with the anti-foreign, xenophobic, 'zealot', yet pro-Temple – even James-like – orientation of the two Letters on Works Righteousness and the Paean to King Jonathan below.

The conclusion appears to be that Qumran represents the archive of a pro-Maccabean nationalist priesthood, one in sympathy with the aims of Judas, John Hyrcanus, Alexander Jannaeus, Aristobulus II, Antigonus, etc., but not Salome Alexandra, nor her son Hyrcanus II with their Pharisaic tendencies. The whole *sitz-im-leben* for these, including 'opposition' (even 'Messianic') and establishment Sadducees, as well as for the two Letters on Works Righteousness and the Paen for King Jonathan was already set forth in R. H. Eisenman's *Maccabees, Zadokite, Christians and Qumran: a New Hypothesis of Qumran Origins* (E. J. Brill) without benefit of these texts in 1983. For more on this subject, see our discussions of these Letters on Works Righteousness in Chapter 6 and the Brontologion and Paean to King Jonathan in Chapter 8.

The reference to 'a Jewish man' or 'Jew' (*ish Yehudi*) in Manuscript D Fragment 4 parallels the similar ones in the Persian Court materials in Chapter 3 and to 'a Jewish woman' below. Again, it shows that this manner of looking at Jews as a distinct people, not as Israelites or in some archaizing tribal notation, was already well in the process of taking hold.

TRANSLITERATION   **Manuscript A Fragment 1**

[א[בעשר [בחודש הששי   ] .1

[בעשרים ואחד]   [בארבעה עשר בו ביא[ת ידעיה בששה עש[ר בו .2

[[בו באית חרים בעשרים ו[שבעה בחודש [הששי .3

[   ] הושיב ג. [   ] 4.
[   ] גו[אים וגם . [   ] 5.
[   ] מ[רורי הנפש . [   ] 6.
[   ] אסורים [   ] 7.

Fragment 2

[   ] ל[חת לו יקר בערב]ים [   ] 1.
[   ] ביום אר[בעה לשבט זה] [   ] 2.
[   ]ה שהוא עשרים בחודש] [   ] 3.
[   ].יסוד באה שלמציון .] [   ] 4.
[   ] להקביל את [פני [   ] 5.
[   ]ב הרקנוס מרד [על אריסטבולוס [   ] 6.
[   ] להקביל] [   ] 7.

Fragment 3

[   ] [...[   ] 1.
[   ] ראש הג[ואים הרג ש] [   ] 2.
[   ] ביום ח[מישי בידעיה ז.] [   ] 3.

Fragment 4

[   ] .ם כרצו[ן [   ] 1.

Manuscript B Fragment 1

[   ]ה בתשע[ה בחודש השמיני ביאת שכניה [   ] 1.
[בששה עשר בה ביאת אלישיב]   [ביום [   ] בשכניה א] [   ] 2.
[[בעשרים ושלו]שה בה ביאת יקים <בשנים ביקים .]   [> וים ר]ביעי ביקים [   ] 3.
[בס..]   יו]ם שני בחודש הת[שיעי [   ] 4.

Fragment 2

[יום רב]יעי בחז]י]ר [זה א]חד בע[שירי] [   ] 1.
[בארבעה בה ביאת הפ]צץ באחד [ע]שר בה [ביאת פתחיה] [   ] 2.
[בשמונה עשר בה בי]א]ת יחזקאל בעשר]ים וחמשה בה ביאת] [   ] 3.
[   ] יכי]ן העו[ב]ודה .]   [יכין [   ] 4.
[   ] בשנים בה] ביאת [גמול [   ] 5.

Fragment 3

[   ] שהוא [   ] 1.
[   ] .[   ] 2.
[   ]ש[   ] 3.
[   ] ות[...[   ] 4.
[   ] אשנ[ים .. [   ] 5.

[.[ונד אר]יסטבולוס   ] .6

[א]מרו בע[   ] .7

[   ] . שבעים [   ] .8

[   ] שהוא [   ] .9

Manuscript C Fragment 1

[בעשרים ושלושה בה] ביאת [אלישיב בשלושים בה ביאת יקים] .1

[אחר שבת ביקים זה אח]ד בש[שי בשבעה בה ביאת חופה] .2

[בארבעה] עשר בה [ביאת ישבאב] .. פות בע[שרים ואחד] .3

[בה ביאת בלנ]ה בעשרים [ושמונה ב]ה ביאת אמ[ר יום] .4

[רביעי באמר זה א]חד בשביעי באר[ב]עה בה ביאת ח[זיר] .5

[יום ששי ב]חזיר שהוא עשרה בשביעי שיום [הכפורים כה] .6

[   ] לברית באחד עשר בשביעי ביאת [הפצץ   ] .7

Manscript D Fragment 1 Column 2

בעשרים ואחד]   .[בל].   [.]   [.]   [יום] .5

[בו]א ביאת ש[עור]ים בעשרים ושמונה בוא ביאת מלכ[יה] .6

vacat   יום רביעי [ב]מלכיה זה אחד בחודש העשירי .7

בא[רבע]ה בע[ש]ירי ביאת מי[מ]ין באחד עשר בוא ביא[ת הקוץ] .8

Fragment 2

ב]עשרים   ] .1

[ואחד בוא ביאת פתחיה בעשרים ושמו]נה .2

[בוא ביאת יחזקאל ביום 3/2/1 בי]חזקאל שהוא .3

31/30/29] בחודש הששי יום] הרג אמליוס .4

[יום רביעי ביחזקאל זה אחד בחוד]ש השביעי .5

[בארבעה בוא ביאת יכין באחד עשר בוא ב]י[את] גמול .6

יום רביעי בגמול ש]הוא   ] .7

[חמשה עשר בחודש השביעי חג הסכות בוא] הרג אמליוס .8

Fragment 3

[   ] . אצל .[ ] [ש]   ] .1

[בעשרים ושמונה בוא ביאת י[שוע יום רביעי] בישוע זה אחד בחודש] .2

[   ] שה[וא עש]רה   [העשירי .3

Fragment 4

[א]איש יהודי א[   ] .1

Manuscript E Fragment 1 Column 1

כוהן ג[ד]ול כ.רי]   ] .1

יוחנן להבי את]   ] .2

Fragment 1 Column 2

[	] .. .1
[	מֶן [.2
[	] .3
[	] .4
[	אנוש [.5
[	ח הזוי. [.6
[	שלמצ>י<ון [.7

TRANSLATION

Manuscript A Fragment 1 (1) . . . on the tenth [of the sixth month (i.e., of the second year of the priestly rotation) . . .] (2) [on the fourteenth of it, the arriva]l of (the priestly course of) Jedaiah; on the sixtee[nth of it . . . on the twenty-first] (3) [of it the arrival of (the priestly course of) Harim; on the twenty]-seventh of the [sixth] month . . . (4) he returned . . . (5) [Gen]tiles and also . . . (6) . . . [b]itter of spirit . . . (7) prisoners . . .

Fragment 2 (1) [. . . to] give him honor among the Arab[s . . .] (2) [on the fou]rth [day] of this course's service . . . (3) which is the twentieth of the . . . month . . . (4) foundation, Shelamzion came . . . (5) to greet . . . (6) Hyrcanos rebelled [against Aristobulus? . . .] (7) to greet . . .

Fragment 3 (2) [. . . the leader of the Ge]ntiles murdered . . . (3) [on the fi]fth [day] of (the service of the priestly course of) Jedaiah . . .

Fragment 4 (1) . . . according to the wi[ll of . . .]

Manuscript B Fragment 1 (1) . . . on the nin[th of the eighth month (i.e., of the second year of the priestly rotation), the arrival of (the priestly course of) Shecaniah . . .] (2) On day . . . of (the service of the priestly course of Shecaniah, [. . . On the sixteenth of it (i.e., the eighth month), the arrival of (the priestly course of) Eliashib]; (3) [on the twenty-thi]rd of it, the arrival of (the priestly course of) Jakim; on the second (day of the service of the priestly course of) Jakim, . . . ; and on the fo[urth] day of (the service of the priestly course of) [Jakim, . . .] (4) the second day of the ni[nth] month . . .

Fragment 2 (1) [. . . the four]th [day] of (the service of the priestly course of) Hez[i]r, [this day is the fi]rst (day) of the te[nth month (i.e., of the second year of the priestly rotation);] (2) [on the fourth day of it (i.e., the tenth month), the arrival of (the priestly course of) Happi]zzez; on the eleve[nth] of it, [the arrival of (the priestly course of) Pethahiah;] (3) [on the eighteenth of it, the arriv]al of (the priestly course of) Jehezkel; on the twen[ty-fifth of it, the arrival] (4) [of (the priestly course of) Jachin . . . Jach]in, the se[r]vice . . . (5) [on the second of it (i.e., the eleventh month)], the arrival of [(the priestly course of) Gamul . . .]

Fragment 3 (1) . . . which is . . . (5) me[n . . .] (6) and against Ar[istobulus . . .] (7) [and] they [sa]id . . . (8) seventy . . . (9) which is . . .

Manuscript C Fragment 1 (1) [on the twenty-third of it (i.e., the fifth month of the fifth year of the priestly rotation)], the arrival of [(the priestly course of) Eliashib; on the thirtieth of it, the arrival of (the priestly course of) Jakim;] (2) after the sabbath, while Jakim is serving, this is the fir]st of the six[th month; on the seventh of it, the arrival of (the priestly course of) Huppah;] (3) [on the four]teenth of it, [the arrival of (the priestly course of) Jeshebeab;] . . . on the twen[ty-first] (4) [of it, the arrival of (the priestly course of) Bilg]ah; on the twenty-[eighth of i]t, the arrival of (the priestly course of) Imm[er; day] (5) [four (of the service of the priestly course of) Immer is the fi]rst day of the seventh month; on the four[t]h of it, the arrival of (the priestly course of) He[zir;] (6) [the sixth day of] (the service of the priestly course of) Hezir, which is the tenth day of the seventh month, this is [the Day of Atonement;] (7) . . . for the Covenant; on the eleventh day of the seventh month, the arrival of (the priestly course of) [Happizzez . . .]

Manuscript D Fragment 1 Column 2 (5) day . . . [on the twenty-first] (6) [of i]t (i.e., of the ninth month of the fifth year of the priestly rotation), the arrival of (the priestly course of) S[eor]im; on the twenty-eighth of it, the arrival of (the priestly course of) Malchi[jah;] (7) the fourth day of (the service of the priestly course of) Malchijah is the first day of the tenth month. (8) On the f[ourt]h day of the te[n]th month, the arrival of (the priestly course of) Mija[m]in; on the eleventh of it, the arriv[al of (the priestly course of) Hakkoz;]

Fragment 2 (1) [. . . on the] twenty-(2) [first of it (i.e., of the sixth month of the sixth year of the priestly rotation), the arrival of (the priestly course of) Pethahiah; on the twenty-eigh]th (3) [of it, the arrival of (the priestly course of) Jehezkel; on the first (or, the second; or, the third) day of (the service of the priestly course of) J]ehezkel, which is (4) [the twenty-ninth (or, the thirtieth; or, the thirty-first) day of the sixth month, the Day] of Aemilius' Massacre (literally, 'Aemilius killed' as below); (5) [the fourth day of (the service of the priestly course of) Jehezkel is the first day of] the seventh [mon]th; (6) [on the fourth of it (i.e., of the seventh month), the arrival of the (the priestly course of) Jachin; on the eleventh of it, the arr]iv[al of] (the priestly course of) Gamul; (7) [. . . the fourth day of (the service of the priestly course of) Gamul, whi]ch is (8) [the fifteenth day of the seventh month, is the Festival of Booths; on that day,] Aemilius killed . . .

Fragment 3 (2) [on the twenty-eighth of it (i.e., of the ninth month of the sixth year of the priestly rotation), the arrival of (the priestly course of) Je]shua; the four[th] day of [(the service of the priestly course of) Jeshua is the first day of the] (3) [tenth month . . . wh]ich is the ten[th . . .]

Fragment 4 (1) . . . a Jewish man . . .

Manuscript E Fragment 1 Column 1 (1) . . . the hi[g]h priest . . . (2) Johanan to bring the . . .
Fragment 1 Column 2 (2) from . . . (5) a man . . . (7) Shelamzion . . .

25. PRIESTLY COURSES IV (4Q325)

This manuscript consists of three fragments, the two largest of which are transliterated here. These fragments belong to the first year rotation in the sexennial priestly cycle. The text records which priestly course is responsible for each sabbath and festival in the period covered. Fragment 1 concerns the period from Passover (1/14) until the first sabbath of the third month. Fragment 2 apparently begins with 5/3 and the Festival of New Wine (heretofore known from the Temple Scroll, but not listed in the Bible or most other calendar texts). The last date indicated in Fragment 2 is 6/23, on which the Festival of Wood Offering began.

TRANSLITERATION   Fragment 1

1. [ביום שלי]שי בשמונה עשר בו שבת ע]ל יויריב [
2. [ביום שלישי] בערב בעשרים וחמשה בו שבת על ידעיה ועלו
3. [מועד] השעורים בעשרים וששה בו אחר שבת רוש החודש הש[ני]
4. [ביום ש]שי על ידעיה בשנים בו שבת חרים בתשעה בו שבת
5. [שעורים] בששה עשר בו שבת מלכיה בעשרים ושלושה ב[ו]
6. [שבת מ]ימין בשלושים בו שבת הקוץ *vacat* רוש החודש
7.   *vacat*   השלישי אחר שבת [ ] [

Fragment 2

1. [החמישי על בלנה בשנים בו שבת א]מר בש]ל]ושה ב]ו]
2. [אחר שבת מועד התירוש ב]תשעה בו שבת חזיר
3. [בששה עשר בו שבת הפצץ בעשרי]ם ושלושה בו שבת
4. [פתחיה בשלושים בו שבת יחזקאל רו]ש החודש הששי
5. [אחר שבת *vacat* בשבעה בו שבת יכין בארב]עה עשר
6. [בו שבת גמול בעשרים ואחד בו שבת דליה בעשרים ו]שנים
7. [בו מועד השמן בעשרים ושלושה בו מועד קרבן הע]צים

TRANSLATION
Fragment 1 (1) [on Tues]day; on the eighteenth the sabbath fa[lls to Jehoiarib . . .] (2) [on Tuesday] in the evening. On the twenty-fifth the sabbath falls to Jedaiah; also during that course's duties falls (3) [the Festival of] the Barley on the twenty-sixth. After the sabbath, the beginning of the

sec[ond] month falls to (4) Jedaiah, [on Fri]day. On the second is the sabbath of Harim. On the ninth is the sabbath of (5) [Seorim.] On the sixteenth is the sabbath of Malchijah. On the twenty-third i[s] (6) [the sabbath] of [Mi]jamin. On the thirtieth is the sabbath of Hakkoz. The beginning of (7) the third month, after the sabbath . . .

Fragment 2 (1) [the fifth (month) falls to Bilgah. On the second is the sabbath of I]mmer. On the th[ir]d, (2) [after the sabbath, is the Festival of New Wine. On] the ninth is the sabbath of Hezir. (3) [On the sixteenth is the sabbath of Happizzez. On the twen]ty-third is the sabbath of (4) [Pethahiah. On the thirtieth is the sabbath of Jehezkel. The firs]t of the sixth month is (5) [after the sabbath. On the seventh is the sabbath of Jachin. On the fo]urteenth (6) [is the sabbath of Gamul. On the twenty-first is the sabbath of Delaiah. On the twenty-]second (7) [is the Festival of Oil. On the twenty-third is the Festival of W]ood [Offering] . . .

26. HEAVENLY CONCORDANCES (*OTOT* – 4Q319A)

As we have seen, the Qumran calendrical texts are based upon an understanding of the Creation narrative of Genesis. No portion is more significant for these texts than Gen. 1:14, which the authors might have understood as 'Let there be lights in the expanse of heaven to separate the days from the night, and let them be for "signs" (*otot*), and for festivals and for days and for years.' Given the belief that this verse had to do with the proper keeping of God's holy festivals and, more generally, with keeping track of time, what did the Qumran authors believe was meant by the term *otot*? Clearly the usual understanding of modern scholars of the text – that the term refers to portents of extraordinary events and divine judgements and to phenomena prognosticating changes in the weather – makes little sense when defining a natural rhythm, the basis of a calendar. Rather than the extraordinary, one then seeks the ordinary.

The author of the present text understood 'sign' to refer to a year in which the sun and moon were once again perfectly aligned at the year's beginning – that is, a year in which the vernal equinox coincided with a new moon. According to the more general scheme of the Qumran calendrical texts that could only happen in Years 1 and 4 of the six-year cycle of priestly rotations. Since Years 3 and 6 were intercalated at year's end, Years 1 and 4 did begin with the heavenlies once again in temporary agreement. The years were named, as was usual in Qumran parlance, after the priestly courses; because the years were always Years

1 and 4 in the cycle, only two priestly courses give their names to *otot* years: Shecaniah and Gamul. Further, the cycle begins with Shecaniah. This oddity results because at the Creation there had been no prior intercalation. Accordingly the reference is to the course in service when intercalation was first necessary in Year 3.

The purpose of the present text is to record all such concordant years until the cycle begins to repeat, and to align that cycle with both the seven-year cycle of sabbatical years and the 'jubilees' that measured longer periods of time. An *otot* cycle of 294 years emerges (6 x 49). The text also counts all the *otot* years and takes special notice when such a year coincides with a sabbatical year. It names each special year by the relevant priestly course and also names each jubilee (in a more complicated way, however, as explained below). But in constructing this alignment of the sexennial priestly rotation with the jubilees, the text encounters a basic difficulty: 49 is not precisely divisible by 6. The *otot* years will therefore not always fall at the beginning and end of jubilee periods. As a consequence the text uses 'jubilee' in two slightly different senses. The term refers first to that period (only approximating to 49 years) that aligns with the cycle of *otot*. We can call this the 'jubilee of the *otot*'. At other times the term denotes the actual period of 49 years. At the end of 294 years the differences are made good as Table 2 illustrates:

Table 2. Lengths of the 'Jubilees of the Otot'

Jubilee	Length in Years	Ends in Year	End of Forty-Nine Year Jubilee
Second	49	49	49
Third	51	100	98
Fourth	51	151	147
Fifth	48	199	196
Sixth	48	247	245
Seventh	47	294	294

The text relates the 'jubilee of the *otot*' to the actual 49-year jubilee in two ways. The first is through its reference to the 'sign of the conclusion of the jubilee'. Only once, in 2:18–19, does the author actually give this special sign a name. In that example, the text says, 'The sign of the conclusion of the fifth jubilee falls during (the priestly course of) Jeshebeab.' The meaning is that Jeshebeab is the course serving in the temple at the end of the fifth actual jubilee – that is, as year 196 (4 x 49) comes to an end. If the author had wished, he could have given the names of all the 'signs of the conclusion of the jubilee' (they are respectively Jedaiah, Mijamin, Shecaniah, Jeshebeab, Happizzez and Gamul). The second way of relating the 'jubilee of the *otot*' to the actual 49-year jubilee involves the names the author gives to the jubilees. These names are always either Gamul or Shecaniah. The writer determined the name according to the sign 'controlling' the actual jubilee year.

Finally, the reader will note that the text never mentions a 'first jubilee', even though it begins its recitation at the Creation. Instead, it counts only Jubilees 2–7. Presumably the explanation for this peculiarity lies in the septimal concept inherent in sabbatical years and 49-year jubilees. The author wanted to emphasize the number seven. Since the priestly rotation in fact required only six years to repeat, the only way to end on the number seven was to begin counting with two.

TRANSLITERATION   Column 1

10. [   ]   אורה באר בעה שב[ת   ] [
11.] ה[בריאה בארבעה בג[מול אות שכניה ברביעית אות גמול בשמטה או[ת
12. שכניה בשלי[שית אות [ג]מול בששית אות [שכניה בשנית אות ג[מול
13. בחמישית או[ת שכניה אחר השמטה אות גמו[ל ברביעית אות שכ[ני[ה
14. בשמטה או[ת גמול בשלישית את שכניה [בששית אות גמ[ו[ל
15. בשנית או[ת ש[כניה] בחמישית אות ג[מול אחר השמט[ה אות
16. שכניה בר[ביעית אות גמול בשמטה אות ס[וף היובל השני אתות הי[ובל
17. השני] אתות ⁊ ||||||| מזה בשמטה אתות ||| [   ]. הבריאה
18.]   או[ת שכ[ני[ה בשנה השלישית אות גמו[ל בששית א[ות שכניה
19. בשנית אות ג[מול בחמ<י>שית אות שכניה אחר הש[מטה אות ג[מול

Column 2

1. [ברביעית אות שכניה בשמטה אות גמול בשלישית אות שכניה]
2. [בששית אות גמול ב[שנ[י]ת א[ות שכניה בחמישית אות גמול]
3. [אחר השמט[ה אות שכניה בר[ביעית אות גמול בשמטה אות]
4. [שכניה בשלישית אות גמול בש[שית אות] שכני[ה בשנית אות סוף]
5. היובל הש{י}ל[י]שי אתות היובל [השלישי אתות ⁊ ||||| [מזה בשמטה
6. אתות || שכניה [בשנה השנית או[ת [גמו[ל בחמישית אות שכניה
7. אחר השמטה או[ת גמול ברביעית או[ת שכניה בשמטה אות
8. גמול בשלישית אות [שכניה בששית אות ג[מול בשנית אות
9. שכניה בחמ<י>שית אות [גמול אחר] השמטה אות שכניה
10. ברביעית אות גמול [בשמטה אות] שכניה בשלישית אות גמול

11. בששית אות שכ]ניה בשנית אות] גמול בחמישית אות שכניה
12. אחר השמטה א]ות סוף היובל הרביעי אתות היוב]ל <הרביעי> אתות ־ ||||||
13. מ]ז[ה <אותות> || בשמטה ש]כניה[בשנה הרביעית אות שכניה
14. [בש]מטה אות גמול ב]שלישית אות שכניה בששית אות גמול]
15. בשנ]י[ת אות שכניה בחמ]ישית אות גמול אחר השמטה אות שכניה]
16. ברביעית אות א]ות ג]מול ב]שמטה אות שכניה בשלישית אות גמול]
17. בששי]ת א]ות ש]כניה בשנית אות גמול בחמישית אות שכניה]
18. אחר ה]שמטה אות נ]מול ברביעית אות שכניה בשמטה אות סוף]
19. [היובל החמיש]י בישיבאב [אתות היובל החמישי ־ |||||| מזה בשמטה]

Column 3

1. [אתות ||| גמול בשנה השלישית אות שכניה בששית אות]
2. [גמול ב]שנית אות שכניה ב]חמישית אות גמול אחר השמ]טה
3. [או]ת שכניה ברביעית אות גמ]ול בשמטה אות שכניה] בשלישית
4. אות גמול בששית אות שכניה [בשנית אות] גמול
5. בח]מי[שית אות שכניה אחר [השמטה] אות
6. גמול ב]ר[ביעית אות שכניה בשמ]טה אות גמול ב]שלישית
7. אות [שכניה בש]שית <אות> סוף [ה]יו[ב]ל הששי אתות]
8. היובל [הששי אתות ־ ||||||][מזה ב]שמטה] אתות || [   ]
9. ה. [   ]
10. וליוב]ל גמול בשנה השנית אות שכניה בחמישית אות גמול אחר]
11. השמט]ה אות שכניה ברביעי]ת אות גמו]ל ב]שמט]ה]
12. [אות שכניה בשלישית אות] גמול בששית או]ת שכניה]
13. [ב]שנית או]ת גמול] בחמישית אות שכניה [אחר]
14. השמט]ה אות ג]מול ברביעית אות שכניה בש]מטה אות]
15. גמול [בשלי]שית אות שכניה בששית אות [גמול]
16. בש]ניה אות שכניה] בחמישית אות סוף היוב]ל ה]שביעי
17. [אתות היובל ה]שביעי אתות ־ |||||| מזה בש]מ]טה
18. [אתות ||] אות הי]ו]בלים [ש]נת יובלים לימ]י [   ]
19. [   ] במימן השלישי י[   ]

TRANSLATION

Column 1 (10) . . . its light on the fourth (day); on the sabba[th . . . (11) the] creation, on the fourth (day) of (the rotation of the priestly course of) Ga[mul, the sign of Shecaniah; in the fourth (year) the sign of Gamul; in the sabbatical year, the sig]n (12) [of Shecaniah; in the thi]rd (year) the sign of [Ga]mul; in the sixth (year), the sign of [Shecaniah; in the second, the sign of Ga]mul; (13) [in the fifth, the sig]n of Shecaniah; after the sabbatical year, the sign of Gam[ul; in the fourth, the sign of Shec]an[ia]h; (14) [in the sabbatical year, the sig]n of Gamul; in the third, the sign of Shecaniah; [in the sixth, the sign of Gam]ul; (15) [in the second, the sig]n of She[caniah]; in the fifth, the sign of Gamu[l; after the sabbatical ye]ar, the sign of (16) [Shecaniah; in the fou]rth, the sign of Gamul; in the sabbatical year, the sign of the con[clusion of the second jubilee. The signs of the [second] jubilee: (17) seventeen signs, of which [three] signs fall in a sabbatical year . . . the creation (18) [. . . the sig]n of Sheca[nia]h; in the third year the sign of Gamu[l; in the sixth, the sig]n of Shecaniah; (19) [in the second, the sign of Ga]mul; in the fifth, the sign of Shecaniah; after the sabb[atical year, the sign of Ga]mul;

Column 2 (1) [in the fourth, the sign of Shecaniah; in the sabbatical year, the sign of Gamul; in the third, the sign of Shecaniah;] (2) [in the sixth, the sign of Gamul; in the] sec[on]d, the sig[n of Shecaniah; in the fifth, the sign of Gamul;] (3) after the sabbatical ye]ar, the sign of Shecaniah; in the fou[rth, the sign of Gamul; in the sabbatical year, the sign] (4) of Shecaniah; in the thi]rd, the sign of Gamul; in the six[th the sign] of Shecani[ah; in the second, the sign of the conclusion] (5) of the thi[r]d jubilee. The signs of [the third] jubilee: six[teen signs,] of which (6) two signs fall in a sabbatical year. (A jubilee of) Shecaniah: [in the second year the sig]n of [Gam]ul; in the fifth, the sign of Shecaniah; (7) after the sabbatical year, the sig[n of Gamul; in the fourth, the sig]n of Shecaniah; in the sabbatical year, the sign (8) of Gamul; in the third, the sign [of Shecaniah; in the sixth, the sign of Ga]mul; in the second, the sign (9) of Shecaniah; in the fifth, the sign [of Gamul; after] the sabbatical year, the sign of Shecaniah; (10) in the fourth, the sign of Gamul; [in the sabbatical year, the sign of] Shecaniah; in the third, the sign of Gamul; (11) in the sixth, the sign of Shecan[iah; in the second, the sign of] Gamul; in the fifth, the sign of Shecaniah; (12) after the sabbatical year, the si[gn of the conclusion of the fourth jubilee. The signs] of the fourth [jubil]ee: seventeen signs, (13) of whi[ch] two signs fall in a sabbatical year. (A jubilee of) Sh[ecaniah:] in the fourth year the sign of Shecaniah; (14) [in the sabbatical] year the sign of Gamul; in the [third, the sign of Shecaniah; in the sixth, the sign of Gamul;] (15) in the seco[n]d, the sign of Shecaniah; in the fif[th, the sign of Gamul; after the sabbatical year, the sign of Shecaniah;] (16) in the fourth, the sign of [Ga]mul; in the sabbatical [year, the sign of Shecaniah; in the third, the sign of Gamul;] (17) in the six[th, the si]gn of Sh[ecaniah; in the second, the sign of Gamul; in the fifth, the sign of Shecaniah;] (18) [after the] sabbatical year, the sign of Ga[mul; in the fourth, the sign of Shecaniah; in the sabbatical year, the sign of the conclusion] (19) [of the fif]th [jubilee, falling] during (the priestly course of) Jeshebeab. [The signs of the fifth jubilee: sixteen signs, of which]

Column 3 (1) [three signs fall in a sabbatical year. (A jubilee of) Gamul: in the third year, the sign of Shecaniah; in the sixth, the sign] (2) [of Gamul; in the] second, the sign of Shecaniah; in the [fifth, the sign of Gamul; after the sabbatical] year, (3) [the sig]n of Shecaniah; in the fourth, the sign of Gam[ul; in the sabbatical year, the sign of Shecaniah;] in the third, (4) the sign of Gamul; in the sixth, the sign of Shecaniah; [in the second, the sign of] Gamul; (5) in the fi[ft]h, the sign of Shecaniah; after [the sabbatical year,] the sign of (6) Gamul; in the [fo]urth, the sign of Shecaniah; in the sabbatical [year, the sign of Gamul; in the] third, (7) the sign of [Shecaniah; in the six]th, the sign of the conclusion of the [sixth] jubi[lee. The signs (8) of the sixth] jubilee: si[xteen signs,] of which two signs fall in a [sabbatical year . . .] (9) . . . (10) And regarding the jubil[ee of Gamul: in the second year the sign of Shecaniah; in the fifth the sign of Gamul; after] (11)the sabbatical[year the sign of Shecaniah; in the four]th, the sign of Gamu[l; in the] sabbatical ye[ar] (12) [the sign of Shecaniah; in the third, the sign of] Gamul; in the sixth, the sig[n of Shecaniah;] (13) [in the] second, the sig[n of Gamul;] in the fifth, the sign of Shecaniah; [after] (14) the sabbatical yea[r, the sign of Ga]mul; in the fourth, the sign of Shecaniah; in the sabbatical [year, the sign] (15) of Gamul; in the th[ir]d, the sign of Shecaniah; in the sixth, the sign of [Gamul;] (16) in the se[cond, the sign of Shecaniah;] in the fifth, the sign of the conclusion of [the] seventh jubil[ee.] (17) [The signs of the] seventh [jubilee:] sixteen signs, of which (18) [two signs] fall in a sabbatical year . . . sign of the j[u]bilees, the [y]ear of (the) jubilees according to the day[s of . . .] (19) in (the priestly course of) Mijamin, the third . . .

NOTES

(22) Priestly Courses I (4Q321)

Previous Discussions: None. Photographs: PAM 43.328 and 43.329, ER 1355 and 1356. Note that for all the texts presented in this chapter, a knowledge of the underlying systems makes restorations virtually certain.

(23) Priestly Courses II (4Q320)

Previous Discussion: J. T. Milik, 'Le travail d'édition des manuscrits du désert du Juda', *Volume du Congrés Strasbourg 1956* (SVT 4) (Brill, 1957) 25. Photograph: PAM 43.330, ER 1357.

(24) Priestly Courses III – Aemilius Kills (4Q323–324A–B)

Previous Discussions: J. T. Milik, 'Le travail', 25–6; idem, *Years*, 73; B. Z. Wacholder and M. Abegg, *A Preliminary Edition of the Unpublished Dead Sea Scrolls, Fascicle One* (Washington, DC: Biblical Archaeology Society, 1991). Photographs: PAM 43.335, 43.336 and 43.338, ER 1362, 1363 and 1365.

(25) Priestly Courses IV (4Q325)

Previous Discussions: None. Photographs: PAM 42.332 and 43.333 (top), ER 1359 and 1360.

(26) Heavenly Concordances (OTOT; 4Q319)

Previous Discussions: Milik, *Books*, 63–4. Photographs: PAM 43.283 and 43.284, ER 1319 and 1320.

CHAPTER 5

Testaments and Admonitions

Life is complicated and always has been. In the ancient world, millennia before the time of the Scrolls, one response to this fact was the development of Wisdom literature. This type of literature expounded principles of life and made judicious observations, often couched in the form of pithy sayings. Wisdom literature in the Bible includes Proverbs, Job and Ecclesiastes.

In the Second Temple period this literature abounded, and new kinds of Wisdom literature developed. One of the new forms was the 'testament'. Testaments had their origin in the farewell discourses common in the Bible, such as Gen. 49 (the last words of Jacob) and 1 Sam. 12 (the last words of Samuel). Thus testaments are speeches delivered in anticipation of death and intended to impart the lessons of a lifetime from a father to his sons. The most famous apocryphal example of this type of literature is the Testament of the Twelve Patriarchs. In this collection (which came down from antiquity in Christian circles written in Greek, although in origin Jewish and Semitic), each of the twelve sons of Jacob speaks in turn. Their words comprise ethical exhortation and predictions about the future.

Testamentary literature is well attested among the new materials from the Scrolls. Testaments attached to Levi, Naphtali, Kohath and Amram have emerged. In addition, other forms of Wisdom literature are ubiquitous in the Scrolls; this chapter presents several examples. When reading the Qumran testaments, the reader may want to bear the following genealogical relationships in mind:

Jacob
Levi – Naphtali (sons of Jacob)
Kohath (son of Levi)

135

Amram (son of Kohath)
Moses — Aaron (sons of Amram)
Priests (descended from Aaron)

27. ARAMAIC TESTAMENT OF LEVI (4Q213–214)

Even though it is possible to harbour reservations about whether all this material of varying emphases can, in fact, ever be made to correspond to a single whole, it is important to note themes and imagery even in well-known texts such as this one, which at once move across the entire spectrum of Qumran literature and are completely harmonious with the Qumran perspective. Here we have the typical emphases on 'Righteousness', 'Truth', 'Judgement', 'Knowledge' and 'Wisdom' as opposed, for instance, to 'Evil' and 'fornication'. The 'Righteousness' and 'fornication' themes at Qumran are, as we have seen, particularly strong. Though it is perhaps possible to identify themes such as these in literature of the Second Temple period generally, their emphasis in documents like this one is particularly telling.

It is also interesting to see the descendants of Levi or the priests denoted in 1.2.2 as 'a Righteous seed'. This has clear 'Zadokite' implications according to some of the definitions we have set forth above, particularly when 'Zadok' is taken in its esoteric sense as denoting 'Righteousness'. The reference to 'Abel Mayin' in 1.2.17 is interesting, too. This is particularly true in view of the visionary materials from 18–21 thereafter.

In 2 Chr. 16:4 Abel Mayin is designated as a city in Naphtali probably on the way to Syria in the northern part of the country. In this text it is probably being seen as the location of Jacob's famous vision in Gen. 28:10–19 of a ladder by which the Angels ascended to Heaven (and descended). The visionary material in 18–21 projects Levi as another of these heavenly voyagers who are so much a part of the literature of Heavenly Ascents. It has much in common with the literature of visionary recitals in Chapter 1 and that of Hymns and Mysteries in Chapter 7.

Lines 5–6 in the first column of Fragment 4 begin with the rather typical emphasis on works Righteousness and Truth. From Line 8 onwards, however, after the reference to '*Torah*' and 'traditional interpretation', the focus quickly moves on to Wisdom, and is hardly distinguishable from texts like the Admonitions to the Sons of Dawn, the Sons of Righteousness, and the Demons of Death below. The reference in Line 4 to Levi as a 'friend of God', if allowed, also parallels similar denotations about Abraham, Isaac and Jacob, already noted in Chapter 3. From Line 16 Column 2, the fragment shifts emphasis to Messianic-style visions of the Kingdom reminiscent both of Dan. 2:44 and Pseudo-Daniel collections.

Fragment 5 is, of course, a typically Righteousness-oriented apocalypse using the by now well-known Qumran nomenclature of 'walking' (either in Light or Darkness) and 'Ways'. It emphasizes two previous, primordial 'Righteous Ones' of the utmost importance to this tradition, Enoch and Noah. Manuscript B Fragment 1, is a mundane, rather typical, recital of the paraphernalia of Temple sacrifice.

TRANSLITERATION
Manuscript A Fragment 1 Column 1

] .8	דן [
] .9	אנה [
] .10	אתרחע]ת וכל
] .11	אדין עיני ואנפי] נטלת לשמיא
] .12	ואצבעת כפי וידי [
] .13	וצלית ו]אמרת מרי אנתה
ידע] .14	א]נתה בלחודיך ידע
] .15	כל] ארחת קשט ארחק
מני] .16	ב]אישא וזנותא דחא
] .17	ח]כמה ומנדע ונבורה
הב לי] .18	לא]שכחה רחמיך קדמיך
] .19	דשפיר ודטב קדמיך [
] .20	א]ל תשלט בי כל שטן
] .21	ע]לי מרי וקרבני למהוא לכה

Fragment 1 Column 2

.8	לע]יניך	[
.9	מרי ב]רכת	[
.10	זרע דק]שטא	שמע נא]
.11	צלות עב]דך לוי	למעבד]
.12	דין קשט לכ]ל עלמין	אל תעדי]
.13	לבר עבדך מן ק]דמיך	[
.14	כאדין נגדת ב]	[
.15	על אבי יעקוב וכד]י	[
.16	מן אבל מין אדין]	[
.17	שכבת ויתבת אנה ע]ל מי דן	[
.18	אדין חזוין אחזית]	[

19. בחזית חזויא וחזית שמ[יא פתיחין וחזית טורא [

20. תחותי רם עד דבק לשמי[א והוית בה ואתפתחו]

21. לי תרעי שמיא ומלאך חד [אמר לי לוי על [

Fragment 3

1.] כהנותך מן כל בשר [ ]

2.] ו]אנה אתעירת מן שנתי אדין

3. [אמרת חזוא הוא דן וכדן אנה מתמה די להוה לי כל חזוה וטמר]ת
אף דן בלבבי ולכל אנש לא

4. [גליתה ועלנא על אבי יצחק ואף הוא כדן ברכני אדין כ]די הוה יעקוב אבי מעשר

5. [כל מה די הוה לה כנדרה לאל אנה הוית קדמי בראש כהני]ה ולי מן בנוהי יהב

Fragment 4 Column 1

1. [ובשנת מאה ותמנה עשרה לחיי היא שנתא ד]מית בה

2. [יוסף אחי קרית לבני ולבניהן ושרית לפקדה] אנון

3. [כל די הוה עם לבבי ענית ואמרת לבני שמעו] למאמר

4. [לוי אבוכן והציתו לפקודי ידיד אל] אנה לכן

5. [מפקד בני ואנה קשטא לכן מחוה חביבי ראש] כל עבדכן

6. [להוה קשטא ועד עלמא תהוה] ק[ימה] צדקתא וקשטה

7.] *vacat* ותעלון עללה בריכה ט[בה דזרע טב טב מעל

8. [ודי זרע באש עלוהי תאב זרע]ה *vacat* וכען ספר ומוסר וחכמה

9. [אלפו לבניכן ותהוה חכמתא עמכן] ליקר עלם די אלף חכמה יקר

10. [היא בה ודי שאט חכמתא לב]סרן ולשיטו מתיהב חזו לכן בני

11. [ליוסף אחי די מאלף הוא ספר ומוס]ר חכמה ליקר ולרב ולמלכין

12. [ ] אל תמחלו חכמתא למאלף

13. [ ].ל.ל גבר די אלף חכמה כל

14. [יומוהי אריכין ושגה לה שומע]א לכל מת ומדינה די יהך לה

15. [אחא   הוה בה ולא מתנכר הוא] בה ולא דמא בה לנכרי ולא

16. [דמא בה לכל זר מן די כלהן יה]בין לה בה יקר כדי כלא צבין

17. [למאלף מן חכמתה רחמו]הי שניאין ושאלו שלמה רברבין

18. [ועל כרסיה די יקר מותבין לה בדיל] למשמע מלי חכמתה

19. [עותר רב די יקר היא חכמתא ל]ידעיה ושימה בה

20. [לכל קניה הן יאתון מלכין] תקיפ[י]ן ועם [רב] חיל

Fragment 4 Column 2

1. מטמוריה ולא יעלון תרעיה ולא [ ]

2. ישכחון למכבש שוריה *vacat* ולא [ ]

3. יחזון שיחתה שימתה ד[לא] ת. [ ]

4. ולא איתי [כ]ל מחיר נגדה כ]   כל אנש [

5. בעא חכמת[א חכ]מתא י[מטא]נה [ ]   ולא[

6. מטמרה מנה [ ]   [א לא] א[

7. ולא חס[י]י[ר]ה   [כל בעי[ן] .]
8. בקשט]   [ספר ומוסר
9. ח[כ]מה ‹די› אלפ[ו]   [תרחין אנון
10. .]   [רבה תתנון
11. [י[קר   *vacat*
12. א.]   [אף בספריא
13. ק.]   [ותהו[ו]ן ראשין ושפטין
14. וד.]   [ב ועבדין
15. [אף כהנין ומלכין [
16. [[ן מלכותכן
17. תה[ו]וה לעלמין .]   לא איתי סוף
18. ת..]   מלכותה לא[תעבר מנכן עד כל
19. ל..]   [ביקר רב .]

Fragment 5

1. [אנ[תן תחשכון]   [
2. [א הלא קבל [ח]נוך]   [
3. [נח ועל מן תהוא חובתא]   [
4. [הלא עלי ועליכן בני ארו ידעתה]
5. [א[ר]חת קש‹ט›א תשבק[ו]ן [ו]כל שבילי
6. [תמחלון ותהכון בחשו[כ]ה [
7. [עקה רבה תתא עליכן [ו]תתי[ה]בון]
8. [[ש.]   [עז ומ]   ]ל תהוון לשכלין

Manuscript B Fragment 1

1. [לאסקה למדבחא הוי עוד תאב ורחע ידיך ורגליך ומקריב עעי]ן מצלחין
2. [ובקר אנון לקד]מין מן כו]ל תולעא וב[אד]י[ן [אסק] אנו]ן ארי]
כדן חזית לאברהם
3. [אבי מזדהר מן] כול לבוך *vacat* [תרי ע]שר עעין א[מ]ר לי [די חזין
ל]אסקא מנהון למדבחא
4. [די ריח חננהון] בסים סלק ואלן שמה[תהו]ן א[רזא ודפ]רנא וסונדא
5. [ואטולא ושיטא ואורנא ברותא ותאנתא ועע משחא ע]רא ארסא ועעי
6. [ע]ר[ק]תא אלן א[נון אמר די] אלן אנון די ח[זין לאסקא מנהון] לתחות עלתא
7. על מדבחא *vacat* ו[כדי תשרה לאסק]א מן [עעי]א אלן על מדבח[א]
ונור[א ישרה]
8. ל[א]ד[ל]קא בהון והא באדין למזרק דמא] על כותלי מדבחא ותוב [רחע]
9. [ידיך ורגליך מן דמא ושרי לאסקא] אברי]ן [מ]לי[ח]ין רא[שה הוי]

TRANSLATION

Manuscript A Fragment 1 Column 1 (8) . . . this (9) . . . I (10) . . . I
[washed myself] and all (11) [. . . then] I raised [my eyes and my

countenance] to Heaven (12) . . . my toes and my fingers (13) [. . . I prayed and] said, 'My Lord, You (14) know . . . You alone know (15) [. . . all] the paths of Truth. Put away (16) [from me . . . Evil and fornication. Turn away (17) [. . . Wi]sdom and Knowledge and strength (18) [give to me . . . [to] find Your Mercy before You (19) . . . that which is pleasant and good before You (20) . . . let [no]t any satan (here, possibly 'enemy') have power over me (21) [. . . up]on me, Lord, and bring me forward to be Your . . .

Fragment 1 Column 2 (8) [Your] e[yes . . .] (9) Lord, [You] bl[essed . . .] (10) a Righ[teous] seed. [. . . Hear, please,] (11) the prayer of [Your] ser[vant Levi . . . to do] (12) a True Judgement for al[l time . . . Do not remove] (13) the son of Your servant from [Your] pre[sence . . .] (14) Then I continued on . . . (15) to my father Jacob and whe[n . . .] (16) from Abel Mayin. Then (17) I lay down and I remained a[t Abel Mayin . . .] (18) Then I was shown visions . . . (19) in the vision of visions, and I saw Hea[ven opened and I saw the mountain] (20) beneath me, as high as to reach to Heav[en, and I was on it. Then were opened] (21) to me the gates of Heaven, and an Angel [spoke to me, 'Levi, enter . . .']

Fragment 3 (1) . . . your priesthood above all flesh (2) [. . . And] I awoke from my sleep. Then (3) [I said, 'This is a vision, and thus I am amazed that I should have any vision at all.'] I [hid] this also in my heart; to no person did I (4) [reveal it. And we went to my (grand)father Isaac, and he also blessed me thus. Then, wh]en Jacob my father was tithing (5) [everything that he owned according to a vow made to God, for the first time I was at the head of the priest]s, and to me of (all) his sons he gave . . .

Fragment 4 Column 1 (1) [And in the hundred and eighteenth year of my life, the year] in which died (2) [my brother Joseph, I called my children and their children and began to instruct] them (3) [concerning all that was in my heart. I said to my children, 'Listen] to the word (4) [of Levi your father, and pay heed to the instructions of God's friend.] I [instruct] you, (5) [my sons, and I reveal the Truth to you, my beloved. The essence] of each of your works (6) [must be Truth. May Righteousness always] re[main] with you, and Truth. (7) [Then you shall have a blessed and g]ood [harvest.] He who sows Good reaps Good, (8) [while he who sows Evil,] his [sowing turns against him.] And now, my sons, [teach *Torah*, its interpretation and Wisdom (9) [to your sons, and Wisdom shall be with you] as an eternal honor. He who teaches Wisdom (10) [will find] honor [therein. He who despises Wisdom] will be given [to con]tempt and disdain. Observe, my sons, (11) [Joseph my brother, who taught *Torah* and interpreta]tion and Wisdom. (He received) honor and became a great man, both to kings (12) . . . Do not exchange Wisdom for a teacher (13) . . . a foreigner. He who teaches Wisdom, all (14) [the days of his life shall be long, and his reputat]ion [shall grow great.] In every land and country to which he goes (15) [he has a brother, and is not like a stranger] in it, nor like a foreigner in it, neither (16) [is he like an unfamiliar person there. For all gi]ve him honor there, because everyone wants (17) [to learn from his Wisdom.] His [friends] are numerous, and many seek his welfare. (18) [They seat him on the seat of honor, in order] to hear his words of Wisdom. (19) [Wisdom is a great richness of honor for] those who know it, and it is a treasure (20) [for everyone who possesses it. If] migh[t]ly [kings come] with a [great] (and) powerful army . . .

Fragment 4 Column 2 (1) (they will not find) its hidden places, and they shall not enter its gates, nor . . . (2) will they be able to conquer its walls. And not . . . (3) they will see its fodder, its treasure that does [not] . . . (4) for which there is [n]o price . . . [Any man] (5) who seeks Wisdo[m, Wi]sdom [will find] him . . . [it will not] (6) be hidden from him . . . (7) and not la[c]king . . . all who see[k] (8) in Truth . . . *Torah* and interpretation, (9) Wi[sd]om that [they] teach . . . they are two (10) . . . great. You will give (11) [. . . h]onor . . . (12) Also in books (13) [. . . you will b]e leaders and judges (14) . . . and servants (15) . . . also priests and kings (16) . . . your Kingdom (17) will l[ast forever . . . there will be no end (18) . . . [the Kingdom will not] pass away from you until (19) . . . in great honor.

Fragment 5 (1) [. . . y]ou will be darkened . . . (2) did not [E]noch complain . . . (3) Noah, and upon whom does the guilt fall? . . . (4) is it not upon me and upon you, my sons? Now, you know (5) . . . the [W]ays of Righteousness you will aba[n]don, [and] all the ways (6) . . . you will renounce, and you will walk in Darkn[ess] (7) . . . great oppression will come upon you, [and] you will be gi[ve]n (8) . . . you will become fools . . .

Manuscript B Fragment 1 (1) to offer up on the altar (anything fitting), wash your hands and feet once again. And offer] split [woo]d. (2) [Examine it fir]st for an[y worms, and t]he[n offer] it up, [for] thus I saw Abraham (3) [my father taking care regarding] anything that might restrain (him from offering the wood). Any of [twel]ve woods [that are fitting] he to[ld] me [to] offer up on the altar, (4) [whose smoke] rises up with a pleasant odor. These are th[eir] na[mes:] ce[dar, jun]iper, almond, (5) [fir, pine, ash, cypress, fig, oleaster, la]urel, myrtle and (6) as[ph]althos. These are th[ose he said] are fitt[ing to offer up] under the burnt offering (7) on the altar. And [when you begin to off]er up one of these [wood]s upon [the] altar and the [fire begins] (8) to bu[rn them, you are to sprinkle the blood] on the sides of the altar. Again, [wash] (9) [your hands and feet of the blood, then begin to offer up] sa[lt]ed portion[s.] As for [its[he[ad,] . . .

28. A FIRM FOUNDATION (AARON A – 4Q541)

The relationship of this text to the Aramaic Testament of Levi above should be clear. In fact, there is no real reason to consider it distinct from it, but rather simply another version or portion of it. The working title, 4QAaron, must be seen as a convention, nothing more, though it does reflect the priestly character of some of the material, particularly the references in Column 2.4 to 'burnt offerings' and being 'a Foundation of peace' and similar allusions, including more 'Foundation' imagery in Columns 4 and 6. The reference in 6.3 to 'brothers', however, would rather suggest a more direct attribution to Levi than Aaron, though the implication might simply be the same general priestly and Levitical thrust of the two Testaments attributed to Kohath and Amram – two more descendants of Levi – below.

The relationship of this text to extant Testament of Levi literature in other languages, as well as to Daniel and Enoch materials – particularly as it turns more apocalyptic in Columns 4–5 – is also strong. These columns parallel the famous eschatological portions of the Greek Testament of Levi 17ff. Apart from the usual allusions to 'Wisdom', 'Mysteries' and some visionary thrust in the first two columns, one should note in 4.1 the emphasis on 'making atonement for all the sons of his generation'.

This 'atonement' imagery is strong in other Qumran literature like the Vision of the Four Kingdoms in Chapter 2 and the Community Rule (viii.6–10). In the latter, it is definitively related to the Council of the Community, who stand as both an 'Inner Sanctum' or 'Holy of Holies' for Aaron and a 'House' or 'Temple' for Israel. It is, of course, strong, too, in early Christianity as we have seen. The use of the imagery of a 'firm Foundation', again so prominent here, is very strong in the Qumran Hymns and the Community Rule as well, the last particularly where the Community Council and spiritualized 'atonement' imagery is concerned. It is even alluded to in the New Testament. It is, of course, generically related to 'Rock' imagery in the latter tradition. In the Qumran Hymns it is not only accompanied by this imagery and that of 'the Cornerstone', but also that of the 'Tower', 'wall' and 'Fortress', of the kind also associated with James, who was called in early Christian tradition both 'Protection of the people' and 'Fortress'.

The use of the word 'swallow' in Column 2.8 is also interesting, because of its relevance to 'swallowing' imagery at Qumran generally. Though this imagery is used here in regard to Wisdom, it usually

Wadi Murabbaʿat on the way to Bar Kochba cave in the Judean Wilderness

Interior of Cave 4 at Qumran

Qumran marl terraces with Cave 4 visible, and the Dead Sea in the distance

Cave 3 at Qumran where the Copper Scroll was found

Cave 4 viewed from Wadi Qumran

Caves 4, 5 and 6 with Wadi Qumran and cliffs in the background

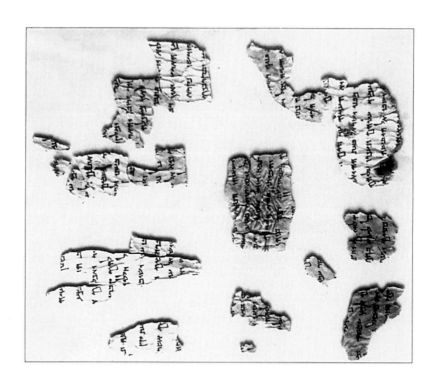

2. Text 2, The Messianic Leader (*Nasi*)

1. Text 1, The Messiah of Heaven and Earth

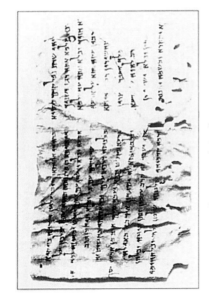

4. Text 12, The Son of God

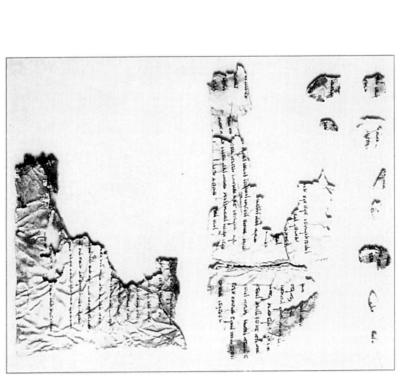

3. Text 6, The New Jerusalem

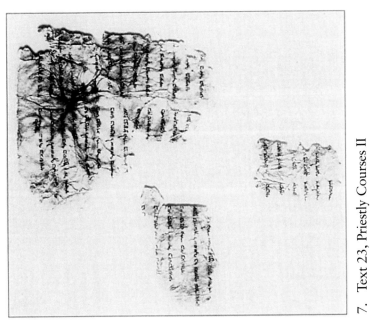

7. Text 23, Priestly Courses II

5. Text 14, A Genesis Florilegium

6. Text 22, Priestly Courses I

8. Text 24, Priestly Courses III – Aemilius Kills

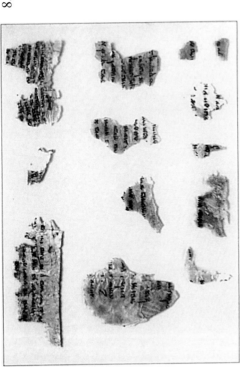

9. Text 29, The Testament of Kohath

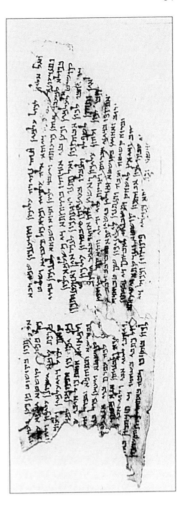

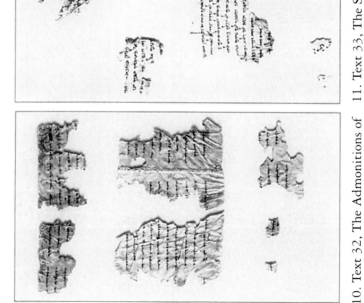

10. Text 32, The Admonitions of the Sons of Dawn (Cryptic)

11. Text 33, The Sons of Righteousness (Proverbs)

12. Text 34, The Demons of Death (Beatitudes)

15. Text 36, Second Letter on Works Reckoned as Righteousness

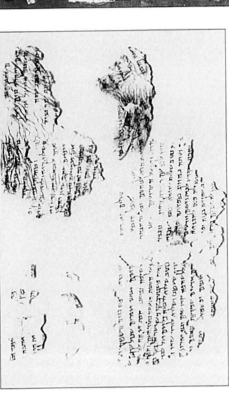

13. Text 35, First Letter on Works Reckoned as Righteousness

14. Text 35, First Letter on Works Reckoned as Righteousness

16. Text 36, Second Letter on Works
Reckoned as Righteousness

18. Text 38, Mourning, Seminal
Emissions, etc. (Purity Laws Type A)

17. Text 37, A Pleasing Fragrance (*Halakhah* A)

19. Text 40, The Last Column of the Damascus Document

20. Text 40, The Last Column of the Damascus Document

21. Text 41, The Chariots of Glory

22. Text 44, The Children of Salvation (Yesha‘) and the Mystery of Existence

23. Text 45, Brontologion

24. Text 49, He Loved His Bodily Emissions (A Record of Sectarian Discipline)

25. Text 50, Paean for King Jonathan (Alexander Jannaeus)

Masada Step Palace with the Dead Sea in the distance

occurs, as we have seen, in connection with 'sons of Belial' or 'sons of Darkness' imagery generally, of the kind one finds in Columns 4–5 of this document. As delineated in some of the *pesharim*, these last together with 'the Liar' are responsible for the destruction of the Righteous Teacher. In this document, too, this imagery in turn moves in Column 4.4ff. into an allusion to 'Lying' and reference to 'violence' generally. This last in Columns 5–6 gives way to the usual emphasis on 'walking', probably in the Ways of Darkness and Light. Even the allusion here to *hamas* ('violence') is widely paralleled in the published corpus, particularly in the Habakkuk *Pesher*, as are allusions to formulae like 'wandering astray' (4.6), usually 'wandering astray in a trackless waste without a Way' as in Column i of the Damascus Document.

The reconstruction involving 'crucifixion' in Column 6 is also interesting, if it is finally to be entertained. Here, combined with the 'firm Foundation' imagery, it moves into a splendid evocation of eternal life in terms of reference to the 'Light' imagery so widespread at Qumran and, of course, the beginning of the Gospel of John. This imagery has much in common with that of the testamental bequests and recitations associated with Kohath and Amram.

TRANSLITERATION   Column 1 (Fragment 6)

[	]ר עמי]קין	] .1
[	] די לא מתכונן וכת]ב	] .2
[	ו]ישחיק ימא רבא מ.]	] .3
[	] אדין יתפתח]ון] ספרי חכ]מתא	] .4
[	] מאמרה וכ]]שין חכ]	] .5

Column 1 (Fragment 2)

מל]ין] [ ] וכרעות	] .1
]נה לי עוד כתב	] .2
מל]לת עלוהי באוחידואן	] .3
] קריב לעלי להן רחיק מני	] .4
] להו]ה ע]מ]יק ח]זוה ....ת פריא	] .5

Column 2

[	]ו[ ]ל[ ]] .1
[	]מ]ן] קודם אל] .2
[	תסב מכא]בין .3
[	ו]ת]בריך עלת]הון ותקים ל]הון יסוד שלמכ]ה .4
] חדי	רוחך ותחד]ה באלהך ונס]ב אנה לכה מתלו]ין .5

6. ארו חכים [יבין די אנא חזה] ומתבונן בעמיק[י]ן וממ[לל   א[ו]חידוא[ן]
7. יואן [לא יבין ומדע חכ]מה יאתה לעליכה די נסיבת   ת[קנה ....]
8. רדף לה ובעי [לה והחסן ל]ה למבלע ארו שני תח[ןדה   שני אתר]

Column 4

1.] וסגה ח]כמתה ויכפר על כול בני דרה וישתלח לכול בני
2. [דר]ה מאמרה כמאמר שמין ואלפונה כרעות אל שמש עלמה תניר
3. ויחזה נורחא בכול קצוי ארעא ועל חש[ו]כא תניר אדין יעדה חשוכא
4. [מן] ארעא וערפלא מן יבישתא שניאן מלין עלוהי יאמרון ושנה
5. [כדב]ין ובדיאן עלוהי יבדון גניאין עלוהי [י]מללון דרה בא<יש>א< יאפיך
6. [ורגז רב] להוה ו[ב]שקר וחמס מקמה [ו]יטעה עמא [ב]יומוהי וישתבשון

Column 5 (Fragment 5)

1.] ומכאבין על מ]
2.] די[ן]כה ולא תהוה חי[ב
3.] נגדי מכאיביכה .]
4.] לא גוע לונכה וכול]
5.]ת לבכה מן ק]ודם

Column 5 (Fragment 1)

1.] ארו אנ]י חזה חדה]
2. דכרין שבעא חזי]ת
3. קצת בנוהי יהכון]
4. ויתיספון על על]יונין

Column 6

1. [ית]קן אל שניא]ן   וידין] שניאן מגליאן א]דין [
2. בקר ובעי ודע מה יונא בכה ואל תמחי להי ביד שחפא [ות]ליא .]
3. וצצא אל [יק]רוב בה ותקים לאבוכה שם חדוה ולכול אחיכה יסוד [מבחן]
4.].א ותחזה ותחדה בנהיר עלמא ולא תהוה מן שנאה   *vacat*

TRANSLATION
Column 1 (Fragment 6) (1) . . . dee[p things] . . . (2) who doesn't understand. And he wro[te] . . . (3) and he stilled the great sea . . . (4) Then the books of Wis[dom] will be open[ed] . . . (5) his word . . .
Column 1 (Fragment 2) (1) . . . wo[rds] . . . and according to the will of (2) . . . to me. Once more he wrote (3) . . . I [sp]oke concerning it in parables (4) . . . was near to me. Therefore, was far from me (5) . . . The visi[on] will be [profou]nd. . . .the fruit . . .
Column 2 (2) [from] God . . . (3) You shall receive the affli[cted ones] . . . (4) [You] shall bless [their] burnt offerings [and You shall establish for] them

a Foundation of Your peace . . . (5) your Spirit, and you will rejoice [in your God. Now] I [am proclai]ming to you parable[s] . . . rejoice. (6) Behold, a wise man [will understand that I am seeing] and comprehending deep Mysteries, thus I am spea[king . . .] parable[s]. (7) The Greek (?) [will not understand. But the Knowledge of Wis]dom will come to you, for you have received . . . [you] will acquire . . . (8) Pursue her (Wisdom) and seek [her and gain possession of] her to swallow (her) down. Behold, you will gla[dden] many . . . many (will have) a place . . .

Column 4 (1) . . . his Wisdom [will be great.] He will make atonement for all the children of his generation. He will be sent to all the sons of (2) his [generation]. His word shall be as the word of Heaven and his teaching shall be according to the will of God. His eternal sun shall burn brilliantly. (3) The fire shall be kindled in all the corners of the earth. Upon the Darkness it will shine. Then the Darkness will pass away (4) [from] the earth and the deep Darkness from the dry land. They will speak many words against him. There will be many (5) [lie]s. They will invent stories about him. They will say shameful things about him. He will overthrow his evil generation (6) and there will be [great wrath]. When he arises there will be Lying and violence, and the people will wander astray [in] his days and be confounded.

Column 5 (Fragment 5) (1) . . . and those who are grieved concerning . . . (2) your ju[dgment] but you will not be gui[lty] . . . (3) the scourging of those who afflict you . . . (4) your complaint (?) will not fail and all . . . (5) your heart be[fore] . . .

Column 5 (Fragment 1) (1) [Behold] I saw one . . . (2) I saw seven rams . . . (3) Some of his sons shall walk . . . (4) They shall be gathered to the Heav[enly Beings] . . .

Column 6 (1) God [will set] right error[s] . . . [He will judge] revealed sins . . . (2) Investigate and seek and know how Jonah wept. Thus, you shall not destroy the weak by wasting away or by [crucif]ixion. . . . (3) Let not the nail touch him. Then you shall raise up for your father a name of rejoicing and for all of your brothers a [firm] Foundation. (4) . . . You shall see and you shall rejoice in the Eternal Light and you will not be one who is hated (of God).

29. TESTAMENT OF KOHATH (4Q542)
(Plate 9)

This text belongs to the genre of pseudepigrapha like the Testament of Levi and A Firm Foundation (Aaron A) above. All of these texts, including the one attributed to Amram below, are associated with one or other of the principal characters in the priestly succession; in fact, we may be witnessing a tradition here not dissimilar to that of the Rabbinical one (e.g. the *Pirke Abbot*), where one after another of the important Rabbinical figures in the line of succession had important sayings attributed to him. Instead of a succession of rabbis, however, this one would have consisted of priestly forebears.

The line can be seen as starting with Noah and Enoch, descending through Abraham to Levi, and from him on down through his son Kohath and his grandson Amram, to Moses and Aaron. From there it moves, presumably through Eleazar and Phineas, to the entire priestly establishment taking their legitimacy in some manner from either their descent or their relationship to these early forebears.

This text derives its name from an allusion to Amram as 'my son' in Line 9 of the Second Column, and to Levi as the 'father' of the speaker in Line 11. (For Kohath's genealogy, see Exod. 6:16ff.) Here, we have as beautifully preserved a piece of pseudepigrapha as one could wish. The instructions it conserves are also of the most high-minded, zealous, and xenophobic kind, presumably in the style of the proverbial Phineas (also a descendant of Kohath), the archetypical progenitor of both Maccabean and Zealot movements. In this regard, one should also note Jesus' 'zeal' recorded in John 2:27 and Acts 21:20's parallel characterization of James' followers as 'zealous for the Law'. These instructions are obviously meant to apply to the entire priesthood relating to the family of Moses, including, one would assume, the Levites themselves.

The text has been dated by those who rely on palaeography to 100–75 BC, but what one has here, regardless of the reliability of such assessments and the typological sequences on which they are based, is not a formal or 'book' hand, but rather a semi-cursive or private one. As such, it is almost impossible to date. A recent, *single* AMS Carbon 14 test done on the parchment yielded a date of about 300 years earlier. This is obviously unreliable, and the inaccuracy is probably connected with the imprecision of such tests generally and the multiple variables that can skew results. It should be noted that C-14 tests in manuscript studies tend to make documents seem older than they actually are, not *vice versa*.

The crucial passage in this text is the one in Lines 5–6 of Column 1 having to do with foreigners coming into the country – particularly, in Line 7, foreign masters who have taken it over – and being humiliated and trampled on by them. It is possible to read the reference to 'violent men' in Line 6 as 'confiscators' or 'expropriators'. As in 1 Macc. 13:36ff., this allusion may not simply relate to violence, but possibly to foreign taxation. It can also be read as 'violent ones' as we have rendered it, which has important overtones with other Qumran texts. A third way of reading it is as a reference to 'men of *mixed blood*' (italics ours). Such a reading would strengthen the relationship of the entire allusion to 'Herodians' – the family of Herod and those owing their positions to them – who were certainly regarded as 'hybrids' or of 'mixed' parentage if not outright foreigners altogether. However this allusion is read – whether in one or a combination of these senses – it is a tantalizing notice, and the antagonism to foreign control, particularly of the priesthood, should be clear. These xenophobic instructions resemble nothing so much as the outlook of 'the Zealots', a militant group in the First Jewish Revolt against Rome (AD 66–70) with roots going back to the Maccabean period and similar uprisings and independence movements in that period (second to first centuries BC).

This nationalistic theme of antagonism to foreigners not only runs across the spectrum of these documents, but can be rationalized to include objections to appointment of high priests by foreigners and their gifts and sacrifices in the Temple, which both the Pharisees and the priesthood dominated by them (i.e. the 'Herodian Sadducees') seemed to have been prepared to accept throughout this period, but which the Zealots and others opposing Roman/Herodian rule in Palestine were not.

In an all-important passage in the *Jewish War*, Josephus describes this unwillingness to accept gifts from and sacrifices on behalf of foreigners in the Temple as an 'innovation' which 'our forefathers' were unacquainted with before (2.409–14). This would include, not only the Roman Emperor, on whose behalf sacrifices were made daily, but also Herodians, looked upon by 'zealot' groups such as these as 'foreigners' because of their Arab and Idumaean origins. For Josephus, these circumstances led directly to the uprising against Rome. From the period 4 BC–AD 7, when most of the first-century revolutionary activity began, the tax issue was a burning one, particularly in the struggle between the upper-class establishment and the masses.

Nor can these objections be seen as unrelated to those in the Damascus Document, nor the two Letters on Works Righteousness in Chapter 6 below, about 'pollution of the Temple' (one of the 'three nets of Belial'). The Damascus Document, vi.16 specifically raises the issue of the pollution of 'the Temple treasure' (followed on the same line by a reference to 'robbing the Meek') and graphically delineates these pollutions in v–viii.

The conditions described in this text could, therefore, apply, not only to the Herodian period (37 BC–AD 70), where we are inclined to place the text, but also to any time prior to that, particularly in the

Maccabean period. However, it must be appreciated that should the text date to the Maccabean period, it, like the Testament of Levi and the Daniel cycle related to it, must be seen as supporting a Maccabean-style priesthood and their 'Covenant of Phineas', that is, a native as opposed to a foreign-imposed one (1 Macc. 2:26–28). New texts such as these, and of course the stark, apocalyptic nationalism evident across the whole corpus from Qumran, are bringing this proposition more and more vividly to light, as opposed to the earlier consensus that led the public to believe that the group responsible for these writings could somehow, quite mystifyingly, have been anti-Maccabean. The Paean to King Jonathan, with which we end this collection, will further corroborate this proposition.

Where paying the Roman tax was concerned, Josephus refers to it when describing the birth of what now goes by the name of 'the Zealot movement' (Josephus calls it 'the Fourth Philosophy'). In fact, the tax issue was central to the split between Herodian Saducees and 'opposition Sadducees' signalled in our discussion of the Priestly Courses/'Aemilius Kills' text above. Josephus presents a high priest, one Joezer the son of Boethus – the obscure priest from Egypt Herod had promoted after marrying his daughter (i.e. a Herodian or *Boethusian* Sadducee) – as successfully convincing the people *to pay* the tax to Rome which the Herodians collected.

Joezer's opposite number – someone Josephus mysteriously refers to as *'Sadduk'* (italics ours) – he portrays as joining Judas the Galilean mentioned in Acts, the proverbial founder of the Zealot movement, in agitating *against the tax* (*Ant* 18.4–5). The Gospels, prefiguring Paul's position thereafter, for their part portray Jesus as teaching the people *to pay* the tax. Paul treated the issue of paying taxes to Rome appropriately in Romans 13. According to one perspective his approach could not be more cynical, yet it is revealing. He applies the key 'Law-Breaker' terminology we find in the Scrolls and the Letter of James to those who *break* Roman law not Jewish. 'God's Law' he calls the law of *the State*, even going so far as to portray Roman officials and tax-collectors as 'God's officers' (Rom. 13:6). According to this view, that Gospels writers after him did not scruple to portray their 'Jesus' as keeping 'table fellowship' with *tax-collectors* – even fornicators – should not be surprising.

As always in these texts, and the Firm Foundation text above, one should note the emphasis on 'Righteousness', 'Truth', 'Judgement' and 'Uprightness', as opposed to 'Evil', 'fornication' and 'deceitfulness'. Part of the second column of this text was previously published under the mistaken identification of the Testament of Amram, presumably because of the mention of Amram in 2.9.

TRANSLITERATION

Fragment 1 Column 1

1. ואל אלין לכול עלמין ו<י>נהר נהירה עליכון ויודענכון שמה רבא
2. ותנדעונה {ותנד'ע[ו]נה} די הוא אלה עלמיה ומרא כול מעבדיא ושליט
3. בכולא למעבד בהון כרעותה ויעבד לכון חדוא ושמחא לבניכון בדרי
4. קוש{ו}ט<א> לעלמין וכען בני אזדהרו בירוחתא די מש<א>למא לכון
5. די יהבו לכון אבהתכון ואל תתנו ירותתכון לנכראין ואחסנותכון
6. לכילאין וחהון לשפלו ולנבלו בעיניהון ויבסרון עליכון די
7. להון תותבין לכון ולהון עליכון ראשין להן אחדו במםר יעק<ו>ב
8. אבוכון ואתחקפו בדיני אברהם ו<ב>צדקת לוי ודילי והוא קד<י>[ש]ין ודכין
9. מן כול *vacat* ברוב ואחדין בקושטא ואזלין בישירותא ולא בלבב ולבב
10. להן בלבב דכא וברוח קשיטא וטבה ותנתנון לי ביניכון שם טב וחדוא
11. ללוי ושמח לי[ע]קוב וד'יאך לישחק ותשבוחא לאברהם די נטרתון
12. והולכתון ירות[ת]א ב]נ<י> שבקו לכון אבהתכון קושטא וצדקתא וישירותא
13. ותמימותא ודכ[ו]תא וק[ו]דשא וכ[הו]נתא ככ[ו]ל די פקדתון וככול די

Fragment 1 Column 2

1. אלפתכון בקושוט מן כען ועד כו[ל עלמין   [
2. מלי ממר קושטא יאתא עליכ[ון   [
3. ברכת עלמא ישכונן עליכון ולהו[ן   [
4. קאם לכול דרי עלמין ול<א> עוד תפ[ן   [
5. מן יסודכון ותקומון למדן דין .]   [
6. למחזיא חובת כול חיבי עלמין הב[[
7. ובאשיא ובתהומ<י>א ובכול חלליא לבלב[[
8. ב[ד]רי קושטא ויעדרון כול בני רשע[א   [
9. וכען לכה עמרם ברי אנא מפקד[[
10. ו[לבנ]יכא ולבניהון אנא מפקד ל[[
11. ויהבו ללוי אבי ולוי אבי לי [יהב   [
12. וכול כתבי בשהדו די תזדהרון בהון]   [
13. לכון בהון זכו רבה באתהולכותהון עמכון] *vacat*   [

Fragment 2 Column 1

5. [	עקרא ו]	[
6. [	]ן בנוהי [	[
7. [	]. באנושא ובחין]ין	[
8. [	ר/דצא [	[
9. [	מרש]	[
10. [	על]יהון ו.	[
11. [	].וכ ולח[	[
12. [	נהיר להן]	[
13. [	ואנא רוז]	[

Fragment 3 Column 1
(written vertically in the left margin of the column)

].ל שורש<ה>

Fragment 3 Column 2

[11. [   ] [בה יקרו אבניא א.]

[12. [ ]ן להון מן זנותא שני מן די]

[13. לחדה די לא אי תאי לה כול כ]

TRANSLATION

Fragment 1 Column 1 (1) . . . and God of Gods for all Eternity. And He will shine as a Light upon you and He will make known to you His great Name (2) and you will know Him, that He is the Eternal God and Lord of all creation, and sovereign (3) over all things, governing them according to His will. And He will give you joy and your sons rejoicing for generations of (4) the Truth, forever. And now, my sons, be watchful of your inheritance that has been bequeathed to you, (5) which your fathers gave you. Do not give your inheritance to foreigners, nor your heritage to (6) violent men, lest you be regarded as humiliated in their eyes, and foolish, and they trample upon you, for (7) they will come to dwell among you and become your masters. Therefore, hold fast to the word of Jacob (8) your father, and be strong in the Judgements of Abraham, and in the Righteousness of Levi and myself. Be Holy and pure (9) from all *vacat* entirely, and hold to the Truth, walking uprightly without Deceitfulness, (10) but rather with a pure heart and in a True and Good Spirit. Thus you will grant to me a good name among you, together with joy (11) for Levi and happiness for J[a]cob; rejoicing for Isaac and blessing for Abraham, inasmuch as you guarded (12) and walked (in) the inheri[tance. My so]ns, your fathers bequeathed to you Truth, Righteousness, Uprightness, (13) integrity, pur[ity, Ho]lliness and the priesthood. In accordance with what you have been commanded, and according to all that

Fragment 1 Column 2 (1) I have taught you in Truth, from now and for al[l Eternity . . . (2) the words of the Truthful saying. There will come upon yo[u . . . (3) eternal blessings shall rest upon you. And there shall b[e . . . (4) enduring to all the generations of Eternity. And no longer shall you . . . (5) from your Foundation, and you shall endure to pronounce Judgements . . . (6) to reveal the sin of all the eternal sinners . . . (7) and the Wicked and in the depths of the sea and in all the hollows of the earth . . . (8) in [gener]ations of Truth, while all the sons of Evi[l] will pass away . . . (9) And now, you, Amram, my son, I appoi[nt . . . (10) and [to] your [son]s and to their sons I appoint . . . (11) and they bequeathed it to Levi my

father, and Levi my father [bequeathed it] to me . . . (12) and all my books
as a testimony, that you take heed of them . . . (13) Great merit [will come]
to you from them as they accompany you in your affairs.
Fragment 2 Column 1 (6) . . . his sons . . . (7) among mankind and among
liv[ing things] . . . (12) a Light. Instead . . . (13) and I . . .
Fragment 3 Column 1 (in the margin) his root.
Fragment 3 Column 2 (11) . . . the stones will call . . . (12) them from all
fornication very much. Whoever . . . (13) exceedingly, for he has no . . .

30. TESTAMENT OF AMRAM (4Q543, 545–548)

The Testament of Amram, if indeed we can call it this – Amram *per se*
is mentioned only in Manuscript C – is one of the most splendid
apocalyptic and visionary works in the corpus. In it, many of the
themes we have encountered in the works discussed above come
together in a fairly rationalized eschatological whole. These include
the usual 'Light', 'Darkness', 'Belial', 'Righteousness', 'Truth', 'Lying'
and 'Watcher' vocabulary, including the very nice allusions to 'sons of
Righteousness' – which we have already identified as a variant of the
'sons of Zadok' terminology – 'sons of Light', 'sons of Darkness' and
'sons of Truth', again widely disseminated through the whole corpus.
Added to these we have the very interesting allusion in Manuscript B
to 'serpents' and 'vipers' encountered in many texts from Qumran (e.g.
CD,v.14), not to mention a well-known parallel imagery in the
Gospels (Matt. 3:7, 23:33, etc.).

Though we cannot be sure that the several fragments and manuscripts represented in this reconstruction in fact belong to the same
composition, nor that they can be sequentially arranged in the manner
shown; there are, in fact, overlaps which seem to indicate multiple
copies of a single work and, in any event, they can be grouped
typologically together. In addition, because of internal and external
similarities, they are probably part of a cycle of literature associated
with Moses' father Amram. This, in turn, is related to the Testament
of Kohath material and the Levi cycle in general.

Manuscript C most fully preserves the beginning of the work, but
has little in common with Manuscript B and Manuscript ?, which on
the basis of content alone obviously belong together. Manuscript ? is
referred to in this way in the literature, no more complete designation
having yet been made. Manuscript C, which includes the names of the
principal *dramatis personae* like Amram, Kohath, Levi, Miriam and

Aaron, pretends to be more historical. It and Manuscript E even give some of the ages of these characters, which are widely out of line with any real chronological understanding of the Exodus sojourn. The surviving fragments do not, however, show any knowledge of a relationship between Miriam and Hur, as suggested in Chapter 3, unless Uzziel and Hur can be equated. One should also note the anachronistic reference to Philistines in 2:19, reflected perhaps too in the Era of Light text in Chapter 8.

It is in Manuscript B, however, and the undesignated one succeeding it, that truly splendid material, which can hardly be referred to as testamentary, emerges. This consists again of a visionary recital of the most intense kind, similar to that in Chapters 1 and 2, the Firm Foundation materials above and in Chapter 7. Here, too, several identifications are made. First, in Line 13 of Manuscript B, the Enochic 'Watchers' are identified with 'the serpent' with 'the visage of a viper' — evidently the same serpent that is connected to the downfall of man in the Adam and Eve story. We have probably already encountered him, as well, in the Tree of Evil text above.

Three more names are accorded him: 'Belial', 'Prince of Darkness' and 'King of Evil'. This latter name, *Melchi Resha^c*, is to be contrasted with the well-known terminology integrally involved with Jesus' Messianic and eschatological priesthood, *Melchi Zedek*/'King of Righteousness', (Heb. 5–7), a subject that has interested scholars heretofore. The latter has two other synonyms, the Archangel Michael, the guardian Angel of Israel, and the Prince of Light (E.3.2).

Tied to these are the other usages, noted above, relating to 'Righteousness', 'Truth', 'Light' and 'Lightness', 'Dark' and 'Darkness', 'Lying' and the like. The 'Way' terminology, again widespread at Qumran and known to early Christianity, is also strong here. All these allusions have their counterparts in their application to the *dramatis personae* of interest to the Qumran writers and their historiography. The text ends with perhaps the most marvellous paean to Light and Dark of any literary work, apart from the Chariots of Glory below and the well-known prologue to the Gospel of John.

TRANSLITERATION   Manuscript C Column 1

1. פרשגן [כתב מלי חזו]ת עמרם בר קהת בר לוי כל
2. די [אחוי לבנוהי ודי פקד א]נון ביום [מותה ב]שנת
3. מאה ותלתין ושת הי]א[שנתא די מותה [בש]נת מא[ה]
4. חמשין ותרתין לגל]ות י]שראל למצרין [ ].בר על]והי ושלח]
5. וקרא לעוזיאל אחוהי זעירא]ואס[כב לה ל]מרי]ם ברת]ה ואמר]

6. אנתה ברת תלתין שנין ועבד משתותה שבעה [יומ]ין
7. ואכל ואשתי במשתותה וחדי אדין כדי אשתציו
8. [י]ומי משתותאא שלח קרא לאהרון לברה ו[הו]א בר שנין
9.]　　　　ואמר] לה קרי ל]]דרי למלאכיה א... מן בית
10.]　　　　.חה לעליה קרא לה

Column 2

11. בארעא דא וסלקת ל.]　　　　　　[
12. למקבר אבהתנא וסלקת]　　　　　　[
13. ל[מ]קם לעמרה ולמבנא .]　　　　　[
14. שניא[י]ן מן בני דרי כחד[א　　　　ומן]
15. עבידתנא [ש]ניאין לח[דא עד במצ]רין מתין]　　　[
16. שמועת קרב ובהלה תאב[ה]תנא לארע מ[צרין　　[
17. לעובד ולא ב[נו קב]ריא די אב[הת]הון ושבקני [אבי קהת למהך]
18. ולמבנה ולמסב לה[ו]ן כל צרכיהון מ[ן ארע כנען]　　וכדי הוו]
19. אנחנא בנין וקר[בא הוא בין] פלשת למצרין ונצח[י]ן　　　[

Manuscript E Fragment 1

1.]　　　　　ל די קרב לוי ברה ל]　　　[
2.]　　　א[מרת לכה על מדב[חא] די אבנ[א　[
3.]　　　　　ע[ל קרבנ]ין　　　　　[

Fragment 2

1.]　　　　　　　]א[　　　　　[
2.]　　　　　[פצית]　　　　　[
3.]　　　　　[בנה]　　　　　[
4.]　　　　[בהר סיני י.]　　　　[
5.]　　　ב[ר]כה רבא על מדבה נהש[א　[
6.]　　בר[ה] יתרם כהן מן כול בני עלמא בא[די]ן　[
7.]　.ח ובנוהי בתרה לכול דרי עלמין בק[ק]ל[שטא　[
8.]　ואנה אתעירת מן שנת עיני וחזוא כתב[ת　　[
9.]　נפקת] מן ארע כנען והוא לי כדי אמר]　[
10.]　מרים ומן באתר[ר] לשנת עש[רי]ן חבת לארע כנען]
11.]　　חון בע]　　　[הויתה]　　　　[
12.]　　　　ה]ו[　　　　　ה]　　　vacat

Manuscript B Fragment 1

9.]　　　　　　חזית עירין]　　　[
10. בחזוי חזוה די חלמא והא תרין דאנין עלי ואמרין]　[
11. ואחדין עלי תגר רב ושאלת אנון אנתון מן די כדן מש[ל]טין　עלי

וענו ואמרו לי אנחנא]

12. [משתח]לטין ושליטין על כול בני אדם ואמרו לי במן מננא אנת[ה
בחר לאשתלטה נטלת עיני וחזית]

13. [וחד] מנהון חזוה דח[י]ל [כפ[תן [ומ]ל[ב]ושה צבענין וחשיך
חשוך] [*vacat*]

14. [ואחרנא חזית] והא [ ]ל[ ] בחזוה אנפוהי
העכן ו]מכסה ב [

15. [לחדה וכול עינוהי [

Fragment 2

1. [ ] מ]שלט עליך [[

2. [ ] וענית ואמרת לה עירא] דן מן הוא ואמר
לי הדן ע]ירא [

3. [ואנון תלתה שמהתה בליעל ושר חשוכא] ומלכי רשע ואמרת מראי
מא ש[ולטן [

4. [ ] וכל ארחה חש]יכה וכל עבדה ח[ש]יך ובחשוכא
הוא].[

5. [ ] אנת]ה חזה והוא משלט על כול חשוכא
ואנה [משלט על כול נהורא]

6. [ ] מן] עליא עד ארעיא אנה שליט על כול
נהורא וכו]ל דאלהא ואנה שליט לאנוש]

Fragment 3

1. [חנה ושלמה ואנה על כול בני נהו]רא אשלטת ושאלתה
[ואמרת לה מה אנון שמהתך]

2. [ ] וענה וא]מר לי דתלתה
שמה]תי אנון מיכאל ושר נהורא ומלכי צדק]

Manuscript ? Column 1

1. [ ] [שבטין] [
2. [ ] תא להון וכל ארח]תה בקשוט [
3. [ ] ויחלם] אנון מן אסיאנהון] [
4. [ ] ח] אנון מן מותא ומן א]בדנא [
5. [ ] ע]ליכון בני ברכתא וש] [
6. [ ] כל דרי ישראל לכל [עלמין [
7. [ ] שי חרא בי די בני צ]דקתא [
8. נתק] [בין בני שקר לבני ק]שוט [
9. אנה [מודע לכון ואף] יצבתא אנה מודע ל[כון ארי כל בני נהורא]
10. נהירין להוון [וכל בני] חשוכא חשיכין להוון [ארי בני נהורא
11. ובכל מנדעהון [לה]וון ובני חשוכה יתא[ב]דון]
12. ארי כל סכל ורש[ע חשיכי]ן וכל [של]ם וקשוט נהיר]ין ארי כל בני נהורא]
13. לנהורא לשמח]ת עלמא לח]דות]א יהכו]ן וכל בני חש]וכה לחשוכה למותא]

[	] לעמא נהירותא ואחוי]לכון	] ולאבדנא יהכון	.14
[	]ן מן חשוכה ארי כל	]וא	.15
[	] וכל בני נהורא	בני]חשוכה	.16

TRANSLATION

Manuscript C Column 1 (1) A copy [of the book of the words of the vis]ion of Amram the son of Kohath, the son of Levi: all (2) that [he revealed to his sons and that he commanded t]hem on the day [of his death, in] the year (3) one hundred and thirty-six, whi[ch] was the year of his death, [in the o]ne hundred (4) and fifty-second year of the exil[e of I]srael to Egypt . . . upon [him, and he sent] (5) to call Uzziel his youngest brother, and [gave] to him [in marr]iage [Miri]am [his] daughter. [For he said] (6) 'You (Miriam) are thirty years old.' Then he gave a wedding feast seven [day]s long, (7) and ate and drank and rejoiced at the feast. Then, when (8) the [d]ays of the wedding feast were completed, he called for Aaron his son. Now, [h]e (Aaron) was a man of . . . years of age (9) [. . . and he said] to him, 'Call . . . and Malachijah . . . from the house of (10) . . . above. He called him . . .

Column 2 (11) in this land, and I went up to . . . (12) to bury our fathers. And I went up . . . (13) to [a]rise, to bind and pile sheaths and to build . . . (14) gre[a]t from the sons of my uncle, all togeth[er . . . and from] (15) our excee[ding g]reat labors, [until in Egy]pt there died . . . (16) the rumor of war and unrest returned . . . to the land of E[gypt . . .] (17) to meet and [they had] not bui[lt gr]aves for their fa[th]ers. Then [my father Kohath] released me [to go,] (18) to build and to get [all their needs] for the[m fr]om the land of Canaan. [And while] (19) we [were] building, wa[r broke out between] the Philistines and Egypt, and . . . was winn[ing . . .]

Manuscript E Fragment 1 (1) . . . that Levi his son sacrificed to . . . (2) I said to you at the alt[ar] of ston[e . . .] (3) [con]cerning sacrifice[s . . .]

Fragment 2 (2) I rescued . . . (3) he built . . . (4) at Mount Sinai . . . (5) a great blessing at the bronz[e] altar . . . (6) from among all the people on earth his [son] will be exalted as a priest. The[n . . .] (7) and his sons after him, for all the generations of eternity in Tru[th . . .] (8) and I awoke from the sleep of my eyes, and [I] wrote down the vision . . . (9) I went out from the land of Canaan, and it happened to me just as he said . . . (10) exalting, and afterwar[d], in the twen[tieth] year, [I returned to the land of Canaan] (11) . . . you were . . .

Manuscript B Fragment 1 (9) [. . . I saw Watchers] (10) in my vision, the dream-vision. Two (men) were fighting over me, saying . . . (11) and holding a great contest over me. I asked them, 'Who are you, that you are thus empo[wered over me?' They answered me, 'We] (12) [have been em]powered and rule over all mankind.' They said to me, 'Which of us do yo[u choose to rule (you)?' I raised my eyes and looked.] (13) [One] of them was terr[i]fying in his appearance, [like a s]erpent, [his] cl[oa]k many-colored yet very dark . . . (14) [And I looked again], and . . . in his appearance, his visage like a viper, and [wearing . . .] (15) [exceedingly, and all his eyes . . .]

Fragment 2 (1) [. `. . em]powered over you . . . (2) [I replied to him,] 'This [Watcher,] who is he?' He answered me, 'This Wa[tcher . . .] (3) [and his three names are Belial and Prince of Darkness] and King of Evil.' I said, 'My lord, what dom[inion . . .?'] (4) ['and his every way is da]rkened, his every work da[rk]ened. In Darkness he . . . (5) [Yo]u saw, and he is empowered over all Darkness, while I [am empowered over all light.] (6) [. . . from] the highest regions to the lowest I rule over all Light, and over al[l that is of God. I rule over (every) man]

Fragment 3 (1) [of His grace and peace. Over all the sons of Lig]ht have] I been empowered.' I asked him, ['What are your names . . . ?'] (2) He [s]aid to me, '[My] three names are [Michael and Prince of Light and King of Righteousness.']

Manuscript ? Column 1 (1) . . . tribes . . . (2) to them and all [his] ways [are True . . .] (3) [and he will heal] them of all their ills . . . (4) them from death and from de[struction . . .] (5) [o]ver you, blessed sons . . . (6) all the generations of Israel for[ever . . .] (7) angry at me, for the sons of Ri[ghteousness . . .] (8) between the sons of Lying and the sons of Tr[uth . . .] (9) I [will make known to you;] certainly I will inform y[ou that all the sons of Light] (10) will be made Light, [whereas all the sons] of Darkness will be made Dark. [The sons of Light . . .] (11) and in all their Knowledge [they will] be, and the sons of Darkness will be dest[ro]yed . . . (12) For all foolishness and Evi[l will be darken]ed, while all [pea]ce and Truth will be made Ligh[t. All the sons of Light] (13) [are destin]ed for Light and [eternal j]oy (and) [re]joic[ing.] All the sons of Dark[ness] are destined for [Darkness and death] (14) and destruction . . . Lightness for the people. And I shall reveal [to you . . .] (15) from Darkness, for all . . . (16) the sons of [Darkness . . .] and all the sons of Light . . .

31. TESTAMENT OF NAPHTALI (4Q215)

The Testament of Naphtali has long been known in its Greek form, which like the Testament of Levi is part of the apocryphal Testament of the Twelve Patriarchs. The original Hebrew or Aramaic version (it was not known which it might be) had, it was long thought, perished in antiquity. Then, in 1894 M. Gaster drew the attention of the scholarly world to medieval manuscripts that contained two slightly different Hebrew versions of the work. The relationship between the Greek and the Hebrew has been a matter of some debate ever since.

The surviving portions of the Qumran version of the work, presented here, will doubtless fuel the debate still further. Column 2 preserves the Hebrew form of the Greek Testament of Naphtali 1:9, 11–12, along with previously unknown details. Column 4 does not parallel any portion of the Greek, and has an eschatological thrust not found in the Greek Testament of Naphtali.

The text, as reconstructed from two separate fragments – and again the reconstruction is not certain – follows the pattern of the Testament of Amram. Here, a more or less straightforward historical narrative is followed by an eschatological presentation of the most intense nature. In fact, this one develops, even in the portion which is extant, into outright Messianism, so that this text, like several others above, could be added to Chapter 1. The prosaic narrative of Column 2 is followed by the ecstatic visionary recital in Column 4.

Only Lines 1–5 in Column 2 parallel Greek Naphtali text 1:9–12. The latter then returns to a rather humdrum admonition, while the present text develops as below. We have inserted the name Rotheos from the Greek text for Bilhah's father in Line 7 for purposes of exposition and not because it actually appears in the Hebrew text. The name itself may have been a comparatively late invention without a Hebrew original, but some name probably does appear in the original.

Here one encounters the usual Messianic vocabulary of 'the Pit' (CD,vi.3–9), *Hassidav* ('His Pious Ones'), 'Knowledge', 'Righteousness', 'Truth', and that predestination implicit in recitals like this in, for instance, the Damascus Document and throughout the already published Qumran Hymns. Here in 4.8, the actions of 'the Righteous' (those 'saved' at the end of time) are known or prepared 'before ever they were created' (see CD,iv.4–7 on 'the sons of Zadok' and 1QH,ix.33–35). Both Paul and James are familiar with this sort of language, and early church literature preserves the tradition that James 'was consecrated ('Holy') from his mother's womb' (*E.H.* 2.23.4). For his part, Paul is familiar with the vocabulary of 'the Service of Righteousness', applying it in the passage from 2 Cor. 11–12 we have already noted above to his opponents among the 'Hebrew' 'archapostles', whom he calls Satan's 'servants' and 'dishonest workmen disguised as apostles of Christ'.

In addition to noting 'the Ways of God' in 4.6, language we shall encounter in the Mystery of Existence text in Chapter 7, the text also draws attention to 'His mighty works'. These 'works' or 'mighty wonders of God' are to a certain extent delineated in the War Scroll. Recast in the New Testament as curings, raisings, speaking in tongues, exorcisms, and the like, at Qumran, in keeping with its more apocalyptic and yet this-wordly approach, they are the battles and final eschatological actions that God has undertaken or will undertake on behalf of His chosen ones, i.e. those He 'loves'.

The text very definitely looks forward to the Messianic era, and in doing so, in 4.4ff., turns more and more ecstatic. This material is not paralleled in the extant Greek version, which turns, as noted, more prosaic at this point. In the first place the text introduces in 4.1 another new expression, 'the Elect of Righteousness', paralleled in Hymns, ii. 13 in a section referring to 'the Way', 'zeal' and 'marvellous Mysteries'. Except for the use of the term 'Wicked'' or 'Evil', the era of which is now past, the text is strictly positive. With the arrival of 'the time of Righteousness', 'the era of Peace' has come, when 'the Laws of Truth' and 'the Ways of God' will be observed to 'all Eternity' (4.4–5).

Connected with this one gets the evocation of the ubiquitous 'Throne' imagery encountered throughout these documents, and the text announces that 'the Rule of Goodness and Righteousness has come' and God has 'raised up the Throne of his Messiah' (4.9). No more triumphant proclamation could be imagined. It is for this reason that we have called the movement responsible for these works 'the Messianic Movement in Palestine'. There is no way this can be gain-said and we stand by this determination.

That the so-called 'Zealot' movement was also permeated by Messianism is confirmed by Josephus at the end of the *Jewish War*, when he contends that the thing that most moved the Jews to revolt against Rome in AD 66–70 was an obscure and ambiguous prophecy – ambiguous because it was capable of multiple interpretations, one Pharisaic like his own and one like that at Qumran – that a World Ruler would come out of Palestine, i.e. the Star Prophecy (6.312–14).

The term 'Elect of Righteousness' in this text is also interesting. Again, in the Damascus Document the 'sons of Zadok' are defined as 'the Elect of Israel, *called by name*, who will stand at the end of time . . . and justify the Righteous and condemn the Wicked' (iv. 3–7; italics ours). The notion of 'the Elect' is an important one at Qumran. This portion of the Testament of Naphtali draws the links between 'the sons of Zadok' and 'the Righteous Elect' even closer. It is, of course, also a variation of 'the sons of Righteousness' terminology.

The usage 'hearts' or 'heart' (4.7) is also an important one at Qumran often connected with these kinds of allusions, denoting

ideological purity. 'The Ways of God and the mightiness of His Works'
in Line 4.6 are those that will reign in the Messianic era; they have their
counterpart both in this document and in others in the 'works' expected of
man. This is 'works Righteousness' with a vengeance.

TRANSLITERATION Column 2 (or later)

.1 עם אחיות אבי בלהה א[מי ואחו]תה דבורה אשר הניקה את רבק[ה]

.2 וילך בשבי וישלח לבן ויפרקהו ויתן לו את חנה אחת מאמהותי[ו ותהר ותלד בת]

.3 ראישונה את זלפה ויתן את שמה זלפה בשם העיר אשר נשבה אל[י]ה [

.4 ותהר ותלד את בלהה אמי ותקרא חנה את שמה בלהה כי כאשר נולדה [ ]

.5 מתבהלת לינוק ותואמר מה מתבהלת היאה בתי ותקרא עוד בלהה

.6 *Vacat*

.7 וכאשר בא יעקוב אבי אל לבן בורח מלפני עישיו אחיהו ומאשר מ[ת רתיוס]

.8 אבי בלהה אמי וינהג לבן את חנה אם אמי ואת שתי בנותי[ה ויתן בת אחת]

.9 [ללאה] ואחת לרחל וכאשר היתה רחל לוא ילדה בנים .. [ ]

.10 [ ] יעקו[ב אבי ונתון לו את בלהה אמי ותלד את דן אח]י [

.11 .[ ] [ל]ש[תי אחיות .. ש...] [ל...] [ ] [לש] [לש] [

Column 4 (or later)

.1 [ ] [...............] .[ ] ב[כור]

.2 וצרת מצוק ונסוי שחת ויצרפו בם לבחירי צדק מח.ל .ש.

.3 בעבור חס[יד]יו כיא שלם קץ הרשע וכול עולה ת[עבו]ר

.4 באה עת ה[צ]דק ומלאה הארץ דעה ותהלת אל בו כ[יא]

.5 בא קץ השלום וחוקי אמת ותעודת הצדק להשכיל [כול אנש]

.6 בדרכי אל ובגבורות מעשיו [יתוסרו ע]ד עולמי עד כול ב[ריאה]

.7 תברכנו וכול אנש ישתחוה לו [ויהיה לב]כם אח[ד] כיא הואה [הכין]

.8 פעולתם בטרם הבראם ועבודת הצדק פלג גבולותם [הגביל]

.9 בדורותם כיא בא ממשל {הצדק} הטוב וירם כסא ה[משיח]

.10 ומודה גבה השכל ערמה ותושיה נכחנו במעש[י] ק[ו]ד[ש]ו[

.11 .[ ] ע.[ ] [

TRANSLATION
Column 2 (or later) (1) with the paternal aunts of Bilhah, my m[other, and
her si]ster, Deborah, who nursed Rebeccah . . . (2) And he (the father) went
into captivity, but Laban sent and rescued him. Then he (Laban) gave him
(Rotheos) Hannah, one of his maidservant[s. And she conceived and bore]
(3) her first [daughter], Zilpah. And he gave her the name Zilpah after the
name of the city to wh[ich] he had been taken captive. (4) Then she
conceived and bore Bilhah, my mother. Hannah named her Bilhah because,
when she was born, (5) she hurried to suckle. So she said, 'My, how my
daughter is in a hurry.' So from then on she was called Bilhah. (6) *Vacat*
(7) And when Jacob my father, fleeing from Esau his brother, came to

Laban, and because [Rotheos], (8) the father of my mother Bilhah, di[ed], Laban took charge of Hannah my grandmother and her two daughters. He gave one daughter (9) to Leah and one to Rachel. When it came about that Rachel was not bearing sons . . . (10) Jaco]b, my father. And Bilhah, my mother, was given to him; so she bore Dan [my] brother [. . . (11) tw]o daughters . . .

Column 4 (or later) (1) [. . . in] the Pit (2) and great distress and devilish trials. And some among them shall be purified to become the Elect of Righteousness . . . (3) for the sake of His Pious [On]es. For the era of Evil has been completed, and all sinfulness will pas[s away]; (4) the time of Rightousness has come, and the earth will be full of Knowledge and praise of God. F[or] (5) the era of peace has come, and the laws of Truth and the testimony of Rightousness, to teach [all mankind] (6) the Ways of God and the mightiness of His works; [they shall be instructed un]til all Eternity. All cr[eation] (7) will bless Him, and every man will bow down before Him in worship, and their he[arts will be] as one. For He [prepared] (8) their actions before ever they were created, and [measured out] the service of Righteousness as their portion (9) in their generations. For the rule of Goodness (Righteousness) has come, and He has raised up the Throne of the [Messiah.] (10) And Wisdom will increase greatly. Insight and understanding will be confirmed by the works of [His] Holiness . . .

32. ADMONITIONS TO THE SONS OF DAWN (4Q298)
(Plate 10)

On the surface, there is nothing astonishing about this text and no reason why it should be written in an unknown script, called earlier by some scholars 'cryptic'. We have been able to decipher it and provide the following chart, which equates the letters used in the text with their corresponding Hebrew forms:

א	ב	ג	ד	ה	ו	ז	ח	ט	י	כ	ל
✗	✗	✗	✗	✗	✗	✗	✗	✗	✗	✗	✗
מ	נ	ס	ע	פ	צ	ק	ר	שׁ	שׂ	ת	Syntactic Marker
✗	✗	✗	✗	✗	✗	✗	✗	None	✗	✗	✗

The letters used are not those of 4Q186, another work using a kind of cryptic script. 4Q186, which has been known for some time, mixes a few words written in the Greek and Paleo-Hebrew alphabets with those in ordinary square Hebrew letters. Furthermore it is inscribed in mirror writing. By contrast, the Admonitions to the Sons of Dawn does not mix scripts, moves from right to left, and relies on 23 more or less arbitrary symbols.

It also uses a character or symbol, perhaps a syntactic marker or null character, which has no equivalent in the Hebrew alphabet. Null symbols serve no other function than to complicate a script's decipherment. In some cases, a script of this kind may not even be 'cryptic' at all, but simply have not come down to us and therefore be 'unknown'. Given the nature of the letters of this script, however, and the correspondences we have worked out, this is unlikely.

Like 'Wisdom' texts generally, the text before us follows a relatively calmer style similar to that of the Sons of Righteousness (Proverbs) and the Demons of Death (Beatitudes) that follow, and large portions of the Children of Salvation (*Yeshaʿ*) and the Mystery of Existence at the end of Chapter 7. In Line 1.2, it is addressed to 'the pursuers after Righteousness . . . and the seekers of Faith'. These are important allusions when the motifs we have been signalling in this work are considered. The first, in particular, is important, when it comes to considering the last column of the Damascus Document at the end of the next chapter. This column ends, as we shall see, with a variation of this usage, well known in Jewish religious activity: *midrash* (seeking/ pursuing or homiletical interpretation).

It contains the usual allusions to 'the storehouse of Knowledge', 'the Glorious abode', 'Meekness', 'humility', 'seeking Judgements', and 'the men of Truth', which are also part of the vocabulary of the next two texts in this chapter and of Chapter 7. Line 3.7 counsels 'the men of Truth' to 'pursue Righteousness and love Piety'. Once again, if the reconstruction is correct, we have an allusion to the Righteousness/Piety dichotomy so much a part of the consciousness of this group. The 'Faith' allusion, too, resonates, however tenuously, with well-known evocations of this notion in Paul/James in early Christianity.

The first and introductory line of this text, however, is *not* cryptic. It is written in normal Hebrew, and evokes an interesting character known from both the Community Rule and the Damascus Document, 'the *Maskil*' — a synonym probably for 'the Teacher' or the Righteous Teacher. The allusion is also widespread, albeit somewhat mysteriously, in Psalms.

The references in the Community Rule and the Damascus Document are interesting in themselves. In 1QS,iii.13, the *Maskil* teaches 'the sons of Light' about 'their works' and ultimate Heavenly or infernal rewards. In ix.12 he is commanded to be 'zealous for the Law and the Day of Vengeance'. The context of these two texts is one that will relate to our discussion of baptismal procedures and the 'Way in the wilderness' with regard to the Sons of Righteousness (Proverbs) text below. In CD,xii.20 and xiii.22, the *Maskil* is to 'walk in the Laws' until the 'standing up of the Messiah of Aaron and Israel in the last days' and the 'visitation of the land'. The eschatological implications of all these allusions coupled with the activities of the *Maskil* are quite explosive.

We have already discussed the terminology 'standing up' as implying possibly either 'being resurrected' or a 'return', as well as the more straightforward 'arising'/'coming'. In CD,xiv.18, this 'Messiah of Aaron and Israel . . . will (or 'did') *atone for their sins*' (italics ours). As we have suggested, contrary to the well-known 'two-Messiah' theory of early Qumran scholarship, these references to 'the Messiah of Aaron and Israel' in the Damascus Document are *singular* not plural. The verbs and verbal nouns connected with them are singular too. This is important, and one possible explanation for it is that it is evoking a Messiah with both priestly and kingly implications, like the somewhat similar recitations of Hebrews.

The doctrines that follow, however fragmented or innocuous, have to be seen as the special provenance of this *Maskil*. The Demons of Death (Beatitudes) at the end of this chapter begins with the related predicate *lehaskil* ('to teach') and reads as follows: 'For He gave me the Knowledge of Wisdom and instruction to teach all the sons of Truth.' It is quite likely, as we shall see, that in this we have a synonym for the sons of Dawn. On the other hand, the kind of activity hinted at in Line 10 Column 3 – 'to understand the era of Eternity and inquire into the past so as to know . . .' (presumably 'the hidden things' of Line 8) – is precisely the kind of activity that the Talmud decries, i.e. those who look into the past and the future will have no share in the world to come (b. Hag 11b). This single reference probably provides a better explanation for the text's cryptology than anything else.

The Hebrew allusion 'sons of Dawn' may also obliquely refer to some kind of all-night community vigils mentioned in the Damascus Document, a part of the backdrop to the Koran as well. This would not be the only Qumran motif that has found its way, tantalizingly, into the latter recitation. Even Sura 89 bears the not unparallel name, 'the Dawn', and quite a few suras refer to these vigils. On the other hand, the phrase may simply have a more esoteric or mystical sense relating to an idea of coming into Light. In fact, the best explanation of it, as we shall also see in our discussion of the Sons of Righteousness (Proverbs) text below, is probably as a synonym for 'sons of Light', though it should be appreciated that esoteric Qumran expressions like these are capable of multiple levels of meaning.

In order to make our discussion of these cryptic Admonitions to the Sons of Dawn complete, we should probably borrow an allusion from the set of admonitions that follow, that is 'the Sons of Righteousness'. There are at least two allusions to 'sons of Righteousness' in the column of the Community Rule referring to the *Maskil* mentioned above (iii.20–22), which early scholars often tried to dismiss as scribal errors. In addition to what we have outlined above, the avalanche of images in these columns in the Community Rule are startling; as they relate to the *Maskil* they are worth recording.

The *Maskil* is 'to make known to and teach the sons of Light' (the sons of Dawn?) 'the Ways of Light' and how to 'be reckoned among the Perfect', including, it would appear, 'justification', 'works' and the like. In particular, he is to instruct them in baptismal procedures, which include being 'purified by the Holy Spirit', 'looking upon the Living Light' (compare this with 'the Living Waters' in the Demons of Darkness and Mystery of Existence texts below in Chapter 7), and 'walking in Perfection in all the Ways of God, which He commanded concerning His appointed times (obviously including those of the calendar in the preceding chapter), and not straying either right or left, nor treading on *even one* of His words' (italics ours).

One should compare this last turn of phrase to Jesus on 'not one jot or tittle of the Law' in Matt. 5:18's Sermon on the Mount and James 2:8 on 'breaking one small point of the Law'. One should also compare it to Paul's attack on these positions (presumably in his response to James) in his development of Abraham's 'Righteousness', being 'sons of God' through faith, and Jesus' being 'cursed by the Law' in Gal. 3–4, which we also set forth below in connection with the end of the Damascus Document: 'You *keep* special days and months and seasons and years', which he calls 'weak and beggarly' (Gal. 4:10–11; italics ours).

A third reference to 'the sons of the *Zaddik*' in another pregnant passage of the Community Rule (ix), mentions the *Maskil*, 'walking in

Perfection', 'the Holy Spirit', and more startlingly even than these, that 'this is the time of the preparation of the Way in the wilderness'. This is specifically tied in exegesis to the *Maskil's* 'preparation of the Way' by 'teaching the Miraculous Mysteries'. The reader will recognize this pregnant passage from Isa. 40:1–3 as that used to describe John the Baptist's activities in the wilderness, including most notably *baptism*. It is clear that these 'Mysteries' and baptismal procedures that 'the *Maskil*' is to teach the sons of Dawn — here delineated in cryptic script — are to be seen as in some way part of the preparation (probably 'in the wilderness') for 'Perfection' and whatever 'Crown of Glory' and 'eternal Light' was envisaged.

TRANSLITERATION   Column 1

.1   [דבר]י משכיל אשר דבר לכול בני שחר האזי]נו לי כ]ול אנשי לבב

.2   [ורו]דפי צדק תבי]נ]ו במלי ומבקשי אמון. ש]מע]ו למלי בכול

.3   [אומ]ץ שימו [לב   יד]עים דר]כי]לה השינ]ו אורך] חיים א[נשי]

.4   [   ] . חקר [   ]עול.. [   ] ..[   ]

.5   [   ] ל. [   ].ב.[   ]

                    Column 2

.1   שורשיה יצ]או   [זבול

.2   בתהום מת]חת   [וכמ.

.3   התבונן]   [עפר

.4   ]   [נתן אל

.5   ]   [בכול תבל

.6   ]   ]. מדר תכונם

.7   ]   ת]חת שם

.8   ]   ת]כונם להתהלך

.9   ]   [אוצר בינות

.10   ]   [מ]]לחי ואשר

                    Column 3

.1   ]י   [ומספר גבולותיה

.2   ]   ]ר לבלתי רום

.3   ].   ]ות את זבול. ועתה

.4   האזינ]ו   [וידעים שמעו ואנשי

.5   בינה ה]   ]ח ודורשי משפט הצניע

.6   לכת י.]   [הוסיפו אומץ ואנשי

.7   אמת רדפ]ו צדק] ואהבו חסד הוסיפו

.8   ענו. ות]   [מעלמי תעודה אשר

9. ‏פתר.. | ‏[‏| בעבור תבינו בקץ
10. ‏עולמות ובקד]מ[וניות תביטו לדעת

Column 4

‏[10. ‏מש]

Column 5

‏[רית   7. [
‏[תכלית   8. [
‏[לדרוך   9. [
‏[10. [

Column 6

‏[7. ‏וא[ ].. [ ]..
‏[8. ‏השחר ו. [
‏[9. ‏גבולותיו [
‏[10. ‏שם גבולות [

TRANSLATION

Column 1 (1) [The word]s of (the) *Maskil* (Teacher) that he spoke to all the sons of Dawn (cryptic script begins): Give e[ar to me], all men of heart (2) and those who [pur]sue Righteousness: you will und[er]stand my words and be seekers after Faith. H[ea]r my words with [all your (3) s]trength. Lis[ten] . . . [kn]owing the ways of . . . [ac]hieve [long] life, men of (4) . . . search out . . .

Column 2 (1) its roots reach [out] . . . a Glorious abode (2) in the depths be[low] . . . and in them. (3) Consider . . . dust (4) . . . God gave (5) . . . on all the earth (6) . . . he measured their setting (7) . . . under the name of (8) . . . their setting, to go about (9) . . . a storehouse of Understanding (10) . . . and which . . .

Column 3 (1) . . . and recounting its boundaries (2) . . . not to be on high (3) . . . the Glorious abode. And now, (4) give ear . . . and knowing, hear. And men (5) of Understanding, . . . and those seeking Judgement, humility, (6) . . . add strength. And the men of (7) Truth, pursu[e Righteousness] and love Piety; add (8) Meekness . . . the hidden things of the testimony, which he (9) solved . . . so that you understand the era (10) of Eternity, and examine the pa[s]t, so as to know . . .

Column 5 (8) . . . destruction (9) . . . to tread . . .

Column 6 (8) of the dawn . . . (9) its boundaries . . . (10) he placed boundaries . . .

33. THE SONS OF RIGHTEOUSNESS
(PROVERBS – 4Q424)
(Plate 11)

In this text, another typical 'Wisdom' text, there is the usual Qumran vocabulary of 'Judgement', 'Riches', 'Knowledge', and in Line 1.9, an additional one – 'zeal for Truth'. This is preceded and followed by an interesting additional evocation of 'deceitful' or 'cunning lips', which will also be of interest in the parallel admonitions which follow next in the Demons of Death (Beatitudes). In 1.13 there is a curious reference to 'swallowing', in this case coupled with a reference on the same line to 'the Kittim'. A conjunction of this kind is always interesting, but its fragmentary nature does not permit any further analysis. Still, the expression *Kittim* has little evident relationship to the rest of the text and usually relates in some way, as we have seen, to foreign, overseas armies coming from the West, either Macedonian or Roman.

We have already extensively discussed the allusion in 3.10 to 'Sons of Righteousness', with which the extant text closes, above. It is not only a verbal parallel, but probably also a synonym for 'the sons of Zadok', particularly when this expression is taken in its esoteric sense. In Lines 2.8–11 the expression is coupled with allusions to 'the removers of the boundary' and 'Riches', both also paralleled in Columns i and iv of the Damascus Document, not to mention the last column of the Damascus Document which we translate at the end of the next chapter. In Line 8, it is preceded by another curious reference: 'zeal' (of a soldier?). It is not uninteresting that this 'zeal' is also paralleled in the all-important aftermath of the exegesis of 'way in the wilderness' in Column ix.24 of the Community Rule discussed above – 'zeal for the Law' and 'the time of the Day of Vengeance'.

TRANSLITERATION   Fragment 1

1. [   ]   ]מ[[
2. [   ]   ]ם[[*vacat*   עם פורה]
3. [   ]   [חוץ ובחר לבנותה ותפל טח קירו גם הו]
4. [י]נתר מפני זרם עם נעלם אל תקח חוק ועם מתמ]ו[טט אל
5. תבוא בכור כי כעופרת כן ינתך ולא יעמור לפני אש   *vacat*
6. ביד עצל אל תפקר אט כי לא יצניע מלאכתך ואל תשלח דב]ר [
7. לקח כי לא יפלס כל ארחותיך   *vacat*   איש תלונה אל תא[מין]
8. לקחת   *vacat*   הון למחסורך   *vacat*   איש לו שפתים אל האמ]ין [

9. משפט[י]ך הלוז יליז בשפתיו אחר אמת לא ירצה]   [

10. בפרי שפתו *vacat* איש רע עין אל תמשל בהו[ן   [

11. ותכן שארכה לחפצך]   [למיתיך]   [

12. ובעת קבץ ימצא חנף קצר אפי[ם   [

13. כתיים כי בלע יבלעם *vacat* איש]   [

Fragment 2

1. ובמשקל לא יעשה פעלתו איש שופט בטרם ידרוש כמאמין בטרם]   [

2. אל תמשילהו ברודפי דעת כי לא יבין משפטם להצדיק צדיק ולהרשיע [רשע]

3. גם הוא יהיה לבוז *vacat* איש שוע עינים אל תשלח לחזות לישרים כ[י איש]

4. כבד אזן אל תשלח לדרוש משפט כי ריב אנשים לא יפלס כזורה לרוח]   [

5. אשר לא תכר כן דובר לאזן אשר איננה שומעת ומספר לנם נרדם ברוח]   [

6. איש שמן לב אל תשלח לכרות מחשבות כי נסתרה חכמת לבו ולוא ימשול כ]   [

7. חכמת ידיו לא ימצא *vacat* איש שכל יקבל ב[ינה] איש ידע יפיק חכמה]   [

8. איש ישר ירצה במשפט *vacat* איש]   [*vacat* ל] איש חיל יקנא ל.[[

9. [ה]וא בעל ריב לכול מסיני גבול]   [.ה לא .. [[

10.]   [דאג לכל חסרי הון בני צדק]   [

11.]   [בכול הון]   [

TRANSLATION

Fragment 1 (2) . . . with a fruitful man . . . (3) outside and chooses to build it, and he covers his wall with plaster, as well as . . . (4) it will fall off under the rain. Don't take legal instruction from a deceitful person and don't go, young man, with someone who is unsta[b]le. (5) For just as lead melts, so before a fire he will not stand. (6) Do not put a slackard in charge of an important task, for he will not carry out your charge. And don't send (him) to pick (7) some[thing] up, for he will not pay attention to your specifications. Do not tr[ust] the complainer (8) to get provisions for your needs. Do not trust the man of cunning lips . . . (9) your Judge[m]ents. He will certainly speak deviously, not being zealous for Truth . . . (10) with the fruit of his lips . . . Do not put the man with a covetous eye in charge of Rich[es . . .] (11) And arrange what remains to suit yourself . . . your dead (?) . . . (12) and in the time of the harvest he will be found unworthy, quick to anger . . . (13) Kittim, because he will surely swallow them . . . A man . . .

Fragment 2 (1) and will not do his work carefully. The man who judges before investigating is like someone who believes before . . . (2) Do not give him authority over those pursuing Knowledge, for he will not understand their Judgement, to justify the Righteous and condemn [the Wicked . . .] (3) he will also be robbed. Do not send the man of poor eyesight to look for the Upright, fo[r . . .] (4) Do not send the poor of hearing to seek Judgement, for he will not carefully consider disputes between men. Like someone winnowing wind . . . [Like a . . .] (5) who doesn't investigate, so is someone who speaks into any ear that doesn't listen or who tries to talk to a drowsy man, who falls asleep with the spirit of . . . (6) Do not send the hard-hearted man to discern thoughts, because his heart's Wisdom is defective, and he will not be able to control . . . (7) nor will he find the discernment of his hands. The clever man will profit from Understanding. A Knowing man will bring forth Wisdom . . . (8) An Upright man will be pleased with Judgement . . . A man . . . A soldier will be zealous for . . .

34. THE DEMONS OF DEATH
(BEATITUDES – 4Q525)
(Plate 12)

This next text has been called 'the Beatitudes', comparing it to famous recitations of a parallel kind in Ecclesiasticus (Ben Sira) and the Sermon on the Mount in the Gospel of Matthew. This is perhaps a misnomer. Once again, we have a typical 'Wisdom' text here, but one also rich in the vocabulary of Qumran. Superficially, the text is fairly straightforward and commonplace. As such, it has much in common with the Sons of Dawn and Sons of Righteousness (Proverbs) materials above – at least Columns 1–3 do.

But as in previous visionary recitals like the Testament of Naphtali, the piece, as reconstructed, grows more apocalyptic in columns 4–5, which are full of the language of Righteous indignation. Though the original order of the portions is speculative and though it might reasonably be queried whether all fragments really belong together, it is reasonable and convenient to assign Fragment 1 to the beginning of the work. The tone of the first three columns – even part of the fourth – is more restrained than what develops towards the end, and we are clearly in the first-person milieu of the admonitions of the *Maskil* in the Sons of Dawn recital above.

Again we come upon the familiar vocabulary of Qumran. For instance, 'the heart of Deceitfulness' language in Line 3 Column 2 is echoed in the Community Rule, viii. 22 and ix. 8 dealing with barring from 'table fellowship', common purse and mutual activity – subjects we shall also have occasion to discuss in Chapter 6 in relation to the end of the Damascus Document. One should note that throughout these translations, the reference to *hok*/*hukkim* as in Line 1 (statutes, ordinances, or laws) is an equivocal one. Often we render it 'statutes', but where the occasion arises it can be rendered 'laws'.

The reason it is important is that in the exegesis of Isa. 40:3 referred to above applied in two places to the activities of the Community in the wilderness, 'zeal' or 'he who is zealous for' is tied to it. In 1QS, ix. 24, following the second exegesis and reference to 'the *Maskil*', the actual words are: 'and he shall be as a man zealous for the Law, whose time is the Day of Vengeance.' The 'Way' terminology is also defined in viii. 15 in the first of these exegeses as 'the study of the *Torah*' (*midrash ha-Torah*), an allusion that will also emerge in the last line of the Damascus Document below.

In this text, too, not only do we have an allusion to 'Way' and 'Ways', and another favourite, 'walking in the Way of', but also 'Watcher', 'Evil', 'Knowledge', 'Mysteries', and 'Perfection' language (cf. Matt. 5:48: 'therefore be Perfect as your Father in Heaven is Perfect', itself tied in documents like the Community Rule to the language of 'walking in the Way of' and, of course, the allusion to Noah as 'Perfect and Righteous in his generation' in Gen. 6:9), and an allusion in Column 4.20, combining both 'Meekness' and 'Righteousness' terminologies – 'the Meekness of Righteousness'. In Column 5.4 there is also the allusion to 'Mastemah' – this time singular – we saw in Chapter 1, a linguistic variation of the word 'Satan' and further adumbration of the 'Devil'/'Belial'/'Watcher' language. There is also in Column 2 (Fragment 4.3) a very interesting note of xenophobic antagonism to foreigners not unsimilar to that encountered in the first column of the Testament of Kohath.

However, it is in Columns 4–6 that really interesting things appear in this text. In the 'blessings' or 'beatitudes' section in Column 2.1, 'holding fast to her Laws' was contrasted with 'the Ways of Evil'; and having 'a pure heart' – by now a fairly familiar allusion – with 'slandering with his Tongue'. This 'Tongue' imagery is widespread at Qumran, particularly in the Community Rule, but also in texts like the Nahum *Pesher*, the Damascus Document, Hymns, and the two Letters on Works Righteousness below. It is generically parallel to the 'Lying', 'spouting' and 'boasting' allusions connected to the 'Lying' Adversary of the Righteous Teacher. Nor is it unrelated to the 'lips' above and the 'uncircumcized heart' – harking back to Ezekiel's strictures about entering the Temple – so widespread at Qumran.

Starting with the very interesting reference to 'atonement for sin' at the beginning of Column 4.2, Lines 4.18–25 generally counsel patience and restraint, clearly identifiable themes in the Letter of James, particularly in 1:3–4 and 5:7–20. The style of James, in fact, recapitulates throughout the tone and substance of these admonitions at Qumran. In this text and against this backdrop, lines 4.25–28 pick up this 'Tongue' imagery again and repeat it several times. In the process they also evoke its variation the 'lips' imagery just encountered and associated with both 'Lying' and the 'Tongue' in 1QS,x.23–25 and Hymns, vii.11–12 (sometimes 'uncircumcized lips').

They do so in such a way that there can be no mistaking the parallel with the famous imagery in Chapter 3 of James, attacking the Lying adversary in terms of this same 'Tongue' imagery. This last follows James. 2:20–24, castigating the 'Man of Emptiness' as not knowing 'that a man was justified by works' and 'faith without works is dead'. The actual language in James. 3:5–9 is extensive and substantial, but its gist is: 'The Tongue is a wicked world all to itself.' No one can 'control the Tongue'; that is, it spouts, and both texts use the very same image to describe the Tongue, 'the stumbling block' (24). There can be no mistaking these language parallels. This is, in fact, very strong imagery at Qumran and found in extremely telling contexts (for instance, in 1QS,iv.11, CD,v.11, etc.).

In the Letter of James, too, this 'Lying' adversary overturns the normal thrust of 'the friend' imagery which all these texts apply to Abraham, that is, by making himself a 'friend of man' he turns himself into an 'Enemy of God' (4:5). In misunderstanding the 'keeping' as opposed to the 'breaking' terminology, he misunderstands that Abraham – the original 'friend of God' – was not saved by faith alone, but also by 'works' (2:23–24).

Column 5 of our text now picks up the language of 'burning' and 'vipers' again (familiar, as we have seen, in both New Testament and Damascus Document recitations). 5.4 again alludes to Mastemah, a variation of Mastemoth, that is, 'the Enemy'. Again this should be compared with 'the Enemy of God' allusion in James. 4:5. In 4:8 the letter actually refers to 'the Devil' as well, thereby further extending the parallels. In discussing the 'Pit' and counselling patience again (5.7), the text before us moves on in 6.4 to an evocation of the Temple. Amid vivid imagery of 'burning', it closes with the inspiring allusion to 'drinking' and the 'Well of deep waters'. This imagery will reappear in texts like the Chariots of Glory and the Mystery of Existence in Chapter 7 as the 'Fountain of Living Waters'.

In the process our text perhaps lays to rest the controversy over the meaning of the phrase 'putting to death', in the Messianic Leader (*Nasi*) text in Chapter 1. In Column 5 Fragment 2, the phrase 'they put to death' once more appears to occur. If our reconstruction is correct, it may be read as referring to 'the putting to death of the Righteous', that is, *hemitu ha-Zaddikim*, in exactly the manner of the allusion to 'they put to death' in the Messianic Leader fragment. Here, too, the accusative participle is missing, as it is in so many such constructions in texts from the Second Temple period, and one possible reading is certainly 'they put the Righteous Ones to death.' If this reading is correct, then the reading of the earlier fragment (depending on where the other references to 'the Leader of the Community' are placed in the reconstruction) can be: 'they put the Leader of the Community to death', just as easily as *vice versa*.

This, too, now turns out to have intriguing repercussions where the Letter of James is concerned. Jas. 5:6, presumably talking about the death of the Messianic Leader, states: 'It was you who condemned the Righteous (One) and *put him to death*, though he offered you no resistance' (italics ours). The language is *exactly* the same as we are encountering here. *Per contra*, see Paul in I Thess. 2:15 about the Jews having 'put the Lord Jesus to death . . . making themselves the *Enemies* of the whole human race' (italics ours). The clear reversal exemplified in this last should by now be familiar; but the usage 'Enemies' (now reversed and applied to the Jews not Paul), relating to the interesting language of Mastemah/Mastemoth we have been encountering in these texts, also has interesting implications. In fact, the order of these allusions in both texts — James and the Beatitudes — where in both cases (if our reconstruction is correct) the use of the startling 'Tongue' imagery is followed by an accusation of an illicit execution of some kind, further reinforces the impression of their parallelism.

One other interesting usage is that of '*hamat*', translated as 'venom' here, i.e. 'venom of vipers' (5.4). In the Habakkuk *Pesher*, xi.4–5, this word has important reverberations relative to the Wicked Priest's destruction of the Righteous Teacher, '*be-cha'as hamato*'in his hot anger' or 'the heat of his anger', he (the Wicked Priest) 'pursued him' in order to destroy him. The reader should appreciate that the Hebrew '*hamat*' can mean *either* 'venom' *or* 'anger', which is the sense of the various plays and interchanges taking place.

This language is reversed in sections of the *pesher* relating to the final eschatological Judgement of God on activities such as these, i.e. 'He (the Wicked Priest) would drink the cup of the Lord's divine wrath', also expressed as '*ḥamat*' (xi.14). This has been further refined in the Book of Revelation, which speaks of Jesus in its epilogue as being 'the root and Branch of David and the bright star of the morning' (22:16), to read in 14:10: 'He will also drink the wine of the wrath of God, which is ready, undiluted in the cup of His anger.' The root of this imagery is to be found in Isa. 51:17 and Jer. 25:15f.

TRANSLITERATION

Column 1

1. [ ]ים[וֹעתה שמעו לי כול בני ואדבר] בחוכמה אשר נתן לי אלוה
2. [ ]כי נתן לי דע[ת] חוכמה ומו[סר] להשכיל [כול בני אמת

Column 2

1. בלב טהור ולוא רגל על לשונו אשרי תומכי חוקיה ולוא יתמוכו
2. בדרכי עולה אש[רי] הגלים בה ולוא יביעו בדרכי אולה אשרי דורשיה
3. בבור כפים ולוא ישחרנה ב[לב] מרמה אשרי אדם השיג חוכמה ויתהלך
4. בתורת עליון ויכן לדרכיה לבו ויתאפק ביסוריה ובנגיעיה ירצה תמ[י]ד
5. ולוא יטושנה בעוני מצר[יו] ובעת צוקה לוא יעוזבנה ולוא ישכחנה [בימי פ]חד
6. ובענוות נפשו לוא ינ[ע[ל]נה] כי בה יהגה תמיד ובצרתו ישוח[ח בתורת אל ובכו]ל
7. היותו בה [יהגה וישיתנה תמיד] לנגד עיניו לבלתי לכת בדרכי [עולה   ]
8. [   ]ה יחד ויתם לבו אלוה[ים
9. [   ] וח[וכמה תרים ראו]שו ועם מלכים תו[שיבנו   ]
10. [י]בטו על מ[   ] אחים יפר[ו   ]
11. vacat
12. [ו]עתה בנים ש[מעו לקולי וא]ל תסורו [מאמרי פי

Column 2 (Fragment 4)

1. [   ] [. [ל]רשתה בלבו]
2. [   ] [זה בלב מרמה ובח[וכמה
3. [   ] אל ת[עזובו [נחלתכמה לזר]ה ונורלכמה לבני נכר כי חכמ[ים
4. [   ] י[שכילו ב.] אלוהים יצורו דרכיה ויתהלכו ב[כול דרכיה]
5. [   ] חוקיה ובתוכחותיה לוא ימאסו נבונים יפיקו [אמרי תבונה
6. [   ] בשלו[ם ילכו תמים יטו עולה וביסוריה לוא ימאסו]   וחכמים[
7. [   ] [בעוז חוכמה] יסובלו ערומים יכירו דרכיה ובמעמקיה [יבינו
8. [   ] יביטו אוהבי אלוהים יצניעו בה]

Column 3

1. [   ] ישוה בה כול ו.]
2. [   ] לוא תלקח בזהב א[ו בכסף

3. עם כול אבני חפץ] [
4. ידמו בת]ו[ר פניה]מה [
5. ונצני ארגמון עם] [
6. שני עם כול בגדי [חפץ [
7. ובזהב ופנינים] [

Column 4

1. [   ] [תכה בת] [ה] [
2. על כפור עון ועל בכות כ.] [
3. ב] [ירימו רואשכה] [
4. תו]ם[מפני דברך ותו]ם [
5. ב] [להדר ונחמד ב] [
6. נגל]ה[בדרכיכה בל תחמוטט] [
7. תתמ]ו[ך בעת מוטך תמצא]חן [
8. ובל תבואכה חרפת שונא]יכה [
9. יחד ומשנאיכה י]ש[סתופפ]ו [ושמח]
10. לבכה והתעננתה על א]ל   [בהא] [
11. למד אב ואלכה ועל במו]תי אויב]יכה תדרוך ו] [
12. נפשכה יחלצכה מכל רע ובל יבואכה פחד [צריכה [
13. וירישך ומלא בטוב ימיכה ברוב שלום תת]ענג [
14. תנחל כבוד ואם נספיתה למנוחות עד ינחלו [כול אוהביכה [
15. ובתלמודכה יתהלכו יחד כול יודעיכה יש]מעו בדבריכה [
16. יחד יאבלו ובדרכיכה יזכרוכה והייתה] [
17. *vacat*
18. ועתה תבין שמעה לי ושים לבכה ל]עשות [
19. הפק דעת לבטנכה ובג.] [הנה] [
20. בענות צדק הוצא אמרו]תיכה[לתתן] [ואל]
21. תשובב בדברי רעיך פן י]ת.[ן לכה] [
22. ולפי שומעכה ענה כמוהו הוצא] [ ]ה[[ואל]
23. תשפוך שיח טרם תשמע את מליהם ו] [ואל תשובב בכול]
24. מואדה לפנים שמע אמרם ואחר תשובב [בתום לבכה ובארך]
25. אפים הוציאם וענה נכון בתוך שרים בל]שון [
26. בשפתיכה ומתקל לשון השמר מואדה בג.] [
27. פן תלכד בשפתותיכ]ה ונ]קשתה יחד בלשו]ון [
28. חיפלה] [ ]ת ממנו ונפלתו] [

Column 5

1. [   ] אופל] [ ]גר רוש ובס] [כול] נולדים [בארץ [
   שמים ואת ר.]
2. [   ] פתנים ב]ו ות]תהלך אליו תבוא רו.] י]היה שמחה [ביום נלות [
   עלמי אלוהים תמ]יד]

3. [   ]   [שרף ובחלח[לות] ידולל פתן בעליו [   ]   ממלכ[ות אלוהים
   [   ]   תני[נים תש[

4. [   ]   [כי יתיצבו אררי[ם לנ[צח וחמת תנינים [   ]   המשטמה [   ]   [
   וזמה תבחר   [

5. [   ]   [צפע ובו יעופפו רשפ[י] מות במבואו תצע[ק פע[ל העוון ה[רשי]ע בו
   יתרוממו ויתהלכו [בדרכיו]

6. [   ]   [הוא רא[ו]שך [מ[סודו להבי גו[פר]ית ומכינתו [   ]   ל[רום
   המגוללים בסאו[ן רשע]

7. [   ]   [יו כלמות חרפה מנעוליו צומי שחת [   ]   [אל[.   ]   ה[רבו
   קורה מקיר   [

8. [   ]   לוא [י]שינו אורחות חיים תב[   ]   [הולכי דרך [   ]   ב[קבוץ
   חרון ובארך [אפים

Column 5 (Fragment 5)

1.]   [השרי[ם
2.]   [בה תעו נבונים [
3.]   [ומוקשים ה[
4.]   [דמים המי[חתו הצדקים
5.]   [במעל יעש[ו
6.]   מ[ות ודל[ים

Column 5 (Fragment 6)

1.]   [תוק[ף
2.]   [בשקיצי[ם
3.]   [קמתה [
4.]   [ובנדת [

Column 5 (Fragment 7)

1.]   עב[דיו פח[דו
2.]   [מלאו כול [הארץ בחמס
3.]   ו[מת תנין מפ[חיד דור ודור
4.]   ושית[נבר סביב [
5.]   [שהו [ע]יר וא[ל[והים

Column 6 (Fragment 9)

1.]   עם [
2.]   התעודה [
3.]   בחסד [
4.]   לכול דו[ר ודור

Column 6 (Fragment 10)

1. פן תביע אמרו]ת עולת
2. לבב האזינו לי ודמ]ו לפני
3. הבינותי ושתו מ]מקור חיים
4. ביתו התה]לכו
5. ביתו שוכן ב]
6. עולם צעדה]
7. אוספיח יקב]צו
8. שרף וכול שית]נתק
9. באר מימי מע]מקים

TRANSLATION

Column 1 (1) [Now, hear me, all my sons, and I will speak] about that Wisdom which God gave me . . . (2) [For He gave me the Kn]owledge of Wisdom and instruc[tion] to teach [all the sons of Truth] . . .

Column 2 (1) [Blessed is he who walks] with a pure heart and who doesn't slander with his Tongue. Blessed are they who hold fast to her Laws and do not hold (2) to the ways of Evil. Bless[ed] are they who rejoice in her and do not overflow with the ways of folly. Blessed are they who ask for her (3) with clean hands and do not seek her with a deceitful [heart]. Blessed is the man who grasps hold of Wisdom and walks (4) in the *Torah* of the Most High and directs his heart to her Ways and restrains himself with her disciplines and always accepts her chastisements. (5) and doesn't cast her off in the misery of [his] affliction[s] nor forsake her in a time of trouble, nor forget her in [days of ter]ror, (6) and in the Meekness of his soul, doesn't despis[e her], but rather always meditates on her, and when in affliction, occupies himself [with God's *Torah*; who al]l (7) his life [meditates] on her [and places her continually] before his eyes so he will not walk in the ways of [Evil] . . . (8) in unity and his heart is Perfect. God . . . (9) and W[isdom will lift up] his h[ead] and sea[t him] among kings. . . . (10) They [shall lo]ok upon . . . brothers will be fr[uitful] . . . (12) Now, my sons, he[ar my voice and do] not turn aside [from the words of my mouth. . . .

Column 2 (Fragment 4) (1) . . . to possess her with his heart . . . (2) with a deceitful heart. And in W[isdom] . . . (3) [You shall not] abandon [your inheritances to a foreign wi]fe or your hereditary portions to foreigners, because those with Wi[sdom] . . . (4) They shall consider . . .(the *Torah*) of God, protect her paths and walk in [all her Ways.] (5) . . . her statutes, and not reject her admonishments. Those with Understanding will bring forth [words of insight . . . (6) (and) walk in p[eace]. The Perfect will thrust aside Evil. They will not reject her chastisements. . . . [Those with Wisdom]

(7) will be supported [by the strength of Wisdom]. The intelligent will recognize her Ways [and plumb] her depths . . . (8) The Lovers of God will look upon her, walking carefully within her bounds.

Column 3 (1) [No] . . . is like her . . . (2) She will not be bought with gold or [silver] . . . (3) nor any precious gem . . . (4) they resemble one another in the be[au]ty of their faces . . . (5) and purple flowers with . . . (6) crimson with every [delightful] garment . . . (7) and with gold and rubies . . .

Column 4 (2) for the atonement of sin and for weeping . . . (3) they shall lift up your head . . . (4) Perfection because of your word and Perfection . . . (5) for splendor and lovely in . . . (6) was revealed in your Ways. You shall not waiver . . . (7) You will be upheld at the time you falter, and you will find [Grace . . .] (8) The reproach of those who hate [you] shall not draw near you . . . (9) together, and those who hate you will be destroyed . . . [Shall rejoice] (10) your heart and you shall delight in [God] . . . (11) God [your] father has taught, and on the [backs] of your [enemies] will you tread. And . . . (12) Your soul shall deliver you from all Evil, and the dread of [your enemies] shall not come near you. (13) He will cause you to inherit, and fill your days with Goodness, and in abundance of peace you shall de[light] . . . (14) You shall inherit Glory. Even though you pass away to (your) eternal abode, [all your loved ones] shall inherit . . . (15) All those who know you shall walk in harmony with your teaching [and] he[ar your words] . . . (16) Together will they mourn and in your ways remember you, for you were . . . (18) And now, understand, hear me, and set your heart to [do] . . . (19) Bring forth the Knowledge of your inner self and in . . . meditate . . . (20) In the Meekness of Righteousness bring forth [your] words in order to give them . . . [Don't] (21) respond to the words of your neighbor lest he give you. . . (22) As you hear, answer accordingly . . . [Do not] (23) pour out complaints before listening to their words. And . . . [Do not respond] vehemently (24) before hearing their words. Afterwards respond [in the Perfection of your heart.] (25) And with patience utter (your words) and answer truthfully before officers (even 'rulers') with a To[ngue of . . . (26) with your lips, and guard against the stumbling block of the Tongue . . . (27) lest you be convicted by your lips and ensnared together with a Tong[ue of . . . (28) impropriety . . . from it and they will be perverse . . .

Column 5 (1) . . . Darkness . . . poison . . . [all] those born [on the earth] . . . Heaven . . . (2) serpents in [it, and you will] go to him, you will enter . . . there will be joy [on the day] the Mysteries of God [are revealed] for[ever]. (3) . . . burn. By poi[sons] will a serpent weaken his lords . . . [the Kingd]om of God . . . [vip]ers . . . (4) In him they take their stand. They are accursed for[ever] and the venom of vipers . . . the Devil (Mastemah) . . . you choose depravity . . . (5) and in him [in his authority] the Demons of Death take wing. At his doorway you will cry out. . . . [He did] Evil. He [acted wick]edly. In him they exalt themselves. They walk [in his ways.] (6) [He is] your he[ad]. [From] his council there are sulph[urous] flames. And from his den are . . . in order to destroy those who wallow in the filth of [sin]. (7) . . . the reproach of disgrace, his bolted (doors) are the fasts of the pit . . . they increase. One calling from the wall . . . (8) They shall not reach the paths of life. . . . the walkers in the way of . . . in simmering anger and in pati[ence . . .]

Column 5 (Fragment 5) (1) . . . the princes . . . (2) in it those who understand wander astray . . . (3) those who ensnare . . . (4) [they shed] blood. They put to de[ath the righteous] . . . (5) [they] act treacherously . . . (6) [de]ath. And the Down[trodden] . . .

Column 5 (Fragment 6) (1) . . . might . . . (2) in the midst of abominations . . . (3) its height . . . (4) and in the pollution of . . .

Column 5 (Fragment 7) (1) . . . his ser[vants] tremb[led] . . . (2) They filled the whole [earth with violence.] . . . (3) The serpent who made [every generation tremb]le died. . . . (4) [He] stationed an Angel around . . . (5) a Wat[cher] and G[od] . . .

Column 6 (Fragment 9) (1) with/people . . . (2) the appointed time . . . (3) in Piety . . . (4) for every genera[tion] . . .

Column 6 (Fragment 10) (1) Lest you bring forth words of [folly.] . . . (2) heart. Listen to me and be sti[ll before me.] . . . (3) I have understood, so drink from [the Well of Life] . . .(4) His Temple. [They walk]ed . . . (5) His Temple is dwelling among . . . (6) forever marching . . . (7) or what grows of its own they shall gat[her . . .] (8) burned, and every weed [He uprooted . . .] (9) a Well of de[ep] Waters . . .

NOTES

(27) Aramaic Testament of Levi (4Q213–214)
  Previous Discussions: J. T. Milik, 'Le Testament de Lévi en araméen: Fragment de la grotte 4 de Qumrân', *Revue Biblique* 62 (1955) 398–406, plate 4; idem, *Books*, 23–4, 214, 244 and 263; Beyer, *Teste*, 188–209. Photographs: PAM 43.241 and 43.243 (Manuscript A), 43.260 (Manuscript B), ER 1277, 1279 and 1296. The Qumran Testament of Levi corresponds at a few points to the Greek Testament of Levi. It is much more closely related to the medieval manuscripts of an Aramaic Testament of Levi from the Cairo *Genizah* probably dating to the tenth or eleventh century AD. Those

manuscripts reside at Cambridge and Oxford. These correspondences have allowed us to restore large missing portions while presenting substantial previously unknown portions as well. The Aramaic was probably the source for the Greek as well.

Manuscript A: For Fragment 1 Column 1, cf. Greek Testament of Levi 2:4b and 4:2; for Fragment 1 Column 2, cf. Greek Testament of Levi 2:5–6; for Fragment 3, cf. the Oxford manuscript Column A and 1Q21, 4–5; for Fragment 4 Column 1–Column 2 Line 1, cf. the Cambridge manuscript Columns E–F.

For Manuscript B: by and large this fragment is identical to Oxford C Line 6 to D Line 4.

(28) A Firm Foundation (Aaron A – 4Q541)

Previous Discussions: É. Puech, 'Fragments d'un apocryphe de Lévi et le personnage eschatologique: 4QTestLévi^{c-d}(?) et 4QAj^{a}', in J. Trebolle Barrera and L. Vegas Montaner (eds), *Proceedings of the International Congress on the Dead Sea Scrolls – Madrid, 18–21 March, 1991* (Universidad Computense/ Brill:Madrid/Leiden, 1992). Photographs: PAM 43.587 and 43.588, ER 1534 and 1535.

(29) Testament of Kohath (4Q542)

Previous Discussions: J. T. Milik, '4Q Visions de ᶜAmram et une citation d'Origène', *Review Biblique* 79 (1972) 97; Beyer, *Texte*, 209–10; R. H. Eisenman, 'The Testament of Kohath', *Biblica Archaeology Review*, Nov/Dec (1991) 64; É. Puech; 'Le Testament de Qahat en araméen de la Grotte 4 (4QTQah)', *Revue de Qumran* 15 (1991) 23–54. Photographs: PAM 42.600 and 43.565, ER 923 and 1513.

(30) Testament of Amram (4Q543, 545–548)

Previous Discussions: J. T. Milik, '4Q Visions de ᶜAmram', 77–97; P. J. Kobleski, *Mechizedek and Melchireshaᶜ* (Washington, DC: Catholic Biblical Association of America, 1981) 24–36. Photographs: PAM 43.566, 43.567, 43.577, 43.578, 43.586 and 43.597, ER 1514, 1515, 1525, 1526, 1533 and 1544. Manuscript C preserves most fully the beginning of the work. Manuscript ? is known thus in the literature; it has never received a more complete official designation. In order to avoid confusion, therefore, we have adopted this admittedly rather silly nomenclature.

(31) Testament of Naphtali (4Q215)

Previous Discussions: Milik, *Years*, 34; idem, *Books*, 198. Photographs: PAM 41.915 and 43.237, ER 512 and 1273. Along with previously unknown details, Column 2 preserves the Hebrew form of the Greek Testament of Naphtali 1:9, 11–12. It is from this Greek parallel that we have derived the name of the father, Rotheos.

(32) Admonitions to the Sons of Dawn (4Q298)

Previous Discussions: None. Photographs: PAM 43.384, ER 1378.

(33) The Sons of Righteousness (Proverbs – 4Q424)

Previous Discussions: None. Photographs: PAM 43.502, ER 1452.

(34) The Demons of Death (Beatitudes – 4Q525)

Previous Discussion: É. Puech, '4Q525 et les péricopes des béatitudes en Ben Sira et Matthieu', *Revue Biblique* 98 (1991) 80–106. Photographs: PAM 43.595, 43.596 and 43.608, ER 1542, 1543 and 1554.

CHAPTER 6

Works Reckoned as Righteousness – Legal Texts

Legal discussion was a major element of Jewish life in the period of the Scrolls, and legal disagreements were a primary factor in the formation of groups and sects. These discussions were grounded in a desire to implement the Commandments of God, and necessary because the Bible's demands were often not complete or entirely clear. Thus interpretation entered the picture, and with it disagreements. Though appearing to dwell on insignificant points, these arguments illustrate how anxious the people were to obey God. Even the smallest details of His requirements had to be obeyed. And no compromise was possible. How could one compromise what God required? Thus competing groups could arise around differences of legal interpretation.

When compared to those of Rabbinic literature, the legal positions of the Scrolls are generally conservative. The Scrolls are relatively harsh, too, often seemingly favouring priests over lay people, that is, if one ignores the esotericism of some of the commentaries. Compare this harshness with a story about Jesus found in the Gospel of Matthew. In the context of a challenge to his practice of healing on the sabbath, Jesus is pictured as asking his audience, 'Suppose one of you has only one sheep and it falls into a pit on the sabbath; will you not lay hold of it and lift it out?' (Matt. 12:11). Clearly the expected answer was that yes, of course, anyone would lift that sheep out. But the author of A Pleasing Fragrance (*Halakah* A) below would not. The sabbath was so Holy in his eyes that one might save a human from a pit, but not an animal. Saving an animal was 'work', and work on the sabbath was forbidden by the Bible.

Some of the works collected below are of the most explosive significance. Though seemingly mired in legal minutiae that to modern readers might appear quite trivial, they actually give a picture of the mindset of the people in Palestine at this critical juncture in the formation of what is now called Western Civilization. We are on fairly safe ground if we imagine this mindset of extreme apocalyptic 'zeal' as being the dominant one – not the mindset of the Pharisees or Herodians, which has been the popular picture up until now, but rather that of 'opposition' groups and others normally thought of as 'sectarian' in the Jerusalem of this time.

Certainly the 'Zealots' were parties to it, as probably were that group now referred to as 'Jewish Christians', i.e., those Jerusalem Church supporters or followers of James the Just called 'zealous for the Law' in Acts 21:21. It would be like imagining, for the purposes of discussion, a non-Muslim venturing into Mecca during the pilgrimage season and seeing the atmosphere of zeal and militancy that would normally be widespread there. Of course, a non-Muslim could not do this; he would not be permitted. But that is just the point.

The same atmosphere held sway in Jerusalem on the Temple Mount in the period we are considering, including the same restrictions regarding 'foreigners' on the Temple Mount, at least where so-called 'Zealots' and the partisans of the literature we have before us were concerned. The use in the two Letters on Works Righteousness, with which we begin this chapter, of the language Paul uses in Romans and Galatians to describe the significance of Abraham's salvationary state (also used in Islam with a slightly different twist to produce similar new departures) is of the most fundamental importance for understanding the foundations of Western Civilization. These two letters are also important for deciphering the sectarian situation in the Jerusalem of this period.

The last document in this chapter is equivalent to the last column of what we have been referring to throughout this work as 'the Damascus Document'. We have been relying on the two copies of these materials found in the Cairo *Genizah* by Solomon Schechter at the end of the last century. Columns representing the first column of this document have now been found in the unpublished materials from Qumran; they are not, however, the first column of the Qumran document, i.e. there is indecipherable material belonging to an additional column or columns to the right of the material paralleling the Cairo version on the unpublished plates. A good deal of the other Damascus Document materials found among the unpublished fragments from Qumran do parallel the Cairo recensions; therefore we have not included them.

This last column does not, though it alludes to passages and themes *in* the Cairo recensions. Therefore, we have included it. We have also included it because it is so interesting and so well preserved.

Revealingly, it is an excommunication text of the most heightened and unbending kind. It absolutely embodies the ethos we have been delineating in this chapter and concern for the *Torah of Moses* – words it actually uses. It would certainly have been directed against someone of the mindset of a Paul, had Paul ever been to the 'Damascus' the Qumran text so reveres.

35. THE FIRST LETTER ON WORKS RECKONED AS RIGHTEOUSNESS (4Q394–398)
(Plates 13 & 14)

('Some of our Words concerning the *Torah* of God')

This text is of the most crucial importance for evaluating the Qumran community, mindset and historical development. Parts of it have been talked about, written about and known about for over three decades. Particularly in the last decade, parts have circulated in various forms, some under the by now popular code 'MMT'. In turn, this is often incorrectly spoken of as 'some words of the *Torah*'. This title would only be appropriate to the First Letter, but the allusion on which it is based actually does not occur until Line 30 of the Second Letter. Its proper translation would be 'some *works* of the *Torah*' (italics ours). Where the history of Christianity is concerned, this is an important distinction.

Our reconstruction, transliteration and translation here are *completely new*. We have not relied on anyone or any other work, but rather sifted through the entire unpublished corpus, grouping like plates together, identifying all the overlaps, and making all the joins ourselves. As it turns out, this is not very difficult, as these group out fairly readily and are quite easily put together. Nor did we rely on the recently published extended Claremont catalogue, because our work was completed before this became available. We also added the calendrical materials at the beginning of the First Letter, which have never been known in any form and are not unimportant, as we have seen, since the control and regulation of society are often based on these.

What we actually have here are two letters, something like Corinthians 1 and Corinthians 2 or Thessalonians 1 and Thessalonians 2 in the New Testament. It would appear from the multiple copies of them, that these letters were kept and recopied as important Community documents. The addressee of the Second Letter looks very like a king of some kind – like the addressee of the Paean to King Jonathan in Chapter 8 at the end of this collection – or, if one prefers 'the Leader of the Community' at the beginning. In our view, if the letter is to be placed in the first century BC and grouped with other texts mentioning historical figures in Chapter 4 and Chapter 8, this could be 'King Jonathan', i.e. Alexander Jannaeus, or his zealot-minded and more populist son, Aristobulus, or either of the latter's two like-minded sons, Alexander or Antigonus, the second having actually been a king.

If placed in the first century, where we would prefer to place it because of its language – a form of 'proto-Mishnaic Hebrew' – and clear typological parallels with similar 'early Christian' efforts; then the addressee is most probably Agrippa I (*c.* AD 40), who according to the extant literature, if nothing else, made a pretence at *Torah* observance, or possibly his son Agrippa II (*c.* AD 60), who was less positively regarded. If it is 'the Leader of a Community', then it is someone who is not at odds with this Community, or who is at least sympathetic enough to be addressed by it in such a comradely and collegial tone.

In the first part the text lays out its calendrical reckonings relating to festivals and sabbaths, ending up with the by now familiar 364-day scheme set forth in the Genesis Florilegium, Jubilees and Priestly texts above, that is, it sets forth the calendar according to the feast days it recommends. Since, superficially, it mentions no other calendar, one must assume the situation had not yet been finally regulated one way or the other and was to a certain extent still in flux. The very fact of its polemic, though, would seem to imply that a lunisolar calendar of the type set forth in Chapter 4 was being used in the Temple.

It then moves on to discuss serious, if seemingly 'nit-picking' legal issues of a different kind – the key words here being 'reckoned as' or 'counted for' in Lines 2, 10, 34, 50, etc. We have seen these words used above in various contexts. Associated with them is an emphasis on 'doing' (cf. Line 62), and of course, the ultimate Hebrew variation of the root of this word, 'works'.

These words 'reckoned as' or 'counted for' are summed up best in the climactic conclusion of the Second Letter, where they are used as follows: 'And finally, we wrote to you about some of the works of the *Torah*, which we *reckoned* for your Good and for that of your people. . .'

(italics ours). The relation of these words to Paul's use of the same language in discussing Abraham's faith in Rom. 3:28: 'We *reckon* that by faith a man is justified and not by *works of the Law*'; or in Rom. 4:9: 'Faith *was counted* to Abraham as Righteousness' based on Gen. 15:6; or finally in Gal. 3:6 to the same effect, is crucial (italics ours). Both the Qumran letters and Paul's are operating in similar ideological frameworks, the only difference being that the Qumran ones are completely 'works' and *Torah*-oriented; Paul's, the opposite.

As Paul puts it: 'If Righteousness is through the Law then Christ died for nothing' (Gal. 2:21, introducing Chapter 3 above). This will have particular relevance to his analysis of why Christ's having taken upon himself 'the curse of the Law' would 'redeem' those Paul is newly converting from 'the curse of the Law' and enable them to be 'adopted sons' and through faith 'receive the promised Spirit' (Gal. 3:13–14 and 4:5–6). We will have occasion to discuss this cluster of allusions relative to such Deuteronomic 'cursing' at the end of the Damascus Document below.

Gen. 15:6's words, 'counted for him as Righteousness', concerning Abraham, were also applied in Ps. 106:31 to the high priest Phineas' act in fending off foreign pollution from the camp in the wilderness. This must have been a matter of some excitement for 'Zealots'. Phineas' 'zeal for God' in killing backsliders because of interaction with Gentiles (a subject too of the present letter) was, as we have seen, an archetypical event for the Maccabean family (cf. Mattathias' farewell speech to his sons in 1 Macc. 2:54), as it was for the so-called 'Zealot' movement that followed. We say 'so-called', because *Ant.* 18:23 never *really* calls it this – only 'the Fourth Philosophy' – and also because it was 'Messianic'. The evocation of critical words such as these in the several various settings above further concretizes the relationships of these movements.

Some of the positions enumerated in the recitation of legal minutiae before us, such as fluids transmitting the impurity of their containers along the course of the poured liquid, have been identified in the Talmud as 'Sadducean'. But the Talmud can hardly be considered historically precise. By 'Sadduki', i.e. 'Sadducee' or 'Zadokite', it often means sectarian generally (*min*) – including even Jewish Christians. The group responsible for these two letters could certainly not have been 'establishment Sadducees' of the Herodian period and the group pictured in the New Testament. Josephus describes these as 'dominated in all things by the Pharisees'. It could, however, have been the Maccabean Sadducees of an earlier period, in so far as they – or their heirs – were not dominated by the Pharisees or involved in the acceptance of foreign rule, foreign involvement in the affairs of the society, or foreign gifts or sacrifices in the Temple.

Maccabees, Zadokites, Christians and Qumran: A New Hypothesis of Qumran Origins, Leiden, 1983, set forth on the basis of Josephus' writings, the Qumran texts, and Talmudic materials a *sitz im leben* for these matters without benefit of either these letters or the Temple Scroll. It identified – at least in the Herodian period – *two* groups of Sadduccees, one 'establishment' and another 'opposition'. The latter can also be called 'Messianic Sadducees'. In the Maccabean period they can be called 'Purist Sadduccees'. These last devolve into groups that are called 'Zealot', 'Essene', or even 'Jewish Christian', depending on the vantage point of the observer, just so long as one understands their 'opposition' nature and their nationalist, unbending and militant attachment to the Law (which Josephus calls 'national tradition'). This is exemplified in the two letters on Works Righteousness which we present here, by the strong attachment to the Law throughout. For instance, if one wants to call attitudes such as these 'Essene', one would have to redefine to a certain extent what one meant by that term.

The group responsible for this First Letter on 'those works of the *Torah* reckoned as good for you', or to use the language of Paul, 'reckoned as Righteousness' or 'reckoned as justifying you', are very interested in the Temple as per the parameters of the Damascus Document and the Temple Scroll, with which it can be typologically grouped. They are particularly concerned with 'pollution of the Temple'. This last, as we have seen, along with 'fornication' – a theme the letter also addresses – constituted two out of the 'three nets' which 'Belial (Herod?) deceived Israel into considering as Righteousness' (CD, iv–v).

The idea that the literature at Qumran was anti-Temple, which developed in the early days of Qumran research from considering the Community Rule only and misunderstanding its splendid imagery, is just not accurate. The 'zeal' shown for the Temple in these letters and other works is pivotal throughout, but this Temple must be one 'purified' of all polluted works. It should be noted that this 'nationalistic' attachment to the Temple in Jerusalem, and a consonant xenophobia related to it, is tangible throughout the document.

Here Gentile gifts (5ff.) and the 'vessels' that bear them (particularly 'skins'; cf. 18ff.) exercise the document's authors to no little degree. This theme, particularly as it relates to the 'skins', also exercises the authors of the Temple Scroll, Columns 46–7, where it is linked to classes of polluted persons barred from the Temple. The same gist is discernible here. In the Temple Scroll such 'skins' are referred to as 'sacrificed to idols'. This theme is again discernible in Line 9 of the present document. It links the whole issue of Gentile gifts and sacrifices in the Temple to idolatry, and is but an adumbration of the more general theme of 'things sacrificed to idols' elsewhere, particularly in the New Testament.

These themes, not to mention the ones of 'works Righteousness' and the Law, are also discernible in extant works relating to James the Just (the *'Zaddik'/'*Zadok'), the leader of the so-called 'Jerusalem Community' from the 40s to the 60s AD — what has retrospectively come to be called 'Jewish Christianity' in Palestine. The movement that seems subsequently to have developed also came to be called the Ebionites (i.e. 'the Poor Ones'), a term of self-designation running the gamut of Qumran documents (see our discussion of it in Hymns of the Poor in Chapter 7). In particular, James is portrayed in the Book of Acts as insisting upon abstention from 'blood', 'fornication' and 'food'/'things sacrificed to idols' (Acts 21:25; also Acts 15). His position on 'works counted' or 'reckoned as Righteousness' is made clear in the letter attributed to his name and the riposte it contains to the Pauline position on Abraham's faith in Romans and Galatians.

The issue of Gentile gifts and Gentile sacrifices in the Temple was a particularly crucial one in the period running up to the war against Rome from the 40s to the 60s AD. Josephus makes this clear in the *Jewish War*, where he describes the barring of these — demanded by 'the Zealots' and presumably other opposition groups — as 'an innovation which before our ancestors were unacquainted with'. Other aspects of this problem, including the barring of Herodians (who were looked upon as Gentiles by groups such as these, though *not by the Pharisees*) and their sacrifices, not only from the Temple, but ultimately from all Jerusalem, was but a special case of this attitude. In the war the Herodian palaces were eventually burned, as were those of the high priests owing their positions to them, not to mention all the debt records.

Though it is possible that Gentile gifts and sacrifices in the Temple were also an issue in the Maccabean period, the literature does not record it. In the end this issue was the one that triggered the war against Rome in AD 66–70 or rather the one that was used by extremists to trigger it; because in AD 66 this war was made inevitable when the lower priesthood stopped sacrifices on behalf of Romans and other foreigners in the Temple, in particular those daily sacrifices which had up to that point been offered on behalf of the Roman Emperor. That is how important these themes are.

This text also refers to the matter of the Red Heifer for particularly important purification procedures, a matter further developed in the text by that name below. In line with the general nationalistic xenophobia across the spectrum of Qumran documents, Ammonites and Moabites are grouped with people like the deaf and the blind, suffering from some serious physical imperfection (47–83). This theme, which is also treated above in the Temple Scroll, in some manner probably involves barring Gentiles from the Temple generally.

This is to be contrasted sharply with the portrait of Jesus' pro-Gentile sentiments or behaviour in the Gospels, where he is even pictured, as noted above, as keeping 'table fellowship' with similar classes of barred persons, including most strikingly 'prostitutes' and 'tax-collectors' – important allusions for this period. Nor should one forget the imagery of Jesus as 'Temple' generally in Paul. In this context, one image in the Gospels, comparing Gentiles with dogs being allowed to eat the crumbs under the table (Matt. 15:27, etc.), is not without resonance in this text. In Lines 66–7, even dogs are barred from *the Temple* because they eat the bones with the flesh still on them, i.e. they acquire the kind of pollution associated with 'things sacrificed to idols'.

These things are related, too, to the issue of 'fornication', which in Lines 83–9 is equated to the one of 'hybrids'. In turn, both appear to be related to intermarrying between Israel and foreigners actually referred to in 87–8. This theme, of course, would be dear to 'Zealots' inspired by the saving act of Phineas warding off such 'mixing' in ancient times. Here, it would seem also to relate to intermarrying between priests and Israelites.

Line 86 uses an allusion from the Community Rule, which we have already referred to – the reference to 'priests' on the Community Council as a spiritualized 'Holy of Holies' leading up to the two allusions to the 'Way in the wilderness' of Isa. 40:3 (viii.5–9 and ix.4). But the reason for the banning of both 'fornication' and intermarriage would appear to be the same: i.e. Israel is supposed to be 'a Holy People', 'a Holy Seed'. It is difficult to conceive of a more xenophobic group than this. The concern for the Temple exhibited in all these passages should be clear throughout.

Where the identifiably 'Sadducean' position on the impurity of poured liquids travelling between vessels is concerned, the infraction relates to that of not 'separating impure from pure', which is fundamental to the

Qumran approach and stated as such in Line 64. This theme is at the root of the problems in the Temple signalled in the Damascus Document too, for instance those relating 'fornication' to Temple 'pollution' (v.6–7). It is also at the root of the exegesis of 'preparing a Way in the wilderness' (1QS,viii.11–13), which is introduced by the injunction 'separate yourselves'.

In the Damascus Document, it is contended that they do not observe proper 'separation' in the Temple (i.e. between 'pure' and 'impure'), and therefore 'pollute' the Temple, because 1) they sleep with women during their periods and 2) because every man of them marries his niece. These two charges are fundamental to the Qumran mindset and are sufficient to develop a *sitz im leben*.

The first charge no doubt relates to the perception of sexual relations with Gentiles; the second, most probably to the Herodian family, as no other group before them can be demonstrably so identified. Niece marriage was a practice the Herodians indulged in habitually as a matter seemingly of family policy. It may well have something to do with their Idumaean/Arab origins, and even today, the practice is not uncommon among heirs to these cultures. This conjunction of antagonism to foreigners and niece marriage becomes most perfectly embodied in the Herodian family and those incurring their pollution by intercourse – sexual or social – with them (see CD,vi.14–15, following the allusion to 'vipers' and 'firebrands': 'No man that approaches them shall be free of their guilt.').

Finally, it should be noted that in one unpublished version of the Damascus Document there appears to be material relating to the problem of 'copper vessels' signalled in Line 6, itself not unrelated to the issue of gifts from Gentiles. Also, the distinction made in Lines 77–8 between intentional and inadvertent sin is discussed at some length in the Community Rule (vi.24ff. and viii.22ff.).

TRANSLITERATION   **Part 1: Calendrical Exposition**

1 1. [בחודש הראשון] 2. [בארבעה] 3. [בו שבת] 4. [בעשתי עשר]
5. [בו שבת] 6. [בארבעה] 7. [עשר בו הפסח] 8. [בשמונה] 9. [עשר בו שבת]
10. [בעשרים] 11. [וחמשה] 12. [בו שבת] 13. [אחר בעשרים]
14. [וששה] 15. [בו הנף העמר]

2 16. [בשניים] 17. [בחודש השני] 18. [בו שבת] 19. [בתשעה] 20. [בו שבת]
21. [בארבעה עשר] 22. [בו הפסח השני] 23. [בששה עשר] 24. [בו שבת]
25. [בעשרים] 26. [ושלושה] 27. [בו שבת] 28. [בשלישים] 29. [בו שבת]

3 .30 [בחודש השלישי] 31. [בשבעה] 32. [בו שבת] 33. [בארבעה עשר]
34. [בו שבת] 35. [אחר] 36. [בחמשה עשר] 37. [בו חג השבועות] 38. [בעשרים]
39. [ואחד] 40. [בו שבת] 41. [בעשרים] 42. [ושמונה] 43. [בו שבת]
44. [עליו אחר] 45. [האחד והשני] 46. יום שלישי 47. [נוסף]

4 .48 [בחודש הרביעי] 49. [בארבעה] 50. [בו שבת] 51. [עשתי עשר]
52. [בו שבת] 53. [בשמונה] 54. [עשר בו שבת] 55. [בעשרים] 56. [וחמשה]
57. [בו שבת]

5 .58 [בשניים] 59. [בחודש החמשי] 60. [בו שבת] 61. [אחר] 62. [בשלושה]
63. [בו מועד התירוש] 64. [בתשעה] 65. [בו שבת] 66. [ב]שש אשר 67. בו שבת
68. בעשרם 69. ושלושא 70. בו שבת 71. [ב]שלו[ש]ים 72. [בו שבת]
73. [בחודש הששי]

6 .74 [בשבעה] 75. [בו שבת] 76. [בארבעה עשר] 77. בו שבת 78. בעשרים
79. ואחד 80. בו שבת 81. בעשרים 82. ושים 83. בו מועד 84. השמן
85. אח]ר בעשרים 86. ו]שלושה] 87. קרב]ן העצים 88. [בעשרים]
89. [ושמונה] 90. [בו שבת] 91. [עליו אחר] 92. [האחד והשני] 93. [יום שלישי]
94. [נוסף]

7 .95 [באחד בחודש] 96. [השביעי] 97. [בו יום זכרון] 98. [בארבעה]
99. [בו שבת] 100. [בעשרה] 101. [בו יום] 102. [הכפורים]
103. [בעשתי עשר] 104. [בו שבת] 105. [בחמשה עשר] 106. [בו חג]
107. [הסכות] 108. [בשמונה] 109. [עשר בו שבת] 110. [בעשרים]
111. [ושניים] 112. [בו שבת] 113. [בו עצרת] 114. [בעשרים] 115. [וחמשה]
115. [בו שבת]

8 .116 [בשניים] 117. [בחודש השמיני] 118. [בו שבת] 119. [בתשעה]
120. בו שבת 121. בשה עשר 122. בו שבת 123. בעשרים 124. ושלושה
125. בו שבת 126. בשל[ו]שי[ם 127. [בו שבת] 128. [בחודש התשיעי]

9 .129 [בשבעה] 130. [בו שבת] 131. [בארבעה עשר] 132. [בו שבת]
133. [בע]שר[ים ואחד] 134. [בו ש[בת] 135. [ב]עשרים 136. ושמונה
137. ב[ו] שבת138. עליו אחר 139. ה]אחד] והשנ[י] 140. [יום שלישי]
141. [נוסף]

10 .142 [בחודש העשירי] 143. [בארבעה] 144. ב]ו שבת] 145. בע[שתי עשר]
146. בו שבת 147. בשמונה 148. עשר בו שבת 149. בעשרים 150. וחמשה
151. בו שבת 152. בשניים 153. בחד[ש] 154. [העשתי עשר]

11 .155 [בו שבת] 156. [בתשעה] 157. [בו שבת] 158. [בששה עשר]
159. [בו שבת] 160. [בעשרים] 161. [ושלושה] 162. [בו שבת] 163. [בשלושים]

164. [כו שבת] 165. [בחודש] 166. [השנים] 167. [עשר] 168. [בשבעה]

169. [כו שבת]

12 170. [בארבעה עשר בו שבת בעשרים ואחד בו שבת בעשרים]

171. [ושמונה בו] שבת על[ל]ו אחר [האחד והשני יום שלישי]

172. [נו]סף ושלמה השנה שלוש מאת ו[ששים וארבעה]

173. יום

Part 2: Legal Issues

1. אלה מקצת דברינו [בתורת א[ל שהם מ[קצת]

2. [ה]מעשים שא א[נח]נ[ו חושבים וכו]לם על [קרבנות]

3. וטהרת {..הר} ו[על תרומת ד[גן ה]גוים שהם... [

4. ומגיע[י]ם בה ש[ ]יהם ומט[מאים... ואין לאכול]

5. מדגן הגוים ואין לביא למק[ד[ש [ועל זבח החטאת]

6. שהם מבשלים [אות]ה בכלי [נחושת הגוים ומטמאים] בה

7. בשר זבחיהם ומ[בשל]ים בעזר[ת המקדש ומטמאים] אות[ו]

8. במרק זבחם ועל זבח הגוים [אנחנו אומרים שהם] זובח[ים]

9. אל הפ[סילה] שא היא[ה] מושכת אליו [ואף על תודת] זבח

10. השל[מים] שמניחים אותה מיום ליום אנ[חנו חושבים]

11. שהמנ[חה נא]כלת על החלבים והבשר ביום ז[ו]ב[חם כי לבני]

12. הכוהנים ראוי להזהיר בדבר הזה בשל שלוא י[היו בני אהרון]

13. מסיא[י]ם את העם עון ואף על טהרת פרת החטאת

14. השוחט אותה והסור[ף אותה והאוס[ף את אפרה והמזה את [מי]

15. החטאת לכול אלה להער[י[בו]ת השמש להיות טהורים

16. בשל שא יהיה הטהר מזה על הטמא כי לבני

17. אהרן ראוי להיות מ[זהרים בדבר הזה   [

18. [ועל] עורות הבק[ר והצאן   [

19. [עורות]יהם כלי[אין]

20. [להביא]ם למקד[ש   [

21. [   ]ה ואף על עורו[ת ועצמות הבהמה הטמאה שהמה עושים]

22. [מן עצמותמה] ומן ע[ו]ר[ות]מה ידות כ[לים אין להביאם למקדש] ואף על ע[ו]ר נבלת

23. [הבהמה] הטהורה [הנוש]א אותה נבלתה [לוא י]גש לטהרת ה[קודש]

24. [   ]על[   ]ת שהמ[ה   ]ה. על ה. וא[ף   [

25. [   ]

26. [   ]

27. [   ]

28. [   ]

29. [   ]

30. [כי לבני]

31. הכו[הני]ם ראוי [להש[מ]ר ב[כו]ל הדברים [האלה בשל שלוא יהיו]

32. משיאים את העם עוון [וע]ל שא כתוב [ושחט על ירך המזבח והמה]
33. [שוחטים] מחוץ למחנה שור [וכש]ב ועז כי מ[קום השחיטה בצ]פון המחנה
34. ואנחנו חושבים שהמקדש [משכן אהל מועד הוא ו]ירושלי[ם]
35. מחנה היא וחוצה למחנה [הוא חוצה לירושלים] הוא מחנה
36. עריהם חוץ ממ[חנה ‹הי›[א] [יר]‹ו›[שלים ועל החט]את שמוצאים את דשא
37. [ה]מזבח ושור[פים אותו מחוץ לירושלים כי] היא המקום אשר
38. [בחר בו] מכול שב[טי ישראל להשכין את שמו עליו   [
39. .   [ה]   [
40. .   [
41. .   [
42. .   [
43. .   [אי]נם שוחטים במקדש
44. [ועל העברות אנחנו חושבים שאין לשחוט א]ת האם ואת הולד ביום אחד
45. [   ]וא[ף על האוכל את הולד אנח]נו חושבים שא יאכל את הולד
46. [שבמעי אמו לאחר שחיטתו ואתם יודעים שהו]א כן והדבר כתוב עברה
47. [ועל העמונ]י והמואבי והממזר ופ[צוע הדכה וכרו]ת השפכת שהם באים
48. בקהל [ו   ונשים] לוקחים [לעשו]תם עצם
49. אחת [[
50. .   [טמאות ואף חושבים אנחנו
51. [שאין ל   ]ואין לבו[א] עליהם
52. .   [ואי]ן להתיכם ולעשותם
53. [עצם אחת   ]ואין להבי[אם
54. .   [   ]ואתם יודעים שמק[צת העם
55. .   [   ]מתוכ[כים
56. .   [כי לבני ישראל ראוי להזהר] מכול תערובת נבר
57. ולהיות יראים מהמקדש [ואף ע]ל סומ[י]ם
58. שאינם רואים להזהר מכול תערו[בת] ותערובת
59. [א]שם אינם רואים
60. ואף על החרשים שלוא שמעו חוק ומשפט וטהרה ולא
61. שמעו משפטי ישראל כי שלוא ראה ולוא שמע לוא
62. ידע לעשות והמה באים לטהרת המקדש
63. ואף על המוצקות אנחנו אומרים שהם שאין בהם
64. [ט]הרה ואף המוצקות אינם מבדילות בין הטמא
65. לטהור כי לחת המוצקות והמקבל מהמה כהם
66. לחה אחת ואין להביא למחני הק[ו]דש כלבים שהם
67. אוכלים מקצת עצמות המ‹ק›ד[ש ו]הבשר עליהם כי
68. ירושלים היאה מחנה הקדש היא המקום
69. שבחר בו מכול שבטי ישראל כי ירושלים היא ראש
70. מ[ח]נות ישראל ואף על מטעת עצי המאכל הנטע
71. בארץ ישראל כראשית הוא לכוהנים ומעשר הבקר
72. והצון לכוהנים הוא ואף על הצרועים אנחנו

‏73. א[ו]מרים שלוא י[בואו {ש}] עם טהרת הקודש כי בדד
‏74. [י]היו [מחוץ למחנות ו]אף כתוב שמעת שינלח וכבס [י]שב מחוץ
‏75. [לאוהלו שבעת י]מים ועתה בהיות טמאתם עמהם
‏76. הצ[ר]ועים באים ע[ם] טהרת הקודש לבית ואתם יודעים
‏77. [שכול שונג שלוא עושה מצוה] ונעלה ממנו להבי<>א {ח}
‏78. חטאת [ועל כול עושה ביד רמה כת]וב שהואה בוזה ומגדף
‏79. [ואף בהיות לה[מ]ה ט[מאות נ[גע] אין להאכילם מהקו[ד]שים
‏80. עד בוא השמש ביום השמיני ועל [טמאת נפש]
‏81. האדם אנחנו אומרים שכול עצם שה[י]א חסרה]
‏82. ושלמה כמשפט המת או החלל ה[וא]   *vacat*
‏83. ועל הזונות הנעסה בתוך העם והמה ב[ני]
‏84. קדש משכתוב קודש ישראל ועל לבושו כתוב שלוא]
‏85. יהיה שעטנז ושלוא לזרוע שדו ו[כרמו כלאי]ם
‏86. בגלל שהמה קודשים ובני אהרון ק[דושי קדושים]
‏87. [וא]תם יודעים שמקצת הכהנים ו[העם מתערבים]
‏88. [והמה] מתוככים ומטמאי[ם] את זרע [הקוד]ש [ואף]
‏89. את [זרע]ם עם הזונות כ]
‏90. [One or more lines may be missing here   ]

TRANSLATION

Part 1: Calendrical Exposition [(1) In the first month, (2) on the fourth (3) of it is a sabbath; (4) on the eleventh (5) of it is a sabbath; (6) on the four- (7) teenth of it is the Passover; (8) on the eight- (9) teenth of it is a sabbath; (10) on the twenty- (11) fifth (12) of it is a sabbath; (13) afterward, on the twenty- (14) sixth (15) of it is the Waving of the Omer. (16) On the second (17) of the second month (18) on that day is a sabbath; (19) on the ninth (20) of it is a sabbath; (21) on the fourteenth (22) of it is the Second Passover; (23) on the sixteenth (24) of it is a sabbath; (25) on the twenty- (26) third (27) of it is a sabbath; (28) on the thirtieth (29) of it is a sabbath. (30) In the third month (31) on the seventh (32) of it is a sabbath; (33) on the fourteenth (34) of it is a sabbath; (35) afterward, (36) on the fifteenth (37) of it is the Festival of Weeks; (38) on the twenty- (39) first (40) of it is a sabbath; (41) on the twenty- (42) eighth (43) of it is a sabbath; (44) after (45) Sunday and Monday, (46) an (extra) Tuesday (47) is added. (48) In the fourth month (49) on the fourth (50) of it is a sabbath; (51) on the eleventh (52) of it is a sabbath; (53) on the eight- (54) eenth of it is a sabbath; (55) on the twenty- (56) fifth (57) of it is a sabbath. (58) On the second (59) of the fifth month (60) is a sabbath; (61) afterward, (62) on the third (63) of it is the Festival of New Wine; (64) on the ninth (65) of it is a sabbath; (66) on] the sixteenth (67) of it is a sabbath; (68) on the twenty- (69) third (70) of it is a sabbath; (71) [on the] thir[t]ieth (72) [of it is a sabbath. (73) In the sixth month, (74) on the seventh (75) is a sabbath; (76) on the fourteenth] (77) of it is a sabbath; (78) on the twenty- (79) first (80) of it is a sabbath; (81) on the twenty- (82) second (83) of it is the Festival of (84) (New) Oil; (85) after[ward, on the twenty- (86) third] (87) is the Offerin[g of Wood; (88) on the twenty- (89) eighth (90) of it is a sabbath; (91) after (92) Sunday and Monday (93) an (extra) Tuesday (94) is added. (95) On the first of the seventh (96) month (97) is the Day of Remembrance; (98) on the fourth (99) of it is a sabbath; (100) on the tenth (101) of it is the Day (102) of Atonement; (103) on the eleventh (104) of it is a sabbath; (105) on the fifteenth (106) of it is the Festival (107) of Booths; (108) on the eight- (109) eenth of it is a sabbath; (110) on the twenty- (111) second (112) of it is the Gathering; (113) on the twenty- (114) fifth (115) of it is a sabbath. (116) On the second (117) of the eighth month (118) is a sabbath; (119) on the ninth] (120) of it is a sabbath; (121) on the sixteenth (122) of it is a sabbath; (123) on the twenty- (124) third (125) of it is a sabbath; (126) on the th[irt]ieth (127) [of it is a sabbath. (128) In the ninth month, (129) the seventh (130) is a sabbath; (131) on the fourteenth (132) of it is a sabbath; (133) on the tw]ent[y-first (134) of it is a sa]bbath; (135) [on the] twenty- (136) eighth (137) of [it] is a sabbath; (138) after (139) S[unday] and Mond[ay,] (140) [an (extra) Tuesday (141) is added. (142) In the tenth month] (143) on the [fourth (144) of it is a sabbath;] (145) on the el[eventh] (146) of it is a sabbath; (147) on the eight- (148) teenth of it is a sabbath; (149) on the twenty- (150) fifth (151) of it is a sabbath. (152) On the second (153) [of the eleventh] (154) mon[th (155) is a sabbath. (156) on the ninth (157) of it is a sabbath; (158) on the sixteenth (159) of it is a sabbath; (160) on the twenty- (161) third (162) of it is a sabbath; (163) on the thirtieth (164) of it is a sabbath. (165-167) In the twelfth month, (168) the seventh (169) is a sabbath; (170) on the fourteenth of it is a sabbath; on the twenty-first of it is a sabbath; on the twenty- (171) eighth of it] is a sabbath; after [Sunday and Monday an (extra) Tuesday (172) is add]ed. Thus the year is complete: three hundred and [sixty-four] (173) days.

Part 2: Legal Issues (1) These are some of our words concerning [the Law of Go]d, that is, so[me (2) of the] works that [w]e [reckon (as justifying you; cf. Second Letter, line 34). All] of them have to do with [holy gifts] (3) and purity issues. Now, [concerning the offering of gr]ain by the [Gentiles, who . . .] (4) and they tou[c]h it . . . and render it im[pure . . . One is not to eat] (5) any Gentile grain, nor is it permissible to bring it to the Tem[p]le. [Concerning the sin offering] (6) that is boiled in vessels [of Gentile copper,] by which means [they (the priests) render impure] (7) the flesh of their offerings, and (further, that) they b[oi]l in the courtya[rd of the Temple and thereby pollute] it (the Temple) (8) with the soup they make—(we disagree with these practices). Concerning sacrifices by Gentiles, [we say that (in reality) they] sacrifice (9) to the i[dol] that seduces them; (therefore it is illicit). [Further, regarding the thank] offering (10) that accompanies peace offer[ings,] that they put aside on one day for the next, w[e reckon] (11) that the gra[in offering is to be ea]ten with the fat and the flesh on the day that they are [off]er[ed. It is incumbant upon] (12) the priests to assure that care is taken in this matter, so that [the priests wi]ll not (13) brin[g] sin upon the people. Also, with regard to the purity of the heifer that purifies from sin (i.e., the Red Heifer): (14) he who slaughters it and he who burns it and he who gathers its ashes and he who sprinkles [the water] (15) (of purification from) sin—all of these are to be pure with the se[tt]ing of the sun, (16) so that (only) the pure man will be sprinkling upon the impure. The sons (17) of Aaron must give wa[rning in this matter . . .] (18) [Concerning] the skins of catt[le and sheep . . .] (19) their [skins] vessels [. . . One is not (20) to bring] them to the Templ[e . . .] (21) Also, regarding the skin[s and bones of unclean animals—for they are making] (22) [from the bones] and from the s[ki]ns handles for ve[ssels—one is not to bring them (i.e., the vessels) to the Temple. With regard to the ski]n from the carcass (23) of a clean [animal,] he who carries that carcass [must not to]uch [holy items] susceptible to impurity. (24) [. . . Al]so concerning . . . that the[y . . . (30) The members] (31) of the pries[tho]od must [be care]ful [about] all [these] matters, [so that they will not] (32) bring sin upon the people. [Con]cerning (the fact) that it is written, ['And he shall slaughter it on the side of the altar . . .,' they (33) are slaughtering] bulls and [lam]bs and she-goats outside the 'camp.' On the contrary, the (lawful) pl[ace of slaughter is at the no]rth within the 'camp.' (34) We reckon that the Temple [is 'the Tent of Witness,' while] Jerusale[m] (35) is the 'camp.' 'Outside the camp' [means 'outside Jerusalem.'] (It refers to) the 'camp (36) of their cities,' outside the 'ca[mp' (which i]s [Jer]u[salem.) Regarding the si]n offering, they are to remove the offal of (37) [the] altar and bur[n it outside Jerusalem, for] it is the place that (38) [He chose] from among all the tri[bes of Israel, to establish His Name there as a dwelling . . .] (43) . . . they are [no]t slaughtering in the Temple. (44) [Regarding pregnant animals, we maintain that one must not slaughter (both)] the mother and the fetus on any one day. (45) [. . . Also, concerning anyone eating the fetus, w]e maintain that he may eat the fetus (46) [that is in its mother's womb (only) after its (separate) slaughter. You know that th]is is the proper view, since the matter stands written, 'A pregnant animal . . .' (47) [With respect to the Ammon]ite and the Moabite and the bastard and the man with cru[shed

testicles and the man with a damag[ed] male organ who are entering (48) the
assembly . . . and taking [wives, to ma]ke them 'one (49) bone' . . .
(50) polluted. We also reckon (51) [that one must not . . . and one must not
have inter]course with them (52) [. . . And one mu]st not integrate them
and make them (53) ['one bone' . . . And one must not bring] them in
(54) [. . . And you know that so]me of the people (55) [. . . integr]ating
(56) [. . . For the sons of Israel must guard against] all illicit marriage
(57) and (thus) properly revere the Temple. [In addition, con]cerning the
bli[n]d, (58) who cannot see so as to avoid polluting mingl[ing,] and to
whom [sin]ful (59) mingling is invisible—(60) as well as the deaf, who hear
neither law, nor statute, nor purity regulation, and do not (61) hear the
statutes of Israel—for 'He who cannot see and cannot hear does not
(62) know how to perform (the Law)'—these people are trespassing on the
purity of the Temple! (63) Concerning poured liquids, we say that they
possess no (64) intrinsic [pu]rity. Poured liquids do not (properly) separate
between the impure (65) and the pure (i.e. vessels), because the fluid of
poured liquids and that of a receptacle used with them (66) is one and the
same (i.e., the pollution travels between the vessels along the path of the
fluid). One is not to bring dogs into the H[ol]y 'camp' because they
(67) eat some of the bones in the Te[m]ple while the flesh is (still) on them.
Because (68) Jerusalem is the Holy 'camp'—the place (69) that He chose
from among all the tribes of Israel. Thus Jerusalem is the foremost of
(70) the 'ca[m]ps of Israel.' Regarding trees planted for food (71) in the land
of Israel, (the fruit of the fourth year) is analogous to a first fruit offering
and belongs to the priests. Likewise the tithe of cattle (72) and sheep
belongs to the priests. In the matter of those suffering from a skin disease,
we (73) s[ay that they should not c]ome with holy items susceptible to
impurity. Rather, they (74) must stay alone [outside the camps. And] it is
also written, 'From the time when he shaves and bathes, let him [st]ay
outside (75) [his tent seven d]ays.' But at present, while they are still
impure, (76) those suf[fering from a skin disease are coming] home [w]ith
holy items susceptible to impurity. You know (77) [that anyone who sins by
inadvertence, who breaks a commandment] and is forgiven for it, must
bring (78) a sin offering (but they are not doing so). [As for the
intentionally disobedient, it is wr]itten, 'He is a despiser and a blasphemer.'
(79) [While th]e[y suffer im]purities caused by [s]kin diseases, they are not
to be fed with ho[lly] food (80) until the sun rises on the eighth day (after
they are cured). Concerning [impurity caused by contact with a dead]
(81) person, we say that every (human) bone, whether it is [skeleton] (82) or
still covered (with flesh), is governed by the statute for the dead person or

those slain in battle. (83) As for the fornication taking place among the people, they are (supposed to be) a (84) Holy People, as it is written, 'Israel is Holy' (therefore, it is forbidden). Concerning a man's cloth[es, it is written, 'They are not] (85) to be of mixed fabric;' and no one should plant his field or [his vineyard with mixed crop]s. (86) (Mixing is forbidden) because (the people) is Holy, and the sons of Aaron are H[oly of Holy]— (87) [nevertheless, as y]ou know, some of the priests and the [people are mixing (intermarrying).] (88) [They] are intermarrying and (thereby) polluting the [hol]y seed, [as well as] (89) their own [see]d, with fornication . . .

36. THE SECOND LETTER ON WORKS RECKONED AS RIGHTEOUSNESS (4Q397–399)
(Plates 15 & 16)

('Some Works of the Law We Reckon as Justifying you')

That this text is a second letter is clearly signalled in Lines 29–30, quoted above, which refer to a first letter already having been written on the same subject – '*works* reckoned as justifying you' (italics ours). Though fragments of the two letters are in the same handwriting, it is not clear that these are directly connected or on the same or succeeding columns. That the same scribe wrote both letters would not be either unexpected or surprising – nor would the possibility that both letters were already circulating as part of the same document or manuscript, as for instance 1 and 2 Corinthians or 1 and 2 Thessalonians noted above. The second letter is, in any event, extant in a single document.

This short epistle of some 35 extant lines is also of the most far-reaching significance for Qumran studies, not only for all the reasons set forth in our discussion of the First Letter, but also because this text is clearly *eschatological*. The question then becomes, when were people thinking in such an eschatological manner, i.e. using expressions *in daily correspondence* like 'the End of Days' (13 and 24) or a less familiar one used here for the first time in the new materials we have been considering, 'the End Time' (15 and 33)? Together these terms are used four times in an extant document of only some 35 lines. This also distinguishes this letter to a certain extent from the first one, where they were not used, at least not in extant fragments.

Besides these points, the exact nature and context of the 'split' between the group responsible for these writings and 'the majority of the people' is delineated here. Its words are pregnant with meaning: 'we broke with the majority of the people and refused to mix with or go along with them on these matters.' The word used in Line 7 is *parash*, the presumable root of the word 'Pharisee', but these are obviously not anything resembling normative Pharisees. The very issue of 'mixing' in Line 8 (cf. Line 87 above) is, of course, related to that of 'improper separation' and not 'separating clean from unclean' just discussed above. This sentence alone – known but not revealed for *over 35 years* – would be sufficient to identify our group as *sectarian* – at least according to their own evaluation. And it definitively identifies them as a group – a movement.

Finally, the issues over which the split occurred are brought into stark relief. These are always firmly attached to 'the Law', repeatedly and unequivocally called here 'the Book of Moses' (11, 16, 24, and compare Line 6 of the last column of the Damascus Document below: 'the *Torah* of Moses'). Added to these are the Prophets, David (presumably Psalms), and some additional writings, probably Chronicles and the like (10–11); that is, we are at a point when the Bible, as we know it, has to a very considerable extent emerged and the Deuteronomic blessings and curses are recognized as being intimately connected with the arrival of 'the last days' (23–24). These 'blessings and curses' will also be the focal point of the last column of the Damascus Document at the end of this chapter.

The vocabulary is rich in Qumranisms throughout, including references to *hamas* ('violence'), *(maʿal)* ('rebellion'), *zanut* ('fornication'), *Sheker* ('Lying'), and 'heart' and 'Belial' imagery. Many of these phrases are to be found in the Damascus Document. For instance, CD,iv.7, as we have seen, actually uses the terminology 'condemning the Wicked' (25) – as opposed to 'justifying the Righteous' – when describing the eschatological activity of 'the sons of Zadok . . . in the last days'.

Probably reinforcing the impression that this is addressed to an actual king, the particular example of David is developed in Line 27ff., as are his works – which were in their view 'Pious' (*Hassidim*). Again the 'Way' terminology, so widespread in these materials, is evoked, a phrase, as we have seen, delineated in the Community Rule in terms of the 'study of the *Torah*' and known to the Book of Acts as a name for early Christianity in Palestine from the 40s to the 60s (22:4,

24:22, etc). Here, forgiveness from sin is found in 'seeking the *Torah*', just as in the Community Rule 'the Way in the wilderness' — applied in the Gospels to John the Baptist's activities — is interpreted as 'the study of the *Torah*' and, immediately thereafter, 'being zealous for the Law and the time of the Day of Vengeance' (note the parallel use of the word 'time' again). This expression 'study of the *Torah*', familiar in Rabbinic Judaism too, will reappear in the last line of the Damascus Document below.

The text ends with a ringing affirmation, as we have noted above, of what can be described as the Jamesian position on 'justification': that by 'doing' these 'works of the Law' however minute (note the emphasis on *doing* again) in the words of Gen. 15:6 and Ps. 106:31 — a psalm packed with the vocabulary we are considering here — 'it will be reckoned to you as Righteousness'. As a result, you will have kept far from 'the counsel of Belial' and 'at the End Time you will rejoice' (32–3). This last most surely means either 'being resurrected' or 'enjoy the Heavenly Kingdom', or both — an interesting proposition to be putting to a king or Community Leader in this time. Note, too, the allusion to this word 'time' paralleling the second exegesis of 'the Way in the wilderness' material in 1QS, ix. 19 above. The tone of the address, like that to King Jonathan below, is again most certainly warm and conciliatory.

TRANSLITERATION

1. [ ]שמ[[[	
2. [עות[ ] שיבואו [[	
3. ומי ישנ] יהיה מת] [	
4. ועל הנשי]ם [....והמעל] [	
5. כי באלה] בנלל] החמס והזנות אבד]ו מקצת [	
6. מקומות [ואף] כת]וב בספר מושה שלו]א תביא תועבה א]ל ביתכה כי]	
7. התועבה שנואה היאה [ואתם יודעים ש]פרשנו מרוב העו]ם ונמנענו]	
8. מהתערב בדברים האלה ומלבוא ע]מהם ע]ל נב אלה ואתם י]ודעים שלוא]	
9. י]מצא ביתו מעל ושקר ורעה כי על [אלה א]נחנו נותנים את [הדברים האלה]	
10. וכתב]נו אליכה שתבין בספר מושה [ובדברי מושה ובדברי הנ]ביאים ובדוי]ד ובדברי]	
11. ימי כול] דור ודור ובספר כתוב [י]ם על]ל שלוא [[	
12. [ ]שה ואף כתוב ש]תסור] מהד]ר]ך וקרת [אותכה] הרעה וכתוב	
13. והיא כי י]בו]א עליך [כו]ל הדברי]ם ה]אלה באחרית הימים הברכה	
14. ו]הקללא [אשר נתתי לפניך והשיבות]ה אל ל]בב]ך ושבתה אלי בכל לבבך	
15. ובכ]ו]ל נפשך באחרי]ת [העת] וח]י]ו]ת ואף]	
16. כתוב בספר] מושה וב]דברי הנביא]ים שיבואו] עליך ברכות וקללות של]ל [	
17. [ ]ית ש [ ]א[[	

18. [Several lines are missing here   ]
19. [   ]
20. [   ]

21. [הבר]כו[ת ש]בא[ו ב]ו ב[י]מ[י]ו ו[ב]ימי שלומוה בן דויד ואף הקללות
22. [ש]באו בו מי[מי יר]ובעם בן נבט ועד גל[ו]ת ירושלם וצדקיה מלך יהוד[ה]
23. [ש]יב[י]אם ב]   [ואנחנו מכירים שבאוו מקצת הברכות והקללות
24. שכתוב בס[פר מו]שה וזה הוא אחרית הימים שישובו בישר[א]ל
25. לת]ורת אל בכול לבם] ולוא ישובו אחו[ר] והרשעים ירש[יע]ו ואמ] [
26. וה]   [זכור את מלכי ישרא[ל] והתבנן במעשיהם שמי מהם
27. שהוא ירא [את התו]רה היה מצול מצרות והם מב[ק]שי תורה
28. [ונסלח]ו עונות זכור את דויד שהוא איש חסדים [ו]אף
29. הוא [מ]צול מצרות רבות ונסלוח לו ואף אנחנו כתבנו אליך
30. מקצת מעשי התורה שחשבנו לטוב לך ולעמך שראינו
31. עמך ערמה ומדע תורה הבן בכל אלה ובקש מלפניו שיתקן
32. את עצתך והרחיק ממך מחשבת רעה ועצת בליעל
33. בשל שתשמח באחרית העת במצאך מקצת דברינו כן
34. ונחשבה לך לצדקה בעשותך הישר והטוב לפניו לטוב לך
35. ולישראל

TRANSLATION

(2) . . . because they come . . . (3) will be . . . (4) and concerning wome[n . . .] And the rebellion [. . . (5) For by reason of these . . . because of] violence and fornication [some] (6) places have been destroyed. [Further,] it is writt[en in the Book of Moses,] 'You [are no]t to bring the abomination t[o your house, because] (7) the abomination is despised (by God).' [Now, you know that] we broke with the majority of the peo[ple and refused] (8) to mix or go along wi[th them] on these matters. You also k[now that] (9) no rebellion or Lying or Evil [should be] found in His Temple. It is because of [these things w]e present [these words] (10) [and (earlier) wrot]e to you, so that you will understand the Book of Moses [and the words of the Pr]ophets and of Davi[d, along with the (11) chronicles of every] generation. In the Book (of Moses) it is written, . . . s[o] that not . . . (12) It is also written, '[(If you turn] from the W[a]y, then Evil will meet [you.'] Again, it is written, (13) 'It shall come to pass that when [al]l [t]hese thing[s com]e upon you in the End of Days, the blessing (14) [and] the curse [that I have set before you, and you ca]ll them to m[in]d, and return to me with all your heart (15) and with [a]ll [your] soul' [. . . at the En]d [Time,] then you will l[i]v[e . . . Once again, (16) it is written in the Book] of Moses and in [the words of the Prophe]ts that [blessings and curses] will come [upon you . . . (21) the ble]ssin[gs that] cam[e upon i]t (Israel) in [his d]ays [and] in the days of Solomon the son of David, as well as the curses (22) [that] came upon it

from the d[ays of Jer]oboam the son of Nebat until the exi[l]e of Jerusalem and Zedekiah the king of Jud[ah.] (23) [For] he may bri[n]g them upon . . . And we recognize that some of the blessings and curses have come, (24) those written in the Bo[ok of Mo]ses; therefore this is the End of Days, when (those) in Isra[e]l are to return (25) to the La[w of God with all their heart,] never to turn bac[k] (again). Meanwhile, the wicked will increase in wick[ed]ness and . . . (26) Remember the kings of Israe[l], and understand their works. Whoever of them (27) feared [the L]aw was saved from sufferings; when they so[ug]ht the Law, (28) [then] their sins [were forgiven] them. Remember David. He was a man of Pious works, and he, also, (29) was [sa]ved from many sufferings and forgiven. And finally, we (earlier) wrote you about (30) some of the works of the Law (see the First Letter above), which we reckoned for your own Good and for that of your people, for we see (31) that you possess discernment and Knowledge of the *Torah*. Consider all these things, and beseech Him to grant you (32) proper counsel, and to keep you far from evil thoughts and the counsel of Belial. (33) Then you will rejoice at the End Time, when you find some of our words were true. Thus, 'It will be reckoned to you as Righteousness' (or in Paul's language, 'reckoned as justifying you'), your having done what is Upright and Good before Him, for your own Good and for that of Israel.

37. A PLEASING FRAGRANCE (*Halakhah* A – 4Q251)
(Plate 17)

This text is typical of the kind of legal minutiae found at Qumran. It further fleshes out our view of the basic legal approach there. In it, there are parallels to both the Community Rule and the Damascus Document. For instance, the enumerations contained in Fragment 1 parallel many in the Community Rule. Those in Fragment 2 parallel similar materials in the Damascus Document. In both cases the parallels are precise, though the language varies. For instance, the penalty for 'knowingly Lying' in Line 7 of Fragment 1 and in the Community Rule are exactly the same, though the offence is described slightly differently (1QS, vii.3).

The same applies to pulling a beast out of a pit or cistern on the sabbath in the Damascus Document (xi.13–14) and pulling a beast out of the water on the sabbath in this document (2.5–6). It is also true for wearing soiled garments on the sabbath (2.3 and xi.3). Since, in fact, there are overlaps in legal issues between the Damascus Document in the Cairo recensions and the Community Rule (e.g. the matter of loud guffaws in meetings of the Community), it is possible that the legal chapters of both, which are more or less rationalized in the present document, originally constituted a single whole.

The reference to 'tent' in 2.4 is interesting too. This is one of the first direct references to living in a 'tent' at Qumran. It may actually give evidence of the style of living in the area of settlements or 'camps' (i.e. the wilderness 'camps') including perhaps Qumran – always somewhat of a puzzle. On the other hand, the reference may simply be a casual one.

Even more interesting in this text are the descriptions of the Council of the Community. The language of 'making atonement for the land' and the reconstructed material about being 'founded on Truth for an Eternal Planting' in 3.8–9 is exactly that of the Community Rule,viii.5–6. If the reconstruction 'fifteen men' in Line 3.7 is correct, then another puzzling problem in Qumran studies is solved – whether the 'twelve men and three priests' mentioned in the Community Rule, viii.1 as 'a Holy of Holies' and 'a House (i.e. a Temple) for Israel' should be exclusive or inclusive: that is, should they be three within the twelve, paralleling Christian reckonings of twelve apostles and a central triad, or three in addition to twelve?

The allusions to 'making atonement for the land' and being a 'pleasing fragrance' (3.9) also directly parallel material in 1QS, viii.5–12, where the imagery of the Community Council as a spiritualized Temple is found, which introduces the exegesis of Isa. 40:3 that this is 'the time of the preparation of the Way in the wilderness'. The reference to being witnesses at the Last Judgement (3.8–9) is also paralleled word for word in these lines in the Community Rule. It strengthens the supernatural aspects of the role of the 'sons of Zadok' in the Damascus Document and the spiritualized atonement imagery generally that moves into Christian theory. The reference to 'Judgement' again at the end of 'the era of Wickedness' in 3.10 further reinforces this.

The text ends with a complete elaboration of the prohibited degrees of marriage, including the important law banning niece marriage (7.2–5), which we have analysed above, and which is so much part of the legal approach and ethos in these texts. This law was probably understood as including close cousins as well, which are not included in the extant text, and was rationalized on the basis of not uncovering the nakedness of one's father or mother, brother or sister. The fragment completely exhausts just about all the aspects implicit in this problem in greater detail than, for instance, either the Temple Scroll or the Damascus Document. Again, it shows the great concern for this matter at Qumran. To us, the application to Herodians, moreover, seems obvious.

TRANSLITERATION

Fragment 1

[   ]   ע[שרת י]מ[ים]   ]   .1

ונענש [   ] שלושים יום [   ]   .2

[את מחצית לחמו חמישה ע[שר יום   .3

ונענש שלושה חודשים א[ת מחצית לחמו ואיש אשר ידבר לפני תכון]   .4

[רעהו וכתוב לפניו והבדיל [מן הרבים   .5

[בם את מחצית לחמו *vacat* איש אשר ..   .6

שלושים יום *vacat* ואיש אשר יכחש במ[דעו ונענש ששה]   .7

[חודשים ונענש במה את מחצית לחמו   *vacat*]   .8

[בדעתו בכול דבר ונענש שלושים יום [את מחצית לחמו   .9

[בדע[תו] יבדילתו ששה חודשים *vacat*]   .10

Fragment 2

[   ] . [   ] הש[בת   .1

ב[יו]ם השבת   אל [יקח איש עליו בנדים] צואי[ם ביום השבת]   .2

[אל [   ]. איש בבנדים א[שר יהיה] בהם עפר או [.3

[בי[ו]ם   *vacat*   השבת   *vacat*   אל [יוציא אי[ש מאהלו כלי ומאכ]ל   .4

ביום   *vacat*   השבת   *vacat* אל יעל איש בהמה אשר תפול   .5

[א[ל] המים ביום השבת ואם נפש אדם היא אשר תפול אל המי[ם]   .6

[   ] [ביום] השבת ישלח לו את בנדו להעלותו בו וכלי לא ישא [.7

[   ] . [   ] ביום] השבת ואם צבא [   ]   .8

Fragment 3

[   ] ביום [השבת   ]   .1

[ביום ה[שבת ולא [   ]   .2

[א]ל יז איש מזרע אהרון מ[י נדה ביום השבת [.3

איש [הפ[סח י]ום נדול וצום ביום [השבת   .4

[א[ת הבהמה ילך אלפים אמ[ה ביום השבת ואל ילך כי אם רחוק מן]   .5

[[המ]קדש שלושים רס אל ימ[.6

[ב]היות בעצת היחד חמשה עש[ר איש תמימים בכול הנגלה מכול התורה]   .7

[והנ]ביאים נכונה עצת היח[ד באמת למטעת עולם ועדי אמת למשפט ובחירי]   .8

[רצון וריח ניחוח לכפר על ה[א]רץ מכ[ול עון   .9

[וספה במשפט קצי עולה והמ[.10

[בשבוע הראיש[ון   *vacat*   .11

[אשר לא הובא אל גן עדן ועצם]   .12

[יהיה לה עד אשר לא הובאה אצ[ל   .13

14. ‫[אל ה]קדוש גן עדן וכול האב אשר בתוכו קודש [אשה כי תזריע וילדה זכר]‬
15. ‫וטמאה שבעת ימים כימי נדת דותה תטמא וש[לשים ושלשת ימים תשב בדמי]‬
16. ‫[טו]הרה ואם נקבה תלד וטמאה [שבועים כנדתה וששים יום וששת ימים]‬
17. ‫[תש]ב בדם טוהרה בכול קודש [לא תגע ואל המקדש לא תבוא‬   [

Fragment 4

1. ‫כי יכה איש את רעהו [בעין [ונפל למשכב אם]‬   [
2. ‫[י]קום והתהלך בחוץ על משענתו ונקה מכה רק] ינתן ש[בתו ורפ]א ירפא‬
3. ‫*vacat*   כי ינח שור את איש או את א[שה והומת השור יסקלהו‬   [
4. ‫ולא יאכל את בשרו ובעל השור נקי   ואם שור נ[גח הוא מאתמול‬   [
5. ‫[שלשום   והודע בבעליו ולא ישמרנה   והמית אי[ש או אשה‬
6. ‫[השור יסקל וגם בעליו יומת‬   [   ]. ש[

Fragment 5

1. ‫דגן תיר[ו]ש ויצהר כי אם [הרים הכוהן‬   [
2. ‫ראשיתם הבכורים והמלאה אל יאחר איש כי]‬   [
3. ‫הואה ראשית המלאה [ה]דגן הואה הדמע .]‬   ‫ולחם [‬
4. ‫בכורים הוא חלות החמץ אשר יביאו [בי]ום ה[בכורים‬   [
5. ‫בכורים הם אל יאכל א[י]ש חטים חדשים]‬   [
6. ‫עד יום בא לחם הבכורים אל]‬   [

Fragment 6

1. ‫...[   ]‬   [   ]
2. ‫[   ]אל ימ.]   [.ט]‬   [
3. ‫מנח]ת העשרון ל[כוהן‬   [
4. ‫בכור האד[ם והבהמה הטמ]אה יפדה‬   [
5. ‫ב[כור האדם והבהמה הטמאה‬   [
6. ‫[הצאן והמקדש מן‬   [
7. ‫הו]א הבכור ותבואת עץ‬   [
8. ‫בשנה הרי[שון והזית בשנה הרביעית‬   [
9. ‫ות[רומה כל חרם לכוהן‬   [

Fragment 7

1. ‫על עריות]‬   [
2. ‫אל יקח איש את א[חותו בת אביו או בת אמו   אל יקח איש]‬   [
3. ‫את בת אחיו ואת בת א[חותו לאישתו   אל יגל]‬   [
4. ‫איש את ערות אחות א[ביו ואת ערות אחות אמו ואל תנתן אישה לאחי]‬   [
5. ‫אביה ולאחי אמה] לאישתו‬   [
6. ‫אל יגל איש ערות]‬   [
7. ‫אל יקח איש בתי נ]‬   [

TRANSLATION

Fragment 1 (1) [. . . t]en days . . . (2) thirty days [. . . he will be fined] (3) half of his food ration for fift[een days . . .] (4) he will be fined for three months [half his food ration. A man that speaks prior to the turn] (5) of his neighbor, though he (the latter) is enrolled ahead of him, must be separated [from the Many . . .] (6) in them half his food ration. A man who . . . (7) thirty days. And a man who tells a lie kn[owingly will be punished for six] (8) months, and fined during that time half his food ration . . . (9) knowingly about everything, his penalty is thirty days and half his food ration . . . (10) kno[wingly, they shall] separate him (from the Community) for six months. . .

Fragment 2 (1) The Sab[bath . . .] (2) on the Sabbath d[ay]. A [man] should not [wear garments that are] soil[ed on the Sabbath day]. (3) A man should not . . . in garments th[at have] dust on them or . . . (4) on the Sabbath day. [A ma]n [should not bring out] of his tent any vessel or food (5) on the Sabbath day. A man should not lift out cattle which has fallen (6) in[to] the water on the Sabbath day. But if it is a human being who has fallen into the wat[er (7) on the day of] the Sabbath, he will throw him his garment to lift him out with it. But he will not lift an implement . . . (8) [. . . on the day of] the Sabbath. And if an army . . .

Fragment 3 (1) . . . on the day of [the Sabbath. . .] (2) on the day of] the Sabbath, and not . . . (3) A man from the seed of Aaron will [no]t sprinkle the waters [of impurity on the Sabbath day. . .] (4) [The Pa]ssover is a (high) holiday, and a fast on the day of [the Sabbath. . . . A man] (5) may take his cattle two thousand cub[its on the Sabbath day, but he may not walk unless he is a distance from] (6) [the Te]mple of more than thirty *stadia*.. A [man] should not . . . (7) [When] there are in the Council of the Community fif[teen men, Perfect in everything which has been revealed in all the Law] (8) [and the Pr]ophets, the Council of the Communi[ty] shall be founded [on Truth for an Eternal Planting and true witnesses at the Judgement, and the Elect] (9) of (God's) favor, and a pleasing fragrance to make atonement for the land, from a[ll Evil . . .] (10) The Period of Wickedness will end in Judgement, and the . . . (11) In the fir[st] week . . . (12) which were not to brought to the Garden of Eden. And the bone of . . . (13) shall be for it forever, which was not brought nea[r . . . (14) to the] Holiness of the Garden of Eden, and all the verdure in its midst is Holy. [When a woman conceives and bears a boy,] (15) she shall be unclean seven days. Just as in the days of her menstrual impurity, she shall be unclean; and th[irty three days she shall remain in the blood of (16) her pu]rification. If she bears a girl, she will be unclean [two weeks, just as in her menstrual period; and sixty-six days (17) she shall rema]in in the blood of her purification. [She should touch] no Holy thing [and should not enter the Temple.]

Fragment 4 (1) [. . . If a man strikes another] in the eye, [and he is bedridden, but gets up and walks around (2) outside on his staff, the one who struck him will merely] compensate [him for his] con[valescence and his medi]cal expenses. (3) [If a bull gores a man or wo]man, the bull will be killed. He will stone it, (4) [and not eat its meat, and the bull's owner shall be blameless. But if the bull had g]ored previously (5) [and the owner had been apprised, but he had not kept it (penned up); and it kills a m]an or a woman, (6) [the bull will be stoned, and its owner will be put to death as well. . . .]

Fragment 5 (1) [. . . grain, new w]ine, or fresh oil, unless [the priest has waved it . . .] (2) their early produce, the first fruits. And a man should not delay (giving) the full measure, for . . . (3) is the firstfruit of the full measure. [And the] grain is the offering . . . [And the bread of] (4) the firstfruits is the leavened bread that they bring [on] the day of the [firstfruits . . .] (5) are the firstfruits. A man should not eat the new wheat . . . (6) until the day he brings the bread of the firstfruits. He should not . . .

Fragment 6 (2) . . . he should not . . . (3) [. . . the grain offer]ing of the tithe is for [the priest . . .] (4) [. . . the firstborn of a ma]n or uncle[an] cattle [he should redeem] (5) [. . . the fir]stborn of a man or unclean cattle (6) . . . the flock, and the sanctuary, from (7) [. . . i]t is like the firstborn, and the produce of a tree (8) [. . . in the fir]st [year], and the olive tree in the fourth year (9) [. . . and the he]ave offering; everything that is set apart for (the support of) the priesthood

Fragment 7 (1) Concerning immoral unions . . . (2) A man should not marry his si[ster, the daughter of his father or the daughter of his mother . . . A man should not marry] (3) the daughter of his brother or the daughter of his si[ster. . . He should not uncover] (4) the nakedness of the sister of his fa[ther or the sister of his mother. Nor should a woman be given to the brother of] (5) her father or to the brother of her mother [to be his wife . . .] (6) A man should not uncover the nakedness of . . . (7) A man should not take the daughter of . . .

38. MOURNING, SEMINAL EMISSIONS, ETC. (PURITY LAWS TYPE A – 4Q274)
(Plate 18)

The contents of this manuscript are remarkable, discussing issues not previously found in any Qumran text. All have to do with matters of ceremonial purity and impurity in accordance with stipulations set forth in legal portions of the Bible. A number of the matters considered here involve impurities that require a seven-day period of purification. Provisions are made for mourners to dwell apart in a special place during the days of their impurity, apparently acquired from contact with the corpse of a loved one. The text stipulates that such people and others, suffering from levitical uncleanness of various sorts, are to dwell to the north-west of the nearest habitations – a law reminiscent of the placement of the latrine in the Temple Scroll (11QT,xlvi. 13–16). The rationale for the north-westerly situation of impure places is still unclear, though the fact of the Temple being north-west of a 'camp' such as that which may have been at Qumran could have something to do with it, i.e. such people were to walk in the direction of the Temple.

Several lines concern women during menstruation. These women are not to 'mingle', but it does not appear that this requires their leaving their homes during this period in order to dwell outside the town. It is surprising to read in 1.7 that a 'scribe' or 'counter' kept records of the number of days of a woman's menstrual cycle, and that the record-keeper could be a female. Since in the ancient world women were much less likely than men to be literate, their inclusion in scribal activity is noteworthy. Much of the text concerns the question of when those suffering the impurities under discussion are allowed to partake of the 'purity' – priestly foodstuffs. The answer is that they are free to do so on the seventh day, after bathing and washing their clothes. The more fragmentary portions of the text apparently concerned impurities that could be transmitted by liquids.

The reference in Line 1.6 to 'the camps of the Holy Ones of Israel' (*Kedoshim*) is also interesting. This allusion calls to mind materials in the War Scroll,vii.3–6 about the extreme purity regulations relating to 'the Holy Angels' actually joining the camps of the Community, i.e. 'in the wilderness'. The same allusion is recapitulated in CD,xv, where the blind, lame, deaf, simple, children, etc. are barred from 'the Community' or these camps, because of the presence of 'the Holy Angels among them'.

The term, taken as another name for the rank and file of the Community and those adhering to this rule, paralleling 'the Many', also calls to mind Dan. 7:21–2's 'Saints' (*Kedoshim*) and 'Saints of the Most High God'. Whatever the conclusion, the allusion at this point in this '*Halakhic*' text brings this movement even closer to the one founded by and centred around Judas Maccabee – thought by many to be the subject of these allusions in Daniel. However this may be, there can be no doubt that the spirit and purpose are the same, i.e. Holy

War, which is, of course, the gist of the War Scroll's statement that 'none of these shall march out to war with them. They shall be . . . Perfect in Spirit and body prepared for the Day of Revenge' (vii.5). The allusion to 'camps', too, besides making it clear that these 'camps' *actually existed*, implies multiple settlements of this kind and resonates strongly with this usage in the apocalyptic and Messianic War Scroll and Damascus Document.

TRANSLITERATION   Fragment 1 Column 1

1. יחל להפיל את תיכונו משכב ינון ישכב ומושב אנחה ישב בדד לכול
הטמאים ישב ורחוק מן

2. הטהרה שתים עשרה באמה כאברו אליו ומערב צפון לכול בית מושב
ישב רחוק כמדה הזות

3. איש מכול הטמאים [ביו]ם [השבי]עי ירחץ במים ויכבס בגדיו ואחר
יואכל כי הוא אשר אמר טמא טמא

4. יקרא כול ימי היו[ת] בו הנג]ע הזבה דם לשבעת הימים אל תגע
בזב ובכול כלי [א]שר יגע בו הזב {יש[ב]

5. עליו} <או> אשר ישב עליו ואם נגעה תכבס בגדיה ורחצה ואחר
תוכל ובכול מודה [א]ל תתערב בשבעת

6. ימיה בעבור אשר ל[ו]א תנאל את מחני קד[ושי] ישראל וגם
אל תגע בכול אשה [זב]ה דם לימים רב[ים]

7. והסופר אם זכר ואם נקבה אל י[נע בזבה] או בדוה בנדתה כי
אם טהרה [מנד]תה כי הנה דם

8. הנדה כזוב יחשב [ל]נוגע בו ואם זוב [מבשרו או ש]כבת הזרע
מגעו וטמא ה[וא והנ]ובע באדם מכו[ל]

9. הטמאים האלה בשבעת ימי טה]רתו א[ל יוכל כאשר יטמא לנפש
[ירחץ במי]ם וכבס ואח[ר]

Fragment 1 Column 2

1. יא[ו]כל   [

2. ושכ[בת   [

Fragment 2 Column 1

1. [א[שר יזו עליו את]ה[ר]ישונה ורחץ ויכבס טרם

2. [ו]ל עליו השביעי ביום השביעי אל יז בשבת בו

3. [בשבת רק אל יגע בטהרה עד אשר ישנה

4. [את בגדיו   הנוגע בשכבת זרע מאדם עד כול כלי יטבול

5. [יטבו]ל והבגד אשר תהיה עליו והכלי והנושא אותו
אשר ישאנה יטבול

6. [.] ואם במחנה יהיה איש אשר לוא השיגה ידו ורג[לו]

7. [ ]ל הבגד אשר לוא נגעה בו רק אל יגע בו
את לחמו והנוגע

8. [ ] ישבו אם לוא נגע בו כבס אותו במים ואם

9. [נגע בו] וכבס ולכול הקדושים יכבס איש את

Fragment 2 Column 2

1. [את בשרו וכן]   [
2. [ואם]   [
3. [אמו]   [
4. [לח..]   [
5. שרץ טמ[אים   [
6. [והנוגע בו]   [
7. וכו[ל   [
8. [ואם א.]   [
9. [אשר .]   [

Fragment 3 Column 1

1. [ ]   [גולת אל את אישון עינו וקר]   [
2. [ ]   [יהם וכול חוק צ]   [ים
3. [ ]   [ול או כול] [.].   [.ל
4. [ ]   [...]   [
5. [ ]   [והיא טמאה] [.ו.]   [
6. [ ]   מקשו [ואל] יוכלהו בטהרה וכול [ ]
7. [ ]   אש[ר ימעכו ויצא משקיהם אל יוכלם איש
8. [ ]   [גע הטמא בהמה וגם מן הירק] .   [
9. [ ]   [או קשות בשלה איש אשר ישק]ה[

Fragment 3 Column 2

1. [ ] [ ] טמאו..]   [
2. vacat]   [
3. וכול אשר יש לו ....]   [
4. לטהור ויתר כול הירק]   [
5. מלחת טל יאכל ואם ל[וא   [
6. בתוך המים כי אם איש]   [
7. הארץ אם יבואו עליה .]   [
8. הגשם עליה אם יגע ב[ה אי]ש   [
9. בשדה בכול מודו לתקופת]   [
10. כול כלי חרש אשר .ל]   [
11. אשר בתוכו]   [
12. המשקה .]   [

TRANSLATION

Fragment 1 Column 1 (1) he is to delay distributing the portions (that he has prepared for the priests). He is to sleep in a bed of mourning and dwell in the house of bereavement, separated with all the other impure persons, twelve cubits distance from (2) the pure food, in the designated part of town, and the same distance to the northwest of any inhabited dwelling. (3) Any man suffering from the various types of impurity should bathe himself and wash his clothing on the [seve]nth [da]y, and afterwards he may eat (the pure food). For this is what it means, "Unclean, unclean!' (4) he should call all the days of his affliction.' As for the woman who suffers a seven-day flux of blood, she should not touch a man suffering from a flux, nor any implement that he touches, (5) nor anything upon which he rests. But if she does touch (these things), she should wash her clothes and bathe and afterwards she may eat (the pure food). At all costs she is [no]t to mingle during her seven (6) days, so that she does n[o]t defile the camp of the Ho[ly O]nes of Israel. Nor is she to touch any woman suffer[ing] a long[standing] flux. (7) And the person that is keeping a record of the period of impurity, whether a man or a woman, is not to to[uch the menstruant] or the mourner during the period of uncleanness, but only when she is cleansed [from her unclean]ness, for (8) that uncleanness should be reckoned in the same way as a flux [for] anyone who touches it. And if someone touches a [bodily] flux [or a se]minal emission, then [h]e should be unclean. Anyone touching any of these types of (9) impure people should n[ot] eat the pure food during the seven days of his puri[fication]. When someone is impure because of touching a corp[se], he is to bathe himself in wa]ter and wash (his clothes) and afterwa[rds]

Fragment 1 Column 2 (1) he may e[at . . .] (2) and sem[inal emission . . .]

Fragment 2 Column 1 (1) . . . who sprinkle upon him for the first time and he should bathe and wash his clothes before (2) . . . on the seventh day. One is not to sprinkle on the sabbath (3) . . . on the sabbath, only he should not touch the pure food until he changes (4) [his clothes . . .] Anyone who touches a human seminal emission must immerse everything down to the last item of dress, and the person that carries the item (5) [. . . must imm]erse, and the garment upon which the emission is found or any item that carries it (the emission) (6) . . . And if there should be found in the camp any man that is incapab[le] (or, that does not have enough) (7) . . . the garment that it/she has not touched, only he should not touch it—his meat—and he that touches (8) . . . they should dwell. If he did not touch it, he should wash it in water, but if (9) [he did touch it] . . . and he should wash (it). Regarding all offerings, a man should wash

Fragment 2 Column 2 (1) his flesh, and thus . . . (2) but if . . . (3) with him . . . (4) to . . . (5) reptile. Impure [people . . .] (6) and he that touches it . . . (7) and eve[ry . . .] (8) But if . . . (9) who . . .

Fragment 3 Column 1 (1) . . . God's revealing the apple of His eye, and (2) . . . every law . . . (3) or every . . . (5) and she is unclean . . . (6) they pour liquid upon and he does not eat eat in purity, and every . . . (7) [(everything) tha]t they will dissolve by rubbing, and whose solvent liquid has evaporated, a man should not eat (8) . . . the impure among them, and also among garden vegetables . . . (9) or a boiled cucumber. A man who [po]urs liquid upon a foodstuff

Fragment 3 Column 2 (1) . . .they are impure . . . (3) and everything that he possesses . . . (4) to purify, and the remains of all the garden vegetables (5) from the moisture of dew he may eat, but if n[ot] . . . (6) in the water, except a man . . . (7) the land, if there comes upon it . . . (8) the rain upon it, if a man touches it . . . (9) in a field by all means he at the turn of the season of . . . (10) every frangible vessel that . . . (11) which is in its middle . . . (12) the foodstuff upon which water has been poured . . .

39. LAWS OF THE RED HEIFER
(PURITY LAWS TYPE B – 4Q276–277)

The two manuscripts presented here are of the most interesting subject matter: the law of the Red Heifer, a subject already referred to in the First Letter on Works Reckoned as Righteousness above. The Red Heifer purification ceremony was one of the most holy in Jewish tradition. It is also, interestingly enough, echoed in the name the Koran gives to its principal Sura, 'the Cow' (2). Most of the laws governing this purification procedure are to be found in Num. 19 and indeed, most of the matters alluded to in these texts are to be found there, though there are some interesting additions in these two Qumran texts.

According to Numbers, the people were to prepare this heifer by burning it with cedar wood, hyssop and scarlet material. The ashes were then gathered and mixed with water. This water, known as 'the water that removes impurity', was sprinkled upon those who had acquired certain types of ritual impurity – including some of the bodily and sexual impurities mentioned in the preceding text. Unlike Numbers, these two texts appear to have a special interest in the clothes worn by those taking part in the heifer's preparation. Apparently these clothes were to serve only for the ceremony and could not be worn for profane tasks. The vessel in which the presiding priest (usually, if not always during the Second Temple period, the high priest) gathered the heifer's blood at a certain point in the ceremony was a special one. The Bible does not make this stipulation. Possibly Manuscript B Line 2 attempts to clarify the meaning of an uncertain phrase in Num. 19:9. The Biblical text says that the ashes of the heifer are to be gathered by a 'pure man'. What, precisely, did this phrase require? According to Josephus, the understanding in the first century was that the phrase was intended to designate a priest for the task, as opposed to a layman. The Qumran text may take a different tack, specifying that the man be innocent of all defiling sins. That is to say, specific sins were understood to be ritually defiling.

TRANSLITERATION   **Manuscript A Fragment 1**

1. [בגדים] אשר לוא שרת בם בקוד[ש]
2. [   ] וחיב את הבגדים ושח[ט]
3. [את ה]פרה לפניו ו<נ>שא את דמה בכלי חרש אשר
4. [לוא נג]ש במזבח והזה מדמה באצבעו[ן] שבע
5. [פעמים א]ל נוכח א[ו]הל מועד והשליך את הארז
6. [ואת האזוב ואת שני] תולע אל תו[ך] שרפתה
7. [ורחצו הכוהן והשורף והאוס]ף את אפר הפרה
8. [וכבסו בגדיהם וטמאו עד הערב והני]חוהו למשמרת
9. [למי נדה החטאת ולחוקת עולם ו]לבש הכוהן

Manuscript B Fragment 1

1. [   ] ואת] האזוב ואת]   [
2. [   ] איש] טהור מכול טמאת עונ]ות   [
3. [   ] ו[ל[בש] הכוהן הכופר בדם הפרה וכול [האנשים בגדים]
4. [אחרים ויכבסו את הכ]ת[נת ואת] החלמה [אש]ר כפרו בם את משפט [החטאת]
5. [ורחצ כל איש] במי[ם וט]מה עד הע[ר]ב והנוש[א ק]לחת מי הנדה יט[מא   [
6. [   ] והזה] איש א[ת] מי הנדה על טמאי נ[דה כ]יא איש כוהן טה[ור יזה]
7. [את מי הנדה עלי]הן כ]יא י]כפר הוא על הטמ[א] ועלול אל יז על הטמא וא[יש]
8. [   ] א[ת מי [הנ]דה יאביאו במים ויט[ה]רו מטמאת הנפש].
9. [   ] א[חרת [יז]רוק עליהם [הכו]הן את מי הנדה לטהר
10. [   ] כ]יא אם יטהרו וט[הור ב]שרם וכול אשר ינע [בו   [
11. [את] זובו]   [   ] ואין שטופות במים [ידים]
12. [ו[טמאו]   מש[כבו ומוש[בו   נגעו] בז]ובו כמגע טמאת [נפש]
13. [ה]נוגע [ירחץ וט]מ[ה עד [ה]ערב והנושא [יכבס את ב]גדיו וטמא עד הערב

TRANSLATION

Manuscript A Fragment 1 (1)[. . . clothes] in which he has not performed (any) sacr[ed] rite. (2) . . . and he should regard the clothes as impure(?).

Then he (a designated man, not the presiding priest) will slaugh[ter] (3) [the] heifer before him, and he (the priest) will take up its blood in a new earthen vessel that (4) [has never drawn] near the altar and sprinkle some of its blood with [his] finger seven (5) [times to]ward the front of the T[e]nt of Meeting. Then he should cast the cedar wood (6) [and the hyssop and the scarlet] material into the mid[st] of its (the heifer's) fire. (7) [Then the priest and the man who burns (the heifer) and the man who gath]ers the heifer's ashes [should bathe] (8) [and wash their clothes, and they shall be unclean until evening. And this they should est]ablish as a ceremony (9) [for that water which removes the impurity of sin, and as an Eternal Law. And] the priest should put on

Manuscript B Fragment 1 (1) . . . and the hyssop and the . . . (2) [a man] pure of all sin[ful] impurity . . . (3) [And] the priest who atones with the blood of the heifer and all [the men should] put [on different clothes (4) and wash their tu]ni[cs and] their seamed robes in which they made atonement in performing the law [governing the removal of sin. (5) Each man should bathe] in wat[er and be un]clean until the eve[n]ing. The man who carri[es the p]ot containing the water that removes impurity will be im[pure . . .] (6) A man [should sprinkle] the water that removes impurity upon those who are imp[ure, in]deed a pu[re] priest [should sprinkle (7) the water that removes impurity on the]m. Thu[s he will] atone for the impure. No wicked man is to sprinkle upon the impure. A m[an] (8) [. . . the water that removes im]purity. They should enter the water and become pu[r]e from the impurity that comes from contact with dead people . . . (9) [an]other. [The pr]iest [should] sprinkle them with the water that removes impurity, to purify (10) [. . . R]ather they shall become pure, and their [fl]esh p[ure.] Anyone who touches [him . . .] (11) his flux . . . and their [hands] unwashed with water, (12) [then] they shall be impure . . . his be[d] and [his] sea[t . . .] they touched his [f]lux, (it) is like the impurity [that comes from contact with dead people.] (13) [The] man who touches (these things) [should bathe and be] impure till [the] evening, and the man who carries (these things) [should wash] his [cl]othes and be impure till evening.

40. THE FOUNDATIONS OF RIGHTEOUSNESS (THE END OF THE DAMASCUS DOCUMENT: AN EXCOMMUNICATION TEXT – 4Q266)
(Plates 19 & 20)

There can be no doubt that what we have here is the last column of the Damascus Document. Though the text as we have it here does not precisely follow any material from either of the two overlapping known manuscripts found by Solomon Schechter in the Cairo *Genizah* in 1897, many of its allusions do. So does their spirit.

The piece is preserved in two copies: one is nicely ruled; the second, in what is called 'semi-cursive', would appear to be a private copy. We present the second, which is the more completely preserved, with occasional help from the first to fill in blanks. That it really is the last column of the document is ascertainable from the blank spaces on the parchment at the left. The edge of a previous column with some stitching is also visible on the right (see Plates 19–20). The Hebrew here is often close to Mishnaic, and apparently superior to medieval recensions. This text also contains one interlinear addition between Lines 4 and 5, as well as one or two corrections.

The correspondences are principally to Columns i, viii and xv of the Cairo version of the Damascus Document. There are also interesting new materials in the present document, e.g. about a convocation of those who 'dwell in camps' on 'the third month' – in Judaism, *Shavu'ot*/'the Feast of Weeks'; in Christianity, Pentecost. The purpose of the convocation would appear not to be to celebrate the revelation and descent of the Holy Spirit, and by implication the abolition of the Law in favour of more Pauline, Gentile-oriented doctrines and devices as in Acts 2:1ff. (see also the picture of Paul hurrying to Jerusalem to be in time for Pentecost below). It is rather *to curse* all those who depart in any manner from the Law or 'the *Torah* of Moses' (17–19).

In fact, the text is an excommunication text, similar to that embedded in the Chariots of Glory in Chapter 7. The words there are to be pronounced by the Community Council. The words here are to be pronounced 'by the Priest commanding the Many' (see our discussion of the *Mebakker* below) on 'anyone who rejects these Judgements based on the (exact) sense of all the Laws found in the *Torah* of Moses' (5–6). 'Rebellion' is referred to in Line 7, and Lines 9–10 contain the actual 'curse' to be pronounced by this 'priest' (high priest?) on the rebellious person being 'expelled from the presence of the Many'.

Preceding this, Lines 2–4, referring to inadvertent sin – already treated in the *Halakhic* texts above – begin by insisting that the penitent bring a sin or guilt offering (presumably to the Temple) to be purified (cf. Lev. 4). It is worth noting that at the time of his final Pentecost visit to Jerusalem, James imposed a similar purification procedure on Paul in the Temple. Here, in the words of Acts 21:21–4, Paul was publicly to exhibit that he was 'still *walking in the Way* and *keeping the Law*' (italics ours).

In Lines 3–5 the passages adduced to support this penance for 'remission of sin', including the interlinear addition mentioned above (5a), are a little esoteric, even ambiguous. One even makes allusion to the pleasing 'fragrance of their offerings' we have seen in the Pleasing Fragrance text above, and in the process, possibly to the Heavenly Ascents of *Hechalot* mysticism (see the reference to 'ascending to the Highest Heaven' in Line 4).

Among many other key usages, one should note the reference to 'the peoples' to designate those who did not follow the Law in Line 10. We have already seen how Paul in Rom. 11:13 uses this key word 'peoples' to describe himself and the people to whom he is addressing his mission. One should also note the key use of the word *ma'as* ('reject') in Lines 5–6 above concerning 'rejecting . . . the *Torah* of Moses' and a parallel word *ga'lah* in Line 7, where the man 'whose spirit rejects the Foundations of Righteousness' is referred to. We have encountered this word *ma'as* repeatedly in key passages throughout the Qumran corpus.

In the Habakkuk *Pesher* it is used to describe the 'Lying Spouter' who 'rejects the Law in the midst of the whole congregation'. The language is paralleled too in the Community Rule, iii–iv, which also describes the behaviour of an archetypical 'son of Darkness' with 'a blaspheming Tongue', whose 'soul rejects the Foundations of the Knowledge of the Judgements of Righteousness', whose 'works are abomination, whose Spirit fornication, whose Ways uncleanness, whose service (mission) pollution . . . who walks in all the Ways of Darkness'.

There is also a parallel in i. 15–16 of the Cairo Damascus Document. Here the 'Foundations of Righteousness' are called 'the Pathways of Righteousness'. This allusion occurs in the midst of a long description of how the Scoffer/Comedian 'poured over Israel the waters of lying'. In it, the allusion to 'wandering astray in a trackless waste without a Way', which the present text uses to describe 'the peoples', i.e. 'the families (of man) and their national languages' in 10 above, is used in i. 15 to describe the effect of the Spouter/Scoffer's 'waters of Lying'.

The same is true for the connections between Lines 12–13 in the Foundations of Righteousness about 'the boundary markers which were laid down' and CD, i. 18: 'removing the boundary markers which the First (the forefathers) laid down as their inheritance that He might call down upon us the curses of the Covenant'. Lines 13–14 of the present text also end by again 'cursing' those who 'cross' or 'transgress' these 'boundary markers'. We will see more about the importance of the language of 'cursing' below. The language parallels in these texts are *exact*. They increase the connections between the process of excommunication being referred to in this text and the subject of the 'Lying Spouter'/'Comedian' in other texts.

There are pregnant parallels of this kind in every line of the text. An interesting parallel in early Christian history would be James 2:10's assertion: 'He who breaks one small point of the Law is guilty of breaking it all.' This passage too is presented against a background of Qumranisms like 'keeping' (keeping the Law), 'breaking'/'Breakers' (breaking the Law), 'Doer'/'doing', 'Light', 'Judgement', etc.

In the context, too, of 'rejecting the Judgements about the exact sense of all the Laws found in the *Torah* of Moses' in Line 6, the text also uses the key word 'reckoned', which we encountered in the two Letters on Works Righteousness above: 'He will not be reckoned among all the sons of God's Truth, because his soul rejected the Foundations of Righteousness.' It would be easy to appreciate how such words could be applied in a mindset of the kind represented by this text to a person teaching 'the Many' that 'the works of the Law' were 'a curse' as in Gal. 3:6–10 (in the section about Abraham's faith we have discussed above) or to someone who, by making himself 'a friend of man', had turned himself into 'an Enemy of God'.

The language at this point in the text is that of Deuteronomy's 'blessing and cursing'. See the parallel in Column ii of the Community Rule. Just as in the Community Rule,v–vii, the expellee is not to participate in the pure food of the Community any longer (or, according to another vocabulary circle, not to keep 'table fellowship' any more), here one is not to 'eat with him' (15). In the Community Rule, too, no one is to cooperate with him in 'common purse' or 'service'/ 'activity'/'ministry'; here one is not to 'keep company with him' in any way or 'ask after his welfare'. Those who do so are to 'be recorded by the *Mebakker*', who is to make sure any additional 'Judgement' with regard to them is carried out (16).

This *Mebakker* or 'Overseer' has already been extensively referred to in Columns xiii–xv of the Cairo Damascus Document and Column 6 of the Community Rule above. In the latter, he is above the Community Council and functions as treasurer. In the Damascus Document he functions as a kind of 'Bishop' and obviously has absolute authority over the Community and its camps. Described as someone between 30 and 50 years old, who 'is the master of all the Secrets of men and all tongue(s) according to its (their) enumerations' (note very carefully the 'Tongue' and 'language' significations here; CD, xiii.13–14). His word is law in everything. He is to examine carefully potential entrants, teach 'the exact sense of the Law', make 'Judgements', and carefully record all the matters mentioned in this document and elsewhere, particularly these 'Judgements'.

The usage 'the priest commanding the Many' in Line 8 (and probably Line 1) should be explained too. Since he also makes 'Judgements' (cf. Lines 1 and 16), he is very likely identifiable with the 'Bishop' just described. If they are identical – and there seems to be every reason to think they are – then this dual role is almost indistinguishable from the dual role accorded to James the Just in early Church tradition. Even James' title, 'Bishop of Jerusalem', and the description of him in almost all early Church sources as 'high priest', reverberates with the materials before us here, particularly if this 'priest commanding the Many' is to be considered a kind of 'opposition high priest' as well.

The issue in Lines 17–18 of 'cursing all those who have departed to the right or to the left from the Torah' at Pentecost is particularly interesting. For Paul in Gal. 3:11–13 above, 'Christ redeemed us from the curse of the Law' by becoming 'a curse' or 'cursed' (by the Law) himself. To explain or show how this could be, he cites Deut. 21:23 (in a discussion flanked by citation of the two key scriptural passages: Gen. 15:6 about Abraham's 'faith' and Hab. 2:4 'the Righteous shall live by his faith'), to the effect that a man hung upon a tree is 'cursed'. The language of the one approach mirrors the language of the other. Both are operating within the framework of the 'blessing and cursing' from Deuteronomy.

Paul, if one can be so bold, is *reversing* the cursing language of his opponents, who, we can assume, have also 'cursed' him, throwing at them the worst affront imaginable, that their Messiah, who for the purposes of argument let us say was 'hung upon a tree', was in a manner of speaking 'cursed' according to the very Law they cursed him with. Therefore, this Messiah has, by taking this 'curse' upon himself, redeemed Paul, and for him and Christianity following him, all mankind as well.

The issues before us are that momentous and one sees how important the context we are talking about here really is. If this suggestion has any truth to it, one can imagine how it would have enraged the interlocutors of the kind illustrated here. James. 3:10, evoking as in 1QS,ii, Paul and Lines 8–14 above the Deuteronomic 'blessing and cursing' backgrounds of the whole issue, of course, ties this 'cursing' to its nemesis 'the Tongue'.

The text ends with the evocation of an annual convocation on

Shav^cuot — in Jewish tradition, classically the commemoration of Moses' receipt of the *Torah* 50 days after going out from Egypt. Here 'the Levites' and the inhabitants of all 'the camps' are to gather every year for the purposes of cursing those 'who depart to the right or the left from the *Torah*' (17). Paralleling this, in 1QS,ii.19ff., they are to curse 'all the men of the lot of Belial . . . as long as the Government of Belial (Herod?) endures year by year in perfect order ranked according to their Spirit'.

In Acts 2:1, Pentecost commemorated the descent of the Pauline 'Holy Spirit' with its 'Gentile Mission' accoutrements of 'speaking in tongues', etc. One should compare this allusion with the abilities of the *Mebakker* in this regard in CD,xiv.9, referred to above, who is to 'master . . . all tongue(s) and its enumerations'. We have already noted the revealing picture in Acts 20:16ff. of Paul hurrying to Jerusalem with his *contributions* to be on time for just such an annual convocation of the early Church (i.e. the Community) at Pentecost. In this context he runs into his last difficulties in Jerusalem with those within the Community of a more 'Jamesian' frame of mind, who cite complaints about his activities abroad and demand absolute adherence to the Law.

In such a presentation, Acts' picture of Pentecost can be seen as the mirror reversal of the 'Pentecost' being pictured here. Lines 17–18 also highlight the phrase 'the exact sense of the Law' — here 'Judgements' — 'in all the Eras of Evil' and 'Wrath', just as the Damascus Document did in xiii.5–6 and xiv.16ff. — these last in relation to the 'Judgements' the *Mebakker* was to make 'until God should visit the earth' and 'the Messiah of Aaron and Israel should arise to forgive their sins. . .' This language of '*doing* the exact sense of the *Torah*' is very important. It is also to be found earlier still in vi.14–15 coupled with a reference to '*the Era of Evil*' and '*separating* from the sons of the Pit' (italics ours). This 'not one jot or tittle' approach to the Law is, of course, prominent in traditions associated with Jamesian Christianity, not least of which is the famous condemnation of 'breaking one small point of the Law' in James. 2:10. Here, too, 'doing' and 'breaking the Law' are prominently mentioned.

The text ends by evoking the phrase *midrash ha-Torah*, i.e. 'the study' or 'interpretation of the Law'. This term also turns out to be the focal point of the critical analysis in 1QS,viii.15 of Isa. 40:3's 'preparing a Way in the wilderness.' Here, too, once again the emphasis is on *doing*, that is, *doing* the 'exact sense of the Law'. The actual words are: the Way 'is the *study/interpretation* of the *Torah* which He commanded by the hand of Moses that they should *do* according to all that has been revealed . . . as the Prophets have revealed by His *Holy Spirit'* (italics ours).

This then ties all these documents and approaches together. Those, who in 1QS,viii.14's words *'separate* from the habitation of the men of Evil and go out *in the wilderness* to *prepare the Way of the Lord'* (italics ours) are none other than the inhabitants of 'the camps' being addressed and described in the present text. The implications are quite startling and far-reaching. One thing is sure: one has in these texts a better exposition of what was *really* going on 'in the wilderness' in these times so pivotal for Western civilization than in any other parallel accounts.

TRANSLITERATION

1. על הרבים וקבל את משפטו מרצונו כאשר אמר ביד
2. מושה ע[ל] הנפש אשר תחטא בשיגנה אשר יביאו את
3. חטת[ו או] את אשמו ועל [י]שראל כתו[ב] אלכה לי
4. אל [קצה ה]שמים ולו אריח בריח ניחוחכם ו[ב]מקום אחר
5a. במקום [אח]ר כתוב קרעו לבבכם ואל בנדיכם
5. כתוב לשוב אל אל בבכי ובצום וכול המואס במשפטים
6. האלה על פי כול החוקים הנמצאים בתורת מושה לו יחשב
7. בכול בני אמחו כי געלה נפשו ביסודי הצדק במרד מלפני
8. הרבים ישתלח וידבר בו הכוהן המופק[ד ע]ל הרבים יעמד
9. [ויא]מר <ברוך את> את הו הכול [ביד]יך הכול ועושה הכול אשר יסדתה
10. [הע]מים למשפחותיהם ולשנות לאומותם ותתעם בתהו ולו
11. {ולו} דרך ובאבותינו בח[ר]תה לזרעם נתתה חוקי אמתכה
12. ומשפטי קודשכה אשר יעשה [ה]אדם וחיה וגבולות הגבלוה
13. לנו אשר את עובריהם ארותה ואנו עם פדותכה וצון מרעיתך<ה>
14. אתה ארותה את עובריהם ואנו הקימונו ויצא המשתלח והאיש
15. אשר יוכל [מ]הונה [ו]אשר ידרוש שלומו להמשתלח ואשר [י]אות עמו
16. ונכתב [ ] דברו על יד המבקר כחרת ושלים משפטו בני לוי
17. [ויושבי] המחנות יקהלו בחודש השלישי וארו את הנוטה ימין
18. ושמאול מן ה[תורה והזה פרוש המשפטים אשר יעשו בכול קץ
19. הרשע את אשר יפק[י]דו [בכו]ל קצי החרון ומסעיהם לכול
20. [יושב מחניהם וכול יושב עריהם הנה הכו]ל הזה ע[ל] [מ]דר[ש] התורה
21. [האחרון   [

TRANSLATION

[. . . before the Priest commanding] (1) the Many, and he freely accepted His Judgement when He said by the hand (2) of Moses regar[ding] the person who sins inadvertantly, 'let such a one bring (3) [his] sin offering [or] his guilt offering.' And concerning Israel it is written, 'I shall ascend (4) to [the

Highest in H]eaven, and there will not smell the fragrance of their offerings.' And in another place (5) it is written, 'return to God with weeping and fasting.' (5a) (In [anoth]er place it is written, 'rend your hearts and not your clothes.') As for every person who rejects these (6) Judgements (which are) in keeping with all the Laws found in the *Torah* of Moses, he will not be reckoned (7) among all the sons of His Truth, for his soul has rejected the Foundations of Righteousness. For rebellion, let him be expelled (8) from the presence of the Many. The Priest commanding the Many shall speak against him. He (the Priest) is to stand (9) and say, 'Blessed are You, You are all, everything is in Your hand and (You are) the maker of everything, who established (10) [the Peo]ples according to their families and their national languages. You 'made them to wander astray in a wilderness without a Way,' (11) but You chose our fathers and to their seed gave the Laws of Your Truth (12) and the Judgements of Your Holiness, 'which man shall do and thereby live.' And 'boundary markers were laid down for us.' (13) Those who cross over them, You curse. We, (however), are Your redeemed and 'the sheep of Your pasture.' (14) You curse their transgressors while we uphold (the Law).' Then he who was expelled must leave, and whosoever (15) eats with him or asks after the welfare of the man who was excommunicated or keeps company with him, (16) that fact should be recorded by the *Mebakker*/Overseer according to established practice and his Judgement will be completed. The sons of Levi and (17) [the inhabitants] of the camps are to gather together in the third month (every year) to curse those who depart to the right or (18) [to the left from the] *Torah*. And this is the exact sense of the Judgements that they are to do for the entire Era (19) [of Evil, that which was com]manded [for al]l the periods of Wrath and their journeys, for everyone [who dwells in their camps and all who dwell in their cities, al]l that [is found in the 'Final M]idra[sh] of the Law.'

NOTES

(35) First Letter on Works Reckoned as Righteousness (4Q394–398)

Previous Discussions: J. T. Milik, 'Le travail d'édition des manuscrits du désert de Juda', (SVT 4) 24; *DJD* 3, 222–5; E. Qimron and J. Strugnell, 'An Unpublished Halakhic Letter from Qumran', in *Biblical Archaeology Today: Proceedings of the International Congress on Biblical Archaeology, Jerusalem,* April 1984 (Jerusalem, 1985) 400–407; idem, 'An Unpublished Halakhic Letter from Qumran', *Israel Museum Journal* 4 (1985) 9–12 and Plate 1; L. H. Schiffman, 'The New Halakhic Letter (4QMMT) and the Origins of the Dead Sea Sect', *Biblical Archaeologist*, (June, 1989) 64–73; R. H. Eisenman, 'A Response to Schiffman on MMT', *The Qumran Chronicle*, 2–3, (Cracow, 1991) pp. 94–104. Most important photographs: PAM 43.477, 43.490, 43.491, 43.492 and 43.521, ER 1427, 1440, 1441, 1442 and 1471. We present an eclectic text that follows no one manuscript where they overlap. Internal analysis shows that this text and the Second Letter were originally separate works, although two manuscripts (4Q397–8) copy them together. Note that several fragments of 4Q398 evidently belong in 'Legal Exposition', Lines 48–56, but cannot be precisely placed and are not represented here. Further note that the calendrical exposition is attested by 4Q394, and it is our perception only that it is an integral part of the First Letter.

(36) Second Letter on Works Reckoned as Righteousness (4Q397–399)

See (35) above. Most important photographs: PAM 42.838, 43.476, 43.489 and 43.491, ER 1045, 1426, 1439 and 1441. Note that 4Q398 is longer at Lines 11–13 than the form of the text that we present. Note also that the ending of the Second Letter differs slightly in 4Q399 as compared with 4Q398. We present the version contained in 4Q398 here.

(37) A Pleasing Fragrance (*Halakhah* A – 4Q251)

Previous Discussions: Milik, *Years*, 111. Photographs: PAM 43.304, 43.305, 43.306, 43.307 and 43.308; ER 1339–43. Milik had originally grouped all the fragments presented here as a single manuscript. According to the *DSSIP*, the portions have subsequently been regrouped into two literary works, to be designated as 4Q251 and 4Q265. The latter work comprises 43.304–6. But all these portions are in the same hand, and for that and other reasons too technical to detail here, we follow Milik's original notion.

(38) Mourning, Seminal Emissions, etc. (Purity Laws Type A – 4Q274).

Previous Discussions: None. Photographs: PAM 43.309; ER 1344.

(39) Laws of the Red Heifer (Purity Laws Type B – 4Q276–277)

Previous Discussions: None. Photographs: PAM 43.316 (Manuscript A on top, Manuscript B below), ER 1351.

(40) The Foundations of Righteousness (The End of the Damascus Document: An Excommunication Text – 4Q266)

Previous Discussions: J. T. Milik, *MS*, 235; J. Baumgarten, '"Scriptural Citations" in 4Q Fragments of the Damascus Document', *Journal of Jewish Studies* 43 (1992) 95–8.

CHAPTER 7

Hymns and Mysteries

This chapter contains some of the most splendid and beautiful texts in the whole corpus. We have grouped them together because of 1) their liturgical quality and 2) because of their relationship to the whole theme of 'Hidden Mysteries' referred to in the last texts of Chapter 5, and evoked variously in the Chariots of Glory, the Hymns of the Poor, and the Sons of Salvation (*Yeshaʿ*) and the Mystery of Existence below. This last text could just as easily have been placed in Chapter 5 under Admonitions, where it typologically belongs, but because of its clear affinities in vocabulary and content with these other texts, we place it here.

The Baptismal Hymns are interesting in themselves, particularly because of the importance of the subject which they treat. The period of the Dead Sea Scrolls was apparently a time of extensive development in the area of liturgy, as these examples and the published Hymns from Cave 1 suggest. This was probably also true of Rabbinic tradition, which was beginning its development in this period as well. Certainly, too, the Eighteen Benedictions, referred to above in connection with the Messiah of Heaven and Earth text, and other elements of Jewish community worship arose during these years.

Unfortunately the extant evidence on these matters is slim. For instance, we did not even know whether it was common in this period to pray together from a set text, that is until the appearance of these materials from Qumran. Now, however, we can certainly be sure that it was common *to curse* together or, at least to expel someone from a set text recited in unison, as we have seen above and will see again below. The *'amen, amen*'s attached to this process, as well as to *blessing* in the texts in this volume and in Column 2 of the Community Rule, are illustrative in this regard.

221

In this section the Hymns of the Poor are related both to the already published Hymns from Cave 1 and their prototype, the Psalms from the Bible. The Paean to King Jonathan in the last chapter is another similar genre. The parchment on which it was found also seems to have contained some additional Hymns known from the Qumran Psalms Scroll as well as compilations in Syriac. Nor are these Hymns to be dissociated from the literature of Admonitions above. There is at best a fine line between them, and other material, as for instance in the cryptic Sons of Dawn or the Demons of Death (Beatitudes) texts.

The reference to 'Miraculous' or 'Secret Mysteries', and the study of the seemingly forbidden subject of 'Being' or 'Existence', including the Sons of Dawn text in cryptic script apparently related to these, relate to a whole genre of literature of this kind like the *Sefer ha-Razim* (*Book of Mysteries*) and other magical texts from the first few centuries AD with a mystic tendency so frowned upon by the Rabbis and yet so much related to *Kabbalah* and the development of medieval and modern Jewish mysticism. The materials in this chapter are a rich source for studies such as these, as well as for Secret Mysteries, as the previously published Songs of the Sabbath Sacrifice already are. As the examples in this chapter illustrate, the sentiments they express are of the most lofty and sublime nature.

41. THE CHARIOTS OF GLORY (4Q286–287)
(Plate 21)

We call this text, which contains some of the most beautiful and emotive vocabulary in the entire Qumran repertoire, the Chariots of Glory to emphasize its connections with Ezekiel's visions and *Merkabah* mysticism. It is a work of such dazzling faith and ecstatic vision that it fairly overwhelms the reader. Of course, it completely gainsays anyone who would challenge the literary audacity, virtuosity and creativity of those responsible for the Qumran corpus.

This work, which has obvious affinities with the already published Songs of the Sabbath Sacrifice, found at both Qumran and Masada, is a work of what goes by the name in Judaism and *Kabbalah* of the Mysticism of the Heavenly 'Chariot' or 'Throne' – so cultivated in the Middle Ages and beyond. If it is not the starting point of this genre, it is certainly one of the earliest extant exemplars of it. Not surprisingly, Line 5 of Manuscript A Fragment 1, as we have arranged the text, also alludes, whether by accident or design, to the word 'Splendour',

(*Zohar*), and a plural variation in Line 3 earlier, 'the Splendours of Nobility'. These in turn are obviously to be equated with 'all Your Secrets' in Line 2. The name *Zohar*, of course, is the title of the best-known work of thirteenth-century medieval Jewish mysticism in Spain.

In Lines 3–5, these 'Secrets' are equated, in an explosion of ecstatic imagery, with 'the feet of Your Glory', 'the Foundations of fire', 'the flames of Your Lamp', 'the fires of Light' and 'the Highness of the Beauty of the Fountain'. This is just a sampling of the vocabulary of this text, one of the most ecstatic visionary recitals of any period, ancient or modern.

The text also operates within the *Hesed/Zedek* dichotomy discussed earlier. These twin concepts, as we have seen, are the equivalent of the two 'love' commandments enunciated in the New Testament as the basis of Jesus' teaching, namely 'loving God' (*Hesed*) and 'loving your neighbour' (*Zedek*). Early Church literature also associates them unmistakably with the figure of James. They are also to be found in Josephus' description of John's doctrines in the *Antiquities* and Justin Martyr's description of Jesus' in *Contra Celsus*. They are cornerstones of Kabbalistic thinking.

Here the text makes allusion, too, to 'the sons of Righteousness', a usage we have already expounded at length in relation to the document by that name. We have delineated it as indistinguishable from and a variation of 'the sons of Zadok' terminology so much discussed in relation to the published corpus. In Lines 7–9 the phrase is used, not surprisingly, in conjunction with wording like 'the Pious Ones' (*Hassidim*) and 'the Congregation of Goodness' – also 'the Pious Ones of Truth', 'the Eternal Merciful Ones' and 'Miraculous Mysteries'.

Calendrical notations, like sabbaths, festivals and jubilees, which Paul in Gal. 4:9–10 refers to as 'beggarly elements', are referred to by ecstatic-sounding titles such as 'the weeks of Holiness', 'monthly flags', 'festivals of Glory' and 'eternal Jubilees'. This fragment ends in Line 13 with the 'Light' and 'Dark' imagery familiar in numerous contexts already mentioned, not least of which is the prologue to the Gospel of John.

A second text, Manuscript B Fragment 1, continues and increases the richness of this vocabulary with allusions like 'the doors of their Wonders', 'the Angels of fire', 'the Spirits of cloud', 'the embroidered Radiance of the Spirits of the Holy of Holies', 'the firmament of the Holy of Holies', 'their wondrous palaces', 'the servants of Holiness' and 'the Perfection of their works' (3–10).

The last two of these are of particular interest. The first echoes a phrase in 2 Cor. 11:15 (also echoed in Rom. 6:22), which we have already noted above and in which Paul complains about Hebrew 'archapostles' who call themselves 'apostles of Christ', but whom he rather calls 'Lying workmen'. These, like 'Satan disguising himself as an Angel of Light', disguise themselves as 'servants of Righteousness'. He ends in a parody of the presumed 'works Righteousness' of 'those proclaiming another Jesus' of the kind we have seen above with regard to 'cursing', namely their 'end shall be according to their works' (11:16).

The second allusion, 'the Perfection of their works' recapitulates one of the most important doctrines at Qumran, 'Perfection'. This term is used in the Damascus Document, viii.28–30, as it is in 2 Cor. 7:11, in conjunction with 'Holiness': 'Perfect Holiness' or 'the Perfection of Holiness'. It is also used, as in the numerous allusions to 'Perfection of the Way' or 'the Perfect of the Way', as a term of self-designation. As such, it resonates with similar allusions in Matthew's Sermon on the Mount. Here, it is combined with the 'works' ideology in a new and different way (10).

Manuscript A Fragment 2 should perhaps be referred to as the Ecology Hymn. It is a veritable Hymn to Nature, one of the most beautiful pieces of nature poetry found at Qumran. On the whole the Qumran literature we have seen thus far has been interested either in Eternal Holy Things or worldly problems related to approaching Eternal Holy Things. In this little fragment, we have one of the first expressions of a sensitivity to nature hitherto missing from the literature. Here the 'hills', 'valleys' and 'streams', 'the land of beauty', 'the depths of forests', 'the wilderness of the desert', 'its wilds' and 'deep wells', 'the highland woods and the cedars of Lebanon' are praised – together with 'all their produce' – in a manner one felt had to be present at Qumran, but up to now was not.

We have entitled Fragment 3.2 'The Community Council Curses Belial'. It is an almost perfect excommunication text of the kind at the end of the Damascus Document encountered in Chapter 6. Though that text was assigned, as we have seen, to 'the priest commanding over the Many' (presumably the high priest designate of the Community) and possibly the *Mebakker*/Bishop, this text is actually assigned to the Community Council. Once again the homogeneity of the literature at Qumran is demonstrated, i.e. this must be the very same Community Council so lovingly detailed in the Community Rule and other texts. It is to be recited by the Community Council in unison, but this Council according to other works is commanded by the

Mebakker. If the latter is to be equated with 'the priest commanding the Many', then once again all our allusions have come full circle.

Like the last column of the Damascus Document, the vehemence and militancy of this text is quite startling. These are no peaceful Essenes, nor do the practitioners of this kind of hatred *love their enemies*; rather in the style of 1QS,ix.21–2 and CD,vi.14–15, they hate 'the sons of the Pit'. There is the usual vocabulary of 'Belial' and 'the sons of Belial', 'cursing', 'Darkness', 'the Pit', 'Evil', all punctuated, as in 1QS,ii, by repetitions of 'Amen, Amen'. In addition one gets new formulations, like 'the Angel of the Pit', 'the Spirit of Destruction', 'the abominations of Sheol'. An allusion to *mastemato* also occurs in 3.2.2, here descriptive of Belial, further confirming the basic circularity of these references to Satan, Belial and Mastemoth. Nor is there any sense of forgiveness here, but rather 'the fury of God's wrath' will last forever (3.2.10).

Throughout the document as we have reconstructed it, one encounters additional familiar vocabulary like 'the Way' imagery, 'Glory', 'the Holy Names', 'the Glorious Names of God', 'mighty works', 'healing' and 'miraculous works'. These last are particularly interesting where the history of Christianity is concerned. But in addition, one has the paraphernalia of Jewish mysticism: 'wondrous Palaces', 'their Secrets', 'secret Truth', 'Treasurehouse of Understanding', and 'Miraculous Mysteries'. There are also 'the Fountain of Understanding' and 'the Fountain of Discovery', which have interesting reverberations with allusions in medieval Jewish poetry, as well as with the title of a treatise, the *Fons Vitae* (*The Living Fountain*) by its most celebrated practitioner, the famous eleventh-century Judeo-Arabic mystic poet of Spain, Solomon Ibn Gabirol.

We have already seen a variation of this imagery in the Demons of Death (Beatitudes) in Chapter 5. This 'Living Fountain' imagery will recur later in this chapter in further hymns, this time 'to the Poor', terminology also important for early Christian history in Palestine. It will be developed to its fullest degree in the Children of Salvation (*Yeshaʿ*) and the Mystery of Existence, with which we close this chapter.

The use of the word 'Glory' in texts such as these is not only interesting because of parallel New Testament usages, but also because of allusions like those in Josephus' description of the beginnings of the Zealot movement. He describes two Rabbis in the disturbance of 4 BC, just preceding the death of Herod, who encourage their followers to strike a blow against Rome and the Herodian family by pulling down the Roman eagle Herod had erected in defiance of all tradition over the entrance to the Temple. They do so in terms of the glory and immortality such zealous acts will gain for their practitioners (*War* 1.650).

Finally the first line of this manuscript begins with allusions to 'the footstools of the feet of your Glory' from Gen. 49:10. The reader will recall this as the Shiloh Prophecy. It was subjected to exegesis in the Genesis Florilegium in Chapter 3, which interpreted the 'Shiloh' in terms of 'the Messiah of Righteousness who would arise at the end of days'. Between these same 'feet' (those of 'the Shiloh') is the *Mehokkek* or 'Law-giver', not to mention 'the Sceptre', which were also interpreted in this context. This 'footstools'/'feet' imagery is carried further in A.1.1 to 'standing' and 'walkway' allusions. The image of 'standing' to great heights is known in Pseudoclementine tradition – those fourth-century Jewish Christian novellas. One of these, called the Recognitions (in which a figure meant to represent Paul attacks James in the Temple) describes someone it calls 'the Standing One', a great redeemer figure which 'stands' to a fantastic height.

But the one surviving line from Manuscript A Fragment 3, which refers to 'the Holy Spirit settling upon His Messiah' has truly remarkable implications, particularly in the setting of the text's rapturous imagery previously. By quoting Isa. 11:2, 'the Spirit of the Lord would settle on him', which it rephrases slightly, it recalls the Messianic Leader (*Nasi*) text from Chapter 1 which quoted Isa. 11:1.

The rephrasing, however slight, is worth noting. 'Him' is now transmuted into 'His Messiah'. But this was the term we encountered in the first line of the first text from Chapter 1, the Messiah of Heaven and Earth. Lest anyone doubted it, Isa. 11:2's 'the Spirit of the Lord' now becomes the more imposing 'the Holy Spirit'. A text of this kind, paralleling the scriptural presentation of Jesus' baptism in the Gospels and related discussions in Hebrews, while at the same time binding all these texts together into a homogeneous whole, reconfirms the basically single, Davidic Messiah ideology at Qumran. It also once more confirms – if such confirmation were by now necessary – the total Messianic thrust of the entire corpus.

TRANSLITERATION
Foundations of Fire   Manuscript A Fragment 1

1. מושב יקרכה והדומי רגלי כבודכה ב[מ]רומי עומדכה ומדר[ך]
2. קודשכה ומרכבות כבודכה ב[ר]וביהמה ואופניהמה וכול סודי[כמה]
3. מוס>ד<י אש ושביבי נרכה וזהרי הוד נה[ור]י אורים ומאורי פלא
4. [הו]ד והדר ורום כבוד סוד קודש ומק[ום ז]ווהר ורום תפארת מ[קור]

5. ‏[עצמ]ות ומקוה גבורות הדר תשבחות וגודל נוראות ורפאו[ת]
6. ‏ומעשי פלאים סוד חוכמא ותבנית דעה ומקור {ע}בינה מקור ערמה
7. ‏ועצת קודש וסוד אמת אוצר שכל מבני צדק ומכוני יוש[ר   [
8. ‏חסדי[ם] ועדת טוב וחסדי אמת ורחמי עולמים ורזי פל[אים]
9. ‏בהר[אותמ]ה ושבועי קודש בתכונמה ודגלי חודשים [[
10. ‏[   ]ים בתקפותמה ומועדי כבוד בתעודות[מה   [
11. ‏[   ] ושבתות ארץ במחל[קותמה ומו]עדי דר[ור   [
12. ‏[   ] וד[רורי נצח ו]   [ל]   [
13. ‏[   ] א[ור וחש]ך   [

Ecology Hymn   Fragment 2

1. ‏[   ]].ה הארץ וכול [יו]שב [   ] יושבי בה אדמה וכול מחשביהמ[ה]
2. ‏[וכו]ל יקומה [וכו]ל גבעות ניאות וכול אפיקים ארץ ציי[ה   [
3. ‏[   ] נ[רנה מצולו[ת] יערים וכול מדברי חור[ב   [
4. ‏[   ]].ותוהוה ואושי מ...תה איים ו[[
5. ‏[   ] פרי[מ]ה עצי רום וכול ארזי לבנ[ון   [
6. ‏[   ] ת[י]רוש ויצהר וכול ת[ב]ו[א]ו[ת   [
7. ‏[   ] וכול תנופות תבל בחדשים שנ[י] עשר [[
8. ‏[   ] *vacat* אמן אמן דברכה ת[[
9. ‏[   ] ומצור ומים מעיני תהום [[
10. ‏[   ] כול נחלים יארי מצ[ול]ות [מ   [
11. ‏[   ] .מים ... ממה.[[
12. ‏[   ] כו[ל] סודיהמה א[[
13. ‏[   ] כה[.   [

Eternal Knowledge   Fragment 3 Column 1

1. ‏[הארצות   [
2. ‏[בחוריהמה.[[
3. ‏[וכול רעיהמה בתהלי   [
4. ‏[וברכות אמת בקצי מ[ועד]   [
5. ‏[כה והנשא מלכותכה בתוך ע[מים]   [
6. ‏[אלי טוהר עם כול מדעי עולמים לה[ן   [
7. ‏[*vacat* אמן אמן [עו]ל[מים] בכול כבודכה שם את לבר[ך   [
8. ‏[כו]ל אמתו   [ל]   [הוסיפו לברך את אל]ל[[

The Community Council Curses Belial   Fragment 3 Column 2

1. ‏עצת היחד יומרו כולמה ביחד אמן אמן *vacat* ואז יזעמ[ו] את בליעל
2. ‏ואת כול גורל אשמתו וענו ואמרו ארור [ב]ליעל במחשבת משטמתו
3. ‏וזעום הוא במשרת אשממה וארורים כול רו[ח]י גו]רלו במחשבת רשעמה
4. ‏וזעומים המה במחשבות נדד [ט]מאתמה כי [המה גור]ל חושך ופקודתמה
5. ‏לשחת עולמים אמן אמן *vacat* וארור הרש[ע בכול] ממשלותיו וזעומים

6. כול בני בל[יעל] בכול עונות מעמדמה עד תוממה [לעד אמן אמן] *vacat*
7. ו[הוסיפו ואמרו ארור אתה מלא[ך השחת ורו[ח האב]דון בכו[ל] מחשבות יצר
8. א[שמתכה ובכול מזמות תוע]בה ועצת רשע[תכה וז[עום אתה במ[מש]ל[ח]
9. [עולתכה ובמשרת רשעתכה ואשמתכ]ה עם כול נ[לולי שאו]ל ועם חרפת ש[חת
10. [ועם כל[מות כלה ל[אין שרית ולאין סל]חות באף עברת [אל לכו]ל
    [עדי עול[ם אמן א[מן]
11. [וארורים כו]ל עוש]י מחשבות רשע[תמה ומקימי מזמתכה [בלבבמה לזום]
12. [על ברית א[ל ול[מאוס את דברי חוזי אמ]תו ולהמיר את משפ]טי התורה]

The Splendor of the Spirits			Manuscript B Fragment 1

1. [ ] [ה כיוריהמ]ה [ ]. [המה] .1
2. [ ] [תיות הדרמה] [המה ע]] .2
3. [ ] [.. כבודמה דלתות פלאיהמה]] .3
4. [ ] [.מה מלאכי אש ורוחי ענן]] .4
5. [ ] זו[הר רוקמת רוחי קודש קדו[שים] .5
6. [ ] ורקיעי קודש [קודשים] .6
7. [ ] חודשים בכול מועד]יהמה] .7
8. [ ] את שם כבוד אלוהותכ]ה] .8
9. [ ]עה וכול משרתי ק[ודש] .9
10. [ ] בתמים מעשיה]מה] .10
11. [ ]ש בהיכלי פ[לאיהמה] .11
12. [ ] כ]ול משרת]יהמה] .12
13. [ ] קודשכה במעו[ן] .13

Fragment 2

1. [ ] אותמה ויברכו את שם קודשכה בברכו[ת] .1
2. [ ]אחה ויברכו[כ]ה כול בריאות הבשר כולמה אשר בר[אתה] .2
3. [ ] ב]המות ועוף ורמש ודג ימים וכול .] .3
4. [ ] א[תה בראתה את כולמה מחדש] .4

Fragment 3

12. [ ] [ם]] .12
13. [ ] נח]ה על משיחו רוח קוד]ש] .13

TRANSLATION
Foundations of Fire
Manuscript A Fragment 1 (1) the seat of Your Honor and the footstools of the feet of Your Glory, in the [h]eights of Your standing and the ru[ng] (2) of Your Holiness and the chariots of Your Glory with their [mu]ltitudes and wheel-angels, and all [Your] Secrets, (3) Foundations of fire, flames of Your lamp, Splendors of honor, fi[re]s of lights and miraculous brilliances,

(4) [hon]or and virtue and highness of Glory, holy Secret and pla[ce of Sp]lendor and the highness of the beauty of the Fou[ntain], (5) [majes]ty and the gathering-place of power, honor, praise and mighty wonders and healing[s], (6) and miraculous works, Secret Wisdom and image of Knowledge and Fountain of Understanding, Fountain of Discovery (7) and counsel of Holiness and Secret Truth, treasurehouse of Understanding from the sons of Righteousness, and dwelling places of Upright[ness . . .] (8) Pious O[nes] and congregation of Goodness and Pious Ones of Truth and Eternal Merciful Ones and miraculous Myst[eries] (9) when th[ey app]ear, and weeks of Holiness in their rightful order and monthly flags . . . (10) in their seasons and festivals of Glory in [their] times . . . (11) and sabbaths of the earth in their divi[sions and appointed] times of jub[ilee . . .] (12) [and] Eternal [Jub]ilees . . . (13) [Li]ght and Dark[ness . . .]

Ecology Hymn

Fragment 2 (1) (Let us praise) . . . the land and all who [dwe]ll . . . who inhabit it, earth and all the[ir] equipment (2) [and al]l its subsistance . . . [and al]l hills, valleys and all streams, land of beau[ty . . .] (3) [Let us] praise the dept[hs] of forests and the wildernesses of Hor[eb . . .] (4) and its wilds and foundations of . . ., islands and . . . (5) [the]ir fruits, highland woods and all the cedars of Leba[non . . .] (6) [new] wine and oil and all the produce of . . . (7) and all the offerings of the land in (the) tw[elve] months . . . (8) Your word. Amen. Amen. (9) . . . and fortress and water, deep wells . . . (10) every stream, de[ep] rivers . . . (11) water . . . (12) [al]l their Secrets . . .

Eternal Knowledge

Fragment 3 Column 1 (1) . . . the lands (2) . . . their young men (3) . . . and all their companions in praises of (4) . . . and praises of Truth in the times of fe[stival] (5) . . . Your . . . and the bearer of Your Kingdom in the midst of Peo[ples] (6) . . . Angels of purity with all Eternal Knowledge, to . . . (7) [to bles]s Your glorious Name for[ever.] Amen. Amen. (8) . . . continue to praise the God of . . . [al]l His Truth . . .

The Community Council Curses Belial

Fragment 3 Column 2 (1) The Community Council shall say together in unison, 'Amen. Amen.' Then [they] shall curse Belial (2) and all his guilty lot, and they shall answer and say, 'Cursed be [Be]lial in his devilish (Mastematic) scheme, (3) and damned be he in his guilty rule. Cursed be all the spir[its of] his [l]ot in their Evil scheme. (4) And may they be damned in the schemes of their [un]clean pollution. Surely [they are the lo]t of Darkness. Their punishment (5) will be the eternal Pit. Amen. Amen. And cursed be the Evi[l] One [in all] of his dominions, and damned be (6) all the sons of Bel[ial] in all their times of service until their consummation [forever. Amen. Amen.'] (7) And [they are to repeat and say, 'Cursed be you, Ang]el of the Pit and Spir[it of Des]truction in al[l] the schemes of [your] gu[ilty] inclination, (8) [and in all the abom]inable [purposes] and counsel of [your] Wick[edness. And da]mned be you in [your] [sinful] d[omi]n[ion] (9) [and in your wicked and guilty rule,] together with all the abom[inations of She]ol and [the reproach of the P]it, (10) [and with the humil]iations of destruction, with [no remnant and no for]giveness, in the fury of [God's] wrath [for]ever [and ever.] Amen. A[men.] (11) [And cursed be al]l who perform their [Evil schemes,] who establish your Evil purposes [in their hearts against] (12) Go[d's Covenant,] so as to [reject the words of those who see] his [Tru]th, and exchange the Judge[ments of the *Torah* . . .]

The Splendour of the Spirits

Manuscript B Fragment 1 (1) . . . as the[ir] teachers . . . (2) their . . . their honor . . . (3) their Glory, the doors of their wonders . . . (4) the Angels of fire and the Spirits of cloud . . . (5) [the] embroidered [Splen]dor of the Spirits of the Holy of Hol[ies . . .] (6) and firmaments of the Holy [of Holies . . .] (7) months with all [their] festivals . . . (8) the Glorious Name of Yo[ur] God . . . (9) and all the servants of Ho[liness . . .] (10) in the Perfection of th[eir] works . . . (11) in [their] wond[rous] Temples . . . (12) [a]ll [their] servant[s . . .] (13) Your Holiness in the habitat[ion of . . .] **Fragment 2** (1) . . . them, and they shall bless Your Holy Name with blessing[s . . . (2) and they shall bless] You, all creatures of flesh in unison, whom [You] have creat[ed . . . (3) be]asts and birds and reptiles and the fish of the seas, and all . . . (4) [Y]ou have created them all anew . . . **Fragment 3** (13) . . . The Holy Spirit [sett]led upon His Messiah . . .

42. BAPTISMAL HYMN (4Q414)

On the heels of this text, we come upon a series of fragments relating to baptism. By baptism, of course, the reader should realize that the proponents of this literature did not necessarily mean anything different from traditional Jewish ritual immersion. The terminologies are synonymous, though the emphasis on baptismal procedures at Qumran is extraordinary. This can be seen not only in texts such as the one represented by these fragments and the well-known Community Rule, iii, 1–4, which in describing baptism makes reference to 'the Holy Spirit', but also the sheer number of ritual immersion facilities at the actual ruins of Qumran – if these can be safely associated with the movement responsible for this literature.

Once again, one is confronted with the vocabulary of 'Glory', this time in terms of 'a law of Glory' (4.3), as well as, if our reconstruction is correct, 'the purity of Righteousness' or 'Justification' (4.4). There is reference to 'making atonement for us', being 'cleansed from pollution' as one 'enters the water', and the usual 'Laws of your Holiness' and 'Truth of Your Covenant'. There is also an interesting allusion to a 'Jewish woman', which parallels the reference to 'a Jewish man' in the calendrical texts, and shows the extent to which the usage 'Jew' had already taken hold in Palestine in the first century BC and the first century AD.

TRANSLITERATION

Fragment 1 Column 1

] .1	.[מר כדבד
] .2	טהורי מועדו [
] .3	[יכה ולכפר לנו
] .4	טהורים לפניכה [
] .5	עתו בכול דבר [
] .6	להטהר מר [
] .7	עשיתנו [

Fragment 1 Column 2

.1	..תכה ...ו לחוקי קוד[ש [
.2	לראשון [ו]לשלישי ולש[ביעי [
.3	כא[מ]ת בריתכ[ה [
.4	להטהר מטמאת] [
.5	ואחר יבוא במים] [
.6	וענה ואמר ברוך א[תה [
.7	כיא ממוצא פיכה] [
.8	אנשי ....] [

Fragment 2

.1	]ריו ובמים] [ ] [
.2	יברך ע] [ ] [
.3	ישראל אשר מ]] [
.4	לפניכה מכול] [
.5	קודשכה] [
.6	עזבח]ה [

Fragment 3

נ[פ] ש[ ].[ ].[1.   [

ההואה]   2.   [

לכם לעם ט[הור   3.   [

וגם אני מב]   4.   [

היום אשר]   5.   [

במועדי טהור]   6.   [

יחד *vacat*]   7.   [

בטהרת [י]שראל ל.]   8.   [

ו[י]שבו]   9.   [

והיה ביום]   10.   [

נקבה יהודיה]   11.   [

ש[   ].[12.   [

Fragment 4

כיא אתה עשיתה את .]   1.   [

]. [ ]כה להטהר לפנ]   2.   [

...ם לו חוק כבוד]   3.   [

ולהיות בטהרת צ[דקה   4.   [

ור]וח[ץ במים והיה]   5.   [

]תם ואחר ישוב]   6.   [

מטהר עמו במימי רוחץ]   7.   [

]. [ ] שנית על עמדו יע[מוד   8.   [

]. [ ] ט[ו]הר]כה בכבוד]   9.   [

] ת[ע]ו [בהיו]ם   10.   [

TRANSLATION

Fragment 1 Column 1 (1) . . . in the word (2) . . . those purified for the appointed time (3) . . . of You and to atone for us (4). . . those who are pure before You (5) . . . his time, in everything (6) . . . to be cleansed during (7) . . . You have made us

Fragment 1 Column 2 (1) Your . . . for the Laws of Holine[ss . . .] (2) on the first [and] third and se[venth (days) . . .] (3) in the Tr[u]th of You[r] Covenant . . . (4) to be cleansed from the pollution of . . . (5) and after he enters the water . . . (6) he will answer and say, Blessed are Y[ou . . .] (7) for from the declaration of Your mouth . . . (8) men of . . .

Fragment 2 (1) his . . . in the day . . . (2) . . . will bless . . . (3) Israel who . . . (4) before You from all . . . (5) Your Holiness . . . (6) you have abandoned . . .

Fragment 3 (1) s[ou]l. . . (2) that . . . (3) for You as a p[ure] people . . . (4) also, I am . . . (5) the day when . . . (6) in the appointed times of purification . . . (7) of the Community. . . (8) in the purity of [I]srael, for . . . (9) [and] they [will] dwell . . . (10) And it will come to pass in the day . . . (11) a Jewish woman . . .

Fragment 4 (1) for You have made . . . (2) Your . . . to be purified befo[re . . .] (3) for Him, a Law of Glory . . . (4) and to be in the purity of Ri[ghteousness . . .] (5) and w[ash]ing in water, and he will be . . . (6) You will . . . And after he returns . . . (7) purifying his people with cleansing water . . . (8) the second one in his place will sta[nd . . .] (9) Your puri[fication] in the Glory of . . . (10) . . . in the da[y . . .]

43. HYMNS OF THE POOR (4Q434, 436)

These texts are appropriately titled. It is important to see the extent to which the terminology *Ebionim* ('the Poor') and its synonyms penetrated Qumran literature. Early commentators were aware of the significance of this usage, though later ones have been mostly insensitive to it. The use of this terminology, and its ideological parallels, *'Ani* ('Meek') and *Dal* ('Downtrodden'), as interchangeable terms of self-designation at Qumran, is of the utmost importance. There are even examples in crucial contexts of the published corpus of an allusion like 'the Poor in Spirit', known from Matthew's Sermon on the Mount in both the War Scroll,xi.10 and the Community Rule,iv.3.

It is clear from the Pauline corpus that in some sense the community following the leadership of James the Just (known in the literature as 'the brother of Jesus', whatever is meant by that designation) – the so-called Jerusalem Church or Jerusalem Community – were called 'the Poor' (Gal. 2:10; also Jas. 2:3–5). Remembering 'the Poor', meaning in some sense bringing a proper amount of monetary contributions back to Jerusalem, is all Paul is willing to say in Galatians above about the conditions laid down on his activities by his ideological opposite James.

As tradition proceeds, it becomes clear that the *Ebionim* (the so-called Ebionites) or 'the Poor' is the name by which the community descending from James' Jerusalem Community in Palestine goes. In all likelihood, it descends from the one we are studying in these materials as well. This movement, called by some 'Jewish Christianity' – the appellation is defective, but we have no other – honoured the person and teaching of this James, otherwise known as 'the Righteous' or 'Just One'. By the fourth century, the high Church historian Eusebius, previously Bishop of Caesarea, is willing to tell us about these Ebionites. Of Palestinian origin and one of the people primarily responsible for the Christian takeover in Rome, he clearly regards the Ebionites he describes as sectarian – sectarian, of course, in contradistinction to that form of Pauline Christianity that he helped promote in Constantine's time.

He tells us in *Ecclesiastical History*, 3.27 that they were 'called Ebionites by the ancients (i.e. a long time before his own era) because of the low and mean opinions they held about Christ'. By this statement he means that the Ebionites do not regard Jesus as divine. He does so, using the 'Wicked Demon', 'Devil' and 'net' language that is so much a cornerstone of the presentation of the charges in the Damascus Document against them. Knowing that Ebionite means 'Poor Man in Hebrew', he jokingly contends that they received this epithet because of 'the poverty of intellect they exhibited', i.e. in following such a primitive Christology.

He knows that they considered Christ born by 'natural' means, 'a plain and ordinary man, who was justified by his advances in Righteousness only . . . They also insisted on the complete observance of the Law, nor did they think one could be saved only by faith in Christ and a corresponding life.' Rather 'they evinced *great zeal* to observe the literal sense of the Law . . . They observed the Sabbath and other ceremonies just like Jews.' Paul they considered 'an *apostate from the Law*' (italics ours).

This description of the Ebionites is crucial to our understanding of these texts and the widespread use of the 'Poor' terminology at Qumran. Though there is more material from other sources about these Ebionites, they are certainly the community that held the memory of James in the highest regard, whereas Paul they considered 'the Enemy' or Anti-Christ (compare this with the terminology *Mastema* we are encountering in these texts). Such a stance is not unparalleled in crucial passages from the letter in James' name in the New Testament. We have already shown that this letter, in responding to some adversary who believes that Abraham was justified only by faith, states that by making himself 'a friend of man', this adversary has turned himself into 'the Enemy of God'. This 'Enemy' terminology is also known in Matt. 13:25–40's 'parable of the tares', perhaps the only anti-Pauline parable in the Gospels, where an 'Enemy' sows the 'tares' among the good seed. At the 'harvest' these will be uprooted and thrown into 'the burning'.

The use of *Ebionim* as a term of self-designation at Qumran is widespread, most notably in the *pesharim*, but also, as we have seen, in the interpretation of the Star Prophecy in Column xi of the War Scroll. Here it is stated that by 'the hand of the Poor Ones whom You have redeemed by Your Power and the peace of Your Mighty Wonders . . . by the hand of the Poor Ones and those bent in the dust, You will deliver the Enemies of all the lands and humble the mighty of the Peoples to bring upon their heads the reward of the Wicked and justify the Judgement of Your Truth on all the sons of men . . .' There is no need to quote further.

The terminology is also used in crucial constructions in the Habakkuk *Pesher*, though it does not appear in the underlying text at all. However its variation, *'Ani* ('Meek') does, but not until Hab. 3:14. Regardless of this, for the *pesher*, the *Ebionim* are the rank and file of the Community led by the Teacher of Righteousness, whose fate they share (xii.6ff). Where scriptural exegesis at Qumran generally is concerned, this is one of the terms from Psalms and Prophets looked for by the exegetes. In the Qumran Hymns, v.23 the term *Ebionei-Hesed* ('the Poor Ones of Piety') occurs as a particularly telling form of self-designation. It combines, as we can see, two important Qumran terminologies: the *Ebionim* and the *Hassidim*.

Found in five identifiable copies, the Hymns of the Poor are delicate poetic creations of considerable beauty. Stylistically, they are similar to the Hymns from Cave 1. They derive their name from the widespread use of the term *Ebionim* and its variants *'Anavim* and *Dal*, 'the Meek' and 'the Downtrodden', throughout. The familiar vocabulary of 'Knowledge', 'Glory', 'Piety', 'the Judgements of the Way', 'the Ways of Truth', 'the Way of His heart', 'zeal', 'anger', 'Light', 'Darkness', 'Gentiles' and 'Violent Ones' again appears.

The interchangeability of the usages 'the Poor', 'the Meek' and 'the Downtrodden' is paralleled in the published Hymns from Cave 1 by the use of *nephesh* − *Ebion* ('soul of the Poor One' − also used here in Line 2.1.1), and *nephesh-'Ani* ('soul of the Meek'), used repeatedly throughout. A parallel, *nephesh-Zaddik* ('soul of the Righteous One'), is to be found in a context of some import at the end of Column i of the Cairo recension of the Damascus Document. Evoking another familiar phrase, 'the Way of His heart', used in these Hymns to the Poor as well, the passage describes a particularly violent attack on 'the soul of the Righteous One' (presumably the Righteous Teacher) and some of his colleagues. These it refers to also as 'walkers in Perfection'.

Line 4 of Fragment 1 of the present text actually uses an allusion hinted at in compilations of Messianic proof texts like the published Messianic Florilegium: *'tinzor Toratecha'* ('to keep Your *Torah*'). The use of this expression as a synonym for the *Shomrei ha-Brit* ('the Keepers of the Covenant'), the definition in the Community Rule, v.2 and v.9 of 'the sons of Zadok', once more confirms the basic circularity of all these usages. It is but a short step from here to the 'Nazoraean' terminology often used as a synonym for Jewish Christians in other sources, and perhaps the root of Matt. 2:23's tantalizing 'Nazarene' epithet.

From 2.1.5–9, one is completely in the context and atmosphere of the Habakkuk *Pesher*, xii, where the Wicked Priest 'plotted to destroy the Poor Ones'. Beginning with the allusion to 'circumcizing the foreskin of their hearts' (4), which the Habakkuk *Pesher*, xi.13 applies in a negative manner to disqualify the Wicked Priest presumably from Temple service, it is quite clear that a Judgement of sorts, similar to that being evoked in the Habakkuk *Pesher*,v, viii, and xii, is being described.

The 'Violent Ones', prominent in both the Habakkuk and the Ps. 37 *Pesher*s are alluded to (5). In the last-mentioned text, they are referred to as 'the Violent Ones of the Gentiles' and take 'vengeance' on the Wicked Priest for what he did to the Righteous Teacher, i.e. 'swallowed him' or 'destroyed him'. In Hymns of the Poor, Line 6, this allusion and one to the 'Wicked' that precedes it are followed immediately by a reference to divine 'wrath' and 'hot anger'. These are used repeatedly by the Habakkuk *Pesher* in the same context and with the same sense. Not only do they describe how the Wicked Priest pursued the Righteous Teacher to 'swallow' or 'consume' him (xi.4–5) – in return for which he too would be ultimately swallowed or consumed (xi.14–15), but they also describe this vengeance as the vengeance of God. The parallels are so exact that it is quite clear the two texts are using the same vocabulary and concepts to discuss the same events. They are also quite possibly *by the same author*. The link between them is that close. Because of their mutual regard for their subject, 'the Poor', both of them could be described as 'Hymns to the Poor', though the Habakkuk *Pesher* is much more than this.

In Lines 1 and 8 of 2.1, the same word, *hizil/hizilam* ('He saved'/ 'He saved them') is also being used that the Habakkuk *Pesher* uses to describe how 'the Righteous' are saved from 'the House of Judgement' or the 'Last Judgement' (viii.2 and xii.14). The latter's eschatological exegesis of the all-important Hab. 2:4, that 'the Righteous shall live by his faith', hinges on the condition that those to whom it applies be both '*Torah*-Doers' and 'Jews' (viii.1–2). Hab. 2:4, with Gen. 15:6

concerning Abraham's faith is, as we have seen, the key scriptural foundation piece of Paul's absolutely fundamental presentations in Rom. 1:17 and Gal. 3:11.

In the Hymns of the Poor, the Poor are 'saved' because of their 'Piety', and God's 'Mercy', and because they 'walked in the Way of His heart'. In Line 4 of 2.1, this proposition is put as follows: 'He saved them because of his Piety (here clearly 'Grace') and directed their foot to the Way.' This exactly parallels the exegesis of Hab. 2:4 in the Habakkuk *Pesher*: 'He saved them . . . because of their *'amal* ('suffering works') and their faith in the Righteous Teacher.' Both are eschatological, the second demonstrably so. The Habakkuk *Pesher* also makes this clear by the reference in the previous exegesis to Hab. 2:3: 'If it tarries, wait for it', which it applies to what is known in early Christianity as 'the delay of the Parousia', i.e. the delay of the 'End Time'.

One should also note the xenophobia inherent in Lines 7–10, and the references, again paralleling the Habakkuk *Pesher*, to 'peoples', 'Gentiles' and the fiery 'zeal' with which God would judge them, i.e. God is as 'zealous' as these presumable 'Zealots'. This is continued into Fragment 3, where, amid the language of 'works', 'atonement', 'Piety' and 'Glory', it is confirmed that God would comfort Jerusalem. Here the nationalist sentiments of the literature are once more completely apparent.

Throughout the Judgement material in Fragment 2, it is made clear that it is from foreign 'nations' and 'peoples' that God would save 'the Poor', as 'He sets His Angel round about the sons of Israel' (12). There are splendid poetic allusions here too, such as, being 'hidden in the shadow of His wings' from Psalms or those who 'walk in the Way of His heart' singing 'like flutes' (7 and 10). In the end, just as in the case of Jerusalem, they would be comforted.

Line 2.6 reverses the Gospels' 'bride and bridegroom' imagery. Whereas in the Gospels this imagery usually ends up in the disqualification of both Israel and the Law, here it is used to bless 'the *Torah* and 'the book of Your Laws' (3.12). Here, too, that 'Throne' imagery, so much a part of *Merkabah* Mysticism and later medieval Jewish poetry, is once again evoked (3.7). As with the War Scroll from Cave 1, there can be no doubting the militancy of these Hymns, nor their nationalism, their zeal for the Law and their xenophobia, which it is possible to think of as becoming inverted in Gentile Christianity as it has come down to us.

TRANSLITERATION   Fragment 1

1. בינה לחזק לב נדכה ולנצח לרוח בה לנחם דלים בעת צרתמה וידי נופלי[ם]
2. לקומם לעשות כלי דעת לתת לחכמים דעה ישרים יוסיפו לקח להתבונן
3. בעלילותיכה אשר עשיתה בשני קדם שני דור ודור שכל עולם אשר
4. [יסדת]ה לפני ותנצור תורתכה לפני ובריתכה אמנתה לי ותחזק על לב[י]
5. [   ]   ללכת בדרכיכה לבי פקדתה וכליותי שננתה בל ישכחו חוקיכה
6. [   ]תה תורתכה וכליותי פתחתה ותחזק עלי לרדוף אחרי דרכי
7. [אמת   ].כה ותשם פי כחרב חדה ולשוני פתחתה לדברי קודש ותשם
8. [   ] מוסר בל יהגו בפעולות אדם בשחת שפתיו רגלי חזקתה
9. [   ]ה ובידכה החזקתה בימים ותשלחני ב.[   ]
10. [ ]ג[ערתה ממני ותשם לב טהור תחתיו יצר רע נע[רתה]

Fragment 2 Column 1

1. ברכי נפשי את אדוני {מ} על כול נפלאותיו עד עולם וברוך שמו כי
   הציל נפש אביון ואת
2. עני לא בזא ולא שכח צרת דלים פקח עיניו אל דל ושועת יתומים שמע
   ויט אוזניו *vacat* אל
3. {ש}ע<פ>תם ברוב רחמיו חנן ענוים ויפקח עיניהם לראות את דרכיו
   וא[וזניה]ם לשומע
4. למודו וימול עורלות לבם ויצילם למען חסדו ויכן לדרך רגלם בד[ו]ב
   צרתם לא עזבם
5. וביד עריצים לא נתנם ועם רשעים לא שפטם ועברתו לא ה[חרה]
   עליהם ולא כלם
6. בחרונו ולא יעף כל חרוני חמתו ובאש קנאת לא שפטם *vacat*
7. שפטם ברוב רחמי משפטי עינו למען בוחנם והרבה רחמ[ו   ]
   הביאם בגוים [מיד]
8. אדם הצילם שפעת גוים לא שפט[ם] ובתוך לאומים ל[א הפיצם]
   ויסתירם ב[צל כנפין]
9. ויתן לפניהם מחשכים לאור ומעקשים למישור ויגל להם עתרות שלום ואמת [ויעש]
10. במדה רוחם מליהם במשקל תכן וישרם כחלילים ולב [שמחה]
    יתן להם וילכו בד[רך לבו]
11. בדרך לבו נם [ה]וא הגישם כי ע..ו את רוחם שליו ויקם
    תעו[דה   ]ל נגע צוה לבל[   ]
12. *vacat* [   ] וי[תן מלאכו סביב בנ]י ישרא[ל פן ישחיתם [בארץ]
13. איביהם [ ]ח[   ]ש עברתו להב[י]א עליהם]את חרונו]ים בהם זו[ ]
14. שנא [ ]ל[   ]ב כבודו ל[   ]

Fragment 2 Column 2

1. כרעה[   ]מו[   ]ל צרה ה[   ].ך[   ]   [
2. עשיתה[ם   ] להם נגד [ב]ני אדם ותצילם למענך [[

3. ויקשו את עונם ואת עון אבותם ויכפרו במ]   [
4. משפטים ולדרך אשר הי..]   [
5. עוד כי א]   [ורתם ב].   [

Fragment 3

1. [   ] [כה   ]].ה. להנחם על אבלה ענוה ה:]
2. גוים [יש]חת ולאומים יכרית ורשעים]   [חרש
3. מעשי שמים וארץ ויניעו וכבודו מלוא]   א]מתם
4. יכפר ירב {ט} טוב ונחמם טוב הש]   [לאכול
5. פריה וטובה   vacat
6. כאיש אשר אמו תנחמנו כן ינחמם בירושל]ם   כחתן] על כלה עליה
7. [   ] [לם ושם   ]   [א כסאו לעולם ועד וכבודו]   [וכל גוים
8. [   ]   [לו והיה] [.. צד] צד]   [ים .[צם חמדה
9. [   ]   [עד תפאר]ת   [אברכה את
10. [שם   ] ברוך שם עליו]ן   [vacat
11. [   ]   ] ר..[[חסדך עלו
12. [   ]   [לתורה הכינותה
13. [   ]   [ספר חוקיך

TRANSLATION

Fragment 1 (1) . . . Understanding to strengthen the downcast heart, and to triumph over the spirit in it; to comfort the Downtrodden in the time of their distress, and as for the hands of the fallen, (2) to hold them up so they can make vessels of Knowledge, to give Knowledge to the Wise, to increase the learning of the Upright, so as to comprehend (3) Your wonders that You performed in former days, in previous generations, the Eternal Insight that (4) You [established] before (establishing) me. And You kept your Law before me, and Your Covenant You confirmed for me, strengthening (it) upon [my] heart. (5) . . . to walk in Your Ways. You commanded my heart, and instructed my conscience not to forget Your Laws. (6) . . . You have . . . Your Law and opened my conscience, and strengthened me to pursue the Ways of (7) [Truth . . .] Your . . . You made my mouth like a sharp sword and opened my tongue to words of Holiness. You have put (8) . . . instruction. Let them not meditate upon the doings of man, whose lips are in the Pit. You strengthened my legs, (9) . . . And by Your hand you strengthened (me) with days. You sent me in . . . (10) (a heart of stone?) You [re]moved from me and put a pure heart in its place, remov[ing] evil inclination

Fragment 2 Column 1 (1) Bless the Lord, O my soul, because of all His wonders forever. Blessed be His name, for He saved the soul of the Poor One (*Ebion*). (2) He has not despised the Meek (*'Ani*), nor has he forgotten the distress of the Downtrodden (*Dal*). (On the contrary), He opened His eyes to the Downtrodden, and, inclining His ears, hearkened to (3) the cry of orphans. In His abundant Mercy He comforted the Meek, and opened their eyes to behold His ways, and their ears, to hear (4) His teaching. And He circumcised the foreskin of their hearts, and saved them because of his Grace, and He directed their foot to the Way. He did not abandon them in their great distress, nor (5) give them into the hand of Violent Ones, nor judge them with the Wicked, nor kindle his wrath against them, nor destroy them (6) in His anger, though the wrath of His hot anger did not abate at all. But He did not judge them in fiery zeal; (7) (rather) He judged them in the abundance of His Mercy. The Judgements of His eye were to test them. In the greatness of His Mercy, He brought them (from) among the Gentiles; from the hands of (8) Man He saved them. He did not judge them in the multitude of the nations, nor scatter them among the Peoples. (Rather), He hid them in the shadow of His wings, (9) and made the dark places Light before them, and the crooked places straight, and He revealed to them abundant Peace and Truth. He made (10) their Spirit by measure, and meted out their words by weight, causing them to sing like flutes. He gave them a heart of rejoicing, and they walked in the Way of His heart. (11) But also, in the way of His heart He led them, because they . . . , their Spirit at rest, and raised up a testi[mony . . .] He commanded a plague to . . ., (12) And He set his Angel around the s[ons of Isra]el lest they be destroyed [in the land of] (13) their enemies . . . His wrath, to bring His anger . . . on them . . . (14) He hated . . . His Glory to . . .

Fragment 2 Column 2 (1) in Evil . . . distress . . . (2) their works . . . for them against the sons of Man, and You saved them for Your own sake . . . (3) And they aggravated their iniquity and the iniquity of their fathers, but they atoned for it in . . . (4) Judgements, and to the Way that . . . (5) again, because . . . their . . . in . . .

Fragment 3 (1) Your . . . to be comforted on account of her mourning; her affliction He . . . (2) nations [He will de]stroy, and peoples cut off, and the Wicked . . . He fashioned (3) the works of Heaven and earth, and they met, and His Glory filled . . . their [Tr]uth (4) will make atonement. Goodness will multiply, and the Goodness of the . . . will comfort them. . . . to eat (5) its fruit and its Goodness. (6) Like a man whose mother comforts him, so will He comfort them in Jerusal[em . . . Like a bridegroom] over the bride, over her (7) . . . and He will put . . . and He will lift u]p His Throne forever and ever. And His Glory . . . and all the Gentiles (8) . . . and there will be . . . desire (9) . . . forever the radiance of . . . I shall bless (10) [the

Name] . . . blessed be the Name of the Most High . . . (11) . . . Your Piety (or 'Grace') upon him (12) . . . for the sake of the *Torah* You established (13) . . . the book of Your Laws . . .

44. THE CHILDREN OF SALVATION (*YESHAʿ*) AND THE MYSTERY OF EXISTENCE (4Q416, 418)
(Plate 22)

If we are justified in grouping all these fragments together, this is one of the longest extant manuscripts in the unpublished corpus. Strictly speaking, the work as a whole has the character of an admonition and belongs in Chapter 5, but because of its eschatological thrust, mysticism, emphasis on the Mysteries of God and parallels with the preceding works and Hymns from Cave 1, we have chosen to place it here.

Again we are in the vocabulary of 'Knowledge', 'Goodness', 'Faithfulness', 'the Glory of the Holy Ones', 'the God of Truth', 'Righteousness', 'works', 'Judgement', 'the Lords of Evil', 'Lying', 'Unfaithfulness', etc. As in the case of the Chariots of Glory above, which it very much resembles, we have separated out the various fragments and given each a subtitle drawn from the most striking and beautiful of these allusions. As in the case of the Hymns of the Poor, here and there it is possible to question the sequence or whether all fragments actually belong together; however manuscript overlaps do seem to assure the sequence of most of the fragments.

Some of the most interesting imagery revolves around the use of the term 'Fountain' already encountered above – 'the Eternal Fountain'/ 'the Fountain of Living Waters' and 'the Eternal Secrets', the 'obscure Mysteries' – even 'the Mystery of Being' or 'the Mystery of Existence'. There can be no mistaking that some of these same images are also being evoked in medieval Jewish mystical texts. The famous philosophical treatise by the celebrated Avicebron (the eleventh-century Jewish mystic poet Ibn Gabirol mentioned above) is, as we have seen, given this title. His poems are even more redolent with this kind of imagery – the most famous of these, *The Crown of the Kingdom*, repeatedly evokes 'Angels', 'the Throne', 'Secrets', 'Mysteries', 'Mighty Wonders', 'storehouses', 'Righteousness', 'the Kingdom', etc. The sense of the Mystery of Existence text also has overtones with the quasi-magical treatise of the early centuries AD, the *Book of the Mysteries* (*Sefer Ha-Razim*), though its vocabulary is less magical.

We also encounter allusions to the 'Eternal Planting' (1.13), which one finds in crucial passages of the Damascus Document, the Community Rule and Hymns. In this regard, one should see the key allusion in CD,i.7 to 'the root of Planting from Aaron and Israel'. In 1QH,vi.15 and viii.6–10, this is combined with 'Branch' and 'Fountain' imagery. In 1QS,xi, it is tied to the imagery of 'the Fountain of Righteousness', 'Perfection of the Way', 'justification' and the Community Council joining 'the sons of Heaven' as a 'Building of Holiness'. One should compare this 'building' imagery with Paul's description of himself as the 'architect' in 1 Cor. 3:6–17. Using 'planting' and 'husbandry' imagery here too, he describes his community as 'the building of God'.

In Line 1 of Fragment 1 of this text, as we have reconstructed it, the addressees are instructed, as per Community Rule and Damascus Document parameters, 'to separate themselves'. They are compared to 'a Fountain' or 'an Eternal Fountain' (1.13), and Paul's spiritualized 'Temple' imagery that the Community Rule applies, as noted above, to the Community Council, is exemplified in the reference to the hearer here as 'a Holy of Holies' (1.4). The addressees are also, it would appear, here and later, given the power of intercession: 'He has given you authority' (1.15; also 10.13 'He has given you authority over an inheritance of Glory').

Perhaps most interestingly, directly after the command in Line 8 to 'love Him', God's 'eternal *Hesed*' ('Piety') is called down upon all 'the Keepers' (1.8). We have elsewhere identified this 'Piety' commandment – loving God – as the first of the two 'love' commandments. With regard to it, one should also see James. 1:12 discussing to 'the Crown of Life which the Lord has promised those who love Him', directly followed in the next chapter by citation of the 'Righteousness' commandment, 'love your neighbour as yourself' (2:8). This 'the Keeper' theme too – here 'the Keepers of His word' – should by now be familiar. It is also, as we have seen, a theme in the early passages in the Letter of James, where much of the language of this treatise can be paralleled, and in the definition in the Community Rule of 'the sons of Zadok', i.e. 'the Keepers of the Covenant'. It is paralleled, too, in the Hymns of the Poor above, by a variant related to the terminology 'Nazoraean'/'Nazarene'.

The 'Fountain' imagery continues into Fragment 2, and after a reference to 'the Righteous' in Fragment 3, Fragment 4 launches into another splendid description of the Last Judgement. Using 'Light' imagery and 'walking in Eternal Light' to describe the lot of the 'seekers after Truth' — also called 'the Elect of Truth' paralleling similar descriptions of 'the sons of Zadok' in the Damascus Document — the most splendid imagery of 'the Foundations of the Universe shouting out Judgement' is used. This powerful allusion is followed by reference to 'the Secret of the Pillars'. Imagery of this kind not only calls to mind characterization of 'the *Zaddik*' in *Zohar*, 59b on Noah, as 'the Foundation of the universe', but also Paul's reference to the central leadership triad, including James the Just, as 'these Pillars' in Gal. 2:9. The play on the *Sod*/*Yesod*, i.e. 'Secrets'/'Foundations', imagery here is also present, for example, in Ibn Gabirol's eleventh-century *The Crown of the Kingdom* mentioned above (lines 14, 112, 164 and 170). We have been following this language throughout the Qumran corpus.

In later fragments, many of these themes are reiterated, and the text now shifts to an emphasis on understanding 'all Mysteries', with particular interest in 'the Mystery of Being'/'the Mystery of Existence'. It is noteworthy that these kinds of inquiries seem to have, at least in theory, been proscribed in Talmudic Judaism. Not only do we have here references to 'the scales of Righteousness', 'Lying', 'swallowing', and 'Ways', but in Fragment 7.3 the ubiquitous *ʿamal* ('suffering works') language appears again. This is to be found, as we have seen, in Isa. 53, and used in the Habakkuk *Pesher* to delineate how one is 'saved'.

In Fragment 9, the most surprising allusion occurs in relation to being 'Righteous' and 'works', and that is the expression *Yeshaʿ* ('Salvation'). It first appears in a construct *Yeshaʿ maʿsaiv* ('the Salvation of His works') in Line 8 in relation to 'not removing the Law of God from your heart' (note once again the ubiquitous 'heart' usage here). Then in Line 11, following another reference to *ʿamal* — this time expressed as a verb (10) — one comes upon the construct 'the children of *Yeshaʿ*' or 'the children of Salvation'. The text then goes on to speak of 'inheriting Glory' and 'everlasting joy'.

The use of the noun '*Yeshaʿ*' or the verbal noun '*Yeshuʿato*' ('His Salvation') is fairly widespread at Qumran and much underrated. One finds expressions such as these in two important contexts in the Damascus Document: viii.43 relating to 'God Fearers' — 'until God reveals Righteousness and Salvation to those who fear His Name' — and viii.57, relating to 'not rejecting the Laws of Righteousness', 'listening to the voice of the Teacher of Righteousness' and 'being forgiven' — 'and they would *see* His Salvation' (italics ours). The verb 'see' here is of prime importance. These terms also crop up in several interesting contexts in the War Scroll (xiii, xiv and xviii) and another equally Messianic section preceding the 'Planting' section in the Qumran Hymns (vii. 19).

Some would feel that such a concept was really quite new for the people of the ancient world; nor had the Greeks yet personified it in various deities. The personification of this concept in the Gospel presentation of Messianic events in Palestine in the first century can in this light be considered a most revolutionary development and one that has not ceased exercising its influence on mankind even now.

In Fragment 9.2/10.1, the theme of 'keeping' is applied to that of 'Mysteries' in conjunction with the parallel one of 'not forsaking the Law' (8). This theme of 'Mysteries' is pursued to the end, particularly the single mystery, 'the Mystery of Existence', amid continued allusion to 'justifying by Your Judgement' — found throughout the Qumran corpus — 'zeal' and a new usage, 'poverty', another obvious variation of the 'Poor' theme, as opposed to 'Riches', in connection with which the 'swallowing' imagery is used again (10.9). The expression *Ebion/*'the Poor One' is actually used on a number of occasions, linking up with the previous work again, and leading to the final message: 'walking in Righteousness', 'lying down in Truth', and 'inheriting Eternal bliss'.

TRANSLITERATION

The Eternal Planting   **Fragment 1**

1. שפתיכה.פתח מקור לברך קדושים ואתה כמקור עולם הלל [כי] הבדילכה מכול
2. רוח בשר ואתה הבדל מכול אשר שנא והנזר מכול תעבות [.] הוא עשה כול
3. ויורישם איש נחלתו והוא חלקכה ונחלתכה בתוך בני אדם [.[
   המשילכה ואתה
4. בזה כבדהו בהתקדשכה לו כאשר שמכה לקדוש קודש[י]ם [.]ל בכול [   ]
5. הפיל גורלכה וכבודכה הרבה מאדה וישימכה לו בכור ב[   ]
6. וטובתי לכה אתן ואתה {ל} הלוא לכה טובתו ובאמונתו הלך תמיד [בכול]
7. מעשיכה ואתה דרוש משפטיו מיד כול ורוב..]
8. אהבהו ובחסד עולם וברחמים על כול שומרי דברו וק[
9. ואתה שכל [פ]תח לכה ובאוצרו המשילכה ואיפת אמת פ>ו<קד [   ]
10. אתכה המה ובידכה להשיב אף מאנשי רצון ולפקוד [
11. עמכה בטרם תקח נחלתכה מידי כבד קדושיו ובט[ו]רם [
12. פתח [   ][שים וכול הנקרא לשמ>ו< קודשו]
13. עם כול ק[צים הדר]י פארתו למטעת עו[לם
14. [ ]ה חב[ ] [ ] יתהלכו כול נוחלי ארץ כי בשמ[ם
15. ואתה מבין אם בחכמת ידים המשילכה ודע[ת]כה
16. אוט לכול הולכי אדם ומשם תפקוד טרפכה ת[
17. התבונן מודה ומיד כול משכילכה הוסף לקח [

18. הוצא מחסורכה לכול דורשי חפץ ואז תבין]   [
19. תמלא ושבעתה ברוב טוב ומחכמת ידיכה[[
20. כי אל פלג נחלת[כו]ל [חי] וכול חכמי לב השכילו]   [

The Fountain of Living Water   Fragment 2

[[אכרים עד כול]   ] .1
[[ש הבא בטנאיכה ובאסמיכה כול]   ] .2
[[ושוה עת בעת דורשם ואל תדם]   ] .3
[[ש כולם ידרשו לעתם ואיש כפי חכ[מה   ] .4
[[כמקור מים חיים אשר הכול אנשי[ם   ] .5
[[למה והיה כלאים [כ]פרד והייתה כלוב[ש שעטנז] .6
[[בשור וב[   ] ונם תבואתכה ת[   ] .7
[[ה] [וק].[   ] הונכה עם בשרכה]   ] .8

All the Eras of Eternity   Fragment 3

[[ט על] [עה כול]   ] .1
[[יחדו] [עו כול אשר ח[   ] .2
[[ותהום פחדו וית[   ] .3
[[ו וכול עולה תתם עד ושלם]   ] .4
[[   ] בכול קצי עד כיא אל אמת הוא[ה   ] .5
[[ל להבין צדיק בין טוב לרע]   ] .6
[[כי]א יצר בשר הואה ומבינים]   ] .7
[[ל] [ל] א   ] .8

The Foundations of the Universe Shout out Judgement   Fragment 4

נ[פחכה   ] .1
מות עם [   ] ותשכיל [   ] .2
[דתם הלוא באמת יתהלכו   ] .3
[הם ובדעה כול גליהם   vacat   ועתה אויל]י לב מה טוב ללוא   ] .4
[ ] [.].[ומה] השקט ללוא הוה ומה משפט ללוא נוסד ומה יאנחו מתים על כ[[
[ ] [אכמ] [ ] [ל נוצרתם ולשחת עולם תשובתכם כי תלך [   ] אתם   [
[ ] [מחשכים יצרחו על רובכם וכול נהיה דורשי עולם אמת ועידי[ם] למשפטכ[ם   [
[ ] [ישמדו כול אוילי לב ובני עולה לוא ימצאו עוד [וכ]ול מחפישי רשעה יבש[ו   [
[ ] [כו]ל אהבי[[ל] במשפטכם ירועו מסודי הרקיע וירעמו כול צ[[
[ ] [שוקד]י   [בינה ב]משפט[vacat   והיתם בחירי אמת ורודפי   :10
[ ] [בכול מ] [   ] על כול דעה איכה תאמרו ינענו בבינה ישקדנו לרדוף דעת ל[.11
[ ] [ול>ו<א עיף בכול {נ}שני עולם הלוא באמת ישעשע לעד ודעה]   .12
תשרתנו ו[כול מלאכי]
[ ] [שמים אשר חיים עולם נחלתם האמור יאמרו ינענו בפעלות אמת ויעפ[נו .13
[ ] [עוד ורוב הדר אתם]   [בכול קצים הלוא באור עולם יתה[לכו .14
[ ] [ואתה ב] vacat [סוד אילים כול] [ברקיעי]   .15

Eternal Glory   Fragment 5

1. [   ] לו]א ישבות אחד מכול צבאם ה]   [
2. [   ] באמת מיד כול אוט אנשים א]   [
3. [   ] אמת ומשקל צדק תכן אל כול]   [ב א.]   [
4. [   ] פ]רשם באמת הוא שמם ולחפציהם ידרש]   [
5. וסתר כול ונם לוא נהיו בלוא רצונו ומח.]   [
6. [   ] משפט להשיב נחם לבעלי און ופקודת]   [
7. [   ] ולסגור בעד רשעים ולהרים ראוש דלים]   [
8. בכבוד עולם ושלום עד ורוח חיים להבדי]ל   [
9. [   ] כול בני חוה ובכוח אל ורוב כבודו עם ט]ו]בו]   [
10. [   ] ובאמונתו ישוחו כול הי]ו]ם תמיד והללו שמו ה]   [
11. [   ] *vacat* ואתה באמת התהלך עם כול [דור]שי]   [
12. [   ] ובידכה אוט]ה]ו ומטנאכה ידרוש חפצו ואתהם]   [
13. ואם לוא ת]ס]שיא ידו למחסורכה ומחסור אוטו]   [
14. [   ] .דו ואל ישים מחפצ]ו] כי אל י]   [
15. [   ] ידכה למותר יפרץ מקניכ]ה   [
16. [   ] עולם ... ל]   [

The Scales of Righteousness   Fragment 6

1. [   ] מקורכה ומחסורכה לוא תמצא ודאבה נפשכה מכול טוב למות]   [
2. [   ] ז]עפה כול היום ואותה נפשכה כי תבוא בפתחיה וקבר]ת] וכס]ית   [
3. [   ]]יכה והייתה למאכל שן ולחומי רשף נגד מי]   [ג]   [
4. [   ] דו]רשי חפץ הונותה בהלוככה ונם אתה ת]   [
5. [   ] ב לכה כי אל עשה חפצי אוט ויתכנם באמת .   [
6. [   ] כ]י במוזני צדק שקל כול תבונם ובאמת]   [ל]   [
7. [   ]]ם ול]   [..]   [

The Angels of God's Holiness   Fragment 7

1. [   ]].. .[[
2. [   ] *vacat* [[
3. [   ] בעמל נכרה דרכיה   תרניע]   [*vacat*   ]   [
4. ושקר יהיה בלב בני [אדם   ] יבטוח בכול דרכיני   *vacat*   [
5. [   ] דעה ולא שחרו בי]נה ודעת ל]א בחרו *vacat* הלוא אל [יתן ד]עות]   [
6. [   ] על אמת להבין כול [רזים   וב]ינה הוא פלג לנוחלי אמת]   [
7. [   ] שקר בא]מת   כול מ]ועש]יו [הלוא שלום והשקט]   [
8. [   ] הלוא יד]עתם אם לא שמעתמה כיא מלאכי קודש [א]ל בשמים]   [
9. [   ] אמת   וירדפו אחר כול שורשי בינה וישקדו על]   [
10. [   ] לפי] דעתם יכבדו איש מרעהו ולפי שכלו ירבה הדרו]   [
11. [   ] כי אנוש הם כי יעצל ובן אדם כי ידמה הלוא]   [
12. [   ] ד והם אחזת עולם ינחלו הלוא ראיתם]   [

The Mystery of Existence   Fragment 8

[
.1] [ ]. אל הנוראים תשכיל ראש .]
.2] [בימי] קדם למה נהיה ומה נהיה במ]
.3] [למה היו {א} ו] [ל] [ ] נהיה במ.]
.4] [יומם ו]לילה הגה ברז נהיה]
.5] [כו]ל דרכיהמה עם פקודים]
.6] [אל הדעות סוד אמת]
.7] [צרה וממשל]ת [ל]
.8] [ל]התהלך ביצר מ[בינתו
.9] [הלכו]

The Salvation (*Yesha*) of His Works   Fragment 9 Column 1

[
.1] [ ]ל עת פן ישמעכה וכד חי דבר בו פן י]
.2] בלוא הוכח הכשר עבור לו והנק}]שר]
.3] ונם את רוחו לא תבלע כיא בדממה ...ות]
.4] ו]תוכחתו ספר מהר ואל תכבוד על פשעיכה]
.5] יצדק כמוכה כיא הואה {כיא הואה} שר ב]
.6] יעשה כיא מה הואה יח<י>ד ובכול מעשה בלתי]
.7] vacat ואיש עול אל תחשוב עזר ונם אין שונא]
.8] ו]ישע מעשיו עם פקדתו ודע במה תתהלך עמו]   תורת אל [
.9] אל תמוש מלבכה ואל לכה לבדכה תרחב
.10] כיא מה צעיר מרש ואל תשמ<ח> באבלכה פן תעמל בחיכה]
.11] נהיה וקח מילדי ישע ודע מי נוחל כבוד ועליו לוא]
.12] ולאבליהמה שמחת עולם [ו]היה בעל ריב לחפצכה ואי]ן
.13] לכול נערות<כ>ה דב[ר] משפטיכה כמושל צדיק אל תקן]
.14] ואל תעבור על [פש]עי]כה [ו]היה פא]ר [...] ב] [ ] משפט]
.15] י]קח ואז יראה אל ושב אפו ועדר על חטאות]כה] לפי]
.16] לוא יעמוד כול ימו וצדק במשפטו ובלי סליחה] י]כה]
.17] אביון ואתה אם תחסר טרף מחסוריכה ומותריכה]
.18] תותיר הובל למחיו חפצו ונחלתיכה קח] מ[מנו ואל תוסף על]יו
.19] ואם תחסר לוא מ] ל] [ ] הון מחסריכה כי לוא יחסר אוצר]ו ועל]
.20] פיהו יהיה כול ואת אשר יטריפכה אכ]ו]ל ואל תוסף ל]
.21] חייכה] [אם הון אנש]ים] תלוה למחסורכה אל]
.22] יומם ולילה ואל מנוח לנפשכה] השיבכה ל] [ ] אל תכזב
.23] לו למה תשה עון ונם מחרפה ל]   ]יד לרעהו
.24] ובמחסורכה יקפץ ידו כחכמ]ה
.25] ואם נגע יפנשכה וא.]
.26]] [ו ינלה ח] [ ]ה]
.27] לוא יכפר בשב]
.28] ע]וד [ונם]

Your Holy Spirit Fragment 9 Column 2 and Fragment 10 Column 1

1. [רחמיו פתח] א[כל מחסורי אוטו ולתת טרף
2. [ואין חי לכל] אם י[קפוץ ידו ונאספה ר]וח כול]
3. [תכן אל בשר]ול בה ו[ב]חרפ[ת]ו תכסה פניכה ובאילך<ה>
4. [כמה מאסור] יצא[ונושה בו] יתן] מהר שלם ואתה תשוה בו כי כי כיס
5. צפינ<י><ה>כה לנושה בך<ה> בעד רעיכה ות..ה כל חייכה בו מהר תן אשר
6. לו יקח כיסכה ובדבריכה אל תמעט רוחכה בכל הון אל תמר רוח ק<ו>דשכה
7. כיא אין מחיר שוה [בנפשכה מו]של אוטכה ברצון שחר פניו וכלשונו
8. [בו דבר] ואז תמצא חפצכה [לו וחוקיכה אל תרף וברזיכה השמר
9. [ ] ה[אם עבודתו יפקוד לכה] ל תנומה לעיניכה עד עשותכה
10. [תכלה] א[ל תוסף ואם רש לה] ואל תותר לו אף הון בלי
11. [ ] עינ]כה יראה כי רבה קנאת
12. [ ]ם[ ]]ם ברצונו תחזוק עבודתו וחכמת אוטו
13. [ ] תועצנו והייתה לו לבן בכור וחמל עליכה כאיש על יחידו
14. כי אתה[ ]רו[ ] א]תה אל תבטח למה .... ואל תשקוד ממדהבכה
15. [וליל]ה דמה לו לע[מו]ל ונם אל תשפל נפשכה [ל]אשר לא ישוה בכה ואז תהי]ה]
16. [לו] [ ] לאשר אין כוחכה אל תגע פן תכשל וחרפתכה רבה מאוד
17. [ ]]ה נפשכה בהון טוב היותכה עבד ברוח וחנם תעבוד נוגשיכה ובמחיר
18. אל תמכור כבודכה ואל תערבהו בנחלתכה פן יוריש גויתכה אל תשביע להם
19. [ ] ואין כסות אל תשת יין ואין אכל אל תדרוש תענוג תענג ואתה
20. [ ] חסר לחם אל תתכבד במחסורכה ואתה ריש .[
21. [ ] אל] תבוז לחייכה וגם אל תקל כלי [ח]וקכה

All the Ways of Truth Fragment 10 Column 2

1. [ ] [
2. [ ] [
3. [אתה ראש כי וזכור] [מחסורכה
4. ל<ו>א תמצא ובמעלכה ת..] [ים פוקד לכה
5. אל תשלח ידכה בו פן תכוה [ ] ו[באשו תבער גויתכה כ] [חי כן השיבהו
6. ושמחה לכה אם תנקה ממנו וגם מכל איש אשר לוא ידעתה אל תקח הון
7. פן יוסיף על רישכה ואם שמו בראיש[כ]ה למות הפקידהו ורוחכה אל תחבל
8. בו ואז תשכב עם האמת ובמותכה יפר[ש לה]ם זכיכה ואחריתכה תנחל
9. שמחה [עד כי] אביון אתה אל תתאו זולת נחלתכה ואל תתבלע בה פן תסוג
10. [מ]עליה ואם ישיבכה לכבודכה התהלך וברז נהיה דרוש מילדיו ואז תדע
11. נחלתו ובצדק תתהלך כי י..הו אל ת..ה בכל דרכיכה למכבדיכה תן הדר
12. ושמו הלל תמיד כי מראש הרים רא<ו>שכה ועם נדיבים הושיבכה ובנחלת
13. כבוד המשילכה רצונו שחר תמיד אביון אתה אל תאמ]ר] רש אני ול]א [
14. אדרוש דעת בכל מוסר הבא שכמכה ובכ]ל חכמ]ה צרוף לבכה וברוב בינת
15. מחשבותיכה רז נהיה דרוש והתבונן בכל דרכי אמת וכל שורשי עולה

16. תביט ואז תדע מה מר לאיש ומה מתוק לגבר כביד אביכה ברישכה
17. ואמיכה במצעדיכה כי כאב לאיש כן אבריהו וכאדנים לגבר כן אמו כי
18. המה כיד הורוכה וכאשר המשילמה בכה ויצו על הרוח כן עובדם וכאשר
19. גלה אוזנכה ברז נהיה כבדם למען כבודכה וכ[אשר   [הדר פניהמה
20. למען חייכה וארוך ימיכ[י]ה   ואם רש אתה כש]ה[
21. בלוא חוק *vacat* אשה לקחתה ברושכה קח מילדו]ת[
22. מרז נהיה בהתחברכה יחד התהלך עם עזר בשרכה]

TRANSLATION

The Eternal Planting

Fragment 1 (1) Open your lips (as) a Fountain to bless the Holy Ones. O ye, bring forth praise as an Eternal Fountain . . . For He has separated you from all (2) bodily spirit. O ye, separate yourself from all that He hates, and keep yourself apart from all Abominations of . . . He made all (flesh), (3) and caused every man to inherit his portion. He set you apart—and your portion—among the sons of Adam . . . He gave you authority. O ye, (4) this was how He glorified it when you sanctified yourself to Him, when He made you a Holy of Holies . . . for all . . . (5) He decided your fate and greatly increased your Glory, and made you as a firstborn for Himself among . . . (6) 'and I will give you My Goodness.' O ye, is not His Goodness yours? So always walk in His Faithfulness in all of (7) your works. O ye, seek His Judgements from every hand, and the abundance of . . . (8) love Him, for with everlasting Piety (*Hesed*) and mercies on all the Keepers of His word, and . . . (9) O ye, He has [op]ened up insight for you, and given you authority over His storehouse, and the accurate value for a measure (*ephah*) He has determined . . . (10) they . . . you. It is in your power to turn aside wrath from the Men of His Favor, and to appoint . . . (11) with you, before you take your portion from the hands of the Glory of His Holy Ones, and in . . . (12) He opened . . . and all who are called by His Holy Name . . . (13) with all the Er[as of] His sub[lime] radiance for an Eter[nal] Planting . . . (14) all those who inherit the land will conduct themselves, for in . . . (15) O ye, because of the Wisdom of your hands, He has given you authority, and [your] Knowledge . . . (16) a storehouse (?) for all humanity. From there you will designate your unclean food, and . . . (17) Seek understanding with all (your) might, and from every hand, take increased insight . . . (18) Bring forth what you lack for all those seeking after (their own) desire(s). Then you will understand . . . (19) You will be filled and satiated with abundant Goodness, and by the skill of your hands . . . (20) Because God has apportioned the inheritance of eve[ry living being,] and all those wise of heart have considered . . .

The Fountain of Living Water

Fragment 2 (1) . . . farmers, until all . . . (2) bring in your baskets, and your storehouses, all . . . (3) and the plain, season by season seek them out, and do not cease . . . (4) all of them seek in their season(s), and according to Wis[dom,] a man . . . (5) like a Fountain of Living Water which all me[n . . .] (6) and it is a hybrid like a mule, or like clo[thing made of two materials . . .] (7) in cattle and in . . . and also, your produce will be . . . (8) your Riches with your flesh . . .

All the Eras of Eternity

Fragment 3 (1) . . . concerning . . . all . . . (2) together with him . . . all who . . . (3) and they feared the deep, and . . . (4) And every sacrifice are you to offer them perpetually, and the peace (offering) . . . (5) in all the Eras of Eternity, because He is (the) God of Truth . . . (6) making the Righteous discern Good from Evil . . . (7) because it is the inclination of the flesh, and those who understand . . .

The Foundations of the Universe Shout out Judgement

Fragment 4 (1) . . . your breath (2) . . . and you will understand . . . death with (3) . . . Shall they not walk in Truth? (4) . . . and all their joys with Knowledge. O ye foolish of heart, what is Goodness without (5) [. . . And how] can there be peacefulness without destruction? And how can there be Judgement without establishing it, and how the dead will groan on account of al[l . . .] (6) you . . . you were created, but your backsliding leads to eternal damnation, because you walk . . . (7) The dark places will be made Light because of Your abundance, and Eternal Being (shall be the lot of) the Seekers of Truth and the Witnesses of Yo[ur] Judgements. (8) All the foolish of heart will be destroyed, and the sons of Wickedness will be found no more, and all those seekers after Evil will be ab[ashed. . .] (9) The Foundations of the Universe will shout out Your Judgement, and all the . . . will thunder . . . all the lovers of . . . (10) You will be the Elect of Truth, and pursuers after [insight with] Judg[ment . . .] those who are watchful . . . (11) according to all Knowledge. How can you say, 'We have worked for insight and stayed awake pursuing Knowledge of . . . in all . . . (12) But He has not tired during all the years of Eternity. Does He not delight in Truth forever? . . . Knowledge ministers unto Him, and [all the Angels of] (13) Heaven—whose inheritance is eternal life—would they ever say, 'We have grown weary in the ministries of Truth, and tir[ed in . . .] (14) for all ages do they not walk in Eternal Light? . . . again, and abundant radiance dwells with them. You . . . (15) in the firmaments of . . . the Foundation (possibly 'Secret') of the Pillars, all . . . O ye, in . . .

Eternal Glory

Fragment 5 (1) [. . . No]t one from all of their host will rest . . . (2) in Truth from the hand of all the storehouses of men . . . (3) Truth, and the measure of Righteousness He meted out to all . . . (4) [. . . dis]tributing them in Truth. He put them in place, and sought out their pleasures . . . (5) and a shelter for all, nor shall they exist without His favor and . . . (6) Judgement to visit repentance upon the Lords of Evil and the visitation of . . . (7) and to shut before the Evil Ones, and to lift up the head of the Downtrodden . . . (8) in Eternal Glory and peace everlasting, and the Spirit of Life to sepa[rate . . .] (9) all the sons of Eve, and with the power of God and the abundance of His Glory, with His Goodness . . . (10) and in His Faithfulness, they shall prostrate themselves continually all the day and praise His Name, and . . . (11) O ye, walk in Truth with all the [See]kers . . . (12) For His storehouse is under your authority, and whoever seeks his own aim (must do so) from your basket, and (to) them . . . (13) And if He does not stretch out His hand for your needs, then will His storehouse (provide) this need . . . (14) . . . and he shall not provide for his own wishes, for He shall not . . . (15) your hand. He will increase you[r] cattle abundantly . . . (16) forever . . .

The Scales of Righteousness

Fragment 6 (1) . . . your Fountain. Nor will you find what you lack, and your soul will languish for want of all Goodness, even unto death. . . (2) [. . . will be trou]bled all the day, and your soul will yearn to come into her (Wisdom's?) gates, and a grave (?) and clo[thing . . .] (3) your . . . And it will be as food to eat and fuel for the flame against . . . (4) For by your conduct you have troubled those who se[ek] pleasure and also . . . (5) for you . . . because God made the pleasures of (His) storehouse, and meted them out in Truth ... (6) [Fo]r in the scales of Righteousness He weighed out all their understanding, and in Truth . . .

The Angels of God's Holiness

Fragment 7 (3) . . . its Ways are carved in suffering. You calm . . . (4) and there will be Lying in the heart of all the sons [of Adam . . .] 'He will trust in all of My Ways . . . (5) Knowledge. They have not earnestly sought Under[standing, nor Knowledge] chosen. Does not God [give Kn]owledge of . . . (6) on Truth, to discern all [Mysteries, and Under]standing did He apportion to those who inherited Truth. (7) . . . Lying. In Tr[uth . . . all His w]orks. Is not peace and tranquility . . . (8) [Do you not k]now? Have you not heard? Surely the Angels of Go[d]'s Holiness are in Heaven . . . (9) Truth. And they pursue all the roots of Understanding, and diligently . . . (10) [according to] their Knowledge, one man will be glorified over another, and according to his insight will his honor be magnified . . . (11) For a man murmurs because he is lazy, and if a son of Adam is silent, is it not (because) . . . (12) And they will inherit an Eternal possession. Have you not seen . . ?

The Mystery of Existence

Fragment 8 (1) . . . to the fearful. You shall teach the first . . . (2) in former [times], why it existed and what existed in . . . (3) why they were . . . existence in . . . (4) [day and] night meditate on the Mystery of Existence . . . (5) [al]l their Ways, with the commands . . . (6) concerning the Knowledge of the Secret of Truth . . . (7) suffering and dominion . . . (8) [to] walk in the inclination of [His] Un[derstanding . . .] (9) walk . . .

The Salvation (*Yesha'*) of His Works

Fragment 9 Column 1 (1) [. . . the] time, lest he hear you. And while he is alive, speak to him, lest he . . . (2) without appropriate reproof for his sake. Is it not bound up . . . (3) Furthermore, his Spirit will not be swallowed (i.e. 'consumed'), because in silence . . . (4) [and] quickly take his reproof to heart, and be not proud because of your transgressions . . . (5) He is Righteous, like you, because he is a prince among . . . (6) He will do. For how is He unique? In all His work, He is without . . . (7) Do not consider the Evil Man as a co-worker, nor anyone who hates . . . (8) the Salvation (*Yesha'*) of His works, together with His command; therefore know how to conduct yourself with Him . . . (9) Do not remove [the Law of God] from your heart, and don't go very far along by yourself . . . (10) For what is smaller than a man without means? Also, do not rejoice when you should be mourning, lest you suffer in your life . . . (11) existence; therefore, take from the children of Salvation (*Yesha'*), and know who will inherit Glory, for it is necessary for Him, not . . . (12) And instead of their mourning, (yours will be) everlasting joy, and the troublemaker will be placed at your disposal, and there will not [be . . .] (13) To all your young girls, spea[k] your Judgements like a Righteous ruler, do not . . . (14) and do not take your sins lightly. Then the radiance of . . . will be . . . Judgement . . . (15) will He take, and then God will see, and His anger will be assuaged and He will give help against [your] sins, according to . . . (16) will not stand up all of its days. He will justify by His Judgement, and without forgiving your . . . (17) Poor One. O ye, if you lack food, your need and your surplus . . . (18) You should leave as sustenance for His flocks according to His will, and [fr]om it, take what is coming to you, but do not add there[to . . .] (19) And if you lack, do not . . . Riches from your needs, for [His] storehouse will not be lacking. [And upon] (20) His word everything is founded, so e[at] what He gives you, but do not add to . . . (21) your life . . . If you borrow Riches from men to fill your needs, do not . . . (22) day and night, and do not for the peace of your soul . . . He will cause you to return to . . . Do not lie (23) to him. Why should you bear (the) sin? Also, from reproach . . . to his neighbor. (24) . . . and he will close up his hand when you are in need. According to Wisdo[m . . .] (25) and if affliction befalls you, and. . . (26) He will reveal . . . (27) He will not make atonement with . . . (28) a[gain]. Furthermore . . .

Your Holy Spirit

Fragment 9 Column 2 Fragment 10 Column 1 (1) He opened His Mercies . . . all the needs of His storehouse, and gave sustenance (2) to every living thing. There is none . . . [If he] closes his hand, and the Spi[rit of all] (3) flesh is withdrawn, you shall not . . . in it, and [with] his reproa[ch] will your face be covered, but by your arbitration (4) [he will go forth] from prison, like . . . And if he receives a loan, he [repays] (it) quickly in full. O ye, recompense him, for your purse (5) of treasures belongs to the one you are obliged to, (even if only) for the sake of your neighbors. You will . . . all of your life with him. (Therefore), quickly return (him) whatever (6) belongs to him; otherwise he will take your purse. In your affairs, do not compromise your Spirit. Do not exchange your Holy Spirit for any Riches, (7) because no price is worth [your soul.] Willingly seek the face of him who has authority over your storehouse, and in his own tongue (8) [speak with him.] In that way will you find satisfaction . . . Do not forsake your Laws, and keep (secret) your Mysteries. (9) . . . If He assigns His service to you . . . (don't allow) sleep (to enter) your eyes until you have done it (10) [all . . . d]o not add. If th[ey] are needy . . . and do not be generous to him. Also, Riches without (11) . . . your [eye] shall see because of the abundant zeal of (12) . . . By His will, devote yourself to His service, and the Wisdom of His storehouse (13) . . . you will advise him, and become for him a firstborn son, and he shall love you as a man loves his only child. (14) Because you . . . [O y]e, do not rely on that . . . and do not stay awake at night because of your money, (15) [and during the night], continue su[fferi]ng because of it. Furthermore, do not demean your soul on account of someone who is not worth it, but rather be (16) to him . . . Do not strike someone who does not have your strength, lest you stumble and greatly humiliate yourself. (17) . . . your soul with the Goodness of Riches. You will be tilling the wind, and will serve your lord in vain; so, (18) do not sell your Glory for money, and do not transfer it as your inheritance, lest your bodily heirs be impoverished. Do not promise them (19) . . . If there are no cups, do not drink wine, and if there is no food, do not request delicacies. O ye, (20) [. . . If you] lack bread, do not glory in your poverty. You are needy . . . (21) [Do not] plunder to stay alive, and also, do not water down (the contents of) a vessel . . . [yo]ur Laws . . .

All the Ways of Truth

Fragment 10 Column 2 (3) So remember that you are needy . . . what you want (4) you shall not find. In your unfaithfulness, you will . . . He has appointed for you. (5) Do not reach your hand out for it, lest you be burned, [and] your body be consumed in His fire like . . . Thus He repaid him. (6) But there will be joy for you if you purify yourself of it. Also, do not take Riches from a man you do not know, (7) lest it only add to your poverty. If (God) has ordained that you should die in [you]r poverty, so He has appointed it; but do not corrupt your Spirit (8) because of it. Then you shall lie down with the Truth, and your sinlessness will He clearly proclai[m to th]em (the recording Angels). As your destiny, you will inherit (9) [Eternal] bliss. [For] though you are Poor, do not long for anything except your own portion; and do not be swallowed up by desire, lest you backslide (10) because of it. And if He restores you, conduct yourself honorably. And inquire among His chidren about the Mystery of Existence; then you will gain Knowledge of (11) His inheritance and walk in Righteousness, for He will . . . Do not . . . in all your Ways. Do homage to those who give you Glory, (12) and praise His Name continually, because out of poverty has He lifted your head, seating you among nobles. (13) He has given you authority over an inheritance of Glory, so seek His favor continuously. Though you are Poor, do not say, 'I am penniless, so I cannot (14) seek out Knowledge.' (Rather,) bend your back to all discipline, and through al[l Wisdo]m, purify your heart, and in the abundance of your (15) intellectual potential, investigate the Mystery of Existence. And ponder all the Ways of Truth, and consider all the roots of Evil. (16) Then you will know what is bitter for a man, and what is sweet for a person. Honor your father in your poverty (17) and your mother by your behavior. For a man's father is like his arms, and his mother is like his legs. Surely (18) they have guided you like a hand, and just as He has given them authority over you and appointed (them) over (your) Spirit, so should you serve them. And just as (19) He has opened your ears to the Mystery of Existence, (thus) should you honor them, for the sake of your own honor. Just as . . . revere them, (20) for the sake of your own life and to lengthen your days. Even though you are in poverty . . . (21) unlawfully. If you take a wife in your poverty, take her from among the daughter[s of . . .] (22) from the Mystery of Existence. In your companionship, go forward together. With the helpmate of your flesh . . .

NOTES

(41) The Chariots of Glory (4Q286–287)

Previous Discussions: J. T. Milik, *MS*, 130–5; P. Kobelski, *Melchizedek and Melchiresha* (Washington, DC: Catholic Biblical Association of America, 1981) 42–8. Photographs: PAM 43.311, 43.312, 43.313 (Manuscript A) and 43.314 (Manuscript B), ER 1346, 1347, 1348 and 1349.

(42) Baptismal Hymn (4Q414)

Previous Discussions: None. Photograph Numbers: PAM 43.482, ER 1432.

(43) Hymns of the Poor (4Q434, 436)

Previous Discussions: None. Photographs: PAM 42.859, 43.513 and 43.528, ER 1048, 1463 and 1478

(44) The Children of Salvation (*Yeshaʿ*) and the Mystery of Existence (4Q416, 418)

Previous Discussions: None. Photographs: PAM 42.758, 43.479, 43.480, 43.481, 43.483, 43.589, 43.511 and 43.512, ER 1006, 1429, 1430, 1431, 1433, 1536, 1461 and 1462. The order of the fragments is certain because of overlapping manuscripts. Fragments 1–3 represent portions from 42.758 and 43.479; Fragment 4 comes from 43.580; Fragments 5–6 appear on 43.481; Fragments 7–8 appear on 43.483; Fragment 9 appears on 43.589; Fragment 10 Column 1 on 43.511 and Column 2 on 43.512.

CHAPTER 8

Divination, Magic and Miscellaneous

The texts in this section represent a cross section of the remaining unpublished corpus. Some present an interesting glimpse into everyday life 2,000 years ago. Though astrology, amulets, magic and the like were frowned upon by the Rabbis and in theory forbidden, it is clear from other sources too that they played some role in the day-to-day life of the people. The material we have here bears this out. How widespread this was or how serious people really were about these things is difficult to assess.

In Graeco-Roman antiquity, astrology and divination counted among their devotees the best minds of the age. The foremost philosophical school in Rome, the Stoics, were astrology's strongest advocates. Among Jews, too, astrological ideas had penetrated to the very heart of the Temple in Jerusalem. Josephus informs us that the seven branches of the *menorah* there symbolize the seven planets then known (among which were counted the sun and the moon). He adds that the twelve loaves of the bread of the Presence embody the signs of the zodiac. Some Jewish writers of the period, such as Artapanus and Pseudo-Eupolemus, went so far as to ascribe the discovery of astrology to the patriarch Abraham. Likewise 1 Enoch makes Enoch himself the discoverer and revealer of this kind of knowledge. Thus it should come as no surprise that among the texts from Qumran one finds a number of astrological writings.

Amulets too were certainly widespread despite the ban on them, though these do not differ in kind from Jewish phylacteries which were and still are widely used. There is one reference to amulets playing a role, albeit negative, among warriors in the Maccabean

256

period (2 Macc. 12:40). Magical incantation bowls and items of this kind from this period and later also seem to have been widespread.

Magical incantations sought to prevent various calamities. Magical incantations against evil spirits were certainly a very significant part of popular religion in Graeco-Roman antiquity. Everyone believed in such spirits, and it was thought prudent to take steps to ensure one's protection. For a slight fee the local magician or scribe would write out a spell or two, often on a bowl, less frequently (so our meagre evidence indicates) on a piece of leather or metal that could be rolled up and kept in a protective case. The inscribed object would then be buried under one's house or somehow affixed at an appropriate location, perhaps near the door. Sometimes people would keep these items indoors.

Texts such as the Brontologion and the Physiognomic ones represented here are almost unique from this era and milieu. This fact alone probably testifies to the somewhat limited nature of their use, but it is surprising that they existed at all among what otherwise seem to be zealous holy warriors. This shows that they must have played a role in the everyday life of the people, as indeed they did in the Roman Empire generally, and as they do today. Like astrological systems, the genres represented by these texts sought to divine the future, the first by searching the Heavens and the astrological signs for thunder and rain; the second by inspecting a person's physical characteristics. It is not clear whether the interests they illustrate were proscribed at Qumran to the extent that they were in Rabbinic circles, though their existence seems to testify that they were not. In this regard, one should note Qumran's interest in 'Secret Mysteries', 'Eternal Secrets', discourses in cryptic script and other tendencies towards esoterica. The kinds of astrological designations present in the Brontologion are also present in Ibn Gabirol's work of medieval Jewish mysticism, *The Crown of the Kingdom*.

The two texts on sectarian discipline and the Paean for King Jonathan actually mention historical people – the disciplinary text quite literally, the Paean or Holy Poem as a dedication anyway or panegyric. With the Priestly Courses III – Aemilius Kills text, also mentioning historical personages, these passages are of profound historical interest. The Paean to King Jonathan is perhaps a missing link in solving crucial historiographic problems relating to the Community's attitude towards Jerusalem. It certainly puts to rest previous theories of Qumran origins envisaging this individual as the Wicked Priest of Qumran allusion.

Why this remained buried for so long, like so many other texts, is difficult to comprehend. Bringing it to light now is final testimony to the felicitous effect unlimited and free access to all individuals can have on the progress of human knowledge. It provides a unique witness to the mindset of the *movement* we have before us in perhaps an earlier formative period and its attitude towards a principal establishment figure of that period.

The disciplinary text which we entitle after an allusion found in the text, 'He Loved his Bodily Emissions', is also of some import. Related to some of the *Halakhic* texts above, it too provides a unique insight into the everyday life of the Community. That the people involved in such activities were serious, and this was not simply an ideal to be followed at some future utopian era, is graphically and vividly attested to. The form of 'Judgement' or 'reproof' being referred to is stark. It is, however, definitely mentioned in the Damascus Document as among those the *Mebakker* or 'Bishop' was actually instructed, not only to make and carry out, but also to record. Clearly we have such a record here.

45. BRONTOLOGION (4Q318)
(Plate 23)

The present work in Aramaic is perhaps the most intriguing divination text found at Qumran, for it is simultaneously a brontologion, a selenedromion and, apparently, a *thema mundi*. Each of these terms requires some explanation. A brontologion is a text that attempts to predict the future based upon where within the heavens one hears the sound of thunder (the Greek *brontos* means 'thunder', hence the name). Examples of such works date back many centuries before the period of the Qumran writings. A selenedromion is a text that plots the movement of the moon (Greek *selene*) through the sky and makes predictions based upon those observations. This Qumran text records the movements of the moon with respect to the signs of the zodiac and combines that approach with the hearing of thunder. Thus the scheme stipulates that if the moon is in a certain sign of the zodiac (and it will be in that sign several times during the year) when one hears thunder, then a certain event of importance to the entire nation will happen.

But the text goes beyond this already interesting combination of divinatory methods in that it regards Taurus rather than Aries as the first sign of the zodiac. It is possible to ascertain this fact simply by noting the regular pattern of the text as preserved and then projecting the same pattern backwards to Nisan, the first month. What does this change in the usual order mean? The reason that Aries is listed as the first sign even in contemporary newspapers and books is that during the Hellenistic period (roughly the fourth through the first centuries BC), when astrology developed essentially into its modern (Western) form, the sun rose in Aries at the vernal equinox. By the year 125 BC, however, a Greek astronomer had discovered the phenomenon of the precession of the zodiac − that the zodiac was slowly moving in relation to the sun. This discovery indicated that over a period of some 2,100 years the sun would move from sign to sign across the zodiac. Thus it would not always rise in the sign of Aries and, long ago, it had not. From about 4500 to 2100 BC, the sun had risen in Taurus. By assigning Taurus the first place in the list of signs, this Qumran work is advocating an astrological system based on *the Creation*. According to the system of Biblical chronology to which the author of this work adhered, God had created the world and the heavenlies some time during the period of Taurus' prominence. Probably he believed that the Creation occurred in the fifth millennium BC. Astrological texts that attempt to build up a sort of horoscope for the world itself are known by the term *thema mundi* − perhaps an appropriate term for the work at hand.

We have used here the familiar Latin equivalents to the names of the months and signs in Aramaic. The last lines of the preserved text from Fragment 2 Column 2 contain some interesting textual information. Even in this genre of literature, the nationalistic and xenophobic sentiments so characteristic of Qumran as a whole are discernible: 'If it thunders on a day when the moon is in Gemini, it signifies fear and distress *caused by foreigners*', or the line preceding it '*nations* will plunder one another' (italics ours). Though Greek texts of this genre express themselves in a not unsimilar manner, it is helpful to look at some of these allusions in a broader context.

The use of the word '*amal* in Line 7 is an interesting one. Here and elsewhere we translate it as 'suffering'. It is an important concept at Qumran. It is also important in early Christianity, because it occurs in the pivotal 'suffering servant' passage of Isa. 53 − referred to in relation to the Messianic Leader Text in Chapter 1 and elsewhere − i.e. the '*amal* of his soul (*nephesh* − see the use of this word tied to *Ebion* in the Hymns of the Poor and elsewhere above) . . . and by his Knowledge will my servant, the Righteous One, justify the Many and bear their sins.'

The term is also used in the Habakkuk *Pesher*, viii.2 in the eschatological exegesis of 'the Righteous shall live by his faith' (Hab. 2:4), which is so important both to Qumran and in Pauline theology (cf. Gal. 3:11 which also mentions Gen. 15:6). Since it is also used thereafter to describe the 'empty' effect of the 'worthless service' and 'works of Lying' with which 'the Spouter of Lies' leads the Community astray in x.12, we have tried to emphasize this eschatological dimension by translating it as 'suffering works'.

The emphasis on thunder in this eschatological scheme is also of interest in view of the many notices to 'rainmaking' connected in the literature. This includes the early Honi the Circle-Drawer, who operated as a 'rainmaker' in the period of Aristobulus, the son of Alexander Jannaeus, just prior to Pompey's storming of the Temple in 63 BC. This Honi, Josephus revealingly also calls Onias *the Just*. As Josephus records it, Honi refused to condemn the partisans of Aristobulus, who, demonstrating their zeal and opposition to foreign rule, were holding out against the Romans in the Temple; he rather condemned the Phariseeizing collaborators of his brother Hyrcanus (*Ant.* 14.22–5). These, the reader will recall, support both the coming of the Romans and by consequence, the rise of the Herodian family that ensues.

As we have seen in our consideration of Priestly Courses III – Aemilius Kills – this is an archetypical moment for the definition of the Qumran mindset and ethos, and crucial historiographically for an understanding of their development. The reference in 2.2.8 of the Brontologion to 'Arabs' is also interesting and complements the reference in the Aemilius text, also to 'Arabs'.

But James the Just (note the parallel to Honi's cognomen) was also reckoned as one of these primordial rainmakers. This is described in a notice from the fifth-century AD historian Epiphanius, probably based on a lost work about James which he mentions – the *Anabathmoi Jacobou* (*The Ascents of James*; *Haeres.* 78:14. Note too the possible allusion to the Mysticism of Heavenly Ascents). Also the letter ascribed to James' name abounds with the imagery of 'rainmaking' in its apocalyptic and climactic final chapter, evoking one of the first archetypes in this tradition connected to apocalyptic 'Judgement', Elijah (Jas. 5:7–18).

This evocation of rain and its connection with eschatological Judgement is strong as well in the War Scroll from Cave 1 at Qumran, where it is again connected to the exegesis of 'the Star Prophecy' and combined with the famous eschatological allusion from Dan. 7 of 'the Son of Man coming on the clouds of Heaven'. The 'clouds of Heaven' here, as we have seen, are the Heavenly Hosts or all the *Kedoshim/*'Holy

Ones' – the 'rain' being the Judgement they bring (see Eisenman, 'Eschatological Rain Imagery in the War Scroll from Qumran and the Letter of James', *JNES*, 1990). Josephus, perhaps sums the situation up very incisively when he observes that it was 'imposters and magicians' of this type who were more dangerous even than the violent revolutionaries, because they were scheming to bring about both 'innovation' (religious reform) and 'change in government' (*War* 2.259).

One should also note the relationship of 'thunder' symbolism to the two 'twins', John and James, called in the New Testament 'Boanerges'/'Sons of Thunder' (Mark 3:17). Whether this epithet has any relevance to the issue we are discussing is difficult to assess, but since the same two apostles were represented as having asked Jesus to be allowed to sit on his 'right hand' (Matt. 20:21; see too Mark 14:62's 'sitting on the right hand of Power and coming with the clouds of Heaven'), one can assume that it does.

The supernatural aspects of the 'sons of Zadok' or 'the Elect of Israel' have also been discussed at length in this work. There is no doubt that these have a role to play in the Last Judgement. The Messiah himself has 'Heaven and Earth' at his disposal in the text by this title with which we begin the work. The *Zaddikim* were 'the Pillars' that upheld the earth; so were presumably 'Pillar' apostles like James (Gal. 2:9). 'The Son of Man' was to come 'on the clouds of Heaven' and the Heavens were 'to rain down Judgement'. Elijah, referred to in the Letter of James, and Phineas, apparently too, before him, were archetypical rainmakers; so was Honi, called 'the Circle-Drawer', because of the circles he drew to bring the rain. James, too, was to *bring the rain* – rain taken both in its mundane sense and eschatologically.

The zodiacal dimension of the notation 'twins' is in a certain sense reinforced by the name in Aramaic of one of the astronomical zodiacal signs mentioned in this text, *Thomiah*, i.e. Gemini. This in turn relates to the name of another of the disciples of Jesus, with regard to whom the 'brother' signification is prominent as well, Judas Thomas/ 'Thomas the Twin'. The 'brother' signification with regard to either or both of the two James mentioned above is also clear.

TRANSLITERATION   Fragment 1

5. [וב]ווווו קשתא בו]וווווווו ובווווווווו גדיא ב־ן וב־ן דולא ב־וו ו וב]

־ווו ו וב־ן ווווו [

6. [נוניא ב־ן ווווו וב־ן ווווו דכרא ב־ן ווווווו וב־ן ווווווווו תורא ב־וו]

ווווווו וב3 וב[13]

7. [תאומיא ב3ו וב3ווו סרטנא ב3ווווו ובו3וו אריא ב3ווווו וב] ווווו3 ווווווו3 וב3ווווווו

8. ‏[בתולתא ב3|||||||||3 וב3¬ וב3¬ ׀ מוזניא |¬3¬]‏   *vacat*

9. ‏[תשרי בו ובו עקרבא בו׀ ובו||||| קשתא בו||||| וב||||||| ובו||||||| גדיא בו||||||||‏

Fragment 2 Column 1

1. ‏ובר||| וב¬ ||| ׀׀ סרטאא בר¬|| ׀|| ובר¬||||||| א[ר¬]י[א] בר¬|||||| [ו¬]בר¬||||||||‏

2. ‏בתו[ל]תא בר¬ ||[||| |||||| וב3¬ וב3¬ מוזניא ב3 ||| וב3 |[עקרבא ב3|||||‏

3. ‏וב3|||||| קש[תא ב3|||||||] וב3|||||| [|] וב3||||||3[||| גדי¬]א ||| וב3 ||3 ||||[‏

4. ‏וב3¬ דול[א]   *vacat*   שבט בו ובו[נוני¬]א ב |||| וב[||||‏

5. ‏[דכרא ב]||||| וב[||||| וב |||||||| תורא בו||| ||||| וב|||||||||| תאומיא] בר¬‏

6. ‏[וב¬||] סרטאא בר¬ || [ו ב]בר¬ ||| ובר¬|||| אריא [בר¬||||| ובר¬|||||| בתולתא]‏

7. ‏בר¬||||||| ובר¬||||||| מוזניא בר¬||||||||| >ו<ב3] וב3 ||3 ע[קרבא ב3||3‏

8. ‏[ו]ב3||| [קש]תא ב3|||| וב3|||||||3[גדיא ב3|||||||] ובר¬ |||||||||3[|] וב3 |||[‏

9. ‏דולא ב3||||||||||3 וב3¬ נוניא   *vacat*

Fragment 2 Column 2

1. ‏אדר בו ובו דכרא בו||| ובו||| תורא בו ||| ובו||||| ובו|||||||| תאומיא]‏

2. ‏בו||||||| >ו<בו||||||||| סרט[נא בר¬ וב¬| וב¬|| א[ר¬יא בר¬|| ובר¬| ||| ובר¬|[‏

3. ‏בתו[לתא] בר¬||||| וב[ר¬|||| מוזניא בר¬|| ||||[>ו<בר¬|||| ||||[עקרבא]‏

4. ‏ב [¬]|| [||||||| וב3 >3|< קש[תא ב3||3] וב3||3 [|] ג[דיא ב3 ||| וב3||||| ובר¬]‏

5. ‏דולא ב3|||||3 וב3 |||||||3[וב3|||||||3][נו[ניא] ב3|||||][וב3¬ וב3¬ |]‏

6. ‏דכרא   *vacat*[אם בתורא] ירעם מסבת על[מא רקן יהוין   [

7. ‏[ו]עמל למדינתא וחר[ב כד]רת מלכא ובמדינת אב[דן   [

8. ‏להוא ולערביא ...]   [.]א כפן ולהוון בזין אלן בא[לן   [

9. ‏אם בתאומיא ירעם דחלה ומרע מנכריא ומ]   [

TRANSLATION

Fragment 1 (5) [and on the 7th Sagittarius. On the eighth and the ninth Capricorn. On the tenth and the eleventh Aquarius. On the twelfth and the] thirteenth and the [four]teenth (6) [Pisces. On the fifteenth and the sixteenth Aries. On the seventeenth and the eighteenth Taurus. On the ni]neteenth, the twentieth and the twenty-[first (7) Gemini. On the twenty-second and the twenty-third Cancer. On the twenty-fourth and the twenty-fifth Leo. On the twenty-sixth], the twenty-seventh and the twenty-eighth (8) [Virgo. On the twenty-ninth, thirtieth and thirty-first Libra.] (9) [Tishri On the first and second Scorpio. On the third and fourth Sagittarius. On the fifth, sixth and seve]nth Capricorn. On the eighth . . .

Fragment 2 Column 1 (1) and on the thirteenth and the [fo]urteenth Cancer. On the fi[ft]eenth and the sixteenth L[e]o. On the seventeenth [and] the eighteenth (2) Vi[r]go. On the [ni]nteenth, the twentieth and the twenty-first Libra. On the twenty-[second and the twenty-t]hird Scorpio. On the twenty-fourth (3) and the twenty-fifth Sagitt[arius]. On the twenty-six[th], the twenty-seve[nth] and the twenty-eig[hth Caprico]rn. On the twenty-n[inth] (4) and the thirtieth Aquari[us]. Shevat On the first and the second [Pisc]es. On [the third and the] fourth (5) [Aries. On] the fifth, [the sixth and the se]venth Taurus. On the eig[hth and ninth Gemini.] On the tenth (6) [and eleventh] Cancer. On the twelfth, thirteenth and fourteenth Leo. [On the fifteenth and six]teenth [Virgo]. (7) On the seventeenth and eighteenth Libra. On the nineteenth, [twentieth and twenty-first S]corpio. On the twenty-second (8) [and] twenty-third [Sagitta]rius. On the twenty-fourth and twenty-fifth Capricorn. On [the twenty-sixth], twenty-seventh and twenty-e[i]ghth, (9) Aquarius. On the twenty-ninth and thirtieth Pisces.

Fragment 2 Column 2 (1) Adar On the first and the second Aries. On the third and the fourth Taurus. On the fif[th, sixth and seventh Gemini]. (2) On the eighth (and) ninth Canc[er. On the tenth and eleventh L]eo. On the twelfth, thir[teenth and fourteenth] (3) Vi[r]go. On the fifteenth and six[teenth Libra. On the seven]teenth (and) eight[eenth Scorpio]. (4) On the [nin]eteenth, twentieth and twenty-first Sagitt[arius. On the twenty-second] and twenty-thi[rd Cap]ricorn. On the twenty-[fourth and twenty-fifth] (5) Aquarius. On the twenty-sixth, twenty-[seventh and twenty-eigh]th Pis[ces]. On the twenty-ni[nth, thirtieth and thirty-first] (6) Aries. [If] it thunders [on a day when the moon is in Taurus], (it signifies) [vain] changes in the wo[rld (?) . . .] (7) [and] suffering for the cities, and destru[ction in] the royal [co]urt and in the city of dest[ruction (?) . . .] (8) there will be, and among the Arabs . . . famine. Nations will plunder one ano[ther . . .] (9) If it thunders on a day when the moon is in Gemini, (it signifies) fear and distress caused by foreigners and by [. . .]

46. A PHYSIOGNOMIC TEXT (4Q561)

This text belongs to a widespread type of divination especially well known from Graeco-Roman examples. Writers infer a person's character from movements, gestures of the body, colour, facial expressions, the growth of the hair, the smoothness of the skin, the voice, idiosyncrasies of the flesh, the parts of the body, and the body as a whole. Ancient medicine in particular valued physiognomical signs. Physiognomy was more important in the Middle Ages and the Renaissance than it was in antiquity, and has not yet fully died out. The Qumran text is unfortunately so fragmentary that it is impossible to specify how many individuals it describes or whether its evaluations are ultimately positive or negative. Enough remains, however, to get some feel for the text's concerns. It is apparently related to another, previously published, Hebrew work from Qumran, 4Q186.

TRANSLITERATION

Column 1 (Fragments 1-4)

1. [ ] ו]הי מערבין ולא שגיא עינוה]י[
2. בין אורין לאכומן אפה נגיד
3. [ו]שפיר ושנוהי שוין ודקנה
4. דק להוה [ו]לא שניא אברוהי
5. [מ]מחקי]ן] וב]ין מה]דמין לעבי]ן]
6. [ ] .
7. די אמן ברין [ ]
8. פתין ושקוהי]יהוין בין דקין]
9. לעבין [ו]כף רגל]והי [
10. נג]יד]. לה רגלה [ ] [
11. [ ]]לת יפל] [
12. [ ] ל]מסף [ ] [
13. [ ]]...[[
14. [ ] כתפה [ ] ר]וח לה
15. [ ] להוון על] [ ] עקא
16. [ ] ולא רב [ ] שערן עבות

Column 2

1. להוה קל]ה [
2. ל.מלי ית] [
3. [ל]א אריך [ ] [
4. שער דקנה ש]גיא [
5. להוון בין עבין ל]דקין [
6. ואגון קטי<נ>ין ו] [
7. כעבין טפרוה]י [
8. לקומתה י] [

Fragment 6

1. [ ]]. [[
2. [ ] לשמקמיק.] [
3. [ ] ב]ררי וסגלגל לה]וה [
4. [ ]]. לה שער רשה [

TRANSLATION

Column 1 (Fragments 1-4) (1) . . . his . . . will be mixed and not numerous. Hi[s] eyes (2) will be intermediate between light and dark. His nose will be long (3) and attractive and nis teeth will be even. His beard

(4) will be sparse [and] not luxuriant. His limbs (5) will be [b]lotch[y, partially mal]formed and partially thick . . . (7) (his) elbows strong . . . (8) broad and his thighs [will be neither thin] (9) nor thick. The soles of [his] feet . . . (10) lo[ng]. His foot . . . (12) [to] finish . . . (14) his shoulder . . . his [sp]irit (15) . . . they will be . . . narrowness (16) . . . and will not be large . . . thick hairs

Column 2 (1) [His] voice will be . . . (3) will [n]ot be extended . . . (4) The hair of his beard will be lu[xuriant] . . . (5) will be neither thick nor [thin...] (6) And they will be small . . . (7) His nails will be somewhat thick . . . (8) As for his height . . .

Fragment 6 (2) . . . be reddish . . . (3) [cl]ear and will [be] round . . . (4) the hair of his head . . .

47. AN AMULET FORMULA AGAINST EVIL SPIRITS (4Q560)

The discovery of this text among the Dead Sea Scrolls is significant not least because it is the earliest known Jewish example, antedating its closest rivals for that honour by several centuries. It is not clear whether this text was part of a larger scroll used as a kind of 'recipe book' by a scribe or magician, or whether it was wrapped up and placed in a case. The reader will also note the several uncertainties in the translation. In part the difficulties arise from the genre of these texts – they intentionally use strange or unusual vocabulary. Many such texts use previously unknown words. The other major difficulty of this text is its broken condition; if we had more context we could gain an improved understanding of several points.

This kind of conjuring or incantation is known in apocryphal literature like the Book of Tobit (Chapters 6, 8, and 11) and the Book of Enoch (Chapter 7), both of which are extant in fragments at Qumran. The *Mishnah* (San. 7:7), like the Old Testament, specifically condemns it. We have already seen how Josephus considered the magicians, imposters and religious frauds (among whom he would clearly include some of the 'prophets and teachers' pictured in Acts) more dangerous even than the revolutionaries.

Apparently, in his time, this kind of knowledge and activity was ascribed, like so much bearing on the provenance of Secret Wisdom, to Solomon, and he actually gives us a picture of such a person (*Ant.* 8.45–9). He describes how a 'countryman' of his named Eleazar in 'the presence of Vespasian and his sons' cured men possessed of demons by putting a ring, having under its seal roots prescribed by Solomon, under their noses 'and reciting that he (Solomon) had composed it'. To prove to Vespasian, who according to Suetonius was very susceptible to these kinds of superstitions, that he had this power, he instructed the demon to turn over a basin of water which he had left a little way off for this purpose when it departed. It did.

It was a group of people like this around Vespasian, including Josephus and interestingly enough Philo's nephew, Tiberius Alexander, who seem to have convinced Vespasian by 'signs and wonders' of this kind – particularly curing the lame and making the blind see – that he was the real 'Star' called from Palestine to rule the world. For Acts 4:6 Tiberius Alexander appears as a persecutor of so-called 'Christians'. Josephus describes him as a turncoat and an apostate from Judaism (*War* 2.220), and Vespasian left him behind to help his somewhat impetuous son Titus as general in charge of the siege that ended in the destruction of the Temple.

Exorcisms and conjuring of this kind were also very popular activities in the Gospels and the Book of Acts.

TRANSLITERATION

Fragment 1 Column 1

[   ] לבכ לנ[   ] 1.
[   ] ילדתה מרדות ילדן פקד באיש ש[   ] 2.
מ[עלל בבשרא לחלח>ל<יא דכרא וחלחלית נקבתא   ] 3.
בשם הנו[שא עואן ופשע אשא ועריה ואשת לבב   ] 4.
ה[בשנא פרך דכר ופ>ר<כית נקבתא מחתורי   ] 5.
[   ] .. ל[   ].[   ]... יעין.[   ] 6.

Fragment 1 Column 2

[   ]... 1.
[קודמו[הי 2.
[   ]...ו 3.
[קודמוהי וממ[4.
[ואנה רוח מומה] 5.
[אומיתך רוחא] 6.
[על ארעא בעננין] 7.
[   ] לל[   ].[   ] 8.

TRANSLATION

Fragment 1 Column 1 (1) . . . heart . . . (2) a new mother, the punishment of those giving birth, a command (of) evil . . . (3) the male poisoning-demon and the female poisoning-demon (is forbidden) [to] enter the body . . . (4) [(I adjure you) by the Name of He who for]gives sins and transgression, O fever and chills and heartburn (5) [. . .and forbidden to disturb by night in dreams or by day] in sleep, the male PRK-demon and the female PRK-demon, those who breach (?) . . .

Fragment 1 Column 2 (2) . . . before h[im . . .] (4) before him and . . . (5) and I adjure you, O spirit . . . (6) I adjure you, O spirit . . . (7) upon the earth, in the clouds . . .

48. THE ERA OF LIGHT IS COMING (4Q462)

This narrative evidently takes as its starting point the prophecy given by Noah in Gen. 9:25–27: 'Cursed be Canaan; he shall be his brothers' meanest slave . . . Blessed by the Lord my God be Shem . . . May God make space for Japheth, and let him live in the tents of Shem.' Shem, of course, was understood as the ancestor of the Jews, while his brothers were regarded as the ancestors of neighbouring peoples. Noah's words, which were read as prophecy, probably relate to the Davidic period. They predict the ultime supremacy of the Jews over their neighbours, an inspiring thought in any time of oppression.

The text could have been placed in Chapter 2 under Prophets and Pseudo-Prophets, but because of its unclear attribution, we place it here. It should be read as a kind of 'Holy History'. Beginning with prophecy, it moves on to Judgement, a Judgement centred, it seems, on Jerusalem. Lines 6–8, 'The Lord is the Ruler . . . to Him alone belongs the sovereignty', are noteworthy in the light of similar slogans attributed by Josephus to 'Zealot' revolutionaries who proliferated before and during the period of the uprising against Rome (AD 66–70).

As Josephus describes them, these refused to call any man 'Lord' and seem to have rallied to a cry that can be characterized by the words 'no king but God', i.e. 'God rules here, not man' (*Ant* 18.23). As a result, they refused to submit to the rule of distant Caesars or, for that matter, to pay the tax required of them, which, as we saw in relation to the Testament of Kohath in Chapter 5, consequently became a burning issue throughout the whole of the first century. Needless to say, they would probably not have deigned to call any Messianic leader 'Lord' either.

In this text, we find the usual imagery of 'Light' and 'Darkness', (the former now tied to the coming, obviously, of the Eternal 'Kingdom'), 'Glory', 'Judgement', etc. If the reconstruction is correct, the

Noahic prophecy is fulfilled with Israel (Jacob) subjecting the Canaanites to forced labour (5), whatever may have been meant by this. The reference from Line 13 onwards to a second captivity in or by the hand of Egypt, coupled with Jerusalem's downfall, is puzzling, particularly as it seems also to relate to 'Philistines'.

Technically, the text seems aware that Egyptians were considered 'sons of Ham' and that the Philistines, though they were also reckoned as 'sons of Ham' in Gen. 10, were actually 'sons of Japhet' or 'Mycenean Greeks'. This is borne out by archaeological data. In this regard, the text does allow 'the Kittim' of Qumran usage as sons of 'Javan' (Greece) too. It is therefore possible that the history we have before us relates to the pre-Maccabean suppression of Jerusalem by Ptolemies from Egypt and Seleucid Greeks from Syria. On the other hand, we may have a veiled reference, of the kind in the War Scroll to 'the Kittim of Egypt' and 'the Kittim of Assyria', to Roman legions from Egypt and Syria at the time of siege of Jerusalem.

However these things may be, the text ends with the usual promise, certainly comforting to the nationalistically minded, that God would not forget Jerusalem and that her humiliation would be manifoldly repaid. This is directly paralleled in texts like the last columns of the Habakkuk *Pesher* or the Hymns of the Poor above. While envisaging the probable destruction of Jerusalem by the Kittim, Hab. xii.2–4 concludes that 'on the Day of Judgement (*sic*) God would destroy from off the earth all idolators (i.e. the nations) and Evil People'.

TRANSLITERATION   Column 1 Fragment 1

] א[ת חם ואת יפת]	[.1
] ליעקוב ויא[מר]נ ויזכור]	[.2
] לש[ום לישרא[ל] *vacat* בכן יאמר[ו	[.3
] לבוש[י]ם ריקמה הלכנו כי לוק.]	[.4
] ויתן בני כנען] לעבדים ליעקוב באהב[ה	[.5
] וי[תנה לרבים לנחלה .... המושל]	[.6
] כבודו אשר מאחד ימלא את המים ואת [הארץ	[.7
] ול[ו] את הממשלה לבדו עמו היה האור עמהם ועלינו היה [החושך	[.8
] יכלה ק[ץ החושך וקץ האור בא ומשלו לעולם על כן יואמר[ו	[.9
] ל[י]שראל כי בתוכנו היה עם האביב יעק[וב ירד מצרימה	[.10
] [על]יהמה ויעבודו ויתקימו ויזעקו אל ....]	[.11
vacat והנה נתנו במצרים שנית בקץ ממלכה ויתק[ן]מו	[.12
[ויתן עיר הקודש ביד יוש[בי פלשת ומצרים לבזה וחורבה	[.13
ו<ועמודיה [נהרסו	
] ת[מיר לרומם לרשע בעבור תקבל טמ[את עוונותיה	[.14

[   ] ‏.15 ‏[ה ועז פניה ותשנה בזיוה ועדה ובנדיה]
[   ] ‏.16 ‏[ים ואת אשר עשתה לה בן טמאת העו]ון
[   ] ‏.17 ‏[שנאתה כאשר היתה לפני הבנותה]
[   ] ‏.18 vacat ‏ויזכור את {ישרא} ירושלם ה[

TRANSLATION

Fragment 1 (1) Ham and Japheth . . . (2) to Jacob and he said . . . And he remembered . . . (3) [to gi]ve to Israel . . . Then they said . . . (4) They went [dress]ed in fine raiment because . . . (5) [And He gave the sons of Canaan] to Jacob as slaves. In love . . . (6) [He] gave it (the land) to the Many for an inheritance. The Lord is the Ruler . . . (7) His Glory which (comes) from (the) One fills the waters and the [land.] . . . (8) To Him alone belongs the Sovereignty. With Him was the Light; with them (the Angels of Darkness?) and upon us was [the Darkness.] . . . (9) [He will end the Er]a of Darkness, and the Era of Light is coming, when they (the Angels of Light?) will reign forever. Therefore, [they] said . . . (10) to Israel, because He was in our midst. In the spring Jac[ob went down to Egypt . . .](11) [upo]n them, and they were put to forced labor, but they were preserved. They cried out to the Lord . . . (12) And behold, they were given unto Egypt a second time, at the end of the Kingdom, but they were preserv[ed . . . (13) And He gave the Holy City into the hand of the inhabit]ants of Philistia and Egypt to spoil and ruin her. [They tore down] her pillars . . . (14) [She (Jerusalem) ex]changed (her loyalty), exalting Evil, so she will receive the poll[ution of her sins]. . . (15) and her defiance, so she was hated. In her beauty, her jewelry and her clothing . . . (16) that which she did to herself. A son of the pollution of Ev[il . . .] (17) her hatred as she was before she was rebuilt. . . . (18) But God remembered Jerusalem . . .

49. HE LOVED HIS BODILY EMISSIONS
(A Record of Sectarian Discipline – 4Q477)
(Plate 24)

This text was evidently meant to be the kind of record the *Mebakker* or 'Bishop' was supposed to keep, as mentioned in the last column of the Damascus Document above, and columns in the extant text, which no doubt preceded it, concerning disciplinary actions and such like 'in the camps'. The presence of one of these records here among the corpus from Qumran not only proves such records were kept, but provides an astonishingly vivid eye-witness testimony to the life that was led in these desert communities preparing for 'the last days' or the 'Time of the End'.

Also impressive is the consistency of its vocabulary with what we have been witnessing throughout these texts. The mindset is fixed, the vocabulary certain, even in mundane or trivial texts and records of this kind.

For these purposes the reference to 'soul' in Line 1.2 has its implications. We have already analysed allusions to this important notation, both in the last chapter and in this one. It is, of course, widespread in the published Hymns and the Hymns of the Poor above. It is usually used in conjunction with allusions to the *Ebionim*, *'Anavim* and *Zaddikim* — 'the Poor', 'the Meek', and 'the Righteous'. It is also used in the Habakkuk *Pesher* to describe the retribution visited on the Wicked Priest for his destruction of the Righteous Teacher and members of his community. It is used in the last column of the Damascus Document with regard to the person who has not confirmed his attachment to 'the *Torah* of Moses' and 'rejected the Foundations of Righteousness'.

Its use in a crucial section of the Damascus Document to delineate an attack on 'the soul of the Righteous'/'Righteous One' and his associates is particularly important. In life-threatening situations like these, and probably related ones in the two collections of Hymns, it probably meant something like 'inner being' or 'being' — even the very *life* of the individual or individuals involved.

In the disciplinary text before us — and it is only a *disciplinary* text, not an expulsion one — we have the usual allusion to 'rebellion' in Line 1.4, no doubt against 'the Laws of Moses'. The allusion to 'rebellion', of course, is as always a negative one. We have seen it in relation to Hyrcanus' 'rebellion' — probably against his brother Aristobulus — in the Aemilius/Priestly Courses text above. We have seen it throughout these texts when considering the rebellion of 'the sons of Darkness'; we have seen it, too, in the rebellion against God highlighted at the beginning of both the Habakkuk *Pesher* and the Damascus Document, and it is no doubt seen as including the rebellion of individuals like the Lying Spouter against the Law. There is even in this context the usual allusion to 'Light', and in Line 2.1 the implication that what we have to do with here is a 'knowing' infraction of some kind, not an inadvertent one of the kind alluded to at the beginning of the last column of the end of the Damascus Document and at length in Column vii of the Community Rule.

The allusion to 'the camps of the Many' (1.3) is also of moment in tying this text to the last column of the Damascus Document and the activities of the *Mebakker* or 'Bishop' there, who is described as recording such infractions and who controls these wilderness 'camps' generally. The reference to 'the Many' with regard to these camps also happens to solve another problem raised above. This is why having *all* the texts at our disposal was so imperative for the critical historian, though perhaps not for the philologist, i.e. someone concerned with the translation of a single manuscript only.

It will be recalled that the term 'Many' was also used to describe 'the Priest commanding the Many' in the last column of the Damascus Document. But the *Mebakker* or Bishop is clearly described in Columns xiii–xiv of the published Cairo Damascus Document as being in absolute charge of 'the camps'; therefore our problem concerning the identity of the two is solved. If the desert 'camps' are 'the camps of the Many' alluded to in passing in this text, then the Priest Commanding the Many and the *Mebakker*/Bishop commanding the camps are the same. Again, the references in early Church literature to James as 'Bishop of the Jerusalem Community' and 'high priest' are not irrelevant.

It is also vivid testimony of the fact of the existence of the 'camps'. Here are *actually* two people who lived in them – the 'inhabitants of the camps' so vividly alluded to in the last column of 4QD, 'Hananiah Nitos' and 'Hananiah ben Shim . . .' (presumably Shim'on or Shemaiah). Moreover, the rank and file of these 'camps' were actually referred to as 'the Many'. This is extremely moving, absolutely immediate testimony.

Again we have an allusion to 'the Spirit of Radiance' of the kind seen in more ecstatic texts like the Sons of Righteousness (Proverbs), the Chariots of Glory, and the Mystery of Existence in Chapters 5 and 7. The allusion in Line 6 of the second column to 'turning aside' is also common in documents like the Damascus Document or the Community Rule, particularly when it comes to 'turning aside' from the Law or 'wandering astray in a trackless waste without a Way'. Such references are omnipresent.

The allusion to 'reproved' in Line 9 ('reprove' in Line 2 Column 1) is not the same as 'expel' in more serious excommunications pronounced in 4QD above, the Community Rule,ii and the Chariots of Glory. The offences treated in this record are not capital or excommunicable ones, but rather more in the nature of those listed in 1QS,vii or CD, xii–xv, presumably preceding 4QD. The allusion recapitulates one already encountered in Jacob's 'reproving' Reuben in the Genesis Florilegium's presentation of Reuben's violation of his father's bedroom arrangements. This is a record of 'picayune' disciplinary 'acts' kept by the *Mebakker* in his role presumably as 'Priest commanding the camps' in the last days.

In Latin usage, the word 'acts' related to real administrative records kept by officials like governors, procurators and the like. Eusebius, for instance, in *Ecclesiastical History* 1.9.3 reveals that he knows about 'acts' circulating under Pontius Pilate's name in his own time — the 300s — purporting to be the *real* administrative records of that individual's procuratorship. The 'acts' or records we have before us in this disciplinary text are *real* administrative proceedings in contradistinction to some others of this genre, hence their thoroughly pedestrian and mundane tone.

Finally the allusion to loving one's 'bodily emissions' recapitulates material about mourning and sexual matters in Purity Laws Type A in Chapter 6. It is completely in accord with the Qumran ethos as we have been following it. Reuben's 'reproval' also had to do with sexual indiscretions. It is in accord with the Qumran concern not to 'mix' with such individuals, because 'the Holy Angels were with them in their camps' — again the reason for the camps themselves. The allusion to the 'Holy Angels being in the camps' is to be found, as we have noted, in both the War Scroll and the Damascus Document — the former particularly with regard to keeping such impurities from the camp 'from the time they (the Holy Ones of the Covenant) leave Jerusalem and march out to war until they return'.

Anyone who thought this scenario was a figment of the imagination of these writers must now think again. The finding of such a fragment here makes it undeniably real. The allusion to 'mixing' is of course interesting as well. It recapitulates allusions of this kind already discussed in the First Letter on Works Reckoned as Righteousness. In that document, this allusion primarily relates to Gentiles and 'mixing' with them, but in the War Scroll and Damascus Document it relates to mixing with 'the sons of the Pit' as well. Of course all of these expressions relate to the 'separation' ideology we have encountered so repeatedly in these texts — 'separating pure from impure', part of the general 'Temple pollution' accusation, but also the general instructions to 'separate from the sons of the Pit' or 'the majority of the people' and 'go out into the wilderness' camps.

TRANSLITERATION   Column 1

[	]יֹם אנשי ה..	] .1
	] נפשמה ולהוכיח א[ת	] .2
	מ[חני הרבים על	] .3
	מעל [	] .4

Column 2

ל [	1.
אשר]	2.
הרבים]	3.
הואה קצר אפים]	4.
[ ] ה הואה ..ס.ש.	5.
] לה[סיר את רוח היח[ה מדרך] ונם לערב א[ת אל]	6.
] ..הוכ[י]חו[ ]א[שר רוע] [עמו ונם אשר איננו ח]	7.
] [ו]רו ונם אוהב את שפך בשרו]	8.
] [ואת חנניה בן שמ] הוכיחו]	9.
] ונ[ם אוהב את ט..] [	10.

(right side column fragments)

2. [ר האור מדע[ת
3. את יוחנן בן ..]
4. העין שמו ונם רוח פארה ע.]   [שמו .]
5. [וואת *vacat* חנניה ניתוס הוכיחו אשר הוא]ה

TRANSLATION

Column 1 (1) . . . the men of the . . . (2) their soul, and to reprove (3) . . . the camps of the Many, concerning (4) . . . rebellion

Column 2 (1) to . . . (2) which . . . the Light, knowing[ly . . .] (3) the Many . . . Johanan ben . . . (4) he was short-tempered . . . his name . . . And also the Spirit of radience with . . . (5) he . . . And Hananiah Nitos they reproved because he . . . (6) turned aside the Spirit of the Commun[ity from the Way], and also to mix the . . . (7) they repr[oved] [be]cause he . . . and also because he was not . . . (8) Furthermore, he loved his bodily emissions . . . (9) Hananiah ben Shim[. . . they reproved because . . .] (10) Furthermore, he loved . . .

50. PAEAN FOR KING JONATHAN (ALEXANDER JANNAEUS – 4Q448)
(Plate 25)

This text completely disproves the Essene theory of Qumran origins at least as classically conceived. It was known for some 30 years, but once again mistranslated and misinterpreted. What is more incomprehensible, the dedication 'to King Jonathan' was missed completely. Once again, it demonstrates the need for open access to all texts and the deleterious effects of opening archives only to a small circle of people.

There were really only two King Jonathans in the history we have before us. These were Jonathan the brother of Judas Maccabee (*c.* 155 BC), and Alexander Jannaeus (d. 76 BC), whom we have referred to in various contexts above. Since the first probably never even was 'king' in the true sense and was never addressed in this manner, we are probably in the realm of the second. We have had occasion to speak of him throughout these texts, but particularly with regard to the Priestly Courses III/Aemilius Kills text in Chapter 4.

To have a text like this Paean, introduced by a dedicatory invocation or panegyric to him – in the words of the Paean itself, a *Shir Kodesh* or 'Holy Song'/'Poem' – is an historical treasure of high magnitude for the study of the Scrolls. Therefore we close our work with it and its interpretation. The fact that it was buried for so long, with the consequence that much of the debate concerning the state of affairs it addresses was misguided and misinformed, cannot be considered anything but reprehensible.

Ten years ago, one of the editors of this volume observed that Qumran had to be considered *pro-Maccabean*, i.e. *pro* Alexander Jannaeus or Jonathan and not *anti*. He concluded from 2 Macc 5:27's picture of Judas and his nine companions out 'in the hills' eating nothing but plants 'to avoid contracting defilement', that the settlement might have been founded by the Maccabees to honour this 'wilderness' experience, not (as in normative Qumran scholarship, which in his view exhibited a definite anti-Maccabean bias) in opposition to them.

It should be noted that both Maccabee Books present the celebration they seem written to commemorate, *Hanukkah*, as a new Feast of Booths or Tabernacles in the wilderness when the Law was either first revealed or rededicated. This editor also noted Alexander Jannaeus' second wilderness sojourn thereafter, when the latter and about 6,000 of his partisans fled to 'the hills' surrounding Jerusalem to resist Demetrius. This Graeco-Seleucid King had been invited into the country by the presumable party opposing Alexander, the Pharisees (*War* 1.92–5).

This invitation by the Pharisaic opponents of Alexander Jannaeus has to be considered a prototypical one for this party and the establishment Sadducees they eventually control. Later it is the Pharisee supporters of Hyrcanus II, presumably referred to disapprovingly in the text on Priestly Courses above, who sided with Pompey and the Scaurus mentioned in that text. They are also presumably involved with Herod's father Antipas, who aided the Roman troops in overwhelming Aristobulus' supporters in the Temple. Josephus comments on the awe-inspiring impression that the zeal of these supporters of Aristobulus made on the Romans as they steadfastly went about their priestly duties in the Temple even as they were being slaughtered there. He also notes that it was the Pharisaic collaborators of the Romans who killed more of these priestly partisans of Aristobulus in the Temple than the Roman troops themselves (*War* 1.148–50).

Josephus also describes two rabbis in the next generation, obviously meant to represent persons of the stature of Hillel and Shammai in Rabbinic tradition. He calls them 'Pollio and Sameas'. During the events of 37 BC, they had advised the people to 'open the gates to Herod', when the latter supported by Mark Antony returned to Jerusalem and again stormed it, finally taking control for himself and his family (*Ant*. 15.2–3). For this, Herod never stopped bestowing favours on Pollio and Sameas and their Pharisee supporters, while he had the other members of the previous Sanhedrin (i.e. the Sadducee-dominated one) executed (*Ant*. 14.175–6). Contrary to popular notion, fostered by the heirs to that tradition over the first millennia, the Pharisee position they represented was *not the popular one*. Rather the people ignored it, as they seemed to do all such advice and typically supported the more nationalist one; so the popular position was *pro-Maccabean*, not vice versa, a position also exemplified in this Song of Praise to King Jonathan we have before us.

Finally, at the time of the uprising against Rome, led presumably by the kinds of forces exemplified in this literature, Josephus specifically notes that it was 'the principal men of the Pharisees, the chief priests (i.e. Herodian Sadducees), and the men of power (the Herodians and their confederates – the intermediary for whom was a mysterious individual he refers to as 'Saul'), who invited the Romans into the Jerusalem to put down the uprising, thus making the momentous events that subsequently transpired and the destruction of the Temple inevitable (*War* 2.411–18). Josephus and Philo's nephew Tiberius Alexander, among others, even presided over this destruction!

There is another text at Qumran referring to these events, the Nahum *Pesher* from Cave 4. This text, whatever it may be interpreted to mean, was obviously written *after* the coming of 'the Kittim' into the country. It appears to refer to Demetrius, mentioned above, as well as 'Antiochus' (probably Epiphanes) at the time of the celebrated events of Judas Maccabee's struggle with him, noting that 'the Kittim' came after the 'Greeks'. Therefore it must have been written *in* the Roman period, and the conclusion would appear to be that in this text, as in the Habakkuk and Psalm 37 *Peshers* related to it, 'the Kittim' refer to the Romans.

In traditional theories of Qumran origins, i.e. the Essene theory and its variations, Alexander Jannaeus is often considered perhaps the most likely candidate for the role of Wicked Priest referred to in these *pesharim* – either him or one of his equally zealous Maccabean predecessors, like Judas, Judas' father Mattathias, his brother Jonathan, or even Alexander's son Aristobulus, who was apparently mentioned in the Aemilius text. It was the aim of *Maccabees, Zadokites, Christians and Qumran* to gainsay this approach. The Paean to King Jonathan now vindicates this position, and supports the opposite.

Since the existence of this Paean came to light, as a result of the efforts of a young Israeli scholar, comments have been made attempting to come to grips with it, like, 'a Sadducee must have joined the Community at Qumran' or the like, mostly from persons trying to salvage the traditional Essene theory. Similar kinds of comments were made in earlier research about the War Scroll, that it was imaginary or allegorical; or about the Copper Scroll for similar reasons, that it was not a real list of the hiding places of Temple treasure. These are preposterous and completely miss the true ethos of the group we have before us.

This group is 'Sadducee', or perhaps even better (to get the nuance of the Hebrew) 'Zadokites'. These are not Sadducees like those portrayed in the New Testament or Josephus. They are of a different stripe altogether. This is also borne out by texts like the two Letters on Works Righteousness in Chapter 6, as well now as the disciplinary text preceding this Paean above. This group was *actually* living out in the wilderness camps.

It is possible to call this group 'Essenes', but to do so one must redefine what one means by 'Essenes' to take into account its militant, nationalist, and resistance-minded ethos, which some would call 'Zealot'. As we have been emphasizing, this group *cannot* have been anti-Maccabean; if anything it was pro-Maccabean. The movement behind the literature at Qumran most likely commemorated the Maccabean 'camp' tradition (the '*booths*' of the new Feast of Tabernacles in the wilderness).

Alexander Jannaeus or other wilderness-fighting characters in the Maccabean tradition cannot have been 'the Wicked Priest'. This is a contradiction in terms, and shows a complete failure to grasp the import of the materials before us. Only an individual with Phariseeizing tendencies, like his more accommodating son Hyrcanus II, discussed in some detail above, could have been referred to in such a manner. The few lines of this splendid little poem *prove* this proposition as nothing else can.

The poem has some interesting characteristics. First it *is* a poem. We have called it a 'Paean' to take into account its laudatory praise of a great figure, as well as the 'Holiness' of the address, signalled in the first dedicatory line. Secondly, it is very old. There is an apocryphal psalm on the top left of Plate 25 above it, which is in different handwriting and distinct from it. At the top of the Plate, too, to the right of this psalm is the scrawled term, again in different handwriting, 'Hallelujah' (praise the Lord). This phrase is found in later portions of the traditional Psalms, and its presence here further increases the sense of religious awe of the document.

The apocryphal psalm at the top of the document is usually referred to as Psalm 154. It is known in Syriac tradition and interestingly enough was attached to the psalms from Qumran found in Cave 11. However it is not found in the Bible. It is a panegyric, glorifying 'the Many', thoroughly in keeping with the Paean to King Jonathan attached on this parchment below it, and repelete with Qumranisms like '*Hassidim*', '*Zaddikim*', 'the Upright', 'the Meek', 'his soul', 'a pleasing fragrance' and a new formulation, 'the Simple', just encountered in the disciplinary text above. A parallel to 'the Poor', it is found in similarly important contexts in the Habakkuk and Nahum *Peshers*. It is also probably paralleled in the Gospels': 'these little ones' (Matt. 10:42, Mark 9:52, etc.). Whatever the role this psalm was to have played in this document, its familiar apocalyptic nationalism is completely in harmony with the ethos of Qumran and it may even have been composed there.

But it is upon the material at the bottom that our attention must focus. There the handwriting is informal and cursive, and the sense laudatory. The dedication comes in an actual nine-line poem in the margin at the right of the main body of material, set forth as Column 1 of our transcription. Each line contains two phrases, though a few contain three, and one evoking 'Israel', contains one. It appears to be complete and totally original, almost like *Haiku* poetry, except instead of 17 syllables, it contains 20 phrases.

This is followed by material in the lower half of Column 2 in the same hand. What we have here may have been some important collection of 'poems' or 'Holy Songs'. They may even have been sung or sent as part of a laudatory dedication to King Jonathan himself. Or they may simply have been a private copy of something someone wanted to keep. It should be observed, however, that the Community shows not reticence in addressing this Alexander as 'King'. Many coins minted in this period bear the logo, 'Jonathan the High Priest of the Jews' (*Yehudim*). Those bearing the logo 'King' are generally in Greek and bear his Greek name 'Alexander'. A few others bear the logo 'the King Jonathan', but reversed from this poem.

The reference in Line 3 of the first column to 'the whole Community of Your People' is interesting in that it reflects the similar terminology Qumran applies to itself, i.e. 'the Community'. So is the fact that Line 5 recognizes the Jews as a *diaspora* people, inhabiting 'the four winds' as it were. However, the two references in Lines 8 and 9 with which the laudatory dedication closes are perhaps most interesting. The reference to 'perfection' in Line 8, of course, recapitulates this terminology as we have been following it in this work. Strictly speaking, it is not exactly the word 'Perfect', but rather a parallel vocabulary allied to it meaning something like 'complete'.

The word *Hever* at the end of Line 9 is used on numerous Maccabean coins from this period, particularly those minted under Alexander Jannaeus. It derives from the Hebrew root, 'friend', or, if one prefers, 'brotherhood'. Jonathan is almost always saluted on coins using this phraseology as 'the High Priest and Head of the Brotherhood (or Council or Sanhedrin) of the Jews'. We have chosen to render this word 'Commonwealth'. Its presence in this text, coupled with fulsome praise for Alexander, accords with the coins from this period and increases the sense of the historical authenticity of the poem itself.

If the laudatory sense of the first column were not sufficiently clear, the laudatory sense of the second column, and, of course, the apocryphal poem above it, makes it even more so. It is difficult to imagine that at some point this group could have become disenchanted with King Jonathan, and the editors reject this position.

This column, as the reader can see, is more obscure, because less has survived. There is a reference to 'love', but the translation of the word at the end of Line 2 'wine' is puzzling in the context of the rest of the extant paean. The word could also be translated 'Greece', but this too would be difficult to understand in the context we have. Without further data, little more can be said about it. The 'Commonwealth' reference in the first column is repeated in Line 6 of the second, including an adulatory reference to 'Kingdom', presumably Jonathan's. The constant reiteration of 'name', intended for the good of the monarch and a blessing is noteworthy.

In this context, the allusion in Line 2.4 to 'visit' is of interest. This is a term we have been following throughout the corpus from Qumran. We have seen it in the Messiah of Heaven and Earth text, referring to God 'visiting the *Hassidim*' or 'calling the *Zaddikim* by name'. Here, too, whether by accident or intent, we have the 'naming' signification again. The allusion to 'visiting' also occurs, as we have seen, in i.6–7 of the Damascus Document. There it relates to the evocation of the 'root of Planting out of Aaron and Israel', which God appears to have caused to grow 'to inherit His land'. In the context of CD, the notion of 'visiting' can be taken to imply this first Messianic figure with roots in both the Davidic and the priestly traditions or backgrounds, who would then be the similar figure who 'stands up', 'arises', or 'returns' at the end of the document. It could also be taken to mean the Community itself. However this may be, the occurrence of this 'visiting' terminology in this Paean to Alexander is striking.

Finally there is the important reference in 2.7 to the 'Joiners in the war' or 'joining the war'. Again the terminology is striking. It is used in a most important context in the exegesis of the Zadokite Covenant from Ezek. 44:15 in Column iv of the Cairo Damascus Document. It is possible to read the allusion in that prophecy to 'the priests, the Levites, the sons of Zadok' as a construct phrase with the sense of 'the priests who were the *Bnei-Zadok* Levites'. But the Damascus Document deliberately breaks this open in favour of its preferred exegesis. 'Ands' are added, so the prophecy now reads: 'the priests *and* the Levites *and* the sons of Zadok', all distinct categories, not descriptive of each other. This prepares the way for the exegesis to follow, which then identifies 'the priests' as 'the penitents of Israel who went out in the wilderness' and the 'sons of Zadok' in the well-known manner.

But the category 'the Levites' is not mentioned in the exegesis. Rather another word, our 'Joiners' (*Nilvim*) here evidently playing on the word 'Levites', is inserted. The interpretation then reads: 'and the Joiners with them' – 'them', it will be remembered, being 'the penitents of Israel . . . in the desert'. This is the term that reappears in this Paean to King Jonathan, but it is now tied to an additional phrase, missing in the Damascus Document, namely 'the Joiners in the war of' or 'those joining in the war of'. 'In the war of' is a significant addition, evoking at once the war-like ethos of this group and that war Jonathan seems to have been involved in against Demetrius, mentioned in the Nahum *Pesher*.

As it turns out, a variation of this terminology also appears in the Nahum *Pesher*, i.e. the verbal usage 'join'. There it is attached to the 'Simple' notation just encountered, and linguistically linked to the expression *ger-nilveh* ('resident alien') – another variation of this usage – in the underlying text. The word '*Nilvim*' actually appears in Esther 9:27, where it is used to refer to 'Gentiles' connecting themselves in some manner to the Jewish Community – therefore the sense of 'join'/'joining', which plays on the word 'Levites' in the Damascus Document. In this, it may even refer to some 'associated', albeit lesser, status, i.e. a cadre of God-fearing Gentiles associated with the

Community. However this may be, the presence of this allusion in this Paean to King Jonathan, the nationalist sentiments of which are patent, with the additional evocation of being connected to war, is of no mean import.

TRANSLITERATION

Column 1

1. ‏[ש]יר קדש‏
2. ‏על יונתן המלך‏
3. ‏וכל קהל עמך‏
4. ‏ישראל‏
5. ‏אשר בארבע‏
6. ‏רוחות שמים‏
7. ‏יהי שלום כלם‏
8. ‏שלם מלפניך‏
9. ‏וחבר בשמך‏

Column 2

1. ‏באהבתך אתימר]‏ [
2. ‏ביום {וע} וערב מיין]‏ [
3. ‏לקרוב להיות ת.]‏ [
4. ‏פקדם לברכה לה.]‏ [
5. ‏על שמך שנקרא]‏ . [
6. ‏ממלכה לחברך]‏ . [
7. ‏נלוים מלחמת ..]‏ [
8. ‏לזכרון שמך]‏ [
9. ‏.ת[ ]ר. [‏ [

TRANSLATION

Column 1 (1) A sacred [po]em (2) for King Jonathan (3) and all the Congregation of Your people (4) Israel, (5) who are (spread) in every (6) direction under Heaven, (7) may they all be well, (8) Perfect before You, (9) and a Commonwealth in Your Name

Column 2 (1) In Your love do I exalt . . . (2) in the day and in the evening, from wine (also possibly 'Greece') . . . (3) to draw near so as to be . . . (4) Visit them for a blessing, to . . . (5) upon Your Name which is proclaimed . . . (6) a Kingdom for Your Commonwealth . . . (7) the Joiners in the war/joining the war of . . . (8) Your Name for a memorial . . .

NOTES

(45) Brontologion (4Q318)

Previous Discussions: Milik, *Years*, 42; idem, *Books*, 187; J. C. Greenfield and M. Sokoloff, 'Astrological and Related Omen Texts in Jewish Palestinian Aramaic', *Journal of Near Eastern Studies* 48 (1989) 202. Photographs: PAM 43.374, ER 1368.

(46) Physiognomic Text (4Q561)

Previous Discussion: J. Starcky, 'Les quatre étapes du messianisme à Qumran', *Revue Biblique* 70 (1963) 503 note 66. Photographs: PAM 43.598, ER 1545.

(47) An Amulet Formula Against Evil Spirits (4Q560)

Previous Discussions: None. The *DSSIP* lists the text as 'Proverbs? ar', but the text is certainly an incantation. Photographs: PAM 43.574 and 43.602, ER 1522 and 1549.

(48) The Era of Light is Coming (4Q462)

Previous Discussion: M. Smith, '4Q462 (Narrative) Fragment 1: A Preliminary Edition', *Revue de Qumran* 15 (1991) 55–77. Photographs: PAM 43.546, ER 1495.

(49) He Loved his Bodily Emissions (A Record of Sectarian Discipline – 4Q477)

Previous Discussion: None. Photographs: PAM 43.562, ER 1510.

(50) Paean for King Jonathan (Alexander Jannaeus) (4Q448)

Previous Discussion: A. Rabinovich, 'A Prayer for King Yonaton', *Jerusalem Post Magazine* (1992) 8, 9–11. Photographs: PAM 41.371 and 43.545, ER 266 and 1494.

Index